Communicating
Effectively

Third Edition

Communicating Effectively

SAUNDRA HYBELS
Lock Haven University

RICHARD L. WEAVER II
Bowling Green State University

McGraw-Hill, Inc.

New York   St. Louis   San Francisco   Auckland   Bogotá   Caracas
Lisbon   London   Madrid   Mexico   Milan   Montreal   New Delhi
Paris   San Juan   Singapore   Sydney   Tokyo   Toronto

Communicating Effectively

Acknowledgments appear on pages 427–430, and on this page by reference.

3 4 5 6 7 8 9 0 VNH VNH 9 0 9 8 7 6 5 4 3 2

ISBN 0-07-016741-9

This book was set in New Aster by Monotype Composition Company, Inc.
The editors were Hilary Jackson, Cynthia Fostle, and Jean Akers;
the designer was Leon Bolognese;
the production supervisor was Kathryn Porzio.
The photo editor was Debra P. Hershkowitz.
Cover photo by Reginald Wickham.
Von Hoffmann Press, Inc., was printer and binder.

Library of Congress Cataloging-in-Publication Data

Hybels, Saundra.
    Communicating effectively / Saundra Hybels, Richard L. Weaver, II.—3rd ed.
        p.   cm.
    Includes bibliographical references and index.
    ISBN 0-07-016741-9
    1. Oral communication.   I. Weaver, Richard L., (date).
    II. Title.
P95.H9   1992
302.2'242—dc20   91-42644

Contents

Part Two
Interpersonal Communication

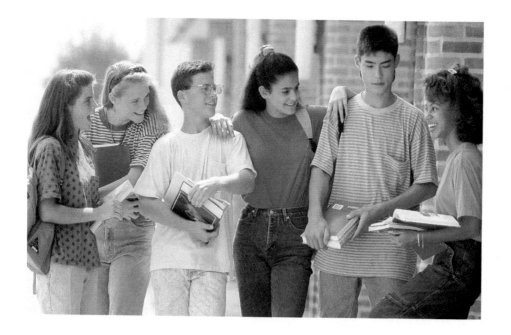

Part Three
Communicating in Groups

Part Four
Communicating in Public

Chapter 12
Finding Speech Material   *278*

Preface

Communicating Effectively, Third Edition, has been written for the introductory course in speech communication. Always with the student in mind, we have tried to show the theories of interpersonal, group, and public communication and how they apply to real-life situations. The introductory chapters present a model of communication and show how language and nonverbal communication work in our interactions with others. In the interpersonal chapters we concentrate on relationships, their dynamics, and how they can be improved. The chapters on small groups focus on decision making in groups and address themselves to how small groups solve problems on the campus and in the community. The public speaking chapters are designed to help the student develop, organize, and present a speech without undue anxiety.

When we set out to write this book, the questions that were always present were: "How do students learn?" "How can we explain concepts in such a way that students will see the applications to their own lives?" "How can we write a book that students find interesting?" "How can this book help enhance the job of the instructor in the classroom?" As well as being the questions that gave us focus and direction for the first edition, they have also guided our revisions in subsequent editions. Our approach to writing has always been to imagine the class members before us and to write as if we are there in the classroom explaining the concept to them.

The best way to help students learn theory seems to be through examples they can relate to. The text, then, relies heavily on examples to explain key concepts throughout the book. To help students identify with the examples, we have drawn them from actual experiences on campus, at work, and in the community. This third edition also has many examples from other cultures.

Students have a chance to try out the theory in a series of *Try This* boxes. In these boxes, students are asked to take the theory explained in the text and try to apply it to some aspect of their lives. In the third edition, many of these boxes have been revised to create even greater motivation for students to try the activity as they are reading the text. Each *Try This* box has questions to help students develop their critical thinking skills. Although the boxes are designed for individual use, many of them can also be used for class discussion.

As well as encouraging students to learn theory through examples and the *Try This* boxes, we have tried to capture student interest by presenting a series of high-interest, short readings from current books, magazines, and newspapers. These readings, called *Consider This,* show how communication theory works in the world outside the campus and classroom. The readings, which present research in lay language, come from communication theory, psychology, and sociology. In order to present students with the most current information, many of the boxes are new to this edition.

Features of the Third Edition

This third edition is a major revision—to the tune of 50,000 new words. The major change in the book is that greater attention has been given to theories and examples that reflect a wider view of race, culture, gender, and ethnicity. Sometimes the changes are small: a Korean or Hispanic name is used. Other times the changes are broad and conceptual. Chapter 2 has the greatest number of changes. It starts with self-perception and ends with one's perception of the world. This chapter also has a model that explains the stages a person goes through when he or she meets a person of another race or culture, and it identifies the stage during which racism or ethnocentrism is most likely to develop. Along the same lines of increasing cross-cultural awareness, Chapter 4, on language, has a new section on bilingualism, and the information interview in Chapter 8 has an interview about Hispanic adjustment to the United States.

Another change throughout the book has been to show how the concept of transactional communication applies to *all* kinds of communication. Responding to requests from reviewers, we have added a discussion of how to write a résumé and have included a sample résumé in Chapter 8. In Chapter 10, we have used some new research findings from organizational behavior to describe how people become leaders and how they receive power to do so.

Several freshly updated sections in the public speaking chapters tell how to use the computer to find speech information. Discussion includes how to use a computer catalog, how to research a topic using a computer database, and how a computer can help find and narrow a topic for a speech. Other changes in the public speaking chapters include broadened sample topics and two new sample speeches, one informative and one persuasive.

Organization

Communicating Effectively, Third Edition, is organized into four parts. Part One sets forth the basic principles of communication in five chapters:

- Chapter 1 discusses the need for communication skills, introduces and explains a model of communication, and focuses on communication as a process and transaction. New material expands on the discussion of communication as a transaction and adds information about concrete symbols.
- Chapter 2 covers intrapersonal communication through a discussion of what makes up self-concept and how perception and self-concept are related. New material discusses how perception can help or hinder people in relating to new cultures, and it introduces a model of the stages people go through when they are introduced to someone from an unfamiliar race or culture.
- Chapter 3 explains how the listening process works. Listening habits and attitudes are discussed. Students are given direction on how to listen for information, how to listen critically and reflectively, and how

to enhance listening for enjoyment. New materials include some memory techniques and discussion of listener responsibility.

- Chapter 4 concentrates on verbal communication. Beginning with a discussion of some theories of language, it emphasizes skill building through a discussion of style, language appropriateness, and language choice. New material includes a discussion of how male and female language differ. In line with the book's increased cross-cultural emphasis, the chapter explores the pros and cons of bilingualism in America.
- Chapter 5 talks about the importance of nonverbal communication. As well as introducing basic principles, the chapter describes various kinds of nonverbal communication. The new material includes information on touch, smell, and color. There are new discussions of how people communicate through what they wear and of gender and cultural nonverbal behavior.

Part Two, which has three chapters, focuses on interpersonal communication.

- Chapter 6 covers interpersonal communication as a transaction, focusing on interpersonal needs, attraction to others, and the importance of self-disclosure. New materials include recent research on empathy and gossip and discussion of perceived gain as a need that affects interpersonal communication.
- Chapter 7 concentrates on relationship stages—how relationships are formed and how they are dissolved. The chapter suggests criteria for evaluating relationships, gives communication strategies to pursue and avoid, and explains a model for resolving conflict. New materials include recent research on giving advice and information about effective and ineffective criticism in relationships.
- Chapter 8, on interviewing, looks at two kinds of interviews: the information interview and the employment interview. The section on the information interview focuses on how a student should prepare and conduct such an interview; the discussion of the employment interview concentrates on how students should prepare for and conduct themselves while being interviewed for a job. New material shows students how to write a résumé and includes a sample résumé.

Part Three has two chapters on small groups and how they work.

- Chapter 9 begins with the characteristics of small groups and proceeds to discuss why groups can often solve problems more readily than individuals. New materials describe the difference between procedural and substantive conflict and also give some insight on some of the cultural values that may influence group behavior.
- Chapter 10 emphasizes leader and participant responsibilities. Beginning with a discussion of leadership styles, it proceeds to a consideration of how a leader should act in group discussions. New materials discuss how leaders get their power and the ways in which they influence group behavior.

Part Four, which contains six chapters, deals with public communication and emphasizes how to research, put together, and deliver a speech.

- Chapter 11 tells the student how to get started on a speech. It focuses on selecting the topic, narrowing it, and choosing a purpose for the speech. The student is given detailed instructions and examples for selecting a general and specific purpose as well as the central idea. The chapter also has a detailed description of how to go about audience analysis. New materials discuss the transactional nature of public speaking and how a speaker's role is defined based on the composition of the audience.
- Chapter 12 tells students how to research a topic using personal experiences, interviews, and library resources. It explains where to look for supporting materials and describes the various kinds of supporting materials students should consider. New materials explain how to use a computer catalog and how to search a database for speech material.
- Chapter 13 is about organizing and outlining the speech. Various patterns of organization are discussed as well as why one pattern might work better than another. Separate sections treat speech introductions and conclusions. The chapter concludes with the mechanics of outlining. New materials include several new speech outlines.
- Chapter 14 tells how to deliver a speech using impromptu, manuscript, memory, and extemporaneous methods. It also discusses how a speaker should look and sound and what kinds of visual aids to use during the speech. This chapter emphasizes the importance of practice and the student's evaluation of delivery. New material expands the discussion of visual aids, which range from using the chalkboard to developing computer graphics. The section on speaker anxiety has been completely rewritten and includes a list of things a student can do to reduce anxiety. There is also a checklist for self-evaluation.
- Chapter 15 focuses on the informative speech. As well as explaining the goals of the speech, it describes some of the more sophisticated ways of developing supporting material. New materials include discussion of how to make large numbers intelligible to readers and a new sample speech.
- Chapter 16 concentrates on the persuasive speech and explains the concepts of speaker credibility and logical and emotional appeals. It also introduces some of the research findings on persuasive speech organization. New materials include the goals of persuasive speaking, information on how to use a database to select a speech topic, and a new sample speech.

Pedagogical Devices

To help students master the words and concepts of speech communication, we have incorporated a number of pedagogical devices. We help students focus on the important ideas in each chapter by beginning with chapter objectives and a list of key terms. The key terms are defined the first time they are used in the chapter and are also included in the glossary. Each chapter concludes with a list of annotated readings that the student can read to follow up on the concepts discussed in the chapter. These readings provide a variety of scholarly and popular materials that students may use for course projects or for additional research. Readings have been revised and updated for this edition.

The *Try This* boxes give students a chance to apply theory to some area of their own experience. These boxes, as well as captions for photographs, all ask students questions that encourage them to think about what they have learned.

The book also comes with an Instructor's Manual. The manual includes course outlines for both semesters and quarters. Each chapter has an overview, discussion questions, and activities that the instructor can do with the class to show how the theory of the chapter works in practice.

Acknowledgments

This edition changed publishers somewhere midstream when McGraw-Hill bought the Random House College Division. Fortunately for us, the book and its authors survived conglomerate America with little trauma. I would like to thank Hilary Jackson at McGraw-Hill for having faith in this book and for all her encouragement in developing this new edition.

Unlike other editions of the book, I revised this book alone because Richard Weaver was on sabbatical and traveling through Australia. Because we have been working together for so many years, we have developed a unified concept that continues through this edition. Although Kathleen Domenig did not edit this edition, her spirit still reigns, and as I was working on this edition I continually heard her voice in my ear saying, "That works," or "This concept still needs a little bit of tinkering."

The new kid on the block is Cynthia Fostle, who joined the book as its editor. Along with being an excellent editor, Cynthia was able to take a fresh look at the book and point out some problems we hadn't noticed. She also had fresh ideas, many of which have been included in this edition.

I would like to thank the following reviewers for their many helpful comments and suggestions: Ruth Aurelius, Des Moines Area Community College; Richard Bartone, William Patterson College; Maresa Brassil, Auburn University; Robert T. Dixon, St. Louis Community College at Meramac; J. Robert Hepler, Broward Community College; Diana Ivy, North Carolina State University; Laurence Kraft, Eastern Washington University; Louise C. Maynor, North Carolina Central University; and Richard W. Thide, Defiance College.

On the home front, I would like to acknowledge Doug Campbell, my department head. Doug's great contribution is that he holds one department meeting a month and never creates busywork for his faculty. What greater gift could one give a writer? I would also like to thank the president of my university, Dr. Craig Dean Willis. He likes the book, uses it to teach his class, and promotes it whenever he can. I would like to add Dr. Esther Jane Carrier, reference librarian, to my personal Hall of Fame. You can't thank her personally because she always says, "I'm only doing my job." However, she goes far beyond what is required of her, and I believe that she can find anything in the library. Jim Bean, my colleague from psychology, was very helpful in leading me to materials about leadership.

Last, and the most, I would like to thank my research assistants Brian Smith and Shawn Gerhardt. Brian worked for me for an entire year. He tracked down obscure references, kept my computer files in order, wrote abstracts of much of the recent research, and even contributed a speech he gave in one of his classes. This book is Brian's, too.

Shawn took over the job after Brian graduated and skillfully and patiently tied up all those loose ends that occur when a manuscript is almost finished.

And then there is Joansin. He was my best friend throughout the whole book. Not only was he a wonderful and amusing companion, he also helped to keep the household running and kept life in perspective.

Saundra Hybels

Communicating Effectively

Basic Principles of Communication

Chapter 1

The Communication Process

CHAPTER OBJECTIVES	KEY TERMS
After reading this chapter, you should be able to: **1.** Explain communication needs and relate them to your life. **2.** Define communication and explain it as a process. **3.** Identify the elements of communication. **4.** Explain how communication is a transaction. **5.** Explain how seeing communication as a transaction helps us to understand it better. **6.** Describe the types of communication. **7.** Discuss the ways you can improve your own communication skills.	abstract symbol channel communication concrete symbol feedback interpersonal communication interview intrapersonal communication message noise nonverbal symbol public communication roles sender-receiver setting small-group communication symbol transactional communication verbal symbol

T ong Hee is the manager of the student food service at the university. Every Monday morning he meets with his entire staff. They discuss such matters as whether students have liked the new foods that were added to the menu and how to move students through cafeteria lines more quickly. Tong Hee doesn't say very much, but he listens to what everyone else says and takes careful notes. Later each week he implements many of his staff's suggestions. Because of his attitude, employee morale is high and turnover is low.

Jackie and Brian are best friends. They first met at the campus radio station and discovered they had the same taste in music. After gaining some experience as disk jockeys, they decided to try out for management positions. Jackie became station manager and Brian program director. Now they spend most of their free time at the station. They make decisions about the music that will be played, they work out the rules that disk jockeys should follow, and they make commercials together. They work so well together that the station is running smoothly and the students are all happy with its operation.

Carmen attends college in a wheelchair. The buildings where her classes are located have all been modified for wheelchairs, but the student center has not. Whenever Carmen wants to go there for a meal or to buy books, she has to ask people to carry her wheelchair up the steps. Carmen decides that she will try to change this situation. She goes to the student government, which runs the center, and asks them to install a wheelchair ramp. The senators of the government all agree that a ramp is a good idea, and the president asks Carmen to get bids from local contractors. At the next meeting she presents the senators with three bids. They vote to hire a contractor and by the end of the semester, the ramp is in place.

Nancy and Steve are going to Poland as exchange students for a semester. In preparation they read several books about Poland and talk to many students who have been there. Through their reading and discussions they discover that Polish society is more formal than American society. They find, for example, that Poles bring flowers to the hostess when they are invited to dinner, that younger people always let older people precede them through doors and into elevators, and that coats and jackets are checked in the cloakroom—even when students are going to class. By observing these and other customs when they arrive in Poland, they fit into the Polish society more quickly and are less conspicuous as outsiders.

Tong Hee, Jackie, Brian, Carmen, Nancy, and Steve all have something in common: they achieved success because of their communication skills. Tong Hee was able to listen and respond to the needs of his employees. Brian and Jackie have remained good friends because they can communicate with each other and with the students who are working at the station. Carmen succeeded because she was able to come up with a plan and present it to a group that could make the change she wanted. Nancy and Steve fit into Polish society because they learned something about the way Poles communicate with one another.

Everyone Needs Communication Skills

People fulfill a variety of needs through communication, and communicating effectively can provide considerable pleasure. A stimulating conversation, participation in a group discussion that leads to solving a problem, a persuasive speech that gains signatures on a petition: all these are instances of successful communication.

Try This Try This Try This

*T*ry to state what you are trying to accomplish in your communication in each of the following situations:

• Presenting an oral report in a class

• Helping a friend who is feeling depressed

• Persuading a potential employer to hire you

How do your goals differ in each of these situations?

Even though we have been communicating since birth, we are not always effective. Sometimes communication doesn't work and we end up frustrated. We get lost from incomplete directions, insult a friend with what we intended as an innocent comment, or bore an audience with a speech. Effective communication is a problem for many of us; that's why a barrage of books, articles, and seminars tell us how to communicate.

Communication is vital in all areas of our lives. We use it for persuasion; to influence relationships; to inform; to share, discover, and uncover information. We want a friend to stop studying and go to a party; we want our friends and family to like one another; we want someone to join our club or to vote for a particular candidate.

Many people believe that effective communication is the most important key to success in our work and in our relationships. In a survey sent to 1000 personnel managers, the managers listed oral communication and listening as the most important skills for gaining employment. For people who were on the job, they said that the ability to work with others and to speak effectively were most important.[1] In another survey, college alumni responded that the most important skills for their jobs were making presentations and handling questions and answers and small-group discussion.[2]

Perhaps our most important need is to maintain and improve relationships. Through communication we discover others' needs and share our own. Any kind of relationship requires open and accurate lines of communication. Only when such lines exist will people feel free to voice important thoughts and feelings.

Communication, then, is vital to our lives. To live is to communicate. To communicate effectively is to enjoy life more fully. On the premise that increased knowledge helps us to do things better, let's begin with a discussion of how communication works.

Communication Is a Process

A Definition of Communication

Communication is any process in which people share information, ideas, and feelings. That process involves not only the spoken and written word, but also body language, personal mannerisms and style, the surroundings—

anything that adds meaning to a message. To see how this process works, consider this exchange.

> *Brenda runs into an old high school friend in the college cafeteria.*
> *"I haven't seen you since school started," her friend says. "What have you been up to?"*
> *"Not much," she says, with a slightly wicked smile.*
> *The smile, an accompanying lift of an eyebrow, and a certain secretiveness in Brenda's manner suggest that she has, in fact, been up to a great deal. So does her outfit—something totally unlike what she wore just a few short months ago. Her hair color has also changed—from a mousy brown to a flaming red.*

Brenda has spoken only two words, but a great deal of communication has taken place. The communication is not only limited to the actual conversation. Because communication is a process and is ongoing,[3] it also occurs before and after the time people actually talk to each other. Brenda's friend came into the conversation with one impression of Brenda and left with another. This new impression will influence their next conversation and their relationship. The friend might think, for example, that she likes the "new" Brenda and that she might want to get to know her even better, or she might be concerned how this change will affect their relationship.

The Elements of Communication

The communication process is made up of various elements. These elements are: senders and receivers, messages, channels, noise, feedback, and setting. Figure 1-1 shows how all these elements work together. The amoeba-like shape of the sender-receiver indicates how this person changes—depending on what he or she is hearing or reacting to.

SENDER-RECEIVERS

People get involved in communication because they have information, ideas, and feelings they want to share. This sharing, however, is not a one-way process, where one person sends ideas and the other receives them, and then the process is reversed. In most communication situations, people are **sender-receivers**—both sending and receiving at the same time.

> *Bobby and Rebecca are discussing baseball. Bobby is sending a message by talking and Rebecca is receiving it by listening. Bobby is enthusiastic, animated, and a little loud as he tells her of his heroics in last night's game. As Rebecca listens, she also sends a message to Bobby. She has one hand on her hip, one eyebrow slightly raised, and an expression which says, "I don't believe a word of this." Both Bobby and Rebecca are sender-receivers.*

MESSAGE

The **message** is made up of the ideas and feelings that a sender-receiver wants to share. In the case of Bobby and Rebecca, Bobby's message was what he

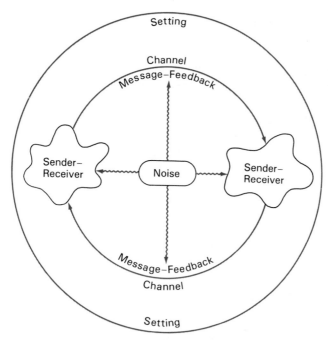

Figure 1-1
The Elements of Communication

was doing and feeling while Rebecca's message was a reaction to what Bobby was telling her.

Ideas and feelings can be communicated only if they are represented by symbols. A **symbol** is something that stands for something else. All our communication messages are made up of two kinds of symbols: verbal and nonverbal.

Every word in our language is a **verbal symbol** that stands for a particular thing or idea. Verbal symbols are limited and complicated. For example, when we use the word *chair*, we agree we are talking about something we sit on. Thus, *chair* is a **concrete symbol,** a symbol which represents an object. However, when we hear the word *chair*, we all might have a different impression: a chair could be a recliner, an easy chair, a bean bag, a lawn chair—the variety is very great.

Even more complicated are **abstract symbols,** which stand for ideas. Consider, for example, the vast differences in our understanding of words such as *home, hungry,* or *hurt*. How we understand these words will be determined by our experience. Since people's experiences differ to some degree, they will assign different meanings to these abstract words.

Nonverbal symbols are anything we communicate without using words, such as facial expressions, gestures, posture, vocal tones, appearance, and so on. As with verbal symbols, we all attach certain meanings to nonverbal symbols. A yawn means we are bored or tired; a furled brow indicates confusion; not looking someone in the eye may mean we have something to hide. Like verbal symbols, nonverbal symbols can be misleading. We cannot control all our nonverbal behavior, and we often send out information of which we are not even aware.

> *Rosa has tried several times to talk to Xavier, who sits next to her in biology class. Each time she speaks to him, his answer has been short and he has turned away quickly. Rosa concludes that Xavier is stuck-up, and so she decides not to pay any more attention to him. The truth is that Xavier thinks Rosa is the most beautiful woman he has ever seen, but every time she talks to him, he becomes hopelessly tongue-tied. By being so, he has inadvertently communicated the wrong message and possibly halted any chance for a relationship.*

Whether or not we are aware of them, nonverbal symbols are extremely important to messages. Some communication scholars believe that over 90 percent of the messages we send and receive are made up of nonverbal symbols.[4]

CHANNELS

The **channel** is the route traveled by a message; the means it uses to reach the sender-receivers. In face-to-face communication, the primary channels are sound and sight: we listen to and look at each other. We are familiar with the channels of radio, television, records, newspapers, and magazines in the mass media. Other channels communicate nonverbal messages. For example, when Denise goes to apply for a job, she uses several nonverbal signals to send out a positive message: a firm handshake (touch); a light perfume (smell); nice clothes (sight); and a respectful voice (sound). In her case, the senses she is appealing to are the channels.

FEEDBACK

Feedback is the response of the receiver-senders to each other. You tell me a joke and I smile. That's feedback. You make a comment about the weather and I make another one. More feedback.

Feedback is vital to communication because it lets the participants in the communication see whether ideas and feelings have been shared in the way they were intended. If Sally tells John, for example, that she will pick him up at 8 P.M. and he is ready and waiting at that time, he shows by his behavior that the message has been understood. However, let's suppose at another time they agree to meet at the intersection of Brown and Keller Streets at 8 P.M. They both arrive on time but wait at different corners. When they finally discover each other, at 9, they have a big fight and each accuses the other of being in the wrong place. In this case they thought they had understood the message but come to realize that not enough feedback had occurred. One of them should have asked, "*Which* corner of Keller and Brown?"

Sender-receivers who meet in a face-to-face setting have the greatest opportunity for feedback. In this kind of setting, they have a chance to see whether the other person understands and is following the message. A teacher working with a child, for example, can readily see by the child's face whether he is confused. She can also see when he is getting bored, by the way he

What are the opportunities for feedback when two people talk?

fidgets and begins to lose attention. A speaker in a large lecture hall, however, is not as aware of the feedback from his audience. Those listeners he can see might look attentive, but the ones in the back rows may be having a quiet snooze. In general, the fewer the people involved in the communication event, the greater the opportunity for feedback.

NOISE

Noise is interference that keeps a message from being understood or accurately interpreted. Noise occurs between the sender-receivers, and it comes in three forms: external, internal, and semantic.

External noise comes from the environment and keeps the message from being heard or understood. Your heart-to-heart talk with your roommate can be interrupted by a group of people yelling in the hall, a helicopter passing overhead, or a power saw outside the window. External noise does not always come from sound. You could be standing and talking to someone in the hot sun and become so uncomfortable that you can't concentrate. Conversation might also falter at a picnic when you discover you are sitting on an anthill and ants are crawling all over your blanket.

Internal noise occurs in the minds of the sender-receivers when their thoughts or feelings are focused on something other than the communication at hand. A student doesn't hear the lecture because he is thinking about lunch; a wife can't pay attention to her husband because she is thinking about a problem at the office. Sometimes internal noise occurs when someone doesn't want to hear what is being said: a child might look attentive when she is being scolded by a parent, but she is working hard on not listening.

Semantic noise is caused by people's emotional reactions to words. Many people tune out a speaker who uses profanity because the words are so offensive to them. Others have negative reactions to people who make ethnic or sexist remarks. Semantic noise, like external and internal noise, can interfere with all or part of the message.

SETTING

The **setting** is where the communication occurs. Settings can be a significant influence on communication. Some are formal and lend themselves to formal presentations. An auditorium, for example, is good for giving speeches and presentations but not very good for conversation. If people want to converse on a more intimate basis, they would be better off in a smaller, more comfortable room where they can sit and face each other.

Setting is made up of several components, which can range from the way a place is lighted to the colors used for decoration. Your local discount store is lighted with fluorescent lights. These lights communicate a message: you are not there to relax, but to do business and move on. On the other hand, if you are going to buy designer clothing in a department store, you are not going to find fluorescent lighting. The lighting will be subdued, and the showroom will probably look more like your living room than like a store.

The color of a room might determine how comfortable you feel. A room that is painted red might be very striking when you first see it, but after you are in it for awhile, you will probably feel nervous and uncomfortable. Public buildings such as schools and offices are often painted "institutional green"— a cool color that means business, not relaxation but has been found by researchers to reduce the restlessness of students.

The arrangement of furniture in a setting can also affect the communication that takes place. For example, at one college, the library was one of the noisiest places on campus. The problem was solved by rearranging the furniture. Instead of sofas and chairs arranged so that students could sit and talk, the library used study desks—thus creating a quiet place to concentrate.

All communication is made up of senders and receivers, messages, channels, feedback, noise, and setting. Every time people communicate, these elements are somewhat different. They are not the only factors that influence communication, however. Communication is also influenced by what we bring to it. That is the subject of our next section.

Communication Is a Transaction

A communication transaction involves not only the physical act of communicating but also a psychological one: impressions are being formed in the minds of the people who are communicating.[5] What people think and know about one another directly affects their communication.

The Three Principles of Transactional Communication

Communication as a transaction—**transactional communication**—involves three important principles. First, people engaged in communication are sending messages continuously and simultaneously. Second, communication events have a past, present, and future. Third, participants in communication play certain roles. Let's consider each of these principles in turn.

PARTICIPATION IS CONTINUOUS AND SIMULTANEOUS

Even if you are not actually talking in a communication situation, you are actively involved in sending and receiving symbols.

Bethany stops a student on the sidewalk and asks the way to the English department. Before stopping the student, she has evaluated her as a reasonable source of information and as a person who is "safe" to talk to. As she listens to the directions, Bethany offers feedback, letting the woman know when she understands and when she is confused. At the same time, she "digests" the information she hears, thinking about whether she can identify the landmarks used as references, deciding just how far the walk will be, and even imagining what she will say when she arrives. She is participating continuously and simultaneously in a complicated situation—one which we all take for granted.

ALL COMMUNICATIONS HAVE A PAST, A PRESENT, AND A FUTURE

We all respond to every situation from our own experiences, our own moods, and our own expectations. Such factors complicate the communication situation.

Jean and Joe, generally a happily married couple, are discussing plans for Thanksgiving vacation. Joe wants to spend a long weekend in Mexico; Jean wants to visit relatives. The discussion has quickly degenerated into a heated argument.

We can only understand this communication by knowing something about its history.

Last year's Christmas vacation was spent with Joe's family; that is in the past. Now Jean is asking him to be fair and spend some time with her family; she is angry because she feels cheated. She realizes that after this trip, the next vacation will be taken up with Joe's business matters, and it may be a year or more before she sees her family; that glimpse of the future is affecting the communication. Joe ignores both the past and the future in favor of his present concern.

Even when you are meeting someone for the first time, you respond to that person based on your experience. You might respond to physical traits (short, tall, bearded, bald), to occupation (accountant, gym teacher), or even to a name (remember how a boy named Eugene always tormented you and you've mistrusted all Eugenes ever since?). Any of these things you call up

How does their body language communicate that these kids know and like each other?

from your past might influence how you respond to someone—at least at the beginning.

The future also influences communication. If you want a relationship to continue, you will say and do things in the present to make sure it does. ("Thanks for dinner. I always enjoy your cooking.") If you think you will never see a person again, this also might affect your communication. You might be more businesslike, leaving the personal aspects of your life out of the communication.

ALL COMMUNICATORS PLAY ROLES

Roles are parts we play or ways we behave with others. Defined by society and affected by individual relationships, roles control everything from word choice to body language.

> *Randy seems to be many different people, depending on the person with whom he is communicating. In the simple matter of finding out some- one's needs, his communication varies wildly: to his younger sister, "Whatdayawant?"; to a customer in his father's store, "What can I help you with, Sir?"; to his girlfriend, "Huh?"*

Roles are not always consistent within a relationship. They vary with others' moods or with our own, with the setting and the noise factor. No two communications are the same. They change to meet the needs of each particular relationship and situation.

Julie's boyfriend picks her up in front of the dorm. "Get in the car," he says. This sentence communicates a great deal about their relationship and how they have defined it. If, instead, he had stepped out of the car, put his arm around her shoulders, and said, "Hi, honey," both of their roles (and their relationship) would be different.

The roles we play—whether established by individual relationships or by society—are also perceived differently by different people. These different perceptions affect the communication that results. For example, Tom, in his role of youth director, is well organized and maintains tight control over the classes he teaches. The kids who take his classes know they have to behave, or they'll be in big trouble. Therefore they speak to him in a respectful voice and stay quiet when they're supposed to. To other kids, however, Tom's discipline indicates rigidity and inflexibility. These kids don't go by the youth center; they choose not to communicate with him at all.

THE PRINCIPLES IN ACTION

Let's see how all three principles of transactional communication work as we listen to a conversation between Jane and Stacy:

Jane: Hey, Stacy. Can I borrow your sweater?

Stacy: (Steps back, slight frown) Well . . .

Try This Try This Try This

*T*ake a look at your attitude toward the instructor for your speech communication course. Since you are at the beginning of the course, you probably don't know very much about him or her. (If you do know each other, pick another instructor you don't know so well.) Now, assume you are going to go to this instructor's office to ask questions about your first assignment.

Past

How will your past experience affect your communication with this instructor? What has been your experience with other instructors in the past? Have they been helpful? Interested in students? Have you heard anything through the student grapevine about this instructor? Will this influence your communication? Do you feel comfortable with college teachers? Will this have an influence?

Future

How do you want this instructor to think about you? What do you want from this instructor in the future? If your answer is "a good grade," do you think it's important to create a good impression?

Jane: (Steps forward) You know. The brown one with the white ducks.

Stacy: (Folds her arms in front of her) What happened to all those new sweaters you got for your birthday?

We know right away in this scene that Stacy does not want to cooperate, even though she never says so. As Jane speaks, Stacy simultaneously and continuously sends out signals: she frowns, she steps back, she folds her arms in front of her—all nonverbal symbols of resistance. Jane reinforces her verbal symbols by stepping forward—a nonverbal way of showing assertiveness.

This scene between Jane and Stacy would probably take no more than thirty seconds in real life, yet it is filled with symbols—some of which nonparticipants would be unable to detect. What are the past and future aspects of this communication? How many times has Jane borrowed things from Stacy? How willing has Stacy been to lend them before? What has been their condition upon return? What is Jane and Stacy's relationship? Do they get along? Do they respect each other and each other's property?

We must also look at the roles that Jane and Stacy play. Their roles seem to be equal because they are friends. From their conversation, however, Jane is willing to play the role of borrower but Stacy is not willing to play the role of lender. The roles they play in this transaction will depend on the experience they have had with these roles in the past. If in the past Jane had returned a dirty sweater, this might make Stacy reluctant to continue in the role of lender.

When we look at this conversation between Jane and Stacy, we can see how complicated even a simple conversation can be. Still, we can never really understand what goes on in communication unless we look at it from a transactional perspective. Then we can begin to see the complexity and uniqueness of each communication event. As Heraclitus, the Greek philosopher, once observed, we cannot step into the same river twice because not only are we different but so is the river. The same is true of communication.

Types of Communication

As you can see in Figure 1-2, there are different kinds of communication. The figure shows the kinds most often used: intrapersonal, interpersonal, interviews, small group, and public.

Intrapersonal Communication

Intrapersonal communication is communication that occurs within us. It involves thoughts, feelings, and the way we look at ourselves. Figure 1-3 shows some of the things that make up the self and, hence, intrapersonal communication.

Because intrapersonal communication is centered in the self, you are the only sender-receiver. The message is made up of your thoughts and feelings. The channel is your brain, which processes what you are thinking and feeling.

INTRAPERSONAL COMMUNICATION

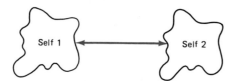

INTERPERSONAL COMMUNICATION AND INTERVIEWING

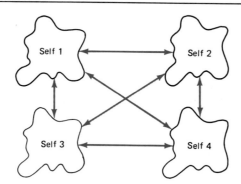

SMALL-GROUP COMMUNICATION

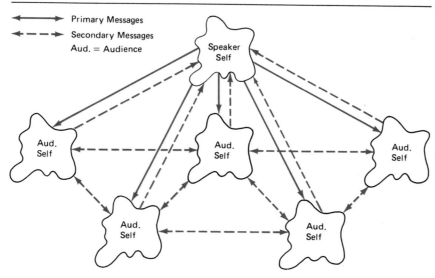

PUBLIC COMMUNICATION

Figure 1-2
Kinds of
Communication

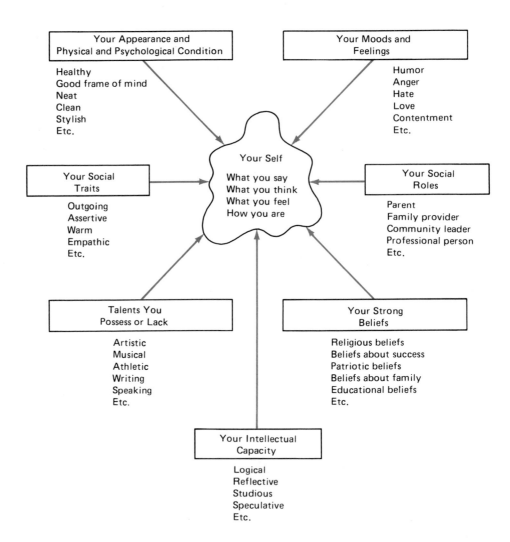

Figure 1-3
Intrapersonal
Communication

There is feedback in the sense that as you talk to yourself, you discard certain ideas and replace them with others.

Even though you are not directly communicating with others in intrapersonal communication, the people and the experiences you have had determine how you "talk" to yourself. For example, if you have had a good day, you are likely to look at yourself in a positive way. If a teacher was disappointed with your work, or if you had a fight with a fellow student, you are likely to focus more on your depression or anger. You can never look at yourself without being influenced by the relationships you have had with others.

Interpersonal Communication

Interpersonal communication occurs when we communicate on a one-to-one basis—usually in an informal, unstructured setting. This kind of communication occurs mostly between two people, though it may include more than two.

Interpersonal communication uses all the elements of the communication process. In a conversation between friends, for example, each brings his or her background and experience to the conversation. During the conversation each functions as a sender-receiver. Their messages consist of both verbal and nonverbal symbols. The channels they use the most are sight and sound. Because interpersonal communication is between two (or a few) people, it offers the greatest opportunity for feedback. Internal noise is likely to be minimal because each person can see whether the other is distracted. The persons involved in the conversation have many chances to check that the message is being perceived correctly. Interpersonal communication usually takes place in informal and comfortable settings.

Interviewing

An **interview** is a series of questions and answers, usually involving two people whose primary purpose is to obtain information on a particular subject. One common type is the *job interview,* in which the employer asks the job candidate questions to determine whether he or she is suitable for the job. Another type is an *information interview* where the interviewer tries to get information about a particular subject.

In interviewing, the sender-receivers take turns talking—one person asks a question and the other responds. Both persons, however, are continuously

Which couple has the closest relationship, the two girls or the girl and the boy? How do you know this?

and simultaneously sending nonverbal messages. Because interviews usually take place face to face, a lot of nonverbal information is exchanged. Feedback is very high in an interview; and because the communication is so structured, concentration is high and there is little noise. Since the interview has a specific purpose, the communication setting is usually quite formal.

Small-Group Communication

Small-group communication occurs when a small number of people meet to solve a problem. The group must be small enough so that each member in the group has a chance to interact with all the other members.

Because small groups are made up of several sender-receivers, the communication process is more complicated than in interpersonal communication. With so many more people sending messages, there are more chances for confusion. Messages are also more structured in small groups because the group is meeting together for a specific purpose. Small groups use the same channels as interpersonal communication, however, and there is also a good deal of opportunity for feedback. In view of their problem-solving nature, small groups usually meet in a more formal setting than people involved in interpersonal communication.

Public Communication

In **public communication** the sender-receiver (the speaker) sends a message (the speech) to an audience. The speaker usually delivers a highly structured message, using the same channels as in interpersonal and small-group communication. In public communication, however, the channels are more exaggerated than in interpersonal communication. The voice is louder and the gestures are more expansive because the audience is bigger. The speaker

Try This Try This Try This

*I*n each of the communication situations listed below, identify the following: the kind of communication, the participants, the message, the channel, the amount of potential feedback, and the likely setting. What are the possible sources of external and internal noise in each situation?

- You meet with a study group to prepare for a biology test.
- You go to the student union for coffee with a friend.
- You are writing a story for the student newspaper and interview the president of the college to see whether there will be a tuition increase.
- A senatorial candidate makes a brief stop in your town and speaks on the courthouse steps. Television cameras are there to cover the event for the local newscast.
- You run into a former boyfriend or girlfriend at the mall.

might use additional visual channels, such as slides, flip charts, and so on. Generally the opportunity for verbal feedback in public communication is limited. The audience members may have a chance to ask questions at the end of the speech, but usually they are not free to address the speaker during the speech. However, they can send nonverbal feedback. If they like what the speaker is saying, they may interrupt the speech with applause. If they dislike it, they may fidget a lot or simply stop paying attention. In most public communication the setting is formal.

Communicating Effectively

Once you understand the process of communication, you can begin to understand why communication does or doesn't work. In an ideal communication situation the message is perceived in the way it was intended. For example, you ask your roommate to pick up a loaf of bread after school and she does so. The message was perceived as you intended it to be. If she comes back without the bread or with the wrong kind of bread, then you have to examine the communication process. If you had wanted her to bring white bread and she brought rye bread, then the verbal symbols in your message were not specific enough. If she forgot the bread altogether, maybe there was a problem with the channel. It wasn't enough to tell her; you also should have written a note. Or maybe internal noise interfered—she was thinking about her class and didn't really hear the message. Your communication could have broken down in any one of these ways. When messages don't work, then, it is useful to ask these questions: Was there a problem with the message? Was the best channel used? Did noise occur? Knowing the right questions to ask is essential to building skills in communication.

Most of us already have considerable communication skills. We have been sending and receiving verbal and nonverbal signals all our lives. Nevertheless, we have all had times when we have not communicated as effectively as we should. We got a lower grade on a paper than we expected, we unintentionally hurt somebody's feelings, or the instructor did not understand our question when we asked it in class.

Where to Begin

The information and research about communication are so vast that most of us could spend a lifetime studying communication and not learn even a fraction of what there is to know. As a beginning student of communication, here are five questions to ask yourself.

WHICH COMMUNICATION SKILLS AM I MOST LIKELY TO NEED?

Find out what communication skills are important to you. What do you intend to do in your life? What kind of work do you expect to do? What communication skills are required in this work? Which of these skills do you already have? Which ones need improvement? Which ones do you need to acquire?

Going into politics, for example, would require a broad range of com-

Try This Try This Try This

*R*emember the time you asked for a particular present for Christmas, but when you got it, it wasn't quite right? The problem was that you weren't precise enough. Now assume that your friend asks you what you want for your birthday and you want a shirt to wear with jeans. Describe what you would like, but don't be too specific—after all, you want to be a little surprised. Some of the things you might want to mention are size, color, fabric, print or solid color, and light or heavy weight.

Once you have a more precise description, ask yourself if you are more likely to get what you want.

munication skills. Public speaking skills would be the most valuable, as well as the ability to talk to strangers and to make an impression on them. Perhaps you are majoring in social work. Since most social workers work one to one with clients, they need both interpersonal and interviewing skills. A career in business requires almost every communication skill. You need interpersonal skills to get along with the people you work with, interviewing skills (especially if you're going to work in personnel), and public-speaking skills for making presentations. Although you may use some communication skills more than others, at one time or another you are going to need every one we have discussed in this chapter.

WHICH COMMUNICATION SKILLS AM I MOST LACKING IN?

Which kinds of communication are most difficult for you? Intrapersonal? Interpersonal? Interviewing? Small-group? Public speaking? Why do you have difficulties in these areas? What problems do you have to overcome before you can perform effectively in these areas?

Probably you would prefer *not* to work in the area that gives you the most trouble. For example, if you are anxious about public speaking, you might feel inclined to avoid any circumstance where you have to give a speech. It will be much more to your advantage, however, if you can conquer this fear by plunging in and practicing the thing that gives you the most trouble. You will find some big rewards in doing so; not only will you learn how to do something, but you will feel much better about yourself.

HOW CAN I GET COMMUNICATION PRACTICE?

Are there situations, other than class, where you can practice communication skills that will be useful to you? Are there groups and organizations you can join that will help you develop these skills? It's always a good idea to take what you have learned in class and try it out on the world. Using new skills helps to develop and refine them.

WHERE CAN I GET HELP?

What people do you know who will help you to develop these skills and give you feedback on how you are doing? Are there people you can ask who will give you support when you try to do something new and scary? Are you willing to ask them to support you? We can usually count on this kind of support from our friends. Most of us have at least one friend who would be willing to listen to one of our speeches and tell us whether it works or where we might improve it. Also, don't forget your instructors. Most welcome visits from students during office hours.

WHAT TIMETABLE SHOULD I SET?

Have you set a realistic timetable for improvement? Knowing that it is difficult to learn new skills or break bad habits, are you willing to give yourself that time? Your speech class is going to last for a semester or a quarter. Although you will be making steady improvement in your speeches, you still might be a long way from making a perfect speech at the end of the term. This does not mean, however, that you will never be able to make a perfect speech; it is a matter of needing more time. The same is true of bad habits. Let's say, for example, that you have asked your friends to remind you to stop saying "he don't." You're not going to break the habit in a couple of weeks; look how long you've been saying it that way. Perhaps the most realistic timetable, then, is one where you say "I'm going to keep working at this until I succeed."

SUMMARY

Everyone needs to communicate effectively. Successful communication helps bring us success and pleasure, helps us to change the way others act and behave, and aids us in maintaining and improving relationships.

Communication is a process in which people share ideas and feelings. It is a process because it is ongoing. The elements of communication include sender-receivers, messages, channels, feedback, noise, and setting.

All communication is a transaction. Viewing communication as a transaction focuses on the people who are communicating and the changes that take place in them as they are communicating. It also implies that all participants are involved continuously and simultaneously; that communication events have a past, present, and future; and that the roles the participants play will affect the communication.

Five kinds of communication are discussed in this book. Intrapersonal communication is communication with one's self. Interpersonal communication is informal communication with one or more other persons. Interviewing is a structured question-and-answer type of communication with the specific purpose of obtaining information. Small-group communication occurs when a small group of people get together to solve a problem. Public communication is giving a speech to an audience.

Communication can be improved if you concentrate on several important areas. You need to find out what communication skills are important to you. You need to discover the kinds of communication that are most difficult for you and work to improve them. You need to seek out people who will help you develop these skills and give you support and feedback. Finally, you need to set a realistic timetable for improvement.

ARNOLD, CARROLL C., AND JOHN WAITE BOWERS. *Handbook of Rhetorical and Communication Theory*. Boston: Allyn and Bacon, 1984. This volume is a useful resource and reference book for serious students of rhetoric and communication. Each of the fourteen chapters presents the state of the theoretical art, including the emergence, development, and present status of that body of theory. Part I treats cultural and scientific presuppositions; Part II deals with communication as facilitator and inhibitor of important human activities.

CAMPBELL, KARLYN KOHRS. *The Rhetorical Act*. Belmont, CA: Wadsworth, 1982. Although this is primarily a book on public communication, we have included it here because it takes a traditional, humanistic approach to public speaking (rhetoric) drawn from the classics. The author's opening chapters on the rhetorical perspective and the rhetorical act provide a clear orientation to this perspective.

GRIFFIN, EM. *A First Look at Communication Theory*. N.Y.: McGraw-Hill, Inc., 1991. This introductory book contains an explanation of thirty-one theories that explain a wide range of communication phenomena along with a discussion of the strengths and weaknesses of each theory. There is also an excellent reading list following each theory for students who want to do more investigation.

HOWELL, WILLIAM S. *The Empathic Communicator*. Prospect Heights, IL. Waveland Press, 1986. Howell's perspective is that communication is an ever-changing, often unpredictable joint venture. We include this book because of his emphasis on empathy, sending and receiving, and messages. Howell explores competence in spontaneous interactions.

IACOCCA, LEE, AND WILLIAM NOVACK. *Iacocca: An Autobiography*. New York: Bantam Books, 1986. From this best-selling book, it is clear that effective communication is a process that Iacocca supports and encourages. He offers numerous suggestions about and examples of successful communication. A powerful book.

LITTLEJOHN, STEPHEN W. *Theories of Human Communication*, 3d ed. Belmont, CA: Wadsworth, 1989. Littlejohn offers a comprehensive examination of major communication theories. His discussion of the strengths and weaknesses of theories is useful; however, the book is designed for the more serious student of communication.

PETERS, THOMAS J., AND ROBERT H. WATERMAN, JR. *In Search of Excellence: Lessons from America's Best-Run Companies*. New York: Warner Books, 1988. One overwhelming theme in this book is the importance that effective communication skills play in America's best-run companies. An outstanding book full of vital information for anyone seeking a business career.

TOMPKINS, PHILIP K. *Communication as Action: An Introduction to Rhetoric and Communication*. Belmont, CA: Wadsworth, 1982. Tompkins challenges the reader to define what it is to be human and how to function effectively in a society that is the sum total of human communicative acts. He discusses interpersonal, group, and organizational communication. This is a textbook for the serious student.

Chapter 2

Self and Communication

CHAPTER OBJECTIVES	KEY TERMS
After reading this chapter, you should be able to:	ethnicity
	ethnocentrism
1. Explain why perception differs from one person to another.	perception
	psychological safety
2. Describe how perception and self-concept are related.	psychological risk
	race
	scripts
3. Explain how each of the following influences perception: our bodies, what people tell us, and what we tell others.	self-concept
	self-esteem
	self-fulfilling prophecies
4. Outline the six steps in the perceptual process and give an example that shows how each step works.	stereotypes
5. Describe the five steps people might go through when they discover someone is racially or culturally different.	
6. Describe some of the ways you can improve your own self-esteem.	

*D*an and Jean sit next to each other in class. They have several interests in common, including an interest in each other. Each would like to see the other outside of class, but neither has made a move in that direction. Now they find themselves in the student center at the same time. Dan sees Jean sitting alone at a table, so he joins her. As they talk casually about the weather and the assignments they have for their class, thoughts about each other are going through their heads. Dan is thinking: "I really would like to ask her out to the movies. I wonder if she would go with me. I'd feel pretty bad if she turned me down." Jean's thinking is taking a similar line. She thinks: "He really is a nice guy. I'd like to get to know him better, but he is so shy. I think he likes me, but I'm really not sure."

Although Dan and Jean's conversation and thoughts seem to be somewhat ordinary, each person is going through a very complicated perceptual process. On one level, what Dan is saying and thinking reflects how he feels about himself. ("In this situation, I am feeling somewhat insecure.") On another level, his thoughts reflect how he feels about Jean. ("I like her and I would like to know her better.") On yet a third level, they are influenced by how he thinks Jean sees him. ("I think she likes me but I'm not sure.") Jean is going through a similar perceptual process. Her thoughts and what she says are influenced by how she sees herself, how she perceives Dan, and how she thinks Dan perceives her.

Like Dan and Jean, whenever we have a conversation with another person, we go through the same six-step perceptual process:

1. How I see myself
2. How I see you
3. How I think you see me
4. How you see yourself
5. How you see me
6. How you think I see you[1]

All these levels make communication a very complicated business. As is true in all transactional communication, many of these levels are occurring continuously and simultaneously. Dan's perception of Jean is influenced by how he sees himself and how he sees his past relationships; Jean is influenced by her sense of self and her experiences with other men. Both of them are also influenced by how they see their roles in a male-female relationship. Jean wants to be more assertive in moving their friendship forward, but based on her idea of the role a woman should play in a relationship, she's worried about being too aggressive. Dan believes that it is his role to move the relationship forward, but he is too shy to do so.

Much of their problem in getting to know each other better is based on how each sees himself or herself. Like them, the way you view the world and communicate about it is greatly influenced by the way you view yourself.

Perception and Self-Concept

Self-concept is made up of the conclusions you draw about yourself; it consists of such diverse elements as the statements you make about yourself, your reaction to yourself when you look in the mirror, and the things you think you can and cannot do. When you add up all the things that make up your self-concept, the good and the bad, you come up with **self-esteem**—how much you value yourself. How you look at others and the world around you is called **perception.**

Self-concept, self-esteem, and perception are so closely related that it is often difficult to separate them. How you look at the world depends on what you think of yourself; what you think of yourself will influence how you look at the world. For example, Min Hee and Bob, who have majored in the same subject, sit around one day and talk about jobs in their field. Min Hee, who had good self-esteem, says, "I looked in the newspaper last night and there were all kinds of jobs I could do." Bob, who doesn't have so much self-esteem, says, "I've had just the opposite experience. Every time I look at the paper, I never find anything. It depresses me so much, I've stopped looking." Because Min Hee's self-concept is one of confidence, her perception of the job market is optimistic. Bob's self-concept is much more negative, so he perceives the world as a much more threatening place.

Your perceptions of what you should notice or ignore will be influenced by your self-concept. For example, Karen sees an announcement that there is going to be an essay contest for African-American history month. Since part of her self-concept is that she's a good writer, she decides to write an essay and enter it in the contest. She mentions the contest to her friend James, and suggests he enter it too. He replies, "No way. I wouldn't have a chance." Since James does not have a good self-concept as a writer, he chooses to ignore the information about the contest.

The messages that we get from others and from the mass media have a lot to do with our self-concept and self-esteem. Probably, the messages we get from others that have the greatest impact come from parents, siblings, teachers, and friends. (See Figure 2-1.)

Try This Try This Try This

W H O   A R E   Y O U ?

Begin with your official story, the one you habitually tell without thinking. Imagine you are sitting beside a stranger on a plane. Introduce yourself ("I am . . ."), using a single word or short phrase that most accurately characterizes you. Try it 10 times, completing the sentences with different predicates that describe you, such as "I am a father," "I am a Republican," "I am a Marx Brothers freak."

Next, write down your 10 predicates and think about what you have chosen to tell about yourself and what you have left out. How many of your descriptive statements have to do with your work? Your home life? Your gender? Your race, religion, or nationality, Your passions? Your possessions?"

Source: Sam Keen, "The Stories We Live By," *Psychology Today.*

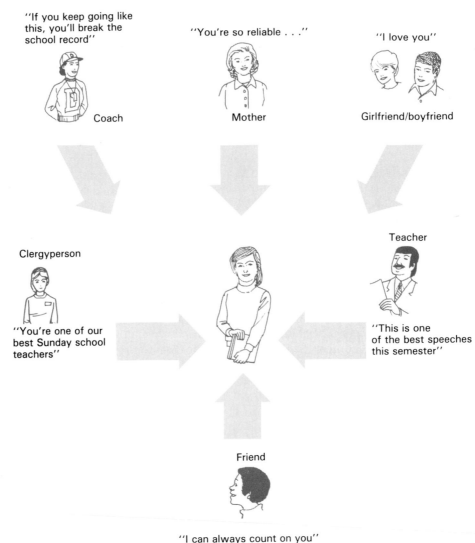

"If you keep going like this, you'll break the school record"

Coach

"You're so reliable . . ."

Mother

"I love you"

Girlfriend/boyfriend

Clergyperson

"You're one of our best Sunday school teachers"

Teacher

"This is one of the best speeches this semester"

Friend

"I can always count on you"

Figure 2-1
**The Development
of Self-Esteem**

Recent research has found that self-esteem is a greater problem for females than for males. When elementary school children were asked how often they felt "happy with the way I am," 67 percent of the boys and 60 percent of the girls responded "always." By high school, however, 46 percent of the boys said "always" but the number of girls who felt that way dropped to 29 percent.[2] Some of this decline in self-esteem can be attributed to problems of adolescence. However, no one has any idea why the self-esteem of girls is so much lower than that of boys.

When we recognize that self-concept, self-esteem, and perception are unique and subjective, it seems reasonable to ask "Why are we all so different?" Where do our perceptions come from? How does self-concept develop? That is the subject of our next section.

The Development of Perception and Self-Concept

Perception and self-concept develop from three areas: the body we are born with, the information people give us about ourselves, and our past experiences.

Our Bodies

Each of us is born with a unique body, and to some extent the body we have influences our perception of the world. Most people have five senses, but those senses are not necessarily equal in all people. For example, most people can see well enough to get through life, but some see differently than others. Why, otherwise, can some children hit a ball better than others? Why do some children learn to read very quickly while other children struggle? Clearly what is seen and how it is interpreted by the brain can differ greatly among people. The same is true of the other senses. In hearing, some people are startled by loud noises while others remain calm. Although tastes can be acquired, people also seem to be born with a taste for certain things. Even babies have their preferences among kinds of baby foods.

The way your body is functioning can affect your perception. Hormones can influence emotional cycles. Health can be a factor, as can such states as tiredness and hunger. When you are feeling good, you are more likely to want to interact with other people. When you are tired or hungry, you are more likely to be irritable.

Physical size can influence perception too. Tall people see tops of heads; short people see bottoms of chins. Where you decide to live, the chairs you choose for your house, the kind of car you drive, the person you choose to marry or date—all might be chosen because of your physical size.

What Other People Tell Us

BODY IMAGE

For most of us, the body we have is perfectly adequate. Our heart beats, our blood courses through our veins, and we have the energy we need to get through our days and nights. How we feel about this body, though, might be an entirely different matter. Researchers have found that when children are teased about their bodies, especially between the ages of 8 and 16, they often go into adulthood with a highly negative body image. The effect of teasing or criticism is particularly powerful if it comes from parents, coaches, or other significant people in their lives.

A negative body image can lead to eating disorders among girls and women. Men are not immune from negative body images either. Ninety-five percent of men in a recent survey expressed dissatisfaction with some aspect of their bodies. Hair loss seemed to be the most devastating to men—especially if they were in their twenties. The most significant finding in body image research has been that the view we have of our body greatly influences our self-concept.

Society sets a standard as well for what is normal or subnormal intelligence. These standards, in turn, are communicated to us by those who take care of us (parents, baby-sitters), by institutions we are part of (school, church), and by the mass media (particularly advertising, television, and movies). Our self-concept is very much determined by whether we measure up to these societal standards of physical attractiveness and intellectual ability.

ROLES

Remember the story of Tarzan? Although Tarzan was a human, he believed he was an ape because he was brought up by apes and had no human experience. Tarzan's story reminds us that we are not born with an identity—it is given to us by someone else. Our parents, or the first people who take care of us, tell us through their words and actions that we are good or bad, stupid or intelligent, lovable or unlovable.

Many of these messages are given to us in terms of the roles we are to play in life. A role, as Chapter 1 noted, is how a person behaves in a particular situation. A role does not mean phony behavior—it merely means that people in different situations act in different ways. In class, for example, you play the role of student. When you relate to your children, you play the role of parent. When you talk to your boss, you play the role of employee.

Every role we play requires certain communication behavior—behavior that has been determined by our society. If you are being interviewed for a job, you are expected to ask some questions and show interest in the job. If you don't do this, you will lessen your chances of getting the job. In your role as a speech student, you are expected to speak up in class and give your

Who is in control of this conversation? How can you tell?

speeches on the day they are due. If you violate any of the expectations of this role, you will probably be in trouble and be punished with a low grade.

Roles and perceptions are closely related. We make judgments of people based on whether we perceive them as playing their roles properly. For instance, Alice says that Dick is a good father because he always listens to his children. Tom, however, does not agree. He thinks Dick is a bad father because he works such long hours. Both Alice and Tom have a precise idea of what the role of "good father" entails, and they evaluate others on the basis of this perception. Judgments based on the perception of how roles should be played are very common.

Most of us want to play our roles properly. This can be difficult, however, because not everyone agrees on how specific roles should be played. Every teacher has an idea of the role of a "good student," but to one teacher it might be a student who is quiet and doesn't disturb the class, while to another it might be a student who asks interesting questions. All bosses value a "hard worker," but one might identify this person as someone who works longer hours than anyone else, while another envisions someone who gets the job done on time.

SCRIPTS

As well as being told how we should play our roles, we are also given lines to speak. These lines are often so specific that some people refer to them as **scripts.**[3]

Some scripts are given to us by our parents, and they contain directions that are just as explicit as any script intended for the stage. We are given our lines ("Say thank you to the nice lady"), our gestures ("Don't point!"), and our characterizations ("You're a good boy"). The scripts tell us how to play future scenes ("Everyone in our family has gone to college") and what is expected of us ("I will be so happy when you make us grandparents").

People outside our family also contribute to our scripts. Teachers, coaches, ministers, friends, even the media—all tell us what they expect from us, how we should look, how we should behave, and how we should say our lines.

SELF-FULFILLING PROPHECIES

Part of our self-concept develops because of **self-fulfilling prophecies.**[4] These are predictions that come true because we (and others) predict them. For example, Professor Farley says to Kevin, "I'm sure you are going to be a very good student." This statement makes Kevin want to be a good student, and so he works hard to live up to Professor Farley's prophecy. Similarly, negative prophecies can have a negative impact. If someone tells a child that he will "never amount to much," there is a good chance the child will do just that.

Children get their self-fulfilling prophecies from others. If these prophecies have been largely positive ("You're a good-looking kid"; "I know you'll do well on your test"; "If you practice, you will be really good"), the child will grow up with a positive self-concept. The opposite is also true: a child who has been subjected to many negative prophecies is unlikely to view himself or herself in a very positive way. The message "You are a bad boy" is likely to be understood and retained as "I am a bad boy."

Consider This Consider This Consider This

Sometimes people are so taken by the roles they play that they can't see beyond them. In this passage of his diary, Rabbi Martin Siegel writes why he and his wife cannot transcend their roles in the eyes of their congregation:

People tend to make me a symbol. They say they know me, but they don't. They know only my roles. To some of them, I am a radical. To some of them, I am a signature on the marriage contract. To some of them I am the man who opposes the indulgence of the psychotic fear of anti-semitism. People see me only as they care or need to see me.

   And poor Judith has to be a wife to all this.

   I can't recognize myself in their eyes, so how could she? We both have to live as exhibits in this community. While people are friendly, we have no friends. We have been made into what they want us to be. . . .

- What roles do people expect you to play? Caring son or daughter? Good student? Loving friend? Hard worker?

- Are any of these roles difficult? If so, why?

- Do you feel that any of these roles hide the real you? If so, which ones?

Source: Michael Rubin, *Men without Masks.*

Our Past Experiences

Our self-concept and many of our perceptions come from our past experiences. On a simple level, a child who gets praise from her parents when she says her first words will be encouraged to try other words—particularly when she discovers words get her what she wants.

   Much of our initial self-concept comes from members of our family. For example, some research has shown that whether we grow up to be optimistic or pessimistic might come from messages we receive from early care givers. If the primary care giver, such as a mother, explains that bad things occur because of a personal flaw, the child is more likely to become a pessimist. If, however, she explains that although a bad thing has happened, it can be fixed, the child is more likely to be optimistic.

   After spending the earliest part of our lives within the family and having our first experiences there, we are ready to step out into the larger world. Then institutions such as school and church begin to play a larger role in shaping us. We start out by taking small steps, and if we are successful with them, we risk taking larger ones. Our past experiences become a road map to our future. Whether they are good or bad, they influence our perception of the world around us. What we do, say, think, and believe will, in many cases, be influenced by our past.

*T*he writer Garrison Keillor has an excellent ear for the messages we get in childhood. How many of these have you heard yourself? What effect do you think these or similar messages have had on your self-concept? Will you give these messages to your own children?

I. I don't know what's wrong with you.
  A. I never saw a person like you.
    1. I wasn't like that.
    2. Your cousins don't pull stuff like that.
  B. It doesn't make sense.
    1. You have no sense of responsibility at all.
    2. We've given you everything we possibly could,
      a. Food on the table and a roof over your head
      b. Things we never had when we were your age
    3. And you treat us like dirt under your feet.
  C. You act as if
    1. The world owes you a living
    2. You got a chip on your shoulder
    3. The rules don't apply to you

II. Something has got to change and change fast.
  A. You're driving your mother to a nervous breakdown.
  B. I'm not going to put up with this for another minute.
    1. You're crazy if you think I am.
    2. If you think I am, just try me.
  C. You're setting a terrible example for your younger brothers and sisters.

III. I'm your father and as long as you live in this house, you'll—
  A. Do as you're told, and when I say "now" I mean "now."
  B. Pull your own weight.
    1. Don't except other people to pick up after you.
    2. Don't expect breakfast when you get up at noon.
    3. Don't come around asking your mother for spending money.
  C. Do something about your disposition.

IV. If you don't change your tune pretty quick, then you're out of here.
  A. I mean it.
  B. Is that understood?
    1. I can't hear you. Don't mumble.
    2. Look at me.
  C. I'm not going to tell you this again.

Source: Garrison Keillor, *Lake Wobegon Days.*

Our Perceptions of the World

Psychological Safety and Risk

Ask some second-semester seniors what they are afraid of. Chances are they will reply that they are very apprehensive about going out into the world. Will they find a job? Can they survive outside of the structure of university life? What is the world like? What is their place in it?

For most of us, **psychological safety**—the approval and support that we get from the familiar people, ideas, and situations is important to us. However, Abraham Maslow, the late psychologist, who worked in the area of self-fulfillment, has pointed out that the needs for safety and growth pull us in opposite directions. In Maslow's view, in order to grow, people have to abandon some of the safe areas of their lives and take some psychological risks. A **psychological risk** involves taking a chance on something new. It could be getting to know someone different from us, trying to understand a different point of view or even moving to a new place. For example, a student going away to college must leave the safety of home, friends, and family. Once in college, students learn new ideas that might be very risky. For example, a student who is pro-abortion will take a big risk if he or she tries to really understand a person who is pro-life. Similarly, it's risky to try to understand why many people believe that Islam is the true religion—especially if you happen to believe that Christianity is. The problem with taking such a risk is that you might be changed. If you do change, your circle of family and friends probably have not changed and you won't fit in completely any more. Inevitably, whenever you take a risk, your circle of safety grows smaller.

Yet anyone who wants to grow must take some risks. For college students, new ideas might be the greatest risk of all. One learns that whole nations of people believe in religions that are different from Christianity and Judaism or that some people don't believe in *any* religion. Or one might learn that some people believe there should be no competitive sports in high school. Our first response to these ideas that conflict with our own is to reject them; if we do, we choose psychological safety. When we take a psychological risk we are ready to consider these ideas from the other person's vantage point.

Our Perceptions within Our Culture

The people we communicate with best are those who see us in pretty much the same light that we see ourselves. With these people we can talk a kind of "shorthand." They know what we are thinking and feeling—they speak our language. These people, however, are small in number and are usually made up of close friends and family members.

In the rest of our daily life—in work and in social gatherings—we have to communicate with people who might not know us very well. Even if we did know them well, we might not share their ways of looking at themselves and the world.

How do we communicate with them? How do we work with them? How do we get through social interactions? How do we deal with differing perceptions? To see how this works, let's look at a common interaction—one

What kind of risk is this child taking? Is anything happening to make her feel safe?

between a student and his professor—following the six perceptual steps we introduced earlier in this chapter.

SELF-PERCEPTION

Jay Brown: Sees himself as a good student. Studies two or three hours a night. Has a 3.1 grade average.

Professor Black: Sees himself as a hard-working professor. Prides himself on preparing material students can understand.

HOW THEY SEE EACH OTHER

Jay Brown: Sees Professor Black as a hard teacher. Believes Black is rigid and unsympathetic to students.

Professor Black: Because he saw Jay Brown falling asleep in class one day, he assumes Jay is lazy and unmotivated.

HOW HE THINKS THE OTHER SEES HIM

Jay Brown: I don't think he likes me very much. Whenever I try to ask a question in class, he seems to ignore me.

Professor Black: If this student sleeps in my class, he must think I'm pretty boring.

Sometimes we aren't able to check out our perceptions of others. If Jay manages to pass the class, he will probably make it a point never to take another class from Professor Black. Let's assume, however, that Jay has failed an exam and has to talk to Professor Black. Based on their perceptions of themselves and of each other, their conversation might go something like this:

Jay: I am having a lot of trouble in your class. The material is hard, and I can't seem to do very well on your exams.

Professor: The material isn't hard. You're probably not studying enough. You can't just skim the book and hope to do well on the exams.

Jay: I study for this class every day. I probably could understand the book better if the lectures were clearer.

Professor: You can always ask questions in class.

Jay: I am so confused I don't even know what questions to ask.

Professor: Well, all I can say is that you should study more.

Jay and Professor Black have reached a dead end. Each entered into the communication with negative perceptions of the other, and these perceptions were reinforced during the communication. Each gave the other a negative message (Jay that the lectures are not clear; Professor Black that Jay doesn't study hard enough).

But what if something had happened in their conversation to change their perceptions of each other? Let's go back to where Jay says: "I am so confused I don't even know what questions to ask." Professor Black changes his reply to: "You might understand more if you could manage to stay awake in class." Now Jay has some information as to how he is perceived by Professor Black. Jay thinks for a minute and says, "Oh, I recall. Remember that day when we had the big rain? The basement of our house flooded, and I was moving furniture out of there all night. You're right. I did fall asleep in class. I'm sorry."

Professor Black now has new information about Jay, and he decides to accept it as legitimate. As his perception of Jay (as a lazy student) begins to change, he tries harder to help Jay with his problems in the class. He asks Jay if he has his lecture notes with him, and Jay hands him the notes. Professor Black is impressed with their thoroughness, but he realizes that Jay is writing down too much information and has a problem distinguishing major points from minor ones. He spends some time explaining to Jay how to take better notes. Jay is so quick to respond and understand that Professor Black's perception of him becomes more and more positive and he begins to see Jay in the way Jay sees himself. The result of the conversation is that both of them leave it feeling better about themselves and each other. A couple of months later, when someone asks Jay if she should take a class from Professor Black, Jay responds: "He's a good teacher. I really learned a lot from him."

Jay Brown and Professor Black are able to communicate because they are willing to take the risk of seeing the perception each one has of the other. By taking this risk, each of them has had to change his opinion. The reward, of course, is that they have greatly increased their mutual understanding. They

might never be in another academic or social relationship. Even so, they can apply what they have learned from this encounter to all their other relationships.

Racism, Ethnicity, and Communication

In recent years there have been several incidents of prejudice against racial and ethnic groups on campuses throughout the country. Since all these incidents involve negative communication of one individual or group toward another, it is useful to try to understand this problem in the context of interpersonal communication.

To discuss racial and ethnic discrimination, we need to start with some definitions. **Race** refers to physical characteristics such as color of skin, eyes, hair, and so forth. Sometimes members of different races share the same culture, but no common culture is found among all members of any racial group. African-Americans, for example, do not share a common culture with Africans.[5]

Ethnicity refers to a shared common history, tradition, and culture. Nationality is often shared, and culture is always shared.[6]

For any accurate communication to occur, the sender-receivers must be operating from the same perceptual point of view. Usually this is not a problem when we are interacting with people from our own race or culture—we share

What steps do we go through in getting to know a person from another race?

the same attitudes, values, and beliefs. When we communicate with someone from a different race or background, however, each sender-receiver might have a different point of view.

One problem involves ethnic or racial **stereotypes**—oversimplified or distorted views of another race or culture. When people have stereotypes, they react to them rather than to reality. In Table 2.1, Teun A. van Dijk identifies and classifies some of these stereotypes.

Another place where misunderstanding is likely to occur is when a person from one culture tries to communicate in a way that is not familiar to people in another culture. When Eva Hoffman immigrates from Poland to Canada as a young girl, she discovers many subtle differences in verbal and nonverbal communication:

My mother says I'm becoming "English." This hurts me, because I know she means I'm becoming cold. I'm no colder than I've ever been, but I'm

---

TABLE 2-1
Prejudiced Attitude Schema

0. *General*
   0.1. I do not like them
   0.2. Others do not like them

1. *Origin and appearance*
   1.1. We should not have invited them
   1.2. They should be sent back
   1.3. Immigration policies should be stricter
   1.4. They look different (color, clothing)

2. *Socioeconomic goals/status*
   2.1. They take our jobs
   2.2. They do the dirty jobs
   2.3. They take our houses
   2.4. They abuse our social system

3. *Sociocultural differences*
   3.1. They have a different lifestyle
   3.1.1. They should adapt.
   3.2. They treat women badly
   3.3. They have too many children
   3.4. They do not speak our language
   3.5. They are dirty (cause urban decay)
   3.6. Their children cause problems at school

4. *Personal characteristics*
   4.1. They are aggressive (violent)
   4.2. They are criminal
   4.3. They are dirty
   4.4. They are lazy (don't want to work)
   4.5. They are noisy

Source: Teun A. van Dijk, *Communicating Racism.* Newberry Park, CA: Sage Publications, 1987, p. 59.

learning to be less demonstrative. . . . I learn restraint from Penny, who looks offended when I shake her by the arm in excitement, as if my gesture had been one of aggression instead of friendliness. I learn it from a girl who pulls away when I hook my arm through hers as we walk down the street—this movement of friendly intimacy is an embarrassment to her.

I learn also that certain kinds of truth are impolite. One shouldn't criticize the person one is with, at least not directly. You shouldn't say, "You are wrong about that"—though you may say, "On the other hand, there is that to consider." You shouldn't say, "That doesn't look good on you," though you may say, "I like you better in that other outfit. . . ,"

My words often seem to baffle others. They are inappropriate, or forced, or just plain incomprehensible. People look at me with puzzlement; they mumble something in response—something that doesn't hit home.[7]

Misunderstanding also occurs when an idea or object exists in both cultures but has a different meaning. *Family* to an American usually means "mother, father, and siblings." To a Nigerian, however, it means "everyone who has a blood tie," and that might involve relatives who are as remote as second and third cousins. In casual conversation this difference in meaning is not critical, but if people enter into a relationship, the difference in meaning becomes very important. For example, let's say that a Nigerian decides to marry an American. Before the marriage, he tells her that he is responsible for his family. Because of her definition of family, this doesn't seem to be a problem. However, once they are married and he decides to spend half of their income by sending his nieces and nephews abroad to study, the different meaning of "family" can lead to considerable semantic noise.

The Development of Racism and Ethnocentrism

Racism and **ethnocentrism** are variations of the same theme: they both imply that one's own race or culture is superior to all others. These feelings come from our family, our peer group, or anyone else who is influential in our lives. In order to experience racism or ethnocentrism, we must identify with the values and beliefs of a particular group: we say, in effect, since my group is the best, other groups must be inferior.

J. E. Helmes has developed a model which shows the process a white person goes through when he or she becomes aware of race and racial problems.[8] Although Helmes developed this model to explain how racism could develop, it may also apply to a person who is experiencing another culture. In the discussion that follows, we will first present the five-step theory, and then with each step we will explain how this might work in real life. We have used the example of encounters between a white American and a black African because this example involves both racial and cross-cultural perception.

The five stages in the model include contact, disintegration, reintegration, pseudo-independence, and autonomy.

CONTACT

In this first stage individuals discover that different races exist. Not conscious of themselves as racial beings, they usually react to people of a different race with curiosity and interest. A typical reaction to a person might be, "Although you are ———, it doesn't make any difference to me. We are all human beings." This, however, is the honeymoon period; sooner or later these people discover that it does matter to society and that society has definite, sometimes negative, attitudes toward a particular race. Since they become aware that race or ethnocentrism may be an issue of conflict, they might decide that they don't want to be involved and that they don't want any more contact than is necessary.

Bethany sits next to Muthoni, a student from Kenya, in her world history class. At the beginning of the semester they often smile and say hello to each other. Once in a while, when the instructor is late, they talk about the class, how they think they are doing in it, and speculate about what the next test will be like. Throughout this exchange Bethany thinks "Kenyan students are just like us. They study, they worry about their grades, and they like a good social life."

One day Bethany and Muthoni get to class and discover it has been canceled. Since the class is just before lunch, they decide to go to lunch together. As they enter the dining room Muthoni leads Bethany to a table where several other African students are sitting. Bethany enjoys talking to them and thinks to herself, "Gee, this is really interesting. If some of those kids I was in high school with could see me now. . . ."

Later that afternoon, Bethany is walking across campus and runs into one of her friends. Her friend says, "Bethany, who were all those black people *you were having lunch with?" Bethany answers that they were African students. Her friend responds, "Why do you want to eat lunch with* them*?"*

DISINTEGRATION

This stage will occur only if the white person decides to continue to try to make friends with people of different races. In this stage the person is forced to acknowledge he or she is white. Now, aware of discrimination, he or she is likely to react with guilt or depression.

When people reach this point, they take one of three routes: One is to overidentify with the racially different people by taking on characteristics of the group such as clothing, dress, or behavior. Another possibility is that they will become paternalistic, deciding that they are the ones to protect this group from abuse. Both of these choices will not work: the individual discovers it is not possible to become like other people. If they are paternalistic, the individuals they are trying to protect will probably become resentful. As in the first stage, the individual might decide that the conflict is too great and will take the third route, a retreat back to his or her own racial group.

Bethany likes Muthoni so much that she accepts when Muthoni invites her to a party which is mostly made up of African students. Many of the students are wearing clothes from their own country, and the food they eat is like nothing Bethany has ever eaten before. Two of the guys suggest they would like to know her a little better and Bethany begins to feel uncomfortable. Now she realizes that there are some real differences between her and the African students. Nevertheless she enjoys the party, and when she goes home, she tells her roommate about it. Her roommate tells her, "If you start hanging out with these people, your friends will think you're really weird."

Bethany gets more and more interested in East Africa. She starts to read articles in the newspaper whenever they appear and begins to borrow some of Muthoni's clothes to wear. She also learns a few words of Swahili and tries to teach them to some of her American friends (who don't seem very interested).

One day when the campus newspaper comes out, there's a letter from an American student who is protesting the scholarships that are being given to African students. Bethany is so annoyed that she writes a letter to the paper and tells why she thinks the university should give scholarships to Africans. Much to her surprise, Muthoni tells her that several African students are angry about her letter: they tell Bethany they can speak for themselves—they don't need her as their spokesperson.

REINTEGRATION

If the individual can not resolve the problems of the disintegration stage, he or she is likely to feel anger or fear and will act with hostility toward the other race. Researchers feel that it's at this stage where people feel prejudice and start to stereotype the other race.

On the other hand, the individual might decide to accept that he or she is white and to understand the implications of being white in a society that is racist. If the feelings of anger and fear eventually dissipate, the person will enter the next stage.

Now Bethany is mad at all her African friends. She thinks, "I was just trying to help them. What right do they have to be upset? If they don't appreciate me, I'm not going to be friends with them anymore."

A couple of days later, she feels calmer about what has happened. She realizes she has become good friends with some of the Africans—Muthoni, in particular—and she doesn't want to break off her contact with them.

PSEUDO-INDEPENDENCE

Individuals who move to this stage become interested in the similarities and differences between the two groups. They are no longer as naive as they were in their first encounter. By trying to understand the problem intellectually, they are able to reduce their anger. At this stage some people might choose to remain friends with people from other groups, but they might choose those members who most resemble their own racial or ethnic group.

Bethany decides to begin by reading some books about East Africa—where most of her friends have come from. She realizes that Kenyans once lived in a country that was ruled by the British, and to gain independence they had to reject their British past. From this book, Bethany realizes how sensitive the Kenyans are to the issue of white control, and she begins to understand that her letter to the newspaper might have been perceived as a form of control. Other books about Africa and racism give her even greater insights. She also attends a series of lectures about South Africa and begins to understand more about the relationships between black and white people.

AUTONOMY

In this stage individuals not only understand the differences between the two groups, they accept them. They see the differences between the two groups as positive. Secure in their own racial identity, they actively seek opportunities to interact with people who are different. They approach other racial and cultural groups with appreciation and respect.

> *Bethany now feels more comfortable with her African friends. She realizes that Kenyans and Nigerians regard their own countries as the best place to live and that it might be an insult to ask them whether they would prefer living in the United States. She becomes so interested in Kenya that she makes an application to go there for a semester as an exchange student.*
>
> *Later in the semester, she meets some students from Sri Lanka. She has lots of questions to ask them. . . .*

Improving Your Self-Esteem

The most difficult thing any human being can do is to change his or her self-esteem for the better. How does one go about doing this? Here are some suggestions that might help.

DECIDE WHAT YOU WANT TO CHANGE ABOUT YOURSELF

Pick one area in which you would like to improve yourself and, hence, your self-esteem. See if you can figure out why you have had problems in this area. Were you given a script saying you were inadequate? Are you living out a self-fulfilling prophecy?

CONSIDER YOUR CIRCUMSTANCES

Are you living in circumstances that are holding you back? Do the people around you support you in risk taking? Sometimes the people we live with try to hold us back—even though they might not be conscious that they are doing so. Tutors who teach adults how to read often discover that a student's spouse is working against him or her. One husband said, for example, "Why do you need to read the newspaper? I'll tell you what's important."

Sometimes we are locked into roles that are uncomfortable for us. Many women feel trapped when their children are small; some people hate their jobs; some students hate school. Are you in a role that you have chosen for yourself, or has someone else chosen it for you? Has someone else defined how you should play this role? Can you play this role in a way that it will be more comfortable for you? Can you change the role so it fits better with your self-concept?

If we are playing roles that don't work for us, we must find a way to change them or to drop them so that we can feel better about ourselves. When we are in relationships and situations that hold us back, we sometimes have to make difficult choices. If we want something badly enough, we might have to break off the relationship or change the situation; we might have to take a big risk and move away from psychological safety.

SET REASONABLE GOALS

Too often, people decide they are going to change their behavior overnight. Students who have habitually gotten poor grades will often announce that this semester they are going to get all A's. This is an unreasonable goal.

If you are going to try to change your behavior, see if you can break the problem down into steps you can handle. Let's say that you are shy but you would like to speak up in class more because you often know the answers.

Try This Try This Try This

*A*mong the following examples, choose one that applies to you:

• You're having difficulty with one of your friends. You've had an argument and you haven't resolved it. You have a lot of pride, and although you know you're wrong, you have trouble admitting it.

• You're in a class where you have to give an oral report or a speech. You feel a lot of dread about this situation. You would like to drop the class, but you have to pass it in order to graduate.

• Whenever you're with your friends you feel you have to compete. If one of them has a problem, you've got a bigger one. If someone got a new car, you have (or are going to get) a better one. It's gotten to the point where people are starting to avoid you.

Now let's assume you would feel better about yourself if you could change your behavior in one of these examples. See if you can answer the following questions:

1. Why do you exhibit this behavior? Is it part of a script you were given when you were young? Does it have anything to do with any of the roles you play?
2. If you were going to change this behavior, would any of your friends or family be upset? Do they influence this behavior in any way?
3. What would be a reasonable goal to set in changing this behavior? Can you really try to pursue this goal—week after week and month after month? If you don't think you can, do you think you should set a more modest goal?
4. What people do you know who might be able to support you in this goal? Are you willing to tell them what you want to do? What people might have a negative influence? Is there a way you can deal with them while trying to reach your goal?
5. If you can accomplish your goal, how will you feel about yourself? Will reaching this goal improve your self-concept?

Why not set a goal to speak up once a week in one class? That is probably a goal you can manage. Once you feel comfortable with that, you might increase it to two or even three times a week. If you keep increasing the times, you will probably find yourself overcoming some of your shyness.

USE A PROGRAM OF SELF-DISCIPLINE

The old saying "Nothing succeeds like success" expresses the importance of self-esteem: as soon as you succeed, you start feeling better about yourself. Sometimes people think they are not successful because they are not motivated enough. Typical thinking might be, "If only I could motivate myself, I would get better grades."

People who think this way are confusing motivation with discipline. There's no way to motivate yourself to shovel the walk, do the dishes, or study your class notes. These jobs can only be done through discipline: you must say "I am going to do this job for one hour—whether I *want* to do it is irrelevant."

This sort of discipline is what leads to success. Then once you have success, you start feeling better about yourself.

PICK PEOPLE WHO WILL SUPPORT YOU

Whenever we try to bring about a change in ourselves, it is very useful to surround ourselves with people who will support us. These are people who understand how difficult it is to change and who understand our need to do so. Let's take the example of speaking up in class. If you are very apprehensive about doing this, you might consider discussing the problem with an instructor you like and trust. Tell him that you are occasionally going to try to say something, and ask for his support. Also tell a couple of your friends in your class what you are going to try to do. Just having other people know what you are trying to do is often good moral support.

When we want to change, it's important to pick our supporters carefully. It is also important that we tell them what we want to do and give them some direction on how they can help us. All of us find it easier to make changes in our lives when we get support from others. Asking others for support is also a way of reaching out and letting people know they are important to us.

SUMMARY

Whenever we communicate, we go through a six-step perceptual process: how I see myself; how I see you; how I think you see me; how you see yourself; how you see me; how you think I see you. This process is part of the transactional nature of communication: it occurs continually and simultaneously, it depends on past and present experiences, and it is influenced by the roles the participants play.

Perception is tied to self-concept; how you see yourself will influence how you perceive the world. Self-concept is made up of the conclusions you draw about yourself. Self-esteem is how much you value yourself. Your self-esteem will also influence your perceptions.

Perception and self-concept come from three sources: the body we are born with, what people tell us about ourselves, and our past experiences. What other people tell us is particularly important because it is made up of body image, the roles we play, the scripts we use, and self-fulfilling prophecies.

How we perceive the world will be influenced by our need for psychological safety countered by our need to take some risks. We can achieve personal growth only if we are willing to take some risks. The greatest risk we can take is to try to see people who are different from us from their own point of view.

Race refers to physical characteristics, such as color of skin, hair, eyes, and so forth. Ethnicity is a shared common history, tradition, and culture. When we encounter a person from a different race or culture for the first time we are likely to go through a five-step process: contact, disintegration, reintegration, pseudo-independence, and autonomy.

All of us can improve our self-esteem if we decide what we want to change, evaluate our circumstances, set reasonable goals, develop discipline, and pick people who will support us.

FURTHER READING

BUTLER, PAMELA E. *Talking to Yourself: Learning the Language of Self-Support.* San Francisco: Harper & Row, 1983. In this book, Butler, a clinical psychologist, provides ways for us to examine our self-talk. She explains how people can change their negative talk to build a language of self-support that can assist in overcoming poor self-images and insecurity.

CAMERON-BANDLER, LESLIE, AND MICHAEL LEBEAU. *The Emotional Hostage: Rescuing Your Emotional Life.* San Rafael, CA: Future Pace, 1986. These authors offer a detailed analysis of human emotions, tell how and why emotions occur, describe how we can control them, and explain how we can use them to our advantage. A useful, but sophisticated, examination.

CUSHMAN, DONALD, P. AND DUDLEY D. CAHN, JR. *Communication in Interpersonal Relationships.* Albany, NY: State University of New York Press, 1985. In this thorough, heavily researched book, Cushman and Cahn discuss the relationship between interpersonal communication and individual self-concepts as well as the development, presentation, and validation of individual self-concepts. An excellent book with useful examples.

ELLIS, ALBERT, AND ROBERT A. HARPER. *A New Guide to Rational Living.* No. Hollywood, CA: Wilshire, 1975. These authors explain the process of rational-emotive therapy (RET), which suggests that people have choices and that through self-conditioning they can reeducate and retrain themselves so that they can surrender most of their serious self-created emotional difficulties. A classic book full of excellent advice.

GLASER, SUSAN R., AND ANNA ABLEN. *Toward Communication Competency: Developing Interpersonal Skills,* 2d ed. New York: Holt, Rinehart and Winston, 1986. Glaser and Ablen's chapters on self-concept, perception, and self-disclosure are valuable because of their practicality. This is a hands-on application-oriented book for students that is full of useful, relevant exercises.

GLASSER, WILLIAM. *Control Theory: A New Explanation of How We Control Our Lives.* New York: Harper & Row, 1985. Glasser explains how we can control our emotions and actions to live healthier and more productive lives. His theory is that everything we do, think, and feel comes from inside us; thus our behavior represents our attempts to get our world to conform to the pictures in our heads. A worthwhile book.

HARRIS, AMY BJORK, AND THOMAS A. HARRIS. *Staying OK*. New York: Harper & Row, 1986. In her readable and enjoyable style, Amy Harris (who does all the writing) explores the things that get in the way of feeling OK and prescribes specific tools for overcoming them. This is a book about maximizing good feelings, minimizing bad ones, and living life to the fullest. It is full of wisdom, insight, and positive help.

HELMSTETTER, SHAD. *What to Say When You Talk to Yourself*. Scottsdale, AZ: Grindle Press, 1986. This is a motivational self-help book. Helmstetter gives readers the techniques to talk to themselves. The book is specific, practical, and full of examples. The ideas here suggest that *we* are in control of our own lives.

HOFFMAN, EVA. *Lost in Translation: A Life in a New Language*. New York: Penguin, 1989. A fascinating autobiography of a woman who immigrated from Poland to Canada when she was 13 years old. This is an insider's look at what it is like to be caught between two languages and two cultures.

JOHNSON, DAVID W. *Reaching Out: Interpersonal Effectiveness and Self-Actualization*, 3d ed. Englewood Cliffs, NJ: Prentice- Hall, 1986. Johnson's chapters "The Importance of Interpersonal Skills" and "Self-Disclosure" are especially helpful. This is a practical book that includes brief, helpful explanations of concepts supported by numerous exercises.

KASSORLA, IRENE C. *Go For It! How to Win at Love, Work, and Play*. New York: Dell, 1984. Looking for an enjoyable, upbeat, motivational, self-help book that will push you toward being a winner? This is a book that offers regular contrasts between winners and losers in doing things for themselves, facing failure, overcoming obstacles, creating luck, competing, becoming more positive, increasing motivation, discovering hidden powers, communicating, and more. A practical, easy-to-read book full of interesting examples.

SELIGMAN, MARTIN E. P. *Learned Optimism*. New York: Knopf, 1991. The author of this book, a psychologist, argues that optimism can be learned—even if one has been a lifelong pessimist. He also points out that optimism is worth learning since pessimists are more likely to suffer from depression and major health problems. Although this book contains a detailed program on how pessimists can change, it has far more depth than the standard self-help book.

Chapter 3

Listening

CHAPTER OBJECTIVES	KEY TERMS
After reading this chapter, you should be able to:	active listener
1. Explain why listening is important.	assessment
	credibility
2. Identify and explain the various parts of the listening process.	critical listening
	listening
3. List the benefits of active listening.	main idea
	passive listener
4. Understand the meaning of listening for information and how to improve your skills in listening for information.	prediction
	reflective listening
	selective attention
5. Understand the meaning of critical listening and how to improve your skills in critical listening.	supporting points
6. Understand the meaning of reflective listening and how to improve your skills in reflective listening.	
7. Understand the meaning of listening for enjoyment and how to improve your skills in listening for enjoyment.	

Why Listen?

Florentina got a part-time job at the local mini-market. After her first day at work, she came home discouraged. She complained to her friend Alma that the manager was teaching her so many new things that she found it hard to listen to everything she said. Alma suggested that Florentina get a small notebook and write down all the things she had to do each day. The next day Florentina started to take some notes and found that once she had notes on the basics, it was much easier to listen when the manager told her new things.

Chris was having trouble in his American government class. Although he took extensive notes and read his textbook carefully, he never got better than a C on an exam. He went to the study skills center to get help and discovered from his tutor that his notes on lectures were too detailed: because he wrote down both significant and insignificant points, he was often unable to distinguish between them. The tutor showed him how to listen for main and supporting points and to take notes in outline form. Chris followed his advice and not only did better on exams, but also found he was taking fewer notes because he was listening more efficiently.

A friend told Charlie that she didn't have time to see him over the weekend. She said that she had a paper to write and wanted to visit her sister and shop for some new spring clothes. After their conversation, Charlie started thinking about what she had said. He realized that they were seeing less and less of each other and that often when he called her to make plans, she said she was too busy. As he thought about some of their recent conversations and the excuses she made, he began to wonder if she was really saying that she did not want their relationship to continue.

Florentina, Chris, and Charlie were all trying to solve problems that involved listening skills. Florentina was listening for information, Chris was engaged in critical listening, and Charlie was wondering if there might be a hidden message behind the message he was hearing.

Like the three of them, we all listen to important information every day. It's not enough to merely hear: **listening** involves responding intellectually and emotionally. Some of the information we listen to is critical: fire drills, first aid, safety instructions on an airplane. Even when the information isn't critical, it can be important to our well-being. Few of us can have successful relationships or be effective in our jobs if we don't develop listening skills.

Sometimes we get clues that we are not listening very well. Have you ever done a class assignment incorrectly while the rest of the class did it right? Have you asked an instructor to reexplain an assignment he or she gave to the class? Have you had trouble finding something even though someone told you where to look? Have you been lost because you didn't follow directions someone gave you? Have your classmates laughed at you when you asked a question that had just been answered? Have you missed an appointment because you got there at the wrong time? Has anyone accused you of not listening?

If you answer yes to one or more of these questions, you are a person who is not listening as well as you could. The next question, then, is what can you do about it?

Listening is a skill that can be learned. Major companies, such as Xerox, Pfizer, 3M, General Electric, and Ford, believe it's so important that they have established listening programs for their employees. Researchers have found that there is a direct connection between good listening skills and productivity on the job. When employees were given training in listening which was followed by training in computer techniques, they were much more productive than employees who had no listening training.[1]

Since we spend so much time listening to others, we often don't listen as well as we should. One barrier to effective listening is that we can think at about 500 words a minute while the normal person speaks at a rate of only 125 to 150 words a minute.[2] Because of the great difference, it's easy to become distracted and not pay attention.

To counteract this kind of distraction, we have to learn to listen. Figure 3-1 shows the percentage of time we devote to the four communication skills: listening, speaking, reading, and writing. Although we spend the greatest amount of time in listening, it is the skill that is taught the least.[3]

Listening, like any skill, has to be practiced. Because we listen every day, we think we know how to do it. Yet, like any skill, we can learn to do it better. We can continue to improve our listening skills throughout our lives.[4] In fact, when researchers polled 450 graduates of business programs as to what kind of communication skills they needed on the job, they responded that listening was the most important skill for success in one's job. When they were asked what communication skill they wished they had been taught in college, listening ranked number one.[5]

If students are to benefit from their classes, they have a responsibility to listen. One teacher tells each new class: "Half the responsibility for good

Figure 3-1
Percentage of Time Devoted to Various Communication Skills

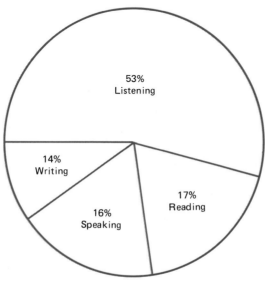

53%
Listening

14%
Writing

16%
Speaking

17%
Reading

Consider This **Consider This** *Consider This*

*I*f you are one of those people who always has to check back with your instructor to confirm whether you have understood the assignment, ask yourself why you are doing this. Is it because you didn't listen when the assignment was given, or is it because your anxiety is high about doing it? Many students check and recheck because of anxiety, not because they didn't listen. If you are one of these students, you might be able to stop all this checking once you realize why you are doing it. Say to yourself, "I understand what I am supposed to do—now I am going to do it."

communication in this class is yours. Do not go to sleep or talk to your classmates while I am talking. I will assume my responsibilities to be clear, to repeat as necessary, to let you argue with me. You must do your part by listening."[6]

Responsible listening does not only involve listening to the teacher. We also have the responsibility to listen to those with whom we might disagree. As one person put it, "We need to make a special effort to hear the voices of those who are not like us, to listen for their truth, and to celebrate both how we are similar and how we are different."[7]

The Process of Listening

Predictions and Assessment

Listening plays a part in the transactional nature of communication. From our past experience with the person to whom we are going to communicate, we make a **prediction** about how he or she is likely to respond. For example, if you go to an instructor with a paper that is late, you know from past experience that she isn't going to be very happy with you and that you will probably have to listen to complaints about your negligence as a student. You also know that your best strategy is to listen—not to talk back.

When you leave your instructor's office, you engage in **assessment**—an evaluation of what occurred. Although she took your paper, you know from her response that you'd better not try to hand in a late paper again: you predict from this experience that she would be really angry and not accept it.

The listener predicts what will happen *before* the listening event takes place and assesses what has happened *after* the event. The actual listening process has four stages: receiving messages, attending to them, assigning meaning to them, and remembering them. In an ideal listening situation, all these stages will be completed. If listening is ineffective, however, the process might break down at any stage. Let us look at each of these stages.

Receiving Messages

In any one day, all of us receive more messages than we need or can process. Some of these messages we mentioned earlier: commercials, someone shouting

Consider This Consider This Consider This

Silence is one of the great arts of conversation.

—William Hazlitt

in the hallway, a lawnmower's drone, an instructor's lecture, a conversation with a friend. We *hear* many of these messages, but we do not *listen* to all of them.

We hear sounds—such as words and the way they are spoken—but when we listen, we respond to far more. It is as if hearing is a mechanical process involving the various parts of the ear, whereas listening is a more composite perceptual process involving our total response to others, with spoken words being just a part of what we respond to.

Thus, receiving messages does not involve hearing alone. Messages come in all forms and from a variety of sources. When we listen, we filter out the irrelevant messages, which brings us to the next step in the listening process— that of attending to what we consider important or interesting.

Attending

We are able to focus our attention on a particular stimulus. A mother, for example, may hear several noisy things occurring around the house. The garbage collectors are picking up the trash, the radio is on, and she is rattling pots and pans in the kitchen. When she hears her baby cry, however, she focuses her perception on that one event and blocks out all other noise.

The ability to focus perception—called **selective attention**—is quite extraordinary. For decades parents have told their children that they can't study with the television set or stereo blaring away. If you like to study that way too, you will think that these parents are wrong—and research will support you. In one study, listeners were seated in the middle of four loudspeakers, all with different messages, and were told to pay attention to the message coming from only one particular speaker. In all cases, listeners were able to show an almost perfect performance in recalling the message from that speaker.[8]

Although we are able to focus our attention in very specific ways, our attention span is very short. Generally people can give full attention to a message for no more than 20 seconds.[9] Something in the message reminds us of something else, or we don't like the message and let our minds wander in a completely different direction. Fortunately we are quickly able to refocus our attention on the message, but every listener and speaker should be aware of just how elusive attention is.

Several other factors may determine how much attention we give to messages. First, we must be receptive to the speaker. We all experience occasions when we don't have time to listen. There are also occasions when we don't want to listen. Children often do not want to listen to their parents; teachers sometimes do not want to listen to their students. Without a receptive attitude to the speaker, however, no attention will take place and, hence, no listening.

Another factor affecting attention is mental alertness. There are days when we are too tired or too preoccupied to listen carefully to other people. When we are tired, it is especially difficult to focus our attention. Under these circumstances, we choose to listen only to messages that are easy and do not challenge us. Or we might be so preoccupied that we are unable to listen. For example, you might not hear a thing if you are trying to remember whether you left your car lights on.

Psychological state affects attention. How open are we to messages we don't want to hear? Every teacher has had students who do not want to listen to criticism of their work—it is too threatening to their self-esteem. All of us tune out messages that are threatening to us by refusing to give these messages our attention.

Assigning Meaning

When we decide to attend to a message, our next step is to *assign it meaning*. This involves assimilating the message—making it part of our knowledge and experience. To assign meaning we must decide what in the message is relevant

---

Try This Try This Try This

You can learn some strategies to improve your memory. One strategy is to use associations. For example, you can associate the word *HOMES* to remember the names of the Great Lakes: **H**uron, **O**ntario, **M**ichigan, **E**rie, **S**uperior. Do you have trouble remembering how to spell "separate"? Remember, there's "a rat" in sep-**a-rat**-e.

If you are trying to remember long lists of things in sequence, try associating the items by linking them together. To do this, you must associate your new information with old information in an exaggerated or ridiculous way. Let's say, for example, that you are going to the grocery store to buy six items: bread, milk, eggs, cat food, grapes, and potato chips. To remember the list, you must form a link between each item. You start with bread and link it to milk by forming a ridiculous mental picture. Picture, for example, a piece of bread lying in a puddle of milk. To link milk and eggs, picture eggs floating in a lake of milk. Link eggs and cat food with a picture of cats rolling eggs down a hill. For your next association, picture a cat lying on a couch holding up a bunch of grapes with one of its paws. Finally, link grapes and potato chips with a picture of you watching television—with one hand in the grapes and the other in the potato chips.

Now that you have the links associated with the mental pictures, see if you can remember the list.

The men who developed this technique say it can be used to remember long lists, as well as abstract concepts and even speeches.

Source: Harry Lorayne and Jerry Lucas, *The Memory Book.*

and how it relates to what we already know. Basically, then, the process of assigning meaning is one of selecting material and trying to relate it to our experience. In assigning meaning we also evaluate. We weigh what the speaker has said against the personal beliefs we hold, we question the speaker's motives, we wonder what has been omitted, and we challenge the validity of the ideas. As well as understanding *what* was said, we also look at *how* it was said. We assign meaning to tone of voice, gestures, and facial expressions as much as we do to words.[10]

Remembering

The final step in the listening process is *remembering*. Again, remembering is a selective process of determining what is important and what is not. As students, few of you would record the whole of an instructor's lecture. Instead you take notes that help you remember the important points.

For effective listening to take place, all these stages must be passed through. It is easy, however, to give the appearance of listening without listening at all. Many people master the art of looking attentive and interested without hearing a word that is said. And as a student, you probably know that it is possible to take notes without understanding what the instructor is talking about.

The extent to which you complete the steps involved in the listening process will depend on who and what you are listening to as well as how important the information is to you. Figure 3-2 shows how a student receives stimuli from three places, selects the one that is most important to him, and acts on it.

Prediction—
"I'm going to need some money to buy Christmas presents."

Assessment—
"I am going there to sell my textbooks."

Receives stimuli—
Noise in the hall, telephone ringing in next room, radio on in room

Remembers stimuli—
"The bookstore will be buying used texts on Monday and Tuesday from 2:00 to 4:00 P.M."

Attends to stimuli—
Radio commercial announces that the campus bookstore is buying used textbooks.

Assigns meaning to stimuli—
"If I sell some of my old textbooks, I'll have money to buy Christmas presents."

Figure 3-2
The Listening Process

Attitudes Toward Listening

People frequently think they are listening, but instead they are doing something that is causing interference with the listening process. Many of us are less-than-perfect listeners. Poor listeners often have bad listening habits.

Poor Listening Habits

THE LAZY LISTENER

Some people believe that listening involves no work. Their attitude is "I don't have to do anything. I can just sit back and listen." These listeners are sometimes found in a classroom. They hear what the instructor says and may even take pages and pages of notes. At exam time, however, they do poorly because they haven't tried to *understand* what was said.

THE TAKE-TURNS LISTENER

Some people don't really want to listen, but they know it is expected of them so they appear to be listening. In reality, they are paying no attention at all. They are only interested when it's their turn to talk.

THE ANXIOUS LISTENER

Some people are so anxious that when they are talking to someone, they are worried about what they will say next. Because they're concentrating on their own anxiety, they usually don't hear what the other person is saying.

THE SELF-CENTERED LISTENER

Some people listen only for messages about themselves. When they hear such a message, they perk up and pay attention. If the subject is about someone or something else, they lose interest.

THE COMPETITIVE LISTENER

Some people regard listening as a competition. If you tell them that you own a 20-pound cat, they will tell you about someone who owns a 25-pound cat. If you tell them you're going to Spain, they will tell you that you really should go to Spain *and* Portugal to make the trip worthwhile.

Active Listening

The way to break all bad listening habits is to become a good **active listener.** You are an active listener when you make a mental outline of important points and think up questions or challenges to the points that have been made. Even though you might not say anything, you are mentally involved with the person who is talking.

People who are active listeners receive greater rewards. As students they get better grades than **passive listeners,** who record but do not evaluate what they hear. In fact, one of the authors of this text had an experience that illustrates this point very well. She was teaching a class where she lectured on a good deal of material that was completely unfamiliar to students. She

Consider This Consider This Consider This

*G*ood listening involves looking for nonverbal signals as well as listening to the words. Imagine being in a conversation with one of your friends. How does his nonverbal behavior communicate nervousness or discomfort? How does he show intense interest or perhaps a lack of interest? or that he is confident? or that he is interested in you? or that he might not be telling the truth?

noticed, with some annoyance, that one student in the class did not take a single note—he didn't even bring anything to class to take notes with. She also noticed, however, that the student was listening carefully. He often asked questions to help him clarify and interpret the material. When the time came for examinations, it was clear this student was an active listener—on all exams he had the highest score in the class. Although most students would consider it very risky to give up note taking in class, this illustration demonstrates that careful listening has a definite advantage over slavishly recording everything the instructor says without evaluating it.

Because active listeners focus on the subject, they are not so easily distracted. All of us can think much faster than we hear. The difference between thinking and hearing is about 400 words a minute.[11] If we use this time gap to distract ourselves, we can easily lose track of what is being said. Our other option is to use this time to think about what is being said and to listen actively to the speaker.

How much do you think children learn by listening to adults?

Active listening also helps to avoid boredom. We are more likely to be bored if we are observing rather than participating in an event. Active listening is a way of involving yourself, and once you are involved, you are likely to get interested. If you use active listening techniques when you listen to a lecture, you might be surprised to find how quickly the time passes.

Active listening, then, involves active participation on the part of the listener. An active listener, however, does not listen in the same way in every listening experience. There are four basic listening experiences you can have, and they all involve different listening skills. These experiences are listening for information, listening critically, listening reflectively, and listening for enjoyment. Let's consider each of these.

Listening for Information

Any college student will find that most of the time in classes is spent in listening, and this listening is primarily for information. Listening to the instructor talk about the reasons for the Civil War, the economic structure of the broadcast industry, or the definition of a paranoid individual are all examples of listening for information.

The business world also requires people to listen for information: the secretary listens to the telephone caller, the customer listens as the salesperson tells her what is stocked in the warehouse, a shipping clerk listens as she is told to ship 100 boxes to Omaha. In business, listening can be seen in dollars-and-cents terms. The Sperry Corporation has pointed out that if each of the

---

Try This Try This Try This

HOW WELL DO YOU LISTEN?

Score each statement in the following way: often (3); sometimes (2); never (1).

1. If I don't agree with someone, I tune him or her out.
2. When a subject is boring, my attention wanders.
3. When a subject is difficult, I have trouble concentrating.
4. When a subject is unpleasant, I have problems listening.
5. As I am listening I often think of what I will say next.
6. When I am the subject of the conversation, I find it easier to listen.
7. I look as though I'm paying attention while I'm really not listening at all.
8. I listen without thinking of questions to ask the speaker.
9. Listening to people's feelings makes me feel uncomfortable.
10. Other people accuse me of not paying attention.

Look at your number for each statement. Statements where you marked a 3 are areas you should work on. You also might need to give attention to the statements where you marked a 2.

100 million U.S. workers made a $10 listening error, the total cost would be $1 billion![12]

Even when it is critical to listen well, some people don't do it. Researchers who tested jurors on how well they understood crucial instructions about the law discovered that only 40 percent correctly applied the rules for circumstantial evidence.[13] Not listening carefully to the rules of circumstantial evidence could result in an unjust life sentence or even death for the accused.

Identifying the Main Idea

What, then, should be the approach to listening for information? If you are listening to a speech or to a lecture, your first approach should be to listen for and identify the **main idea**—the central thought that runs through the passage. Then you listen for **supporting points**—the materials that reinforce the main point. It is important to identify the main idea because all the other points will relate to it. Identifying the main idea also aids memory. If you remember the main idea, then the supporting points will follow. If you remember only the latter, you will have unrelated points that make no sense; and because they make no sense, they will be easily forgotten.

With interpersonal communication, the main point is not always evident, and in some cases there might not be one. Still, when a friend comes to visit or calls you on the telephone, you probably are predicting what he or she wants. Main points are more likely to be present when you are having a heated discussion or an argument. A mother, for example, might have a main point when she tells her teenager why he can't have the car that night. Two men who are arguing about the best football team might each come up with a main point to support his side.

When small groups are working to solve a problem, they will work more effectively when they identify the main point. If you have ever been in a group that didn't accomplish very much, it's probably because the group strayed away from the main point. For example, the food committee meets with the purpose of making suggestions on how the campus food service can improve. If they stick to this point, the group will be likely to come up with some useful advice. However, if the group members sit around and swap horror stories about the terrible meals they have had, they won't accomplish much.

Identifying Supporting Material

In listening to a speech, once you have identified the main point, your next step is to look for material that supports the main idea. The purpose of supporting points is to build evidence for the main point. Supporting points often consist of illustrations and examples that make the main idea clearer to the listener. Let's suppose that a speaker is explaining why the legislature has passed a law requiring that children be strapped into car seats. Her main idea would be that children who are not strapped into these seats have a much greater chance of being killed or seriously injured if the car is involved in an accident. One supporting point she might give is actual figures about children killed in accidents who were not strapped into car seats. Another supporting point might be the number of strapped-in children who were able to survive accidents. By way of illustration, she might describe an accident where a child was actually killed.

Supporting material is not really relevant to most interpersonal communication unless you are using it to support an argument. In small groups, however, it's often useful to break down the main topic into smaller, more manageable units. For example, the committee to improve campus food might want to offer supporting material in the form of new recipes that include more fresh fruits and vegetables and use cooking methods other than frying.

Forming a Mental Outline

When you are listening to a speech or a lecture, try to *form a mental outline.* Identify the main idea and then listen for the supporting points. The idea and its supporting points are the information to remember. The illustrations are examples that help you remember the supporting points better. In the overall organization of the speech, however, the examples might be trivia. If you remember only the details of how the child was killed and do not remember *why* the child was killed, you were not listening well.

Predicting What Will Come Next

Earlier we discussed the role of prediction in the listening process. When you are listening for information, it helps to focus your attention by *predicting what is coming next.* Once you hear the speaker's main point—that children who are not strapped into car seats are more vulnerable in case of accidents—you might logically predict that she is going to give figures about children involved in accidents. Prediction might seem difficult, but you do it all the time. The next time you are listening to a joke, notice how much predicting you are doing—it will continue right up to the punch line.

Relating Points to Your Experience

Another useful way to listen is to try to *relate the points to your own experience.* When a speaker makes the point that professional football is getting too violent, you might try to remember any particularly violent games you have seen. All good listeners attempt to relate material to their own experience— it's part of being an active listener.

Looking for Similarities and Differences

Your understanding of a subject is often aided if you can discover the *similarities* and *differences* in relation to what you already know. Sometimes the similarities and differences are obvious. When you hear that 95 percent of marriages in India are arranged by parents, this is an obvious difference from the American custom. A more subtle difference begins to emerge when you examine the role that parents play in marriage in both countries. You might ask, for example, why Indians of marriageable age permit their parents to arrange their marriages. And this question might lead you to ask whether parents and children relate differently in Indian society than they do in American society.

Questioning and Paraphrasing

Questioning is an important aid to active listening. As you listen, you may ask questions of yourself. If you cannot answer them, then it is important that you ask them of the speaker. Even if you have answers to your questions, you might want to ask them anyway so that you can check your perceptions with those of the speaker. Another useful method for ensuring that your information is correct is *paraphrasing*—simply restating in your own words what you believe the other person has intended.

We also listen for information in interpersonal and small-group settings. Many of the methods for active listening outlined above are appropriate for such settings, too; however, relating points to your experience, looking for similarities, and especially questioning and paraphrasing would probably be the most applicable.

Critical Listening

Critical listening requires all of the ingredients of informative listening. The listener still should identify the main idea and the supporting points. But in

---

Try This Try This Try This

*H*ave you ever thought that a class might be giving you difficulty because you are not listening properly? Test this out by taking your most difficult class and applying this strategy:

- *Predictions:* Before you go to class, try to predict what the class will be about. If your instructor follows a syllabus, what will the topic be? Is the subject likely to be connected to a chapter in the textbook? Review your class notes for the last class period. What were they about and where are they likely to lead?

- *Listening:* Rather than take notes on everything your instructor says, concentrate on writing down the main points and listing supporting points below them. Is the instructor writing anything on the board? Does this help you to identify main points?

- *Interaction:* As you are listening, try to put in your own words what the instructor is saying. Think of some questions about the material he or she is discussing. Even if you don't answer these questions aloud, coming up with them will help you to play a more active role in the class.

- *Assessment:* After the class is over, look at your notes. Are your main points really the most important information? Do your supporting points really illustrate the main point? Do you need to make improvements in your note taking?

critical listening, the listener also should evaluate and challenge what has been heard. These challenges might take place in the listener's mind or they might be expressed directly to the speaker.

Ideally, all communication should be listened to critically. When you are receiving new information, however, it is sometimes difficult to evaluate it critically because you do not know very much about the subject—and possibly about the speaker either.

The area of *persuasion* offers the greatest opportunity to use critical listening skills. Products are advertised every day with the promise that they will bring romance, adventure, or success into our lives. It takes no genius to be critical of those sorts of messages! But commercials are not the only persuasive messages that we are subjected to. A candidate wants our vote, we are asked to sign a petition to build a dike on the river, a friend tries to persuade us to stop studying and go shopping. All these messages require evaluation and critical thinking.

Determining the Speaker's Motives

When we use critical listening, our first job is to *question the communicator's motives*. With commercials, it's easy. Someone wants to sell a product. With political candidates, the motive is more complex. Obviously they want to be elected to office. So then the question is: Why? Are they after money or power? Do they want to bring about social change? Do they want to keep things the way they are?

A petition to build a dike on the river is even more complex and requires more in-depth questions. It also requires the questioner to have some background knowledge on the subject: How much will it cost? Who will pay for it? Will taxes be raised? Will it solve the problem of flooding?

Even when a friend tries to persuade us to stop studying and go shopping, we must address a number of questions. What are his or her motives? What are the effects likely to be? When we are involved in persuasive situations, questioning the persuader's motives is a normal, proper response. In public speaking situations we often check the speakers' motives by examining their backgrounds. Some give lengthy introductions that are designed to establish their **credibility,** or believability. Not every speaker has to be an expert; it is enough if he has done the proper amount of homework needed to give a credible speech.

Challenging and Questioning Ideas

Critical listening also involves *challenging ideas* and *questioning* the validity of ideas. Where did the speaker get her information? Did it come from a source that is generally regarded as credible? Is the speaker quoting the information accurately or is she taking it out of context? Does she identify her sources of information so they can be checked later by her audience?

In persuasive situations, speakers sometimes omit information that does not support their cause. If you have information contrary to what a speaker presents, keep it in mind so you can ask questions later. You can assess whether information has been omitted by asking questions about the speaker's

sources. In a political speech, for example, is all the supporting material from one particular party or viewpoint—say liberal or conservative? Does this mean that important information may have been omitted?

Distinguishing Fact from Opinion

Part of challenging ideas and questioning their validity is the ability to *distinguish fact from opinion*. A *fact* is something that can be verified. Everyone who applies the same test should be able to get the same information. Today's temperature is a fact. If we put several thermometers in the same place, they should all show the same temperature. A fact is always true, whereas an *opinion* is someone's belief. Because people sometimes present opinions as facts, it is important that you, as the listener, make the distinction. The statement "Women should stay home and take care of children" is an opinion—regardless of how authoritative the speaker may sound.

Although all facts are equal, some opinions are more reliable than others. We are more likely to trust the opinions of speakers who have been right before, who have a high degree of authority or credibility, or whose opinions have been (or are) supported by others.

Recognizing Our Own Biases

Sometimes there are messages we don't want to hear because they contradict our own attitudes and beliefs. If you're a Democrat, you don't go to Republican rallies; if you're a religious liberal, you don't go to revival meetings. If, for some reason, you were forced to go to either of these, you would probably tune out most of what you heard.

In some cases, we might not even be aware that we are blocking out messages. Earlier we mentioned that although jurors had heard instructions about the rules of circumstantial evidence, only 40 percent correctly followed these instructions. The authors concluded that this misunderstanding of the law was not merely a matter of poor listening. They believed that jurors were likely to misinterpret the law when they didn't believe in it. Their interpretation was compatible with the view they held of the law.[14] This tendency to interpret information in the light of our beliefs can lead to distorting the information we hear. As listeners, we have to be aware of our own values and attitudes—especially when we hear information we might resist or disagree with.

Assessing the Message

Earlier in this chapter, we discussed listening as an ongoing process that includes *assessment* of the communication. This assessment can take place while the event is happening and can continue long after the event is over. Assessment is basically a critical process; it is chewing over what you have heard before you swallow it. An idea that may seem acceptable when we first hear it may not be so palatable when we have had time to think about it. For important ideas, it is essential to reflect on them before they become part of us and of our thinking. We must learn to *suspend judgment*—delay taking a position—until all the facts and other evidence are in, until we have had a chance to test the facts in the marketplace of ideas, and until they have been chewed over sufficiently for digestion.

Reflective Listening

When we are involved in interpersonal communication, talking to one other person or to a group of friends, we can use our skills in listening for information. We ask, for example: What is the cheapest way to get to California? Should we buy new tires or retreads? What did the instructor say in class today? We

---

Try This Try This Try This

*L*ook for a politician speaking on the nightly newscast or on CNN (or if it's election time, look for a commercial for a candidate). Ask yourself the following:

• Is there anything the candidate has said that you suspect is not true?

• When does the candidate use fact? Opinion?

• Do you have a bias of your own that interferes with hearing what the candidate is saying?

Consider This Consider This Consider This

*B*ore, n. A person who talks when you wish him to listen.

— Ambrose Bierce

---

also listen critically to friends. We favor increased taxes for schools; our friend is against them. As we discuss school systems, we challenge and question the validity of each other's ideas.

One day, however, we see that a friend is very upset. He knows what he's upset about—he is failing a class—and he is looking for a good listener. Now your skills in informative and critical listening are not going to be very helpful. In this situation it is not listening for main points or criticizing ideas that is called for but *listening for feelings*. This kind of listening is called **reflective,** or empathic, **listening.**

Listening for Feelings

We are often asked or expected to listen for feelings, and we often want to share our feelings with others. We are all upset or happy at one time or

Consider This Consider This Consider This

*I*n the following passage, a well-known author, John Wideman, writes about the problems of listening to his brother—a brother who had often been in trouble with the law and who had spent much of his life in prison. Can you identify the main reason he finds it difficult to listen to his brother?

The hardest habit to break, since it was a habit of a lifetime, would be listening to myself listening to him. That habit would destroy any chance of seeing my brother on his terms; and seeing him in his terms, learning his terms, seemed the whole point of learning his story. However numerous and comforting the similarities, we were different. The world had seized on the difference, allowed me room to thrive, while he'd been forced into a cage. Why did it work that way? What was the nature of the difference? Why did it haunt me? Temporarily at least, to answer these questions, I had to root my fiction-writing self out of our exchanges. I had to teach myself to listen. Start fresh, clear the pipes, resist too facile an identification, tame the urge to take off with Robby's story and make it my own.

I understood that, but could I break the habit? And even if I did learn to listen, wouldn't there be a point at which I'd have to take over the telling? Wasn't there something fundamental in my writing, in my capacity to function, that depended on flight, on escape? Wasn't another person's skin a hiding place, a place to work out anxiety, to face threats too intimidating to handle in any other fashion? Wasn't writing about people a way of exploiting them?

Source: John Wideman, *Brothers and Keepers.*

another, and if we share these feelings with someone else, it permits us to reveal ourselves. Sharing our feelings also helps us to cope with them. Often when we talk our feelings over with other people, we can gain control of them or deal with them better. Listening to other people's feelings is a way of giving emotional support, and the ability to do this is what creates intimacy with others.

But many of us do not do a very good job of listening for feelings. Because it is one of the most common forms of listening, we assume we can do it easily. You will probably be surprised to learn, however, that you might not be listening as effectively as you could be. Let's look at some of the responses you might make that hamper your effectiveness as a listener.

Negative Listening Responses

In order to look at negative listening responses, let's assume that your best friend has been feeling depressed for the last few days. You ask her what is wrong and she responds that she is having a terrible time at her job because her boss is picking on her so much. Here are some possible ways you could respond—responses that we all use, but none of which is very helpful.

DENYING FEELINGS

If you respond, "You shouldn't feel that way—everyone knows how hard it is to get along with him," you are focusing on the personality of the boss rather than on what your friend is feeling. When our feelings are very intense, we want them recognized. We don't want them pushed aside while other, less important, items are dealt with.

EVALUATING

If you respond, "Why don't you just stop trying? There are other jobs" or "He really doesn't appreciate all the work you do," you are making an evaluative response—one that passes judgment on and offers an opinion of either your friend or the boss. Often an evaluative response is a way of trying to dispose of another's problems. The listener does not take the time to listen to the problem; he or she just makes some generalizations that are designed to make the problem go away.

BEING PHILOSOPHICAL

The philosophical response is so broad and sweeping that it does nothing to solve the problem. In this kind of response, you might say, "All bosses are hard to get along with; it's the nature of the boss-employee relationship." Like an evaluative response, this response ignores the problem and the feeling of the person with the problem.

GIVING ADVICE

"Go out and get a new job. Your boss will never get any better." This is concrete and specific advice. When people have problems, however, it is better to let *them* find their own solutions. Your job is not to give advice but to listen in such a way that your friend can solve the problem on her own. Deborah

Tannen points out that many men are more interested in "fixing" problems than in listening to them.[15]

DEFENDING THE OTHER PERSON

Sometimes we think it might be helpful to present the other person's viewpoint: "Well, you have to understand his side. He has a lot of employees to supervise." But your friend with the problem doesn't want to hear any defense of the boss. If you defend him, she might wonder where your loyalties lie.

EXPRESSING PITY

Sometimes we are tempted to give total sympathy: "I really feel sorry for you. It must be terrible to work for a person who treats you so badly." But with a response like this, your friend is going to feel even worse.

QUESTIONING

Sometimes our response to a friend's problem is to ask a series of questions: "What did you do to make him disapprove of you?" "Is there anything you can do to make the situation better?" Question asking can be a valuable interpersonal skill but not when emotions are very high. Once the *feeling* has lost some of its intensity, questions might be useful to help solve the problem.

All these responses are weak because they do not deal with the problem of feelings. They all, in one way or another, lead the person with the problem away from her feelings. How, then, can we respond in such a way that we focus on feelings?

The Reflective Listening Response

The best way to listen for feelings is through *reflective listening*—where you try to understand what the person is feeling *from his or her point of view* and reflect these feelings back. As the listener, your job is to put aside your own feelings and enter into the feelings of the person who is speaking. In order to do this you need to recognize what feelings are involved, let the person tell you what has happened, and then encourage him or her to find the solution to the problem.

IDENTIFY THE EMOTION(S)

First, and this is often the most difficult part, you need to "hear" what the person is really saying. If, for example, your roommate comes home and bursts through the door saying, "I would really like to kill Joe!" he is obviously not saying that he literally wants to kill Joe. When we are listening reflectively, we first need to identify what the speaker is feeling. In this case, it would be reasonable to assume he is feeling anger, and we respond with, "Boy, you really sound mad." With this kind of response, it is almost certain your roommate will tell you what has happened.

LISTEN TO THE STORY

The second part of a reflective response is to listen to what the person has to say. As the whole story comes out, there is no need to respond with anything very specific. This is the point where the person just wants to be listened to. You can show your interest by paying attention and looking sympathetic.

Let's go back to your roommate and his problem with Joe. What did Joe do to make him so mad? You discover that Joe borrowed your roommate's favorite shirt—the one he got from his girlfriend for his birthday. While Joe was wearing the shirt, he stopped to pick some blueberries and got blueberry stains all over it.

After your roommate has told you the whole story, he is not quite so mad, but he is still pretty upset. As you listen, you discover other feelings in addition to anger. Because the shirt is a gift from your roommate's girlfriend, he may be feeling guilty, that he betrayed her by lending it to Joe. He may also be feeling upset because he will have to tell his girlfriend what happened to it. Usually people do not feel just one emotion—they have a whole assortment of them.

If you can let your roommate talk through the entire problem, without making judgments but offering support, it is likely that the full range of the problem will be revealed. One way to reach this point is through *paraphrasing*— restating the other person's thoughts or feelings in your own words. If your roommate says, "My girlfriend is really going to be mad when she finds out," an appropriate paraphrased response might be, "You sound worried about your girlfriend's reaction." This response not only helps to identify the feelings; it also helps to find out whether you have been hearing accurately and shows you are paying attention. A paraphrased response provides a mirror for the other's remarks.

LET THE PERSON WORK OUT THE PROBLEM

Sometimes just listening for people's feelings and letting them explain what is upsetting them largely solves the problem. We often hear someone say, "I feel better just because I've talked to you." People frequently just want to vent their feelings, and once they have done so, they feel better.

But sometimes mere listening is not enough; your friend has a problem, and he or she wants some help in solving it. In such a situation, the best approach is usually to trust in the other person and in his or her ability to work out the problem. This does not mean, however, that you ignore the problem. Reflective listening includes helping the other person find a way to solve the problem.

The last step in reflective listening, then, is to give the person a chance to work out the problem. In the case of the roommate, you don't want to say, "You should make Joe buy you a new shirt." Let your roommate decide what he wants to do. If the emotion in the situation has died down, it might be appropriate to ask some very broad and general questions, such as, "What are you going to do now?" It might also be possible to ask some questions that might lead to a solution the other person has not thought of: "Do you think the dry cleaners might be able to get the stains out?" "Has Joe offered to do anything about the shirt?"

The important thing to remember at this stage is that you do not have to solve the other person's problem. If you try to solve every problem that people bring you, you put a heavy burden on yourself. Think of the person with the

*I*dentify the emotions you hear in the following statements. Then check your answers in section A. Now think of a reflective response you would make to each statement. Check your answer with section B. (Your answer doesn't have to be exactly like the answers given, but it should reflect the general sense.)

1. "Boy, am I upset. I read the assignment before I went to class, but when Mr. Parker asked me three questions, I didn't know the answer to any of them."
2. "I thought I had saved enough money to go to Florida over spring break. Now I have to pay to have my car fixed and I won't be able to go."
3. "I really would like to go to the fraternity party tonight, but I don't know if I want to go alone."
4. "I'm never going to lend my sweaters to Carol again. She always stretches them."
5. "I'll never go to the cafeteria again. Today I slipped and fell, and my tray of food went all over the place."

Section A

1. embarrassment, humiliation
2. disappointment
3. anxiety, insecurity
4. resentment, anger
5. humiliation, embarrassment

Section B

1. "You must have felt embarrassed."
2. "It must be a real disappointment to you to not be able to go."
3. "You sound like you feel insecure about going alone."
4. "You must feel resentful when they come back stretched."
5. "You must have felt humiliated."

problem as *owning* that problem. This attitude also will help the other person to grow in his or her ability to deal with problems. If parents, for example, tried to solve all their children's problems, the children would not learn to live independent lives.

If you are the kind of person who feels burdened because everyone comes to you with problems, you are probably taking on more responsibility than is required. Rather than focusing on solutions, try focusing on feelings and listening reflectively. You will be surprised at how well this system works.[16]

Reflective listening can be very useful in many situations, but there are times when it might not work very well because you, as the listener, are feeling too much stress and conflict. If you are really angry with someone, it is very difficult to use reflective listening because you are not interested in the other person's feelings; you are interested in your own. But if you are not under stress and are able to listen to another person without feeling threatened in any way, reflective listening can work very well.

The important thing to remember is that when strong emotions are involved, people often just need a sounding board. To be there and to utter an occasional "Oh," "Mmm," or "I see" is often enough. Much comfort is derived from just being listened to.

Listening for Enjoyment

Few of us have any difficulty when we listen for enjoyment. We turn on the television or stereo, lean back, and relax. The information is easy to listen to because we have chosen it. If we like what we hear, we don't even have much problem remembering it. We can often recite, with perfect fidelity, song lyrics from a recording or a dialog from a movie.

As college students, however, your instructors often ask you to enjoy information that is complex and difficult to listen to. When your English teacher puts on a recording of a famous actor reading from *Hamlet,* he hopes that you will both understand and enjoy it. Your theater instructor does not stick to uncomplicated Broadway plays and musical comedies; she also wants you to enjoy George Bernard Shaw and Eugene O'Neill. As a student, you too are probably interested in increasing your ability to listen with enjoyment to more complex information.

When we want to listen to something for enjoyment but it is too complex to understand, we can try listening in the same way we listened critically for information and listened for feelings. A course in music appreciation is a good example of a place to employ all these skills. Since most of us enjoy music, it is not unreasonable to assume that we will enjoy some of the music we hear in such a class. In addition to enjoying the music, however, we will

---

Try This Try This Try This

Go to a play or a movie, or watch a television drama, with the idea of reviewing it. Concentrate on answering some or all of these questions:

- *Informative:* What was the play, movie, or drama about? Who were the principal actors? What roles did they play? What were the sets and costumes like?

- *Critical:* Did the actors play their parts in a way that was believable? Were the sets and costumes appropriate for the period? Did the drama hold your attention?

- *Emotional:* Did you identify with any of the characters and what they were feeling? Did you respond emotionally to this drama? What emotions did you feel?

- *Enjoyment:* Did you enjoy the drama? Did others enjoy it too? How do you know? Did your reasons for enjoying it come from any of your answers to the above questions?

also be asked to use other listening skills. Our informational skills might be tested: Can you identify the theme? What is the rhythm of the piece? What does *allegretto* mean? Our critical skills might be tested if we are asked to listen for the way two different composers treat the same theme or to indicate whether we agree with the way the musician interprets the piece. Since music involves feelings, we are asked to listen for the mood of the piece: Is it solemn or light? How does it make the listener feel? By requiring listening skills other than those needed for enjoyment, the music instructor is hoping to increase your enjoyment of music—because the more one knows about music, the more one is able to appreciate and enjoy more complex forms of it.

Listening for enjoyment, then, can be a more sophisticated process than merely sitting back and letting the sounds wash over us. Complex material, even when we enjoy it, involves greater listening skill. In music, for example, if we had not worked on these skills, we would all still be listening to "Twinkle, Twinkle, Little Star."

The same skills can be applied when we listen to a play. Listen for information: What is the play about? What is the plot? Listen critically: Do the scenes flow into one another? Are the characters believable? Listen reflectively: What is the character feeling? How does she relate to the other characters?

Listening is often more enjoyable if we can relate what we are hearing to our own experience. Someone who plays the violin can enjoy a violin concerto because he knows what to look for and is aware of the discipline and practice that it takes to play such a piece. Watching a play, we can sometimes think "I have felt that way too."

You will find it worthwhile working to enjoy more complex information. Remember, however, that listening for enjoyment can require skills just as complex as those needed in any other listening situations. The only difference is in the rewards. What could be better than listening to enjoy yourself?

SUMMARY

All of us are surrounded by hundreds of messages every day. Because we are surrounded by so much information, it is often difficult to listen, and many of us become poor listeners.

Listening is a skill, and like any other skill it must be learned and practiced. It is also a process and a transaction. We make predictions about messages before we hear them, we listen to them, and then we assess what we have heard. How well we listen is determined by the attention we give to a message. We are able to tune out unwanted messages through the process of selective listening. Once we hear a message, we must assign meaning to it by selecting and organizing the material we have heard. Our final step in listening is to select what we need to remember.

In order to be good listeners we must become actively involved in the process of listening. As active listeners we evaluate and criticize the material as we listen to it. When one listens actively, one is less likely to be distracted or bored. In many situations we have a responsibility to listen carefully.

There are four kinds of listening: listening for information, critical listening, reflective listening, and listening for enjoyment. Listening for information involves listening for facts. In this kind of listening it is important to identify the main point and distinguish it from the supporting points. Critical listening involves evaluating the material one hears. To listen critically, one listens for the motives of the speaker and mentally challenges the speaker's ideas and information. Critical listening is especially effective when one is listening to persuasive messages.

Reflective listening is listening for feelings. This kind of listening is most often done in interpersonal communication, and it often has the purpose of helping the speaker to cope with his or her feelings and problems. Listening for enjoyment is most often the listening that we choose to do. We can learn to enjoy complex material by using all the other listening skills.

FURTHER READING

BANVILLE, THOMAS G. *How to Listen—How to Be Heard.* Chicago: Nelson-Hall, 1978. Banville explains how feelings and emotions are part of total listening, and he offers specific techniques to improve your ability to listen actively.

BURLY-ALLEN, MADELYN. *Listening: The Forgotten Skill.* New York: Wiley, 1982. The author provides exercises and techniques designed to improve the way we listen to others. She examines listening, why we listen as we do, various barriers, how to listen to ourselves, making listening work for us, and, finally, how to get others to listen to us.

FLOYD, JAMES J. *Listening: A Practical Approach.* Glenview, IL: Scott, Foresman, 1985. Floyd presents a skills-approach to listening improvement. In a mere 137 pages, he addresses the importance of listening, the nature of the listening process, how to become aware of undesirable listening habits, and how to modify those habits through recognition, refusal, and replacement. Finally, he treats each listening skill area: attention, understanding nonverbal and verbal messages, analysis/evaluation, and feedback.

LORAYNE, HARRY, AND JERRY LUCAS. *The Memory Book.* New York: Dorset Press, 1989. This book is one of the classics on memory techniques. It has many techniques you can use to help you remember items for tests, long lists, concepts, and people's names.

STEIL, LYMAN K., LARRY L. BARKER, AND KITTY W. WATSON. *Effective Listening: Key to Your Success.* New York: Random House, 1983. These authors build awareness, understanding, and appreciation of listening excellence. This book offers a guide for listening improvement for professionals in business and industry. A useful introduction to listening.

WOLFF, FLORENCE I., NADINE C. MARSNIK, WILLIAM S. TACEY, AND RALPH G. NICHOLS. *Perceptive Listening.* New York: Holt, Rinehart and Winston, 1983. This is a comprehensive textbook in listening at the college level. It explains current theory and offers researched-based principles. The authors emphasize motivated practice and performance and analyze in detail the entire spectrum of normally experienced listening situations. A fine, well-researched textbook loaded with useful information.

WOLVIN, ANDREW D., AND CAROLYN GWYNN COAKLEY. *Listening,* 3d ed. Dubuque, IA: Brown, 1988. This complete textbook on listening examines the need for, process of, and types of listening. The authors look at appreciative, discriminative, comprehensive, therapeutic, and critical listening. This is a useful, well-documented resource.

Chapter 4

Verbal Communication

CHAPTER OBJECTIVES	KEY TERMS

After reading this chapter, you should be able to:

1. Explain how thought processes and language are linked.

2. Explain what is expected of a speaker in a particular language environment.

3. Give examples of the ritual use of language.

4. Explain the function of role in a language environment.

5. Define style.

6. Describe how role and style are interrelated.

7. Distinguish between report-talk and rapport-talk.

8. Explain the advantages and disadvantages of dialect.

9. Describe the ways in which speaking is more transactional than writing.

10. Define and give examples of metamessages.

11. Describe some of the ways to make your verbal style clearer, more powerful, and more vivid.

KEY TERMS

bilingualism
connotative meaning
denotative meaning
dialect
language environment
metamessages
rapport-talk
report-talk
ritual language
style

Words are all around us. Some we hear or read; some we perceive only as background noises; others we miss altogether. The radio blasts out commercials; our roommate or spouse calls out to us from another room. The bulletin board outside the classroom holds notices filled with words; the library holds the most words of all. We type words on the computer; we make a telephone call and use more words.

Even when we are not talking out loud, we use words. It would be difficult to think something through without using the symbolism of language. Our dreams and daydreams, indiscernible to observers, consist of images that depend on language.

Ideally, language is used to achieve mutual understanding and communication with others. Sometimes, however, language is manipulated by its users. A hotel advertises "spectacular views" without mentioning that a guest has to climb halfway up a mountain to see *any* kind of view. "Easy to assemble" means you have to put it together yourself—and it could take you days to figure out how. Language can also be used in such subtle ways that even when it is accurate, it can still distort meaning. McDonald's, for example, calls one of its hamburgers the "Quarter Pounder"—language designed to make the four ounces sound like an unusually ample portion.

It is important to remember that even though we use language in most communication situations, what we mean to say is conveyed by more than the words themselves. We usually add all sorts of nonverbal communication to our words, and the two become so interrelated that it is difficult to tell where one begins and the other leaves off. Moreover, words can have more than one meaning, and nonverbal communication can contradict words. For example, if you and your teacher are talking about a paper you wrote and she says, with little enthusiasm, "This paper has some potential," you will probably figure out from her words and her tone of voice that she doesn't like your paper very much.

This chapter is largely concerned with the language behavior of speakers and listeners; to divorce words from how they are spoken and how they are heard is to look at them in isolation—and words are never isolated in oral communication. It is impossible, for this reason, to discuss language behavior without discussing the people who are using the language. This applies equally to both speaker and listener. Successful communication depends on the completion of the transaction, and much of the emphasis in this chapter is on the two ends of the communication chain: the speaker and the listener.

Part of the communicator's effectiveness in conveying thoughts and emotions is derived from his or her language.

An understanding of language will help you express what you really want to say, honestly, clearly, and straightforwardly. When messages are misunderstood or when a communication has no effect on the listener, it may be the language of the speaker that is at fault. And no matter how skillful it may be in other ways, any communication that is not understood cannot be successful.

How Words Work

When you use a word orally, you are vocally representing something—whether that thing is a physical object such as your biology textbook or an abstract

As her father teaches her words in the book, is this child more likely to be learning denotative or connotative meanings?

concept such as peace. The word is, as Chapter 1 noted, a symbol; it stands for the object or concept that it names. This is what distinguishes a word from a random sound. The sounds that are represented in our language by the letters *c a t* constitute a word because we have agreed that these sounds will stand for a particular domestic animal. The sounds represented by the letters *z a t* do not make up a word in our language because these sounds do not stand for anything.

A word that stands for a concrete and emotionally neutral thing—such as the word *mailbox*—can usually be interpreted with good fidelity because most people respond primarily to its **denotative meaning**—that is, the dictionary definition.

Other words stand for abstract concepts about which people may have strong feelings. Words such as *freedom* and *love* are easily misunderstood because they carry a lot of **connotative meaning**—the feelings or associations we have about a word. For example, when we hear the word *love*, we don't just think about the word; we associate it with a person, an experience we have had. The connotative aspect of words may cause problems in communication because a single word may evoke strong and varied feelings in listeners. Think, for example, of the many different reactions people have to the word *abortion*.

Although we need abstract connotative words to express ideas, precise denotative words work better when we want to convey information or get things done. Figure 4-1 shows the usefulness of precise, concrete words.

When you study a language, whether it is your native tongue or a foreign one, you must learn what the words stand for in that language; that is, you have to know both their denotative and their connotative meanings. Another thing you need to know is how to put the words together to make the clauses and sentences that express relationships among the words. This is the grammar of a language.

When you say that another person understands your language, you mean that he or she knows what your words stand for and how the words are put together to express ideas and relationships. You and that person both interpret the same verbal sound in approximately the same way. Each of you has

Figure 4-1
**Using Precise,
Concrete Words**

Consider This *Consider This* Consider This

*L*anguage is always based on experience. The national experience of baseball has offered many colorful expressions to our language. Few Americans are likely to misunderstand these expressions, but what if you used these expressions with a foreign student who comes from a country where baseball is not commonly played? Would there be any way the student could understand what you're talking about?

- He was born with two strikes against him.

- He couldn't get to first base with that girl.

- He sure threw me a curve that time.

- I'll take a rain check on it.

- He went to bat for me.

- He was way out in left field on that one.

- I think you're way off base on that.

- It was a smash hit.

- I hope to touch all bases on this report.

- Could you pinch-hit for me?

- He doesn't even know who's on first.

- I just call 'em as I see 'em.

- He has a lot on the ball.

- No game's over until the last man's out.

Source: Adapted from Willard R. Espy, *Say It My Way.*

learned the connection between the sound and what it represents, and each of you can use the sound intelligibly.

Notice, however, that your idea of an object or a concept is never exactly the same as another person's, because each individual has had different experiences. Your notion of what "cat" means comes from all the cats you have ever known, read about, seen on television, heard others talk about, and so on. This composite cat is unique to you, but you can use the sound of the word to refer to cats in general because cats have certain qualities on which we all agree.

A theory of language developed by Edward Sapir and Benjamin L. Whorf suggests that language helps us determine how we see and think about the world. They believe that language restricts the thoughts of people who use it and that the limits of one's language become the limits of one's world.[1]

In Whorf's study of the Hopi language, for example, he realized that the language had limited tenses and made no distinction between the concepts of time and space. English, however, has many tenses, and it is common to look at events from the point of view of when they happened. One author, commenting on these differences, says that the Hopi language would enable a child to understand the theory of relativity while a native English-speaking child could more easily understand history.[2]

People Determine Meanings

For the listener to understand what the speaker intends, the speaker should have something definite in mind. If the idea or impression is vague in the speaker's mind, what he or she is trying to say to someone else will be confused and ambiguous. Understanding is the core of meaning, and understanding is a two-way process; that is, the speaker is responsible for presenting the idea clearly, and the listener is responsible for trying to understand it accurately. Meanings are determined in people, not by words.

Sometimes, for meaning to occur, we have to use a very specialized vocabulary before we can talk about a subject. A medical student who calls each of the various bones in the leg the "leg bone" is in trouble; the language is not specific enough. People who buy home computers find they must learn a new language if they want to understand the instruction manual or talk to other computer users. Most important, however, is that this language must be learned even to *think* about the subject.

Another example of different language use often occurs in communication between parents and children. The world of adults is different from the world of children or adolescents. A parent might wish, for example, that his or her child were popular. But *popular* to a teen-ager means "being able to stay out late and use the family car"—possibly unacceptable conditions to the parent.

Try This Try This Try This

*H*ere are three examples where meaning went astray. Figure out why it happened in each case.

1. "Please hand me my shoes."
   "There aren't any shoes here."
   "Are you blind? There they are—the gray-and-white ones."
   "Why didn't you say you wanted your sneakers?"
2. A Micronesian student who was studying in America was told he could bring a crib sheet to his physics exam. When he got to the exam, he was amazed to see that everyone had brought in a sheet of paper with physics formulas. He didn't know that "crib sheet" meant a list of formulas, so he failed the exam.
3. An American who traveled to London decided he needed some clothes for relaxing. He went to a department store and told the clerk he wanted a casual pair of sports pants, a matching vest, and a pair of suspenders. Much to his surprise, the clerk returned with underpants, an undershirt, and a woman's garter belt.

Because the experiences of the teen-ager and parent are so different, their values and vocabulary also differ.

New meanings are continually created by all of us as we change our ideas, our feelings, and our activities. As we think, read, travel, make friends with others, and experience life, the associations and connections that words have for us are changed.

The Language Environment

All language takes place within a particular environment. A minister speaks in the environment of a church, two friends have a conversation in the student center, an instructor gives a lecture in a classroom. Language that is appropriate to one environment might appear meaningless or foolish in another. The language you use in a dormitory, for example, might be completely inappropriate in a classroom.

People, Purposes, and Rules

According to Neil Postman, a writer about language, the **language environment** is made up of four elements: people, their purpose, the rules of communication by which they achieve their purpose, and the actual talk being used in the situation.[3] To illustrate these elements, let's take the simple example of John and Mary seeing each other on the street. Their purpose in communicating is to greet each other.

Mary: "Hi. How are you?"
John: "Fine. How are you?"
Mary: "Good."

The rules for this sort of conversation are well known to all of us, since we often participate in it ourselves. If John had failed to follow the rules, however, and had stopped to talk for five minutes about how miserable he felt, Mary would probably have felt annoyed, because John would have gone beyond the limits of that sort of conversation.

The kind of conversation Mary and John had illustrates language as a ritual. **Ritual language** takes place when we are in an environment where a conventionalized response is expected of us.[4] Greetings are a ritual; we briefly respond to each other—usually only half-listening to what the other person has said—and then go about our business.

Rituals

The rituals we use are determined by the language environment. If we are at a funeral, we are expected to respond in conventional, ritualized ways to the family of the person who has died: "He was a wonderful man and I will miss him"; "She had a rich and full life"; "It's a blessing he is no longer suffering."

At a wedding we wish the couple happiness and tell the bride that she looks beautiful.

Every society's language rituals are determined by the cultural values of that society. In rural East Africa, it would be rude to pass someone you know well with a brief "Hello." You are expected to stop and inquire about the person, his home, his livestock, and his health. In some cultures it would be appropriate to tell the couple at their wedding that you hope they will have many sons; in American society, such a response would be considered highly inappropriate.

We learn ritualized language when we are very young, and we learn it from our parents or other adults around us. Research indicates that young children often do not make the conventional response of "Hi," "Good-bye," or "Thanks" unless they are prompted by their parents. In a study of twenty-two children who ranged in age from two to five, only 27 percent of them responded to "Hi," 25 percent to "Good-bye," and 7 percent to "Thanks." After being prompted by their parents, 44 percent said "Hi," 86 percent said "Thanks," and 84 percent said "Good-bye." The researchers concluded that children do not use politeness rituals spontaneously; they use them on the insistence of adults.[5]

As children grow older, they begin to assimilate and use ritual language. Anyone who has handed out candy on Halloween can tell you that although the younger children may have to be prompted, this is no longer necessary with the older children; they will offer their thanks spontaneously.

Appropriate Language

Through social conditioning, then, children learn appropriate language. They also learn, often dramatically, not to use inappropriate language. Do you remember the first time you used an obscene or a blasphemous word in your home? If the reaction to your word was typical, you were probably severely reprimanded or even spanked by one of your parents. You may have been surprised by the vehemence of the reaction to the word because you didn't know exactly what the word meant. You learned something from that experience, however. You learned never to use *that* word with *them* ever again!

By the time we enter college, we have a good idea of the appropriate language for a particular language environment. We have been thoroughly socialized as to what is appropriate and inappropriate in language choices. Whether we *want* to use the words that are prescribed for us is largely irrelevant. The language environment dictates the language that is *expected* of us. If we violate these expectations, we run the risk of having people respond to us negatively.

Specialization

Language environments can often be very specialized. A doctor who tells a patient that he or she has a hematoma is likely to be met with a blank stare. The patient would have understood if the doctor had used the word *bruise—*

Try This Try This Try This

*T*ake out a piece of paper and divide it into three categories: a close friend, a parent, an employer. Now write down how you would describe the following situations to each of these persons:

- A party you attended where you had a very good time

- Your most embarrassing moment

- How you have spent your money over the past three or four weeks

Do you find that your language changes from one communication situation to another? Are there things you say to one person that you wouldn't say to the other two? Why? Are you conscious of finding the appropriate language when you talk to each person?

a layperson's term for hematoma. Many other areas, especially those of work, have specialized vocabularies. Computer scientists, cooks, and teachers all use a language that is special to their particular environment.

Even where a highly specialized language is used, there may be variations in the language used within a language environment. Most of us are familiar with stock market terms such as *bull market* and *bear market*. People who work in the stock market, though, use all sorts of words that are known only to insiders. Many of them are animal words: *lambs* are unsophisticated customers; an *alligator spread* occurs when commissions eat up profit; *mouse-milking* means spending a lot of time on a small account.[6]

Sometimes people create a special language when they feel they don't have as much power as the people around them. Quite often this is a language that those in power do not understand, and it is deliberately used to keep information from them. Students, especially those in high school and college, are one example of special-language groups. They use slang or a special meaning to exclude outsiders or members of the adult establishment. For example, on the streets of New York City, kids use such expressions as *basing* for arguing; *coming in face* for direct confrontation; and *chilling hard* for hanging out.[7]

Other groups develop a special language to hide unpleasantness or to distract people from the truth. For example, government and industry commonly refer to serious accidents as "incidents" or "events." When a restaurant in Taiwan wanted to serve dog meat, the owners knew that it would offend some people, and so rather than admit what it was they called it *fragrant meat*.

When a group has created a special language, we usually cannot step into that group and use its language unless we have some legitimate claim to membership. How we speak in a language environment depends on the role we are playing. Students, for example, might be using their own variations of the language, but if a teacher joins the group, the language and the language environment will change because the roles have changed. A similar change occurs when an adult joins a group of children.

Whenever we shift roles, we are also shifting our language environment. Let's say that, in a single day, you talk to your roommate, you go to class, and you speak to your mother on the telephone. Your role will have shifted three times: from *peer* relating to peer, from *student* relating to instructor, and from *child* relating to parent. Each circumstance has entailed a different language environment, and you have probably changed your speech accordingly—often without realizing it.

The important thing to remember about language environment is that we must choose language that is appropriate to the particular environment. The language used in one environment usually does not work in another. When we think about the environment, we need to ask ourselves with whom we are going to be talking and in what context our language is going to occur. If we don't adapt to the environment, our language will not work, and we will lose the chance for effective communication.

Style: Your Role and Your Verbal Image

The words you use are determined by all your past experiences, by everything in your individual history. You learn words in order to express thoughts, and thought and language develop together. The way you think and the way you talk are unique; they form a distinctive pattern. In a sense, you *are* what you say because language is the chief means of conveying your thoughts. Neither language nor thought can be viewed in isolation. They are related and constantly growing. Together, they determine your verbal style.

Style is the result of the way we select and arrange words and sentences. People choose different words to express their thoughts, and every individual has a unique verbal style. Styles not only vary among different people; each person uses different styles to suit different situations. In the pulpit, a minister often has a scholarly and formal style. At a church dinner, however, his or her style is likely to be informal and casual. When a football player signs autographs for fans, he speaks to them in the role of athlete—even though he might drop this role when he is with friends and family.

Sometimes style can negate a communicator's other good qualities. We all know someone who is so shy that he or she can speak only in a faltering manner. We also know very bright people who can never seem to get to the main point. Style, because of its power and influence, is as important to the acceptance of ideas as all the other aspects of communication. Even if we have the proper information, the right occasion, and a listener interested in our message, what we have to say may be lost if our style is inappropriate.

Impressions of personality are often related to verbal style. When you characterize a person as formal and aloof, your impression is due in part to the way that person talks. Since your style partially determines whether others accept or reject you as a person, it also influences how others receive your messages. Style is so important that it can influence people's opinion of you, win their friendship, lose their respect, or sway them.

Like language environment, verbal style is very much connected with role. Professionals, for example, are expected to speak grammatically correct English—both in private and in professional life. A college student is also expected to use correct grammar. Yet if he takes a factory job during summer vacation, using correct grammar might get him into trouble with his fellow workers, for his verbal style could identify him as a "college kid."

Should we always speak in the style that is expected of us? Could our adaptation to others' expectations cause us psychological harm? To answer these questions, it might be illuminating to look at two different examples of groups that historically have not been very powerful in our society: African-Americans and women.

At one time, many linguists believed that the mass media, particularly radio and television, would lead to standardized speech throughout the country. Among African-Americans, however, this has not been the case. A recent study shows that their dialect is moving further and further away from standard English. The linguists who conducted the study believe that this has happened because they are becoming increasingly segregated from whites—particularly in urban areas. They point out that African-American children often do not meet a white person until they enter school. This segregation has led to a dialect with unique sentence structures and idioms that are not found in standard English.[8]

African-Americans are not the only group to have developed a language that differs from the dominant language. In recent years there have been numerous studies of the different language styles used by men and women. Deborah Tannen, a sociolinguist, has found that men and women have an almost completely different style of speaking. In fact, she maintains that their languages are so different that they might as well come from different worlds.[9]

According to Tannen, when women have conversations their goal is the language of *rapport-talk*. This language is designed to lead to intimacy with others, to match experiences, and to establish relationships. Men, however, speak *report-talk*. The goal of this type of speech is to maintain status, to demonstrate their knowledge and skills, and to keep the center-stage position.[10]

Because of their different ways of speaking, men and women may have problems when they try to talk to each other, Tannen says. For example, a stock cartoon shows a man and woman at the breakfast table with the man reading the newspaper and the woman trying to get his attention. For him, the newspaper is a source of information he needs for future report-talks. The woman, however, is looking for interaction.

Tannen also notes that men are more likely than women to look at problems in terms of "fixing them." A woman, for example, might want to talk to her husband about a problem at work. Her husband is likely to respond with a solution: "You should try . . . ." For the woman, this is not a satisfactory answer; she would prefer some statement of understanding or some expression of empathy.[11]

How are these differences reflected in actual speech? Researchers found that when men and women talk together, men are more likely to interrupt ("Let's go on to the next topic") and give directives ("Why don't you write this down?"). Women used more personal pronouns and more intensive adverbs ("I really like her"). The researchers also found that women used more questions and more justifiers ("The reason I say this . . .").[12]

Robin Lakoff, a linguist, has found that even some words are gender-specific. Females, for example, make use of the "empty" adjectives ("cute," "nice," "divine," "fascinating"). Women are also likely to turn a declarative sentence into a question. ("It's a nice day, isn't it?" or "We'll have dinner at six?") Other characteristics of female speech include modifiers and hedges ("sort of," "I guess," "kind of"). All these are examples of the language of

---

Consider This Consider This Consider This

Two California sociologists, Candace West and Donald Zimmerman, found that men interrupt women far more often than they interrupt other men—and more frequently than women interrupt anybody.

When psychologist Pamela Fishman recorded many hours of male-female conversation, she found that topics introduced by men succeeded (that is, developed further) 96 percent of the time, whereas those brought up by women were only 36 percent successful.

The effect constant interruption has on women is that they become silent [says sociologist Jennifer Coates, author of Men, Women, and Language]. *It isn't solely that the male view of conversation is that it is a contest (''which means that, once men have made a point, they expect to be attacked—and do the same'') but also as a clash of styles.*

''We all think we know what a question is. But with men and women, it triggers different reactions. Men think questions are requests for information, whereas women think they are part of the way in which a co-operative conversation works—in other words, I feed you a question so that you can have a turn. Women don't like it if one member of a group isn't speaking; they always try to draw him or her in.

''Thus, if a woman asks a man a question, she's trying to keep the conversation going, while the man thinks this is a request for information so he gives her a lecture,'' she explains.

In social situations, Coates says, this cross-purpose view of the polite inquiry often can cause a certain amount of bad feelings. ''The woman thinks, 'What's his problem? I don't want a run-down on company accountancy,' and the man thinks, 'Why is she looking so upset? If she didn't want to know, why did she ask?' ''

*C*an you remember a conversation you had with a member of the opposite sex that wasn't very satisfactory? Do you think that one of you might have used report language while the other one used rapport language? Did one member of the conversation seek a greater intimacy than the other member wanted? Do you think that gender differences were important in this conversation?

Source: Extract from Anne de Courcy, "Between Us: Male and Female English Spoken Here." *Chicago Tribune.*

submission: a woman does not like to commit herself to a position until she is certain that the position is acceptable to the listener, who is often a male.

Children learn gender-specific language from the social world of their peers. Tannen reports that one researcher who observed preschool children found that when the children wanted to do something, the girls would start with "Let's . . . ," while the boys would give direct commands ("Sit down.").[13] In looking at videotapes of second graders, Tannen says that in language and behavior, second-grade girls were more similar to adult women than they were to second-grade boys.[14] When the same second graders were put in pairs and asked to talk about "something serious," the girls did so. The boys, however, resisted or mocked authority.[15] Since language behavior starts so young, it's not surprising that it soon becomes automatic.

One encouraging aspect of "gender-appropriate" speech is that women are not locked into it. Once a female plays a role equal to that of a male, her language becomes more similar to male speech. Faye Crosby and Linda Nyquist discovered, for example, that when women are in positions of authority, they use basically the same speech as their male counterparts.[16] Their study indicates that language strongly reflects the role we play in society, and as our role changes, so does our language.

Dialect

Toward the end of the summer in central Pennsylvania, many of the cooks begin to fry or preserve *mangoes*. Outsiders are always surprised that Pennsylvania cooks are so interested in this tropical fruit. What they don't know is that a "mango" in this part of the country isn't a fruit at all—it's what everyone else calls a *green pepper* or a *bell pepper*.

The central Pennsylvanian's use of the word *mango* is an example of dialect. A **dialect** is the habitual language of a community. It is distinguished by a unique grammatical structure, certain words, and figures of speech. The community members who use the dialect may be identified by region or by such diverse factors as education, social class, or cultural background.

Linguists refer to dialect as a nonstandard form of language. As well as using unique words, a dialect often uses nonstandard grammar. Linguists generally try to avoid such questions as whether dialect is a correct form of speech or whether one dialect is superior or preferable to another. The debate over dialect is often heard in the schools, however—especially when a dialect uses nonstandard grammar. For example, there is some evidence that African-American children who use dialect have difficulty understanding some concepts in science and mathematics because many of the words in their dialect have different or opposite meanings to standard English.[17]

One of the richest areas of dialect in the United States is in the south. As Figure 4-2 shows, there are three distinct dialects in these states.

Bilingualism

One of the most passionate debates in America over the last decade has been whether we should become a **bilingual** nation. Because our population

Figure 4-2
Vocabulary of the South
Samples from the three principal southern dialects.

General American	HILL	PLAINS	COASTAL
Dragonfly	Snake feeder	Snake doctor	Mosquito hawk
Large porch	Veranda	Piazza	Gallery
Skin mite	Chigger	Chigger/red bug	Red bug
Burlap bag	Tow sack	Crocus sack	Crocus bag/grass sack
Cling peach	Plum peach	Press peach	Press peach/cling peach
Andirons	Dog irons	Fire dogs	Fire dogs/andirons
Harmonica	French harp	Mouth harp	Mouth organ
Small tomatoes	Tommytoes	Salad tomatoes	Cherry tomatoes
Mantel	Fireboard	Mantelpiece	Mantelpiece/mantel
Pancakes	Fritters	Battercakes	Battercakes/pancakes
Burrowing turtle	—	Gopher	Gopher
Closet	Closet	Closet	Locker
Paper bag/sack	Poke	Bag/sack	Bag/sack
Wishbone	Pulley bone	Pulley bone	Wishbone

includes many Puerto Ricans, Cubans, and Mexicans, many people argue that Spanish should be officially recognized as another language in America.

Much of the debate has centered in the schools. When children come to schools speaking Spanish, how much of their learning is jeopardized if they have to learn in English? People have questioned whether these children should be taught in Spanish or whether Spanish should be only a transitional language until they learn English.

Those who argue for Spanish as a transitional language say that the English language has always been the language of the United States and that people will never be able to function fully if they don't speak English. Critics of this argument say that Americans are too ethnocentric: that they don't realize that other cultures and languages are just as rich as English and that use of another language would add a valuable diversity to the American experience.

Try This Try This Try This

*C*hoose one of the people from the following list and analyze his or her verbal style. How does the way in which the person selects and arranges words affect your impressions of this person's likeability, trustworthiness, and competence? What does the person's speech suggest about education, social class, and cultural background? Is there anything in his or her style that gives you a bad impression?

Roseanne Barr	Willie Nelson
Barbara Bush	Joan Rivers
Arsenio Hall	Mr. Rogers
Jesse Jackson	Bart Simpson
Ralph Kramden	Oprah Winfrey

This attitude that another language adds diversity is reinforced by a study conducted in Detroit. People who came from different backgrounds and different generations were asked whether they thought ethnic and minority groups should maintain their traditional ways of life or be assimilated into the American mainstream. The people surveyed strongly endorsed ethnic groups, maintaining their ethnic heritage and mastering their ethnic language along with English.[18] As Jesse Jackson once remarked, perhaps we are wrong to think of America as a melting pot. In reality it is a mixed salad, with each ingredient distinguishable from the others.

Speaking and Writing: A Transactional View

We use language in both speaking and writing, but the transactional nature of speaking makes it much different from writing.

When two people are engaged in conversation, both of them interact continuously and simultaneously. Both get and give information, form impressions, and respond to each other. Based on each other's responses, both can change their comments to explain, backtrack, hurry up, slow down, or do whatever is necessary to be understood.

Sometimes their conversation may reflect their past knowledge of each other. They can use a kind of shorthand because of the experiences they have had together. If they are in a close relationship or if they desire one, they know that the words they speak may affect their present and future relationship. If the relationship is more impersonal, then the choice of words might not be so important.

Finally, they can change their language to reflect the circumstances. If one person gets negative feedback, he or she can change language to appease the other. In other cases the person might use simpler words or concepts if he or she sees that the other person doesn't understand.

This kind of adaptation occurs with every person you talk to. Whether you are talking to your father, a professor, or a friend, your language will

Is the disk jockey likely to get
any feedback from her audience?
If yes, what kind?

reflect your impression of this person, the kinds of experiences you have had
together, and the role you are playing.

In contrast, it's not so easy to change your written language. When you
are speaking, people are reacting to you as the message *occurs*. Writers,
however, never have an immediate reaction from their audiences. In fact,
they usually don't have a reaction at all. The message flows one way—from
writer to reader—and the writer has no chance to revise based on the reader's
reaction.

Writers also have no way of taking the past, present, and future aspect of
their words into account. When Salman Rushdie's novel was condemned by
the Ayatollah of Iran who "gave permission" for any Moslem to kill the author,
Rushdie had no way of predicting that his words would provoke such an
extraordinary response.

Also, a writer can play only one role at a time. He or she is a term-paper
writer, a romance-novel writer, or a humorist. Words are chosen from the
point of view of that role.

Writers, however, enjoy one advantage over speakers. They have the time
to go over their words, polish their phrases, and check their grammar. The
reader has more time too. He or she can always reread the words when the
meaning is not clear the first time.

Speech, on the other hand, must be understood as soon as the listener
hears it. As a result, speakers must take care with vocabulary and make sure
that their train of thought is logical and easy to follow. If they present complex

ideas, they must allow time for feedback—that is, for questions from the audience.

Working on Your Communication

When we set out to communicate verbally we are more likely to be successful if we use words and ideas that have the same meaning to us as they do to the person with whom we are communicating. Unfortunately, although we think we are being clear, the other person often does not perceive what we think we have communicated. Communication can break down at various stages. Let's look at some of the places where this might happen.

What Do You Want to Say?

In 1938 Orson Welles wrote a radio play about Martians invading the United States called *War of the Worlds*. We can assume that in writing this play, Welles had the intent of entertaining his audience. Although Welles's intent was clear to him, at least 1 million people misunderstood his intent and believed the play was real—they believed that Martians really had landed and that their lives were in peril. By the time the misunderstanding was cleared up, many people had already reacted to the play by leaving their homes and trying to find a place of safety.

Although this is an extreme example of intent going astray, most of us have had times when people responded to us in a way different from what we intended. You intend to tell your roommate to buy a loaf of whole wheat bread; she buys white bread instead. You intend to make a joke and end up insulting someone. When we are involved in one-to-one communication, we often have a chance to clear up misunderstandings. We see that the other person looks confused or annoyed, or the verbal response we get indicates that we have not communicated something as precisely as we intended, and we have a chance to clarify what we have said.

When we are talking to an audience, however, it is not so easy to clear up misunderstandings. In a public-speaking or mass communication setting, we don't have a chance to respond to feedback—or at least we usually can't do it until the communication is over. Therefore, when we are going to communicate to a large audience, we have to engage in much more thought and preparation than in an interpersonal setting.

The first thing we must consider then is: What exactly do we want to say? Students who are new to public speaking often do not think out this step

Consider This Consider This Consider This

*T*he difference between the right word and the almost-right word is the difference between lightning and the lightning bug.

—Mark Twain

clearly enough. Let's say that you are going to give a speech about satellites. Do you want to describe what a satellite is? What it does? Do you want to persuade your audience to have a certain view of satellites? Answers to these questions will help bring into focus your intent in giving the speech.

How Do You Want to Say It?

Once we have decided on our intent, we must choose the language we are going to use. A speech on satellites might entail the use of a highly specialized vocabulary that our audience does not know. To what extent do we have to define and explain our terms? If we have highly technical information to impart, how can we modify the language so that our audience will understand our concepts on the basis of their own experience?

If descriptive and informative language have to be carefully chosen, we run into an even greater problem when we are dealing with abstractions. In speaking about justice, for example, we have to consider our language very carefully. "Justice" is not only an abstract word but an emotional one, and it might have as many different meanings as there are members in the audience. One person might think about a low grade she felt she didn't deserve; another might think of prison reform; still another might think about the backlog of cases in the courts. It would therefore be a mistake to think that people know what you are talking about when you use this word. When we use the language of abstraction and emotion, we must be careful to define our language from our *point of view* as it relates to the subject we are talking about.

To Whom Are You Talking?

When you seek a specific response from a listener, your words have to have meaning within the person's experience. If you were talking about snow to a student who had lived all his life in Puerto Rico, for example, he would have little idea of what it means to live with snow—even though he might understand the concept intellectually. By the same token, a professor lecturing to a beginning psychology class would probably assume that students do not know the words *affective* and *cognitive* and therefore would define them as she lectured. Some knowledge of the listener's (or audience's) interests, experiences, and expectations will help the speaker to choose the words and arrange the ideas in the way that will be most effective.

Metamessages

Most of us choose our words carefully when we are making a public presentation. It might not occur to us, however, to be so careful when we are talking to a friend or conversing with a small group of people. Yet we sometimes have conversations that make us feel uneasy—the words all *sounded* right but there was something else going on.

What we are hearing is a **metamessage**—a meaning apart from what actual words express. For example, one friend tells another, "A lot of people say you're cold, but I believe you're acting professionally." This message provides little comfort. Its recipient suddenly imagines everyone talking about her behind her back. She also realizes that the person who told her this is feeling some hostility toward her. This feeling that comes across is a meta-message.

Metamessages take many forms. At a graduation ceremony, the president of the university introduced everyone on the stage but missed one of the deans. The dean realized this was more than a simple oversight, that he might be in serious trouble. He was right—he was fired the next semester.

Sometimes metamessages don't involve words at all. Deborah Tannen believes that men refuse to ask directions because it puts them in the inferior

---

Consider This Consider This Consider This

M E T A M E S S A G E S

*J*udith Martin, who writes about manners, points out some of the meanings behind metamessages:

- *How do you do? How are you?* Both of these mean *Hello.* The correct question, when you want to know how someone's digestion or divorce is getting along, is *Tell me, how have you really been?*

- *Call me.* This can mean *Don't bother me now—let's discuss it on office time,* or *I would accept if you asked me out* or *I can't discuss this here* or *Don't go so fast.*

- *I'll call you.* This has opposite meanings, and you have to judge by the delivery. One is *Let's start something* and the other is *Don't call me.*

- *Please stop by some time and see me.* Said to someone who lives in the same area, it means *Call me if you'd like to visit me.* Genuine dropping in disappeared with the telephone, so if you want to encourage that, you have to say *I'm always home in the mornings. Don't bother to call; just drop by.*

- *We must get together.* Watch out here, because there are several similar expressions. This one means *I like you but I'm too busy now to take on more friendships.*

- *We must do this more often.* Another variation. This one is really *This was surprisingly enjoyable, but it's still going to happen infrequently.*

Try these expressions on a foreign student or professor on your campus to see how he or she understands them. Ask "What do you understand Americans to mean when they say ". . ."?" Then ask yourself what the answers tell you about communicating with someone who comes from a different culture.

Source: Judith Martin, *Miss Manners' Guide to Excruciatingly Correct Behavior.*

position of not having information. Asking another person puts that person into the superior position.[19]

Sometimes metamessages are recognizable to people within a specific culture but not to outsiders. A Polish professor told an American colleague that when she was in the United States, one of her colleagues kept saying, "Let's have lunch sometime." When she tried to pin him down, he looked annoyed. What she didn't realize until much later was that this is a statement that Americans commonly use to terminate a conversation. The "Consider This" box in this section shows other expressions that we use in this country that might be misleading to outsiders.

Language is filled with metamessages, and we have to listen for this kind of talk and understand its meaning if we are going to have accurate communication. We also should be aware of sometimes using metamessages ourselves. For example, it is not unusual for a student speaker to begin his or her speech by giving some indication that the speech will not be very good: "I just finished this speech this morning," "I couldn't find any research on this topic," or "You'll have to excuse me because I am feeling sick." If we say anything of this sort, we may be engaging in a metamessage; what we may really be saying is "I am feeling extremely nervous and anxious about giving this speech."

Language Choices

Although we are often told that we should use clear and precise language, most of us wouldn't know how to go about it. Command of the language requires years of practice and study. Since it is impossible to lay down strict rules that govern the choice of language for all occasions and for all circumstances, the discussion here is limited to four important aspects of language choice: clarity, power, vividness, and morality.

Clarity

Sometimes our meaning is unclear when our sentence structure is faulty: For example, if we say "Having taken his seat, we started asking him questions" and our listeners look baffled, we can try again. There are other times, however, when the need to speak as clearly and precisely as possible is more urgent. If we are saying something of special importance or if we are in a formal speaking situation, clarity is essential since a second opportunity to make our point clear probably will not arise.

Some language is so specialized that it is inappropriate to use outside the field in which it has come into use. *Interface* is a word from science, and it shouldn't be used for human interactions. "I would like to work with you" is certainly better than "I would like to interface with you." Doctors often use a highly specialized language to describe illnesses and injuries. Although one doctor can communicate with another doctor, sometimes he or she has problems communicating with patients. For example, many newspapers carry a column in which a doctor answers questions from readers. Many of these readers ask the newspaper doctor to explain something their doctors have said.

Other language that might not be clear to everyone is slang. Slang has its place when you are talking informally with your friends. However, many words in slang have such broad and vague meanings that they could apply to almost anything. If you use the word *awesome* to apply to someone's shirt and use it again to describe outstanding scenery, you reduce everything to a common element.

Sometimes people feel that they should use long and complicated words when they know them. On a bottle of fluoride, the consumer is advised to "hold the solution in the mouth for one minute and then expectorate." In case the consumer doesn't understand the word *expectorate*, the phrase "spit it out" follows in parentheses. Since the purpose of this message is to communicate with the consumer, the simpler words, "spit it out," should have been used in the first place.

Use more complicated words when it helps to make the meaning clearer. For example, if you want your car painted red, you'll be happier with the final results if you use a more precise description than "red." What shade do you prefer? Burgundy? Crimson? Vermillion?

One of the delights of language is that it offers many subtleties and shades of meaning. Choosing jargon to express all our ideas is like eating Big Macs for dinner every night. Language is a marvelous banquet providing us with a vast array of choices for anything and everything we want to say.

Powerful Talk

Many communication researchers have been looking into the issue of powerful talk. Powerful talk, they agree, is talk that comes directly to the point—talk that does not use hesitation or qualifications. People who engage in powerful talk are found to be more credible, more attractive, and more persuasive.[20]

To achieve powerful talk, one should avoid certain communication behaviors. First, avoid hedges and qualifiers—expressions such as "I guess," "kind of"—because they weaken the power of the words. Next, eliminate hesitation forms such as "uh," "you know." These words make speakers appear to be less powerful. Third, stay away from tag questions—comments that start out as statements but end as questions ("It would be nice to go on a picnic, wouldn't it?"). Tag questions make the speaker seem less assertive. Finally, do not use disclaimers. These are words and expressions that excuse or ask the listener to bear with the speaker. Examples are "I know you probably don't agree with me but . . ." and "I'm really not prepared to speak today. . . ."[21]

Many of us dilute our conversations and speeches with these words and expressions. However, the use of these expressions is mainly a matter of habit. Once we recognize our habits, we can start work on breaking them.

Besides using powerful language, there are several techniques you can use to make your language more lively. A sense of urgency is communicated mainly by verbs—the action words of the language. "Judy slapped him" and "The children jumped up and down" are both sentences that have energy and excitement. Adjectives and adverbs slow the language down, as in "The

Try This Try This Try This

*O*ne piece of advice often given to people who want to describe something is "show, don't tell." Look at the phrase that *tells* and change it into a phrase that *shows*—using the picture as a guideline. The first one is done for you.

Phrase That Tells   Phrase That Shows

The girl jumped into the icy water and saved the drowning child.

The heroic girl

The naughty girls

The accident-prone boy

The tired old man

The vicious dog

How does your language change when you rewrite these phrases? Do you use more or fewer words? Do you use words with opinions or words with fact? Which version is the most descriptive?

outraged Judy slapped him soundly." Language is also livelier when you put sentences in the active rather than in the passive voice. "The boy hit the ball" is more energetic than "The ball was hit by the boy."

Many of us slow down our speech by using complicated words when simple ones would be more vivid. The weather forecaster who says "There is a 10 percent chance of rain" sounds much livelier than the one who says "The probability of precipitation is 10 percent." *Fire* is a more active word than *conflagration*. The verb *left* has more action than the verb *departed*.

Language also has more energy when the speaker avoids tired, worn-out phrases. *Blushing bride, Mother Earth,* and *busy as bees* are all examples of *clichés*—phrases that have been used so much they have lost their impact.

Vividness

Think back on some of the ghost stories you heard when you were a child. The best ones were those that filled you with terror—the ones laced with blood-curdling shrieks, mournful moans, mysterious howling. They were usually set in dark places, with only an occasional ghostly light or a streak of lightning. If any smells were mentioned, they were sure to be dank and musty.

A ghost story is usually told by the person who had the experience. Any narrative told from the point of view of "I was there" or "It happened to me" is particularly vivid. By re-creating an experience for your listeners, you can often make them feel what you felt. Thus the quality of vividness in communication is a result of the re-creation of a personal experience.

Vividness also comes from unique forms of speech. Some people would say that a person who talks too much "chatters like a magpie," a phrase that has become a cliché. To one Southern speaker, however, this person "makes a lot of chin music." When we say that language is vivid, we often mean that someone has found a new way of saying old things. Children often charm us with the uniqueness of their language because they are too young to know all the clichés and overused expressions. One of the best places to look for vivid language is among poets and song writers. Although more words have been written about love than any other subject, many song writers have given us new expressions and therefore new ways of looking at the experience. Their unique perspectives make an old idea sound original and exciting.

Moral Choices

When the leader of the rap group 2 Live Crew was put in jail for using obscene lyrics, he responded by saying he didn't know why everyone was upset. It was just "a bunch of words," he said.[22] What the rap group leader didn't realize was that he had chosen words that created a world where women were subject to humiliation and degradation.

C. Ray Penn, a communications professor, points out that "a choice of words is a choice of worlds."[23] Unfortunately, Penn says, one can cause considerable damage to others by choosing the wrong words. For example, if one is asked to remember his or her most painful moment, the response will most likely be something someone *said*.

Penn asks us to consider whether "our analogies create a self-fulfilling prophecy that will ultimately keep us from relating to others unless we get our way." For example, how often in life do we talk of "winners" and "losers," condemning the "losers" to permanent failure? On the international scene, does calling Saddam Hussein "another Hitler" create a self-fulfilling prophecy? When political figures in the Middle East call us "Satan" or "the devil," does such labeling influence the way we might react to them?

Penn also warns us that language choices can influence people's perceptions of how they see themselves. Insulting words, he points out, can reduce an individual to a mere trait ("four eyes," "fatty"); it can reduce one to less-than-human status ("pig," "chicken"); or it can tell the person, "I know all about you and you have no mystery" by means of labels ("hillbilly," "redneck," "women's libber").[24]

Penn's ideas are a reminder that we make moral choices in our use of language. Many of the choices we make will not only determine how we present ourselves to others but will decide the nature of our relationships in the years to come. For this reason, it is important that we choose our words wisely and well.

Improving Your Verbal Style

Your verbal style says a good deal about you. If you make a favorable impression, do well in a job interview, or make a good grade in a class, some of your success has come about because of your verbal style. Thus it is to your advantage to pay attention to the way you talk and to question whether you can improve.

Three ways to improve your verbal style are by increasing your vocabulary, by adapting your speech to the language environment, and by making a determined effort to break bad verbal habits. You can actively pursue one or all of these goals in the course of daily interactions.

Increasing Your Vocabulary

Since you hear thousands of words every day, you can benefit from this continuous access to other people's vocabularies. By becoming more conscious of the words used by the telephone or radio advertiser and how skillfully and subtly he tries to sell his product, or of the politician and how she presents her ideas, or of the teacher and how she teaches a lesson, you can take advantage of a resource that is readily available.

When you hear a new word, try to understand it in its *context*—that is, from the words or actions that precede or follow and that are directly connected with it. Although you may not always be able to stop another person to ask what he or she means by a certain word, it is sometimes helpful to do so if possible. People sometimes use words incorrectly, of course, and contexts can be deceiving or misleading. When you hear a word that is unknown to you or when you hear a word in an unfamiliar context, check its meaning. You can also develop sensitivity to the meanings of words by paying attention to people's feelings as they are revealed in verbal expression and in nonverbal cues. This will help you become more aware of the emotional content in the messages of others.

Another way to build your vocabulary is by reading and by looking up and remembering the meaning of any new words you encounter. When you are reading, just as when you are listening to your friends talk, try to be aware of new words—then find opportunities to fit those words into your own conversation. A word that is not actually used will not be remembered for long.

When you increase your vocabulary, you increase your chances of getting your intended meaning across to your listener. The more words you have at your command, the more precise you will be. This does not mean that you should search for big words; on the contrary, familiar words are often the best. But by increasing your vocabulary, you will enrich your conversation.

In addition to building your vocabulary, note how the words you read and hear are used in combination. It is the combination of words that makes style effective or ineffective. Thus you should not examine just the individual trees—the words—but the way the trees combine to make up the forest—the sentences, phrases, and the ideas themselves. Thoughts are expressed in groups of words—seldom as words alone.

Adapting Your Oral Language

As you talk to people, become conscious of them as particular individuals for whom you need to adapt your message. Note the language environment in which your conversation is taking place, and make the adaptations that are necessary. Also, be aware of the topic you are discussing, since it too can influence your choice of words. Be conscious of what you are saying. This added consciousness will increase your sensitivity to other people as well as your awareness of language choice and use.

Sometimes people confuse personal authenticity with inflexible language usage, and they equate undisciplined speech with spontaneity. "Telling it like it is" becomes an excuse for allowing the first words that come into your head to spill out in a torrent. Such language choices reflect a kind of self-centered indulgence that says to your listener "Never mind who you are; listen to me." Adapting your language to the individual with whom you are talking can result in a more satisfying exchange.

Breaking Bad Habits

Although we are sometimes told that we are making language mistakes, such as using poor grammar or misusing or mispronouncing certain words, it is difficult for us to correct ourselves because we are so accustomed to talking this way. If we live in a language environment where these mistakes are constantly being made, it is even more difficult, because the errors are reinforced by hearing them so often. The only way to correct such mistakes is to have someone point them out to you—someone with whom you spend a lot of time. In using this method, it is advisable to tackle only one wrong usage at a time. Once you get that one cleared up, then you can begin to work on the next one. All habits are hard to break, and when you are trying to break one, you need all the help you can get.

SUMMARY

A word is a symbol; it stands for the object or concept it names. In order for us to understand one another, we must agree on what the particular word symbols stand for.

Language is directly linked to our perception of reality and to our thought processes. Our perceptions and our thought processes begin in our earliest childhood. Each person creates meanings for words, as ideas, feelings, and activities change.

Because meanings are determined by each person, it is important for the speaker to present ideas as clearly as possible while the listener tries to understand accurately. For language to be successful it must be appropriate to the language environment. The language that we should use in a particular environment is often determined by the role we are playing in that environment. Certain language rituals are predetermined for us by the values of our society. We learn these and other forms of appropriate language during our childhood.

Style, the way we express ourselves, is an important aspect of language. The style that is expected of us is often determined by the role we play. If we do not modify our language to fit our role, we may speak in ways that are inappropriate to the occasion.

Language styles may differ by gender, role, geographic region, or ethnic background, and we must be aware of these different styles if we are to communicate effectively. These differences can be as simple as talking for information as opposed to talking for interaction or as complicated as speaking a different dialect.

Speaking and writing differ in that oral communication is more transactional. In oral communication, people interact continuously and simultaneously and their conversation reflects their past knowledge of each other.

It is impossible to lay down strict rules for making good language choices. But language that is clear, powerful, vivid, and shows that the speaker has made responsible choices will be most effective. You can improve your use of language by making a conscious effort to become more aware of these qualities.

FURTHER READING

BATE, BARBARA, AND ANITA TAYLOR, EDS. *Women Communicating.* Norwood, NJ: Ablex, 1988. This book has a collection of essays on various aspects of women's talk. The essays all deal with issues important to women—ranging from talk about athletics to talk about victimization.

BAUGH, JOHN. *Black Street Speech: Its History, Structure, and Survival.* Austin, TX: University of Texas Press, 1983. Baugh takes an intriguing look at African-American street speech, the nonstandard dialect that thrives within the African-American street culture and frequently varies depending on the social context. Baugh's procedures draw on linguistics, ethnography, and sociology. This is an important work for those doing research in spontaneous speech and conversation interaction.

CONDON, JOHN C., JR. *Semantics and Communication*, 3d ed. New York: Macmillan, 1985. A useful introduction to semantics that examines the world of semantics and semiotics, moving from experience to symbol, words, symbolic transformation, how symbols work, "nice" words and "bad" words, creativity, how we organize our experience, and what happens when we talk with people. A book that will cause readers to confront the many functions of communication.

ELGIN, SUZETTE HADEN. *Staying Well with the Gentle Art of Self-Defense.* New York: Prentice-Hall, 1990. This work is the fifth book in a series about verbal self-defense. The series covers in detail what to do when under verbal attack, how to identify verbal abuse, and how to remove it from your environment.

HAMMERBACK, J. C., R. J. JENSEN, AND J. A. GUTIERREZ. *A War of Words: Chicano Protest in the 1960s and 1970s.* Westport, CT: Greenwood Press, 1975. Speeches of four Mexican-Americans make up this book. The book analyzes these speeches, and also discusses symbols and issues of special importance to the Chicano movement.

HAYAKAWA, S. I. *Language in Thought and Action*, 5th ed. New York: Harcourt Brace Jovanovich, 1989. First published in 1939, this book has become a classic. It is a clear, cogent, highly readable, and intelligible introduction to the principles of semantics. Hayakawa combines sound scholarship with an engaging, lively style and numerous practical applications. Truly an outstanding book.

KILPATRICK, JAMES J. *The Writer's Art.* New York: Andrews, McMeel & Parker, 1985. This is a finely crafted, witty guide to writing well. Intended for the layperson and professional alike, it highlights techniques and examples of good writing and includes more than 200 personal judgment calls on word usage that are often controversial as well as funny. The book is very useful, interesting, and readable.

MORAIN, MARY, ED. *Bridging Worlds through General Semantics: Selections from the First 40 Years of* ET CETERA. San Francisco: International Society for General Semantics, 1984. Here is a fascinating, eclectic introduction to the world of general semantics—its background, its contribution, its application in daily living, and its value in communication in the larger society. Numerous (34) brief articles lend variety and make this an interesting volume (347 pages) to read.

ORR, ELEANOR WILSON. *Twice as Less.* New York: Norton, 1987. Orr, a high school teacher, explains how African-American students are hampered in learning math and science because many of the words they use are different from standard English. She suggests strategies that would be useful both to students and teachers.

PEARSON, JUDY CORNELIA, AND LYNN H. TURNER. *Gender and Communication*, 2d ed. Dubuque, IA: Brown, 1991. This work focuses on how women communicate. This well-researched textbook offers both theory and practice.

TANNEN, DEBORAH. *You Just Don't Understand.* New York: Morrow, 1990. A fascinating look at the differences in language between men and women. Many examples in the book will strike a responsive chord in the reader. This book is fun to read as well as informative.

VAN HORNE, WINSTON A., AND THOMAS V. TONNESEN, EDS. *Ethnicity and Language.* Madison: University of Wisconsin System Institute on Race and Ethnicity, 1987. Several authors write about ethnic groups and language. Some essays cover the importance of ethnic language to the groups that speak it.

Chapter 5

Nonverbal Communication

CHAPTER OBJECTIVES	KEY TERMS
After reading this chapter, you should be able to:	adaptors
1. Explain the differences between verbal and nonverbal communication.	body movement (kinesics)
	displays of feelings
	emblems
2. List the various functions of nonverbal communication.	illustrators
	mixed message
3. Explain the basic principles that govern nonverbal communication.	nonverbal communication
	paralanguage
	pitch
4. Describe the various types of nonverbal communication.	proxemics
	quality (of voice)
	rate (of speech)
5. Be more sensitive to your own use of nonverbal cues.	regulators
	territory
	vocal fillers
	volume (of vocal sound)

*D*o women prefer to date tall or short men? Researchers found that on first dates they preferred tall men—but once they got to know a man, it didn't matter whether he was tall or short. Men, on the other hand, said that the height of their dates didn't matter. However, when they were asked to rate women on attractiveness, they reported that the short women were more attractive.[1]

Many people believe that when talking, women gesture with their hands, more than men do. Not true, say the researchers: men use their hands just as much. Women, however, tend to gesture more rapidly.[2]

How do you know whether you have a chance of getting a job? Look at the number of times the interviewer touches his or her foot, says the research. The more the interviewer touches the foot, the better your chance of getting the job.[3] You might ask what touching a foot has to do with getting a job. The researchers of this study speculate that once interviewers decide to hire someone, they become more relaxed in their posture and therefore are more likely to sit in a position where they can touch their foot.

All these studies point to one conclusion: **nonverbal communication**, the information we communicate without using words, is extremely important in human interactions.

Albert Mehrabian, a contemporary writer on nonverbal communication, has determined from his research that as much as 93 percent of communication is nonverbal.[4] Thus the way a person uses voice, body movement (for example, eye contact, facial expression, gesture, and posture), clothing and body appearance, space, touch, and time is an essential part of every message that he or she sends.

The Importance of Nonverbal Communication

Nonverbal Communication as a Transaction

The transactional nature of communication comes through very strongly in nonverbal communication. Without saying a word you could be communicating by your clothing, your facial expressions, your posture, or any other number of nonverbal signals. In just the simple act of walking across campus, you are giving and getting signals from passersby you might not even know. You think: "Nice coat—wonder where he got it," "Pretty girl—I'd like to know her better," "He's really tall—basketball player?" As these passersby see you, they may be making similar assessments of you.

When you attend a class for the first time, some of the judgments you make of the instructor stem from her nonverbal behavior. She hands out the syllabus and then discusses some of the assignments for the class. As you listen to her, you think, "She sounds tough. I'd better get my work in on time." In making these assessments, you are comparing her with past instructors you have had who may have looked and acted the way she does. You are also predicting what you will have to do to get a good grade. At the same time she may be assessing you—judging you by your posture and clothes, thinking about past students you may resemble, and predicting whether you'll be a good student.

Information about roles is communicated nonverbally as much as it is verbally. If you are walking with an instructor from the classroom to his

Consider This Consider This Consider This

*S*ome of the most fascinating research in nonverbal communication has to do with smell: how it can affect our emotions, promote a general sense of well-being, relieve stress, and increase productivity.

Researchers have found that the smell of spiced apple can reduce systolic blood pressure an average of three to five points. Others have found that because taste is 80 percent smell, people can reduce their food cravings by spraying the taste they crave on their tongue. For example, a chocolate-flavored mist works well for chocolate lovers. Pleasant odors such as plum or peach have been successful in reducing pain.

The Japanese have experimented with scent in the workplace. In their experiment, they began the day with a lemon scent, intended to rejuvenate workers. At midday, the scent was changed to light floral to aid in concentration. The afternoon scents were the aroma of a forest—used to relieve stress—followed by more lemon before work ended.

The researchers who developed this technique claim that the light floral scent led to 21 percent fewer errors and faster work, while general productivity throughout the day increased by 14 percent.

The New York Times Magazine and *The [London] Times.*

office, you will probably let him enter the door first and wait until he invites you to sit down. If you're smart, you won't plop your book bag on his desk since that would be an invasion of his territory.

Verbal and Nonverbal Differences

Verbal and nonverbal communication differ in seven important ways: environment, feedback, continuity, channel, control, structure, and acquisition. Let us consider each of these differences in turn.

ENVIRONMENT

Unlike much of verbal communication, in nonverbal communication there are times when we don't have to be around at all for people to get an impression of us. For example, if someone were to go into your room without your being present, she could learn quite a bit about you from your environment. Your tapes or CDs would give information about the music you like; the photographs on your desk would show the important people in your life; your clothes in the closet would give an idea of whether you were a dress-up or informal kind of person. Because one's environment can give so much information, we often feel we cannot get to know a person until we visit the place where she lives.

FEEDBACK

As well as reacting verbally to others, we also give a lot of nonverbal feedback. We show we are interested in what someone is saying by smiling or nodding our head; we show a lack of interest by fidgeting or sneaking a look at our watch. Much of our emotional response is expressed by our facial expressions and the positioning of our bodies.

CONTINUITY

Verbal communication begins and ends with words, whereas nonverbal communication is continuous. Imagine the waiting room of a dean's office. Several students are waiting to see the dean, and although some of them might occasionally talk to each other, they are all engaged in continuous nonverbal communication. Several students are looking at magazines—and occasionally at their watches. One person sits for a few minutes, then gets out of his chair and paces a few steps before he sits again. All these students, then, are continuously sending out nonverbal messages about how they are feeling in this situation.

CHANNEL

Verbal communication requires a single channel—words—whereas nonverbal communication uses several channels. In the doctor's office, as we watch a mother with her sick child, she is communicating her state of mind through several channels: her posture is tense, her facial expression is worried, and her gestures try to comfort and reassure the child. She is also communicating information other than her concern about her child. Her clothing tells us something about her socioeconomic status, her hairdo might indicate that she has recently been to a hairdresser, and if she speaks, one might get an impression of how educated she is.

CONTROL

Whereas verbal communication is under our control because we can choose our words, nonverbal communication is under our control only part of the time. We have control when we choose the clothes we are going to wear or when, on greeting someone, we smile and put out our hand. We don't have control, however, over many of our emotional responses. When we are happy, surprised, or angry, many of our nonverbal signals are spontaneous, arising out of the occasion.

STRUCTURE

Verbal communication is structured. It follows formal rules of grammar. Because so much of nonverbal communication occurs unconsciously, however, there is no planned sequence. If you are sitting and talking to someone, you don't plan when you will cross your legs, get up out of your chair, or look at the other person. These nonverbal actions will occur in response to what is happening during the conversation. The only rules that govern nonverbal communication are those which determine whether the behavior is appropriate or permissible. A child, for example, learns that to stare at people or to point at them is rude behavior.

ACQUISITION

Many of the formal rules for verbal communication, such as grammar, are taught in a structured, formal environment, such as a school. We also learn

Consider This Consider This Consider This

*T*he idea that a particular set of gestures, a particular way of crossing the feet or legs, a particular way of wrinkling the forehead, can be relied upon to have the same meaning all the time in every person you encounter is a myth. People who write books on the subject rarely mean to give that impression and can usually be counted on to tell you that they are talking about most of the people in a specific cultural or ethnic group, most of the time. But magazine articles, quick spots on television talk shows or news programs, newspaper stories and reviews with quotes taken out of context as well as speeches by "instant experts" all tend to overlook these warnings. You get the idea that you can memorize a list of gestures, expressions, and postures along with a list of their "meanings" and then rely on that universally. This is totally false. You cannot even rely on such a list for *one* person in a single culture all of the time.

Source: Suzette Haden Elgin, *More on the Gentle Art of Verbal Self-Defense.*

what style is appropriate to particular situations—that formal English is required for essays, whereas informal English is more suitable for speech. In contrast, much of nonverbal communication is not formally taught; we pick it up through imitating others. Young children commonly imitate the nonverbal communication of their parents, siblings, or peers.

The Functions of Nonverbal Communication

Nonverbal communication has four functions. Nonverbal cues *complement* a verbal message when they add to its meaning. When you meet someone for the first time you might say "I am really glad to meet you. I've heard a lot about you." If you say this with a warm smile and shake his or her hand, your nonverbal behavior complements your verbal message.

Nonverbal cues also *regulate* verbal communication. If you are talking to your boss or one of your teachers, how does she tell you that it's time for the conversation to end? She might get up out of her chair, or she might look pointedly at the clock on the wall—two ways to indicate that the conversation is over.

Nonverbal messages can also *substitute* for verbal messages. The secretary waves you into the boss's office without telling you to go in. We raise a hand in greeting instead of saying hello, or we give someone a hug—a wordless way of saying we like that person.

Often nonverbal messages *accent* what we are saying. The politician pounds the lectern to make sure everyone realizes his or her message is important. A mother tells a child he is a bad boy and shakes a finger at him to emphasize the point. Whenever people are communicating something they consider important, they are likely to accent it with a nonverbal message.

The Principles of Nonverbal Communication

Four fundamental principles underlie the workings of nonverbal communication. The first is that the nonverbal communication we use is largely that used by other persons in our culture. Second, verbal and nonverbal messages may be in conflict with one another. Third, much of nonverbal communication operates at a subconscious level—we are not even aware of it. Fourth, our nonverbal communication shows our feelings and attitudes.

Nonverbal Communication Is Culturally Determined

Much of our nonverbal behavior is learned in childhood, passed on to us by our parents and others with whom we associate. Through the process of growing up in a particular society, we adopt the traits and mannerisms of our cultural group. When meeting people for the first time, Americans put a high value on eye contact and limiting their touch to firm handshakes. A Polish man, however, in meeting a woman for the first time, might kiss her hand. People from the Micronesian islands in the Pacific neither speak nor touch when they meet; instead, they greet a person by raising their eyebrows or giving a nod.

As well as belonging to a broad cultural group such as a nation, we also belong to cultural subgroups. Puerto Rican and African-American children might grow up with a broad American cultural conditioning, but they also belong to subgroups that have nonverbal behaviors of their own. For example, when they are with people from their own cultural group, they will probably touch each other more. Other groups, formed because their members have something in common other than ethnic or national identity, might have specific nonverbal communication that enables members to identify and communicate with one another. Street gang members wear specific gang colors and mark their territory with gang symbols; members of a bowling team wear identical bowling shirts to signal their membership. All these nonverbal signals say, "I belong to this group."

In American culture, there is a good deal of difference in the way men and women position their bodies. As Deborah Tannen observed after watching videotapes of communication between girls, boys, men, and women, both girls and women sit closer and look directly into each other's faces. Boys and men, on the other hand, sit at angles to each other and hardly look at each other directly.[5]

Tannen also says that research shows that men usually sit in a relaxed, sprawled-out way—whether they are with groups of men or in mixed groups. In contrast, women sit in ladylike poses when they are in mixed groups, but when they are in all-female groups, they also sprawl out and relax.[6]

Nonverbal Messages May Conflict with Verbal Messages

Nonverbal communication is so deeply rooted, so unconscious, that we can say something verbal and then directly contradict it with a nonverbal message. For example, Will gathers up his courage and goes to talk to his economics

Does the way
these kids are sit-
ting support Tan-
nen's theory of
how males and fe-
males sit when
they are in each
other's company?

professor. To Will, the professor seems like a calm, reasonable man who likes students. What Will doesn't know is that his professor has just gotten off the phone with his mechanic, who has told him that his car needs $1400 worth of work. When Will walks into the office, he finds the professor glaring at him, with his arms crossed tightly over his chest and both feet planted firmly on the floor. The professor is giving off the air of someone who can't be questioned about anything.

Now Will is confused. He has received a **mixed message**. The professor had told his class one thing ("I'm always willing to help students"), but his nonverbal behavior communicates something else ("Don't bother me").

Often in the case of mixed messages, the nonverbal communication is more reliable than the verbal. We learn to manipulate words, but it is difficult for us to manipulate our nonverbal communication. Will's professor probably was not aware of the negative nonverbal message he was giving. The message, however, was coming through loud and clear.

Nonverbal Messages Are Largely Unconscious

Your mother calls you to see how you are doing. Right after the "Hello" and "I'm fine," she says "What's wrong?" She has sized up your emotional state on the basis of vocal tone alone. Did you know tone of voice could be so revealing?

Often we don't recognize our own nonverbal behavior: we stand farther away from people we don't like than we do from people we like. Our body position, such as our crossed arms, might show that we are resistant to what is being said. We use our head and eye movements to begin and end conversation with others.

Consider This Consider This Consider This

Research in color seems to indicate that colors bring out different emotions in people. Blue, Americans' favorite color, has a tranquilizing effect—perhaps due to a hormone secreted by the brain. Because navy blue commands respect, Carlton Wagner, Head of the Wagner Institute for Color Research, recommends it as the best color for substitute teachers and lawyers to wear.

Wagner also says that people feel secure in green settings and that they get fewer stomachaches than people who live and work in rooms of other colors. Brown is a color that leads to informality and invites people to open up. Wagner suggests that these qualities make it a good clothing color for reporters and marriage counselors.

No one will be surprised that white is associated with goodness and virtue. A nurse who wears white is seen as more competent than those who wear uniforms in other colors. Black, Wagner says, signifies dignity, sophistication, power, and authority. However, he cautions that black doesn't work for airplanes: the public perception is that light colors help them to fly better.

Source: Adapted from Bernice Kanner, "Color Schemes," *New York Magazine.*

When we consider all these nonverbal behaviors, it is hardly surprising that we are unaware of much of our nonverbal communication. Research has shown, however, that outgoing, aggressive people notice nonverbal cues more than shy and passive people.[7]

Nonverbal Communication Shows Our Feelings and Attitudes

The expression on our face, our gestures and body movement, and the way we use our eyes—all communicate our feelings and emotions to others. The feelings and emotions others can detect in our faces include happiness, sadness, surprise, fear, anger, disgust/contempt, and interest.[8] Research has also shown that most people can accurately identify emotions expressed by

Try This Try This Try This

Watch a TV drama, comedy, or soap opera that you don't ordinarily watch. Turn off the sound, concentrate on one character, and see how much you can discover about him or her from nonverbal behavior.

- Is there anything that tells you what this character's role is in relation to the other characters?

- Can you tell anything about the character's socioeconomic status?

- What nonverbal behavior does this character use to communicate emotion?

the voice.[9] If the emotion in the face and voice is combined with similar body movements, nonverbal communication becomes a powerful means of expression. You may have heard stories of legendary actors who could bring their audiences to tears while merely reciting the alphabet. These were actors who understood how to use nonverbal communication.

Types of Nonverbal Communication

Paralanguage

Paralanguage is the way we say something. There is a clear distinction between a person's use of words (verbal communication) and a person's use of paralanguage (nonverbal communication). Paralanguage includes such vocal characteristics as rate (speed of speaking), pitch (highness or lowness of tone), volume (loudness), and quality (pleasing or unpleasing sound). When any or all of these factors are added to the words, they can modify the meaning. Albert Mehrabian estimates that 39 percent of the meaning in communication is affected by vocal cues—not the words that are spoken but the way in which they are said.[10]

RATE

The **rate** (speed) at which one speaks can have an effect on the way a message is received.[11] Researchers have studied people speaking at rates varying from 120 words per minute (wpm) to 261 wpm. They discovered that when a speaker uses a faster rate, he or she is seen as more competent.[12]

PITCH

Pitch refers to the highness or lowness of the voice. Pitch can determine whether a voice sounds pleasant or unpleasant. Some people believe that high-pitched voices are not as pleasant as low-pitched ones. However, the same researchers who studied rate of speaking also found that speakers were judged more competent if they used a higher and varied pitch.[13] Lower pitches are more difficult to hear, and people who have low-pitched voices may be perceived as insecure or shy because they don't seem to speak up. Pitch can be changed, but it requires working with someone who has had professional training in voice modification.

VOLUME

The meaning of a message can be affected also by its **volume**—how loudly we speak. A loud voice is fine if used for the appropriate purpose and in moderation. The same is true of a soft voice. Notice how parents and teachers who are effective increase their volume when dealing with children.

VOCAL FILLERS

Vocal fillers are the sounds we use to fill out our sentences or to cover up when we are searching for words. Nonwords such as *uh, er, um* are a nonverbal way of indicating that we are temporarily stuck and are searching for the right word. We all use vocal fillers; they become a problem only when they become excessive or if they are distracting to listeners.

QUALITY

The overall **quality** of a voice is made up of all other vocal characteristics—tempo, resonance, rhythm, pitch, and articulation. A change in voice quality can indicate some kind of change. When people are under stress, for example, their voices often get tighter and higher.

Many of us do not have a very good idea of how we sound. When students see and hear themselves on videotape they are almost always more unhappy with how they sound than with how they look. Voices can be changed, with hard work and professional assistance.

Body Movement

Body movement, also called **kinesics,** is responsible for a lot of our nonverbal communication. Paul Ekman and W. C. Friesen, researchers on nonverbal communication, divide body movement into five categories: emblems, illustrators, regulators, displays of feeling, and adaptors.[14]

EMBLEMS

Emblems are body movements that have a direct translation into words. The extended thumb of the hitchhiker is an emblem that means "I want a ride." Making a circle with the thumb and index finger can be translated into "O.K." These emblems are known by most of the people in our society, and they are used to send a specific message. Emblems often cannot be carried from one culture to another. If you shake your head back and forth in India, for example, it means yes!

Emblems are often used when words are inappropriate. It would be impractical for a hitchhiker to stand on the side of the road and shout, "Please give me a ride!" Sometimes emblems can replace talk. We cover our faces with our hands if we are embarrassed, and we hold up our fingers to show how many we want. Also, subgroups in a society often use emblems that members of the group understand but whose meanings are intentionally kept from outsiders—the secret handshake of a fraternity is an example.

Try This Try This Try This

*W*hat emblems might accompany or substitute for the following words or phrases?

- Yes.

- Who cares?

- Maybe.

- Stop.

- Shame on you.

ILLUSTRATORS

Illustrators accent, emphasize, or reinforce words. If someone asks how big your suitcase is, you will probably describe it with words and illustrate the dimensions with your hands. If someone is giving you directions, she will probably point down the road and gesture left and right at the appropriate points. Illustrators can help to make communication more exact. If someone tells you he has just caught a fish, you will have an idea of how big the fish is by how far apart he holds his hands. He could tell you the size in inches, but somehow you will get an even better idea if he uses his hands as illustrators. But not all illustrators are gestures. If an instructor underlines something she has written on the blackboard, she is telling you that this point is particularly important. A car salesperson emphasizes that a car is well built by slamming the door so that you can hear how solid it sounds.

REGULATORS

Regulators control the back-and-forth flow of speaking and listening. They include the head nods, hand gestures, shifts in posture, and other body movements that signal the beginning and end of interactions. At a very simple level, a teacher uses a regulator when she points to the person she wants to speak next. On a more subtle level, someone might turn slightly away when you are talking—perhaps indicating "I don't like what I'm hearing" or "I don't want to continue this conversation."

DISPLAYS OF FEELINGS

Displays of feelings show, through our faces and our body movements, how intensely we are feeling. If a student walks into a professor's office and the professor says "I can see you are really feeling upset," he or she is responding to nonverbal cues the student is giving about his feelings. The student might have come in tearfully or with a body posture indicating "We really are going to fight this out"—clenched fists, a jutting jaw, or a variety of other body movements showing that the student was feeling upset.

Adaptors are nonverbal ways of adapting to a communication situation. We each use such a wide variety of adaptors and they are so specific to our own needs and the individual communication situation that they are difficult to classify or even describe. Let's look, however, at how they work in some specific communication situations.

You have rented your first apartment and your mother has come to visit. While she is there, she spends a good deal of time moving objects and furniture around. By moving things around, she is using adaptors. What does her nonverbal behavior mean? On a simple level, she might be telling you that you are not very tidy. On a more complicated level, she might be telling you that you are still her child and that she, your mother, is still in charge.

People often use adaptors when they are nervous or uncomfortable in a situation. We might play with jewelry, drum on the table, or move around a lot in our seats. Each of these behaviors is an adaptor—a way of helping us to cope with the situation. We all use adaptors, but we are generally not aware of them unless someone points them out.

Body Type

Our body type communicates a message. No matter how we may perceive ourselves, others tend to judge us by our body type. Ernst Kretschmer, a professor of psychiatry and neurology, made the first known effort to classify

---

Try This Try This Try This

*L*ook through your wardrobe and identify three outfits: the one that is your favorite, the one you like least, and the one you wear when you want to feel comfortable but don't care how you look.

- *Your favorite:* Why do you like this outfit? Do you get compliments when you wear it? Would other people's reactions to it influence how you felt about it? How do you feel about yourself when you are wearing it?

- *Your least favorite:* Why don't you like this outfit? How do other people react to it? Do you feel comfortable when you wear it? How do you feel about yourself when you are wearing it? Do you plan to get rid of it anytime in the near future?

- *Your most comfortable:* What is the condition of this outfit? Where do you wear it? Do you care how other people react to it? Has anyone tried to persuade you to get rid of it? If so, what was your response?

After you look at these outfits, see if you can draw any conclusions about your clothing. Do you pick clothes for style or comfort? How do other people's reactions influence what you decide to wear? How does what you wear reflect who you are? Do you think you could change the way that people react to you by changing your clothing? Would you be willing to do this?

body types as early as 1925.[15] Those with skinny, bony, narrow bodies are *ectomorphs*. *Mesomorphs* have athletic, hard, firm, muscular bodies. *Endomorphs* have oval-shaped bodies with heavy, large abdomens. In the 1940s, William Sheldon related body type and temperament.[16] His work has been updated by researchers W. Wells and B. Siegel.[17] They asked subjects to make judgments about silhouettes of each of Kretschmer's body types. Ectomorphs (thin people) were rated as more ambitious, younger, more suspicious of others, more tense and nervous, more inclined to be difficult, more pessimistic, and quieter. Mesomorphs (athletic people) were seen as stronger, more adventurous, more mature, more self-reliant, younger, and taller. Endomorphs (fat people) were considered to be more old-fashioned, lazier, weaker, more talkative, older, more warmhearted and sympathetic, more good-natured and agreeable, more dependent on others, and more trusting. This research shows that people might have a strong impression of us before we have a chance to say a single word.

Attractiveness

People who are perceived as attractive get a more positive response from others than people who are not perceived as attractive. In our society, greatly influenced by what we see on the television screen, attractiveness consists of being thin, tall (especially if you're a man), and having a lot of hair.

Not surprisingly, attractive people have an easier time in life. Researchers have discovered that women perceived as attractive have more dates, receive higher grades in college, persuade males with greater ease, and receive lighter court sentences.[18] Men or women rated as attractive are also perceived as being more sensitive, kind, strong, sociable, and interesting.[19] In business, attractiveness pays off in several ways, including finding jobs and obtaining higher starting salaries.[20]

Clothing

Because clothing gives such a strong and immediate impression of its wearer, it is enormously important to nonverbal communication. Clothing projects a message and, by having chosen the clothing, the wearer has committed himself or herself to the statements the clothing makes.[21] The viewer responds not only to the clothing itself but also to what it says about the wearer in terms of status, affiliation, norms, and conformity. For example, if we see a man walking down the street in a well-tailored suit, we will probably assume that he is a white-collar worker and that he might work for a bank or a big company. If we see a young woman on the same street in jeans and a T-shirt and carrying a book bag, we will probably assume that she is a student.

Clothing falls into four categories: uniforms, occupational dress, leisure clothing, and costumes. Each of these categories conveys a somewhat different meaning.[22]

UNIFORMS

A uniform is the most specialized form of clothing. It tells us that the wearer belongs to a particular organization. The most common uniforms are found in the military. By showing rank, these uniforms tell what positions the users hold in the military hierarchy and what their relationships are to others in the organization. The uniform also implies that its wearer will follow certain norms.[23] For example, one would expect someone in military uniform always to be respectful of the flag.

OCCUPATIONAL DRESS

Occupational dress is clothing that employees are expected to wear. Unlike uniforms, occupational dress is not as precise. Occupational clothing indicates participation in a certain kind of job, and it is designed to present a specific image of the company.[24] In some cases, the clothing is quite specific: letter carriers, airline pilots, and train conductors have little choice about their clothing. On the other hand, some employees have choices: flight attendants are required to wear several pieces of specific clothing, but they can mix them according to their own preference. Nurses might be required to wear white, but they can select the style they like. People who wear business clothing have even greater choices. The company might expect its employees to wear suits, but the employee can choose both color and style.

Required school clothing, another form of occupational clothing (even if it is called a *uniform*), is also a way of making everyone equal. In recent years some of the big-city public schools have required students to wear uniforms. These uniforms take away the status students get from wearing designer clothes, fancy running shoes, and expensive jewelry.

Power and control are important to organizations (or individuals) who demand a uniform or some sort of occupational dress. Upon joining the military or the staff of a fast-food restaurant, a person gives up some individuality by agreeing to wear the designated clothing. Sometimes wearers are required to wear clothing they dislike. Women who work in bars, for example, might be required to wear clothing which is sexually provocative and which may bring unwanted attention from men. On the nonwork level, parents control children when they decide what they should wear. Even when teenagers make their own clothing choices, they are limited by the amount of money they have.

LEISURE CLOTHING

Leisure clothing is used when work is over. Because this kind of clothing is left to choice, individuals can assert their own identity by wearing it.[25] However, even some leisure activities require a kind of "uniform." Many teenagers will wear only a particular brand of jeans and when the group agrees on the brand, it becomes the new uniform. Skiers might use a certain brand of skis, parkas, and goggles—even though others would work equally well. The mass media have had such a great influence on leisure clothing that it's hard to separate media influence from individual preference.

COSTUMES

Costumes are a form of highly individualized dress. One example of a costume might be an imitation of cowboy dress: boots, bandanna, and hat. By putting on a costume, the wearer announces, "This is who I want to be." Such a

How would you classify the clothing in each of these pictures: uniforms, occupational dress, leisure clothing, costume?

costume might have symbolic importance—the cowboy costume announcing a macho kind of individuality.[26] Not many people are interested in wearing costumes. Not only do costumes require thought about the image they convey, but they also go against many norms. As one student shrewdly observed as he changed his shoes for a job interview at a supermarket, "I had better not wear my cowboy boots. They look too aggressive."

Space and Distance

The study of space and distance, called **proxemics**, concerns the way we use the space around us as well as the distance we stand or sit from others. The minute you enter a classroom, you are faced with a decision that relates to how you use space. You have to decide where to sit. You may choose to sit in the back because you do not want to be noticed, because you feel it is a "safer" distance from the teacher, because you do not want people behind you staring at you, or because it will give you an opportunity to see other students' reactions and thus give you confidence. On the other hand, you might select a front-row seat because you have a lot of confidence or because you want to be noticed.

What is interesting about your choice of seating is that you might be sending your instructor a message. When he sees you sitting in the back row in the far corner, he might decide you are not very interested in the subject and are looking for a place to go to sleep. If you are in the front row, he might conclude that you are an unusually bright and attentive student and that he should give you special attention. You could also be sending your

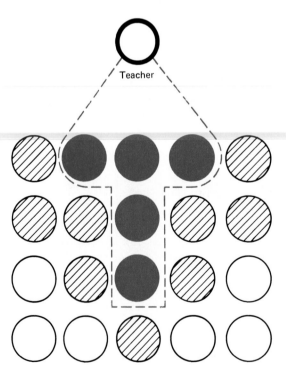

Figure 5-1
In a traditional classroom arrangement, those students occupying the colored seats will account for a large proportion of the total interaction that occurs between teachers and students. Those in the striped seats will interact some; those in the white seats will interact very infrequently. The area enclosed in dotted lines has been called the "action zone."

classmates a message. They might interpret the front-seat choice as a way of trying to win points with the instructor. If you are more toward the back of the room, you are one of them—since that's where most students decide to sit—yet that's where least interaction with the instructor is likely to take place (see Figure 5-1).

We also map out certain spaces as our territory. **Territory** is the space that we consider as belonging to us—either temporarily or permanently. For example, you would probably be upset if you came into the classroom and found someone sitting in "your chair." Most of us have territories that we consider our own, and other people can enter into them only with our permission. A bedroom, for example, is usually considered to be the territory of the person who sleeps there. People whose houses have been burglarized commonly report that not only do they feel distress at losing personal possessions, but they also feel anger at having their personal territory violated by strangers.

We make judgments about how others are thinking and reacting to us by the way they use space. It was Edward T. Hall, author of *The Silent Language* and *The Hidden Dimension*, two popular books on nonverbal communication, who labeled the study of space and distance proxemics.[27] From his observations and interviews, Hall has discovered that North Americans use four distance zones when they are communicating with others: intimate distance, personal distance, social distance, and public distance.[28]

INTIMATE DISTANCE

In *intimate distance*, people are in direct contact with each other or are no more than 18 inches apart. Look at a mother with her baby. She picks him up, caresses him, kisses him on the cheek, puts him on her lap. All her senses are alert when she is this close to the baby. She can touch him, smell him, and hear every little gurgle he makes. We also maintain an intimate distance in love relationships and with close friends. Intimate distance exists whenever we feel free to touch the other person.

When our intimate distance is violated by people who have no right to be there, we feel apprehensive. If we are on a crowded bus, subway, or elevator, and people are pressed against us, they are in our intimate distance. We react by ignoring these people and by not making eye contact. In this way we can protect our intimate distance—psychologically if not physically.

PERSONAL DISTANCE

In *personal distance* people stay anywhere from 18 inches to 4 feet from each other. This is the distance we keep most often when we are in casual and personal conversations. It is close enough to see the other person's reactions but far enough away not to encroach on intimate distance. If we move closer than 18 inches, the person will probably back away. If we move farther away than 4 feet, it will be difficult to carry on a conversation without having the feeling that it can be overheard by others.

SOCIAL DISTANCE

When we do not know people very well, we are most likely to maintain a *social distance* from them—that is, a distance of 4 to 12 feet. Impersonal

People's distance zones are affected by culture. The top picture shows American
police officers standing in line; the bottom picture, Guatemalan voters. How would
you feel if you were standing in the line in the bottom picture?

business, social gatherings, and interviews are examples of situations where we use social distance.

Whenever we use social distance, interaction becomes more formal. Have you ever noticed the size of the desks in the offices of important people? They are large enough to keep visitors at the proper social distance. In a large office with many workers, the desks will be social distance apart. This distance makes it possible for each worker to concentrate on his or her work and to use the telephone without affecting others in the office. Sometimes people will move back and forth from social distance to personal distance. Two coworkers might, for example, have desks that are 10 feet apart. When they want to discuss something more privately, they will move into each other's personal distance.

PUBLIC DISTANCE

Public distance—a distance of more than 12 feet—is typically used for public speaking. At this distance, people usually speak more loudly and use more exaggerated gestures. Communication at this distance is more formal and permits few opportunities for people to be involved with each other. Figure 5-2 shows the dimensions of the four distance zones.

SPACE/DISTANCE AS AN INDICATOR OF INTIMACY

When we observe the distances that people maintain between themselves and others, we can tell which people have close relationships and which people have more formal relationships. If you enter the college president's office and she remains behind her desk, you can assume that your conversation is going to be formal. If she invites you to the corner where there are easy chairs and you sit side by side, she has set up a much more intimate situation, and consequently, the conversation is going to be more informal.

Figure 5-2
The Four Distance Zones

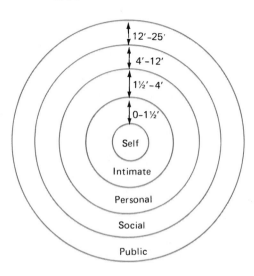

Try This Try This Try This

*I*magine that you are in the following situations. How much distance would there be between you and:

- Someone you have been dating for a long time?

- Your boss at a business function?

- Your professor in her office discussing your poor grade?

- Your professor in the hallway?

- Your dentist who is working on your teeth?

- Your best friend listening to a new CD?

As we get to know people better, we are permitted into their more personal space. Remember when you were in junior high and went with a boy or a girl to the movies for the first time? When your hands met in the popcorn box, you were exploring the possibilities of moving from a personal to an intimate distance. The opposite can also happen. A married couple experiences a lot of intimate distance. If there are problems in the marriage, however, the couple's communication will be conducted mostly at a personal distance. If they start to negotiate a divorce, they will probably carry out most of their negotiations at a social distance.

SPACE/DISTANCE AS AN INDICATOR OF STATUS

Besides degrees of intimacy, degrees of status are communicated through the use of space. Executives, presidents of colleges, and high government officials all have large offices with expansive windows and elaborate furnishings, whereas their secretaries and support staff are in smaller spaces—spaces that are often used by many people. In a household, children have the least amount of space. Even if they have their own room, that space is often controlled by

Try This Try This Try This

- What spaces do you regard as your personal territory? Are they where you sit in the classroom, a room in your house, a certain space in the place where you work?

- Have others ever invaded your territory? How did you feel when this happened? Did you give any indication that they should not be in your territory?

- Are you sensitive to other people's territory? Are there any people in your life whose territory you respect and would ask permission to enter?

adults. It is planned and decorated by an adult, and the adult sets the rules for how the space will be used. Adults also punish children by depriving them of space. Commands such as "Go to your room" or "Stay out of my room" limit children's access to space within the household.

Touch

The closer we stand to one another, the more we increase the likelihood of our touching. We are all familiar with the use of touch in intimate situations. We kiss babies, hold hands with loved ones, and hug family members.

When and where we touch one another is governed by a strict set of societal rules. Richard Heslin has described five different categories of touch behavior.[30] The first is *functional-professional touch*, in which you are touched for a specific reason, as in a physical examination. This kind of touch is impersonal and businesslike. *Social-polite touch* is used to acknowledge someone else. The handshake is the most common form. Although the two people move into an intimate distance to shake hands, after the handshake is over, they move away from each other. In close relationships people use the *friendship-warmth touch*. This kind of touch involves hugs and casual kisses between friends. In more intense relationships the *love-intimacy touch* is common. Parents stroke their children; lovers and spouses kiss each other. The final touch Heslin describes is *sexual-arousal touch*—touch used as an expression of physical attraction.[31]

As in distance, the kind of touch that is used communicates information about the relationship. The more intense the relationship, the more frequent

Consider This Consider This Consider This

Most of us know intuitively that touch is an important way for humans to relate to each other. Recent research has found that touch is also critical for humans to grow.

The conventional treatment of premature babies has been to touch them as little as possible so they don't get agitated. Researchers, however, have found that touch is important because it releases brain chemicals that promote growth. When premature infants were massaged three times a day for 15 minutes, they gained weight 47 percent faster than those who were left alone in their incubators. They were also able to leave the hospital an average of six days earlier. Eight months later, they still held their advantage in weight and did much better in tests of mental and motor ability.

Researchers also believe that touching between parents and children is important to psychological development. Physical contact makes children feel safer. When parents touch children through roughhousing, children generally have a more positive feeling about their bodies.

Source: Daniel Goleman. "The Experience of Touch: Research Points to a Critical Role," *The New York Times.*

and more intimate the touch. Often we can tell how much others are involved and what kind of relationship they have by how much they touch each other. For example, nurses know that if a mother does not frequently touch her child, something is wrong in the relationship.

Time

People seem to be divided into those who are always on time and those who are always late. Have you ever noticed that certain students always come late, whereas others are always in their seats when the class begins? From the viewpoint of an instructor, the person who is always late may be communicating considerable negative information: he is really not interested in this class, he doesn't respect the instructor, and so on. By the same token, students might resent an instructor who is always late. They might think he doesn't plan well enough or that he doesn't respect the class.

In one instance or another we all use time for psychological effect. If you have a date with someone you don't know very well, you probably will not arrive too early because this might make you appear too eager. If you dent the family car, you wait for the right time to tell your parents about it. Our control of time, then, is an important form of nonverbal communication.

Often time is connected with status: the higher our status, the more control we have over our time. A child has little control over time. His higher-status parent interrupts his play to have him eat dinner or makes him go to bed far earlier than he wants to. Professionals in our society often make others wait for them. How long do you wait in the doctor's office before you can see him or her? Students have little say in how their time is spent. If they want a particular class and it is only offered at 8:00 A.M., they have little choice but to take it then. They also have no choice about when papers are due or when

---

Consider This Consider This Consider This

*I*f you look at the people on any crowded street, you will notice that women are carrying babies, groceries, shopping bags, and a variety of other items while men are seldom loaded down with much more than a briefcase. Letty Cottin Pogrebin writes that the amount one carries has a good deal to do with one's status:

The ability to keep one's hands free implies not only status and economic privilege but real physical freedom. It is much easier for the unencumbered to use their hands, defend themselves, be mobile, run, or stand tall and retain their dignity. . . . Historically and cross-culturally, women have been weighted down by babies in their arms and baskets on their heads while men, carrying only their weapons, move freely in the world. In modern society as in ancient cultures, noticing who schleps and carries tells us a lot about who is usually left holding the bag.

Source: Letty Cottin Pogrebin, *Hers, through Women's Eyes.*

they have to take examinations. If we want to discover who has the most status in our society, we might do well by watching who waits for whom.

Improving Your Nonverbal Communication

Because our nonverbal behavior is so tied in with our social and cultural conditioning, it is not very easy to change it. Fortunately, most of us don't need to make any drastic changes. We should be concerned with nonverbal communication that distracts us from what we want to say or that contradicts our verbal messages. If we find that people regularly misunderstand us, we might do well to ask whether this might be due to nonverbal cues people are picking up—remembering that as much as 93 percent of what we are communicating may be nonverbal.

If we want to change our nonverbal behavior, it is important to pay attention to feedback we get from others. "Why have I been misunderstood?" "Why do people see me as unfriendly, rigid, unhappy. . . . ?" For example, if a number of people tell you that when they first met you they thought you were a snob, you can learn a lot by asking what you did to make them feel that way. Once you have this feedback, you will be able to make concrete plans for changing your behavior.

If you realize that you have distracting mannerisms (playing with your hair, saying "you know" too much), it might be useful to have friends and family members remind you when you are doing these things so that you can break the habit.

Probably the single most important tool for discovering negative nonverbal behavior is videotape. Most people who see themselves on tape know immediately what their bad habits are. If you have access to a videotape recorder, take advantage of it. Have someone tape you giving a speech or in conversation with another person. You will be amazed at what you can learn about yourself. If you have a chance to tape your voice, don't spend all your time reacting to it emotionally; see if you can figure out what there is about your voice you don't like and how you might be able to change.

Observe people in the roles they play. How do bosses act? How much of their communication is nonverbal? What nonverbal elements are desirable? Undesirable? When you get to be a boss, which of these behaviors would you want to imitate? Which people *don't* you want to be like? Is it their nonverbal behavior that turns you off? Do you do any of these same things? Can you stop doing them?

Time and space are two forms of nonverbal communication over which you can take some control. What does your room, apartment, or house look like? What will people think of you when they see your space? How about time? Are you sensitive to other people's time, or do you make them wait for you? How do you think they feel about you when they have to wait?

Our greatest problem with nonverbal communication is that we don't think about it enough. When we realize how important a part of our total communication it is, we are more likely to realize that we should all pay careful attention to it.

SUMMARY

As much as 93 percent of the impact of a message can depend on its nonverbal elements. Verbal communication and nonverbal communication often reinforce each other, but there are clear differences as well. Verbal communication begins when a word is uttered and requires a single channel. It is under your control, is structured, and is formally learned. Nonverbal communication is continuous, is multichanneled, is mostly habitual and unconscious, is largely unstructured, and is learned informally.

Nonverbal communication serves important functions. With respect to the verbal message, it can complement it, regulate it, substitute for it, or accent it. In addition, basic principles tell us that most nonverbal communication is culturally determined, may conflict with verbal messages, is sent subtly, perhaps even unconsciously, and communicates feelings and attitudes.

There are several types of nonverbal communication. They include: paralanguage, body movement, clothing and body appearance, space/distance, touch, and the use of time.

Much of nonverbal communication is difficult to change, but through feedback from others, it is possible to modify some of our nonverbal behavior—particularly that which is distracting to others. Videotape and audiotape recorders are valuable tools for discovering the nonverbal cues we are sending to others.

FURTHER READING

ACKERMAN, DIANE. *A Natural History of the Senses.* New York: Random House, 1990. This is a fascinating book about how we perceive, savor, and experience the world through our senses. Each chapter contains a series of short essays about each sense, and so if the reader doesn't have time to read the whole book, he or she can pick and choose the sections that are the most interesting.

ELLISON, RALPH. *Invisible Man.* New York: Vintage Books, 1989. This now-classic novel is about a man who, because of his race, seems invisible to those around him. The book illustrates brilliantly how a person's self-concept is defined on the basis of how people react to his or her physical appearance.

HALL, EDWARD T. *Hidden Dimension.* Garden City, NY: Anchor Books, 1969. In this paperback book the author deals with spatial experience as it is dictated by culture. The "hidden dimension" is people's use of space, and the author is very convincing in presenting the idea that virtually everything a person is and does is associated with the experience of space. This is an immensely interesting and exciting book full of examples and illustrations that develop the concepts of social and personal space and how they are perceived.

————. *The Silent Language.* Westport, CT: Greenwood Press, 1980. This paperback book examines the cultural component of nonverbal communication, especially how American behavior differs from that of people in other cultures. The author is an anthropologist and uses numerous examples and anecdotes to examine the world of nonverbal communication. The book will stimulate you to make your own observations and analysis of the nonverbal behavior of others.

HICKSON, MARK L., III, AND DON W. STACKS. *NVC: Nonverbal Communication—Studies and Applications,* 2d ed. Dubuque, IA: Wm. C. Brown, 1989. Although this book contains what is found in other nonverbal textbooks, the authors here also emphasize the interaction between biological and sociopsychological functions.

In addition, they illustrate how the research may be used in real-life situations. Well documented, interesting material.

JOSEPH, NATHAN. *Uniforms and Nonuniforms: Communication through Clothing.* New York: Greenwood Press, 1986. A fascinating account of how our clothing communicates our rank, status, and place in the world. The book covers the meaning of uniforms, nonbureaucratic clothing, occupational and leisure clothing, and costumes. The book is particularly valuable because it is entertaining and at the same time based on solid scholarship.

KNAPP, MARK L. *Essentials of Nonverbal Communication.* New York: Holt, Rinehart & Winston, 1980. Although brief, this book is comprehensive and well written. The research base is large.

LEATHERS, DALE G. *Successful Nonverbal Communication: Principles and Applications.* New York: Macmillan, 1986. This is an introductory textbook; however, Leathers focuses on how knowledge of the informational potential of nonverbal cues can be used to communicate successfully in the real world. A very complete, well-written and researched textbook.

MALANDRO, LORETTA, LARRY BARKER, AND DEBORAH BARKER. *Nonverbal Communication,* 2d ed. New York: Random House, 1989. The authors provide examples, applications, research findings, a historical perspective, contemporary information, and complete reference lists. This textbook is enjoyable to read. It is also intellectually and emotionally challenging.

RICHMOND, VIRGINIA P., JAMES C. MCCROSKEY, AND STEVEN K. PAYNE. *Nonverbal Behavior in Interpersonal Relations,* 2d ed. Englewood Cliffs, NJ: Prentice-Hall, 1991. The authors present nonverbal communication as a unique blend of social, scientific, and humanistic study. In the first ten chapters they consider the traditional categories of nonverbal behavior. After a chapter on how these categories relate to immediacy, they consider four essential nonverbal contexts: female/male relationships, superior/subordinate relationships, teacher/student relationships, and intercultural relationships.

Interpersonal Communication

Chapter 6

Interpersonal Relationships

CHAPTER OBJECTIVES	KEY TERMS
After reading this chapter, you should be able to:	affection
	attitudes
1. Define interpersonal communication.	beliefs
2. Identify and explain interpersonal needs.	control
	gossip
3. Tell why people are attracted to each other.	inclusion
4. Discuss how roles influence interpersonal communication.	interpersonal communication
	Johari Window
5. Give some ways of beginning a conversation.	proximity
6. Explain the uses of small talk and gossip.	self-disclosure
	small talk
7. Define self-disclosure and tell why it is important.	
8. Describe the four panes of the Johari Window.	

*L*eo spent the morning talking to his friends about what they would like to do for Black History Month. He went out for lunch with the Affirmative Action adviser and discussed with her some ideas for speakers during the month. After his two afternoon classes, he stopped and had coffee with a friend. When he got home, he called his girlfriend and made arrangements to meet in the library to study together. Later that night, he called his mother and told her that he wouldn't be coming home that weekend.

During the course of his day, Leo had a lot of communication with various people. This was ***interpersonal communication***—communication where one talks to people on a one-to-one basis, usually in an informal setting. In Leo's case, he talked to several friends during the morning, the adviser at lunch, another friend at coffee, and later his girlfriend and his mother. All these conversations took place in the course of a single day. Leo's extensive use of interpersonal communication is not unusual: if we were to keep track of our own conversations, we might find that we had as many as Leo, for interpersonal is the kind of communication we use most often. It occurs whenever we are in a relationship with another person or persons. Talking to a friend, arguing with a spouse, scolding a child, negotiating a business deal—all are situations in which we use interpersonal communication.

Scientists have found that interpersonal contacts with friends will help us live longer. In a study of loneliness and health, researchers at the University of Michigan's Institute for Social Research examined biomedical and survey data collected over two decades and discovered that isolation from others was as detrimental to health as smoking, high cholesterol counts, and lack of physical activity.[1] Polls have shown that Americans put a high value on friendship. In a Harris poll, 97 percent of the 3001 respondents, when asked what they wanted for their children, replied they hoped their children would have lots of friends and would be well-liked. In a Roper poll, eight out of ten persons said it was absolutely essential to have friends who respected them.[2]

Interpersonal Needs

Interpersonal communication is valuable to people because it serves so many important purposes. We use it for personal discovery, for involving ourselves with others, for meeting our needs for love and affection, and for keeping control in our lives. Interpersonal communication, more than any other kind of communication, is needed to fulfill the social needs that allow us to survive.

Personal Discovery

Interpersonal communication helps us discover who we are. As John Powell writes, "I must be able to tell you who I am before I can know who I am."[3] If we were to live in complete isolation, we would have no sense of self. For example, if parents took care of a newborn's physical needs but completely ignored his emotional needs, the child would grow up to be emotionally disturbed. Our self-concept depends on our relationships and how those in our relationships respond to us. When we are small children, our parents label us as "good" or "bad." Our teachers say "You are not living up to your

Consider This Consider This Consider This

*E*mpathy, the ability to share someone's feelings, has always been regarded as highly desirable. As well as helping us to form relationships, empathy helps us to respond with concern to the welfare of others.

Recent research has shown that children develop empathy in surprising ways. The most important finding is that the more time a father spends with his children, the more likely they are to grow up to be empathic adults. Even after 25 years, the father's influence was still felt.

Another researcher found that setting limits on children's behavior was much more important to developing empathy than warmth and nurturing. The researcher interprets these results by saying, "A child has to learn to give something up; it takes self-control to donate or help. To teach empathy, you have to teach kids there are times they have to control their own impulses so as to help others."

Source: Daniel Goleman, "Studies on Development of Empathy Challenge Some Old Assumptions," *The New York Times.*

potential." Our friends tell us that they like us because we have certain qualities that appeal to them. All these reactions add up to how we see ourselves. If the reactions are positive, then we are likely to have a positive sense of self.

As we look at the development of our self-concept we are again reminded of the transactional view of communication. All of these past experiences that tell us who we are will influence both our present and future relationships. Our self-concept will also determine the roles we play and the roles we expect others to play in relation to us. William Schultz writes that we all have certain needs in our interpersonal relationships. We need to feel included, to receive affection, and to be in control.[4]

Inclusion

The need for **inclusion**—involvement with others—is one of the most powerful human needs. Do you have childhood memories of being chosen last on the team or of all the other kids going off without you? Remember how terrible you felt because you weren't included?

Some people have their most powerful feeling of being excluded in high school. Penelope Eckert, who has studied social interactions in high school, points out that American public high schools have always divided into what everybody recognizes as the "leading crowd." This crowd is made up of what she calls "jocks." These are people who consider athletics as a way of life. They either participate in sports or attend sports events, follow a "clean" life style and generally hold American ideals about fair play and competition.[5]

Students who do not like or participate in athletics are left out. They might choose to join groups of students who rebel against the school, or they may gravitate toward groups that have no status. Many of them, however,

Were you ever excluded from a group? What happens to your self-esteem when this occurs?

have an acute sense of not being included, and sometimes their resentment and pain about this exclusion stays with them long after they have left high school—even when they have achieved great success in the world. The pain of not being included is just as great for an adult as it is for a child. Adults, however, are better able to avoid situations from which they might be excluded.

Affection

Affection, the feeling of warm, emotional attachment to other people, is another important interpersonal need. Whether it is expressed nonverbally (hugging, pats on the back) or verbally ("I'm really glad you called me today"), affection is important to human happiness.

Affection is a one-to-one emotion. Unlike inclusion, which usually occurs in situations where several people are present, affection is a matter of singling out a particular person. People vary in their ability to express affection.

Control

If we are going to have a good relationship with another person, it is important that we have some control. In an interpersonal sense, **control** means having options and choices in life rather than always being manipulated by others and submitting to people and circumstances.

Control is exercised in various forms. It might relate to simple decision making: deciding which movie to see or which restaurant to eat in. It can also be more broad-ranging: how to raise the children, where to live, how money is spent. Control can also be used to dictate emotional responses: "I hate it when you cry"; "I am willing to discuss this, but only if you act in a more rational manner."

Recent research on control has found that people who have control over their lives are healthier—both mentally and physically.[6] Students learn better when teachers give them some autonomy, and workers feel better about their jobs and the place they work when they can make some decisions about how their work should be done. Elderly people lived longer in nursing homes if they had some say about what they wanted to eat and how the furniture in their room was arranged.[7]

Attraction to Others

In the course of a week, most of us have hundreds of casual encounters with other people. With most of the people we meet, we conduct our business and go on our way. Most of us, for example, will not remember the waitress who

---

Try This Try This Try This

*W*hen you are entering into a new emotional relationship, especially one in which you will be living with a new person, it would be useful to compare notes on your emotional styles. Try out these introductory statements with a roommate. Both of you should respond before you move to the next item.

- What I am like when I'm down or upset about something . . .

- How hard it is for me to let people know what I am feeling or what I need . . .

- Something that will usually cheer me up when I'm down . . .

- How I am when things are going really well . . .

- Times when I would prefer to be left alone . . .

- How I usually let people know when I am angry . . .

- What my mood is like most of the time . . .

- Something that can make me tense or uptight . . .

- What I'm like when I feel pressured . . .

- Something that is likely to annoy me . . .

- My idea of relaxing after being tense . . .

Source: Dan J. Peterman, Mary Ann D. Sagaria, and James E. Sellers, *The Roommate Starter Kit.*

served us the last time we ate out or the bank teller who cashed our check. These people recede into a kind of human landscape. Occasionally, however, we have an encounter where we think "I would like to get to know that person better." Out of all the people we meet, how do we pick out some we want to know better? What ingredients make up our attraction to others? What do we have to gain?

Physical Attraction

Often we are attracted to others because of the way they look. We like someone's appearance and want to get to know the person better. In some cases physical attraction may be sexual attraction. In most cases, however, it goes beyond that. Sometimes we are attracted to people because of the way they dress. They choose a style of clothing that is our own style or is a style we would like to imitate. They have a certain "look" that we like very much.

Since physical attraction is superficial, it usually recedes into the background as we get to know the person. Physical attraction, then, is a reason for getting to know someone; it alone is seldom the basis for a relationship.

Perceived Gain

Sometimes we are attracted to people because we think we have something to gain from associating with them. In high school, for example, a student might try to hang out with popular students so that he or she can be popular too—whether these students are likable may be irrelevant.

In college a student may join a particular sorority or fraternity because some of the members are influential in campus life. Another student might join a business management club because she believes that meeting certain people might give her an advantage in getting a job. Some people like to make friends with those who have status or power, hoping that this association will confer status and power on them too.

Similarities

Often we are attracted to people because we like what they say. We are attracted to people because they seem knowledgeable about subjects we also find interesting and significant. Even more important, we are attracted to people because they share our beliefs and attitudes. Our **beliefs** are our convictions; our **attitudes** are the deeply felt beliefs that govern how we behave. Although we like to think that opposites attract, when it comes to a strongly felt belief, we look for people who believe as we do. For example, it would be difficult for a Palestinian and an Israeli to be close friends—their politics are too far apart. Although a born-again Christian and an Orthodox Jew might share similar ideas, they would be so far apart in religious beliefs that they probably would not seek each other out.

An advantage of sharing similar beliefs and attitudes with another person is that you can make accurate predictions about each other. For example, Bob doesn't have to consult Alice when he plans the evening. He knows her well enough to know that she will enjoy a Mexican restaurant and a cops-and-robbers movie. Stacy does not even bother to ask Marie to play Scrabble with her. She knows that Marie doesn't like word games of any sort.

Someone's emotional style might also be a reason why you are attracted to him or her. Researchers are discovering that people have very different ways of reacting to what is going on around them. Some people are in emotional tumult even when ordinary things are happening, while others stay calm when extraordinary things occur.[8] Some of us choose friends who have an emotional style that is much like our own; others like the challenge of friends who are different.

Differences

Although two people who have very different beliefs are unlikely to form a strong and lasting relationship, people with different personality characteristics might well be attracted to each other. For example, a person who doesn't like making decisions might be attracted to a strong decision maker. Because these qualities complement each other, they might help to strengthen the relationship.

Sometimes people might be attracted to people of a different race or culture. Although the culture or race may differ, important beliefs might be the same. For example, a white American may share similar beliefs about child rearing with a black American. In other cases, association with a group might bring people together. An American Rotary member would have a different cultural background from a Rotary member from India. However, that they both belong to Rotary may bring them together.

Proximity

Often we get to know and like people because of **proximity**—because we live or work close to them. Even when people might not otherwise have been attracted to each other, they may begin to know and like each other because they are together so much. This often happens when people work together. After sharing an office or standing next to each other on an assembly line, they begin to share on a day-to-day basis what is happening in their lives. This leads to their becoming friends.

Sometimes people who are attracted to each other form a strong friendship but lose touch with each other when they no longer have proximity. Typically, friends who move to different cities vow to stay in touch. However, if they can't afford telephone calls or if they aren't letter writers, it's not unusual for contact to drop to a yearly holiday card. Proximity, then, is important not just for starting relationships but also for keeping them going.

Who Likes Whom?

When sizing up others, the reaction of others to us is also important. It isn't clear whether we like others *because* they like us or whether the knowledge that others like us strengthens our attraction to them. We might be attracted to people because we think they like us.[9]

Try This Try This Try This

*T*hink about a person you met who you thought might make a good friend. Analyze your attraction to this person by answering the following questions:

1. Was there anything you noticed about this person that was physically attractive?
   a. Did you notice his or her clothing?
   b. Did you notice anything about his or her nonverbal communication?
2. Did this person say something that interested you?
   a. Was it about a subject you were interested in?
   b. Was it about something you also believed in?
3. Was this person in close physical proximity?
   a. Could you see him or her every day?
   b. At least once a week?
4. How would you describe this person's emotional style? Is it different from or similar to your own?
5. Did this person give signs that he or she liked you?
6. Did you notice desirable qualities in this person that you would like to have yourself?

Talking to Each Other

Roles, Relationships, and Communication

All relationships are governed by the roles that the participants in the relationships expect each other to play. Sometimes these roles are tightly defined; other times the participants have more flexibility in defining them. A conservative boss, for example, might expect his employees never to engage in personal conversations during working hours and to receive and make no personal telephone calls. In this case, the roles of boss and worker are traditionally defined. In another office, the boss might not interpret the roles so rigidly. She might like to be on a first-name basis with the people who work for her, and she might not care about personal conversations and phone calls as long as the work gets done.

Often the roles we know best are those that are the most traditionally defined. We have certain expectations of teachers, coaches, and bosses. In families, parents decide what time young children should go to bed and whether they should be permitted to eat junk food. In institutions, the state, the school board and principals, and the teachers decide what children should learn. Doctors decide what is best for a patient. Even though the people who work in these roles might want more flexibility than is provided by the traditional definitions, there is often social pressure to conform to traditional roles and thus to traditional behavior.

As roles get farther away from the nuclear family or the institutions of society, they are not so tightly defined. Often at the beginning of a peer relationship, we can choose the roles we are going to play. Friends, for example, often decide on the role they will play within the friendship. Once the relationship is established and functioning, however, the role expectations become fixed and friends expect each other to react in certain ways.

Our roles and relationships determine how we communicate. Depending on the role we play, certain communication is expected of us. Teachers expect children to speak in a respectful manner. A boss expects employees to perform their jobs conscientiously. Friends and spouses expect the other person in the relationship to disclose inner thoughts and feelings. We can see, then, that much of our success in playing a role will depend on how we meet others' communication expectations.

Beginning Conversations: The Art of Small Talk

Much of the basis for establishing a relationship rests on reducing uncertainty.[10] For example, a new social situation might make you feel uneasy. You may wonder whether you will be able to begin a conversation and whether you will find people you like and people who like you. The uncertainty you are feeling will probably be shared by other people in the room. How do you go about reducing it?

When most people begin conversations, they engage in **small talk**—social conversation with others about unimportant topics that allows a person to maintain contact with a lot of people without making a deep commitment. We are often in situations where it would be uncomfortable to stand around without talking. Therefore, there are all sorts of conventions in small talk. We can talk about the situations we find ourselves in ("What do you think of this party?"). We can talk about our jobs, our recent experiences and those of others, our gardens—or if all else fails, the weather.

In new social situations the best way to get started in a conversation is by asking questions. Some questions are to find out information, others are to find a way of establishing common ground with others. We also ask questions in certain situations just to fill time or to be sociable. Since most people like answering questions about themselves, they are flattered when someone shows interest in them.

When you are talking to a stranger, there are certain conventions to be followed. The main rule is that questions should be more general than personal. "Where do you live?"; "How do you like that instructor?"; "What kind of work do you do?" are all examples of general questions. The best response to questions is to pay attention to the answers. Have you ever had a conversation with someone who was giving you only half attention while looking over your shoulder to see who else was around? This kind of response indicates that the person is just passing time until someone better comes along. It's probably better to ask no questions than to communicate this kind of attitude.

Because small talk and questions are socially sanctioned, they are safe procedures. They provide us with a chance to establish who we are with others. They also permit us to find out more about ourselves through the eyes of others. Although personal information is superficial in small talk, the image we give to others can be reflected in the way others react to us.

The Value of Gossip

When people first meet, they often try to find common ground by engaging in low-level gossip. If you find that a person whom you have just met knows your good friend Diane, it might be a natural response to tell a good story about Diane—something the other person hadn't known. This story, then, would be a form of gossip.

Gossip is talk of a personal or intimate nature about another person. Unlike small talk, gossip has never been socially sanctioned by everyone. Some people feel it should be discouraged because it is an invasion of another person's privacy. Others, however, are beginning to look at gossip in a new light and feel it has a valuable function in society.

According to Sam Keen, a writer about psychological topics, gossip is gaining a better reputation.[11] He sees gossip as a communication network that keeps us informed about healthy and unhealthy relationships ("Did you know that Amy and Kevin have broken up?").

Gossip, says Keen, allows us to share confidences with others and to share ideas, experiences, and stories. Sometimes we can test our own values with gossip. When, through our gossip, we condemn a couple that is going through a divorce, we affirm our own attitude about the importance of marriage and of working out problems within the marriage.

Keen also believes that gossip is a valuable way of finding out information that might protect us. A student warns another, "Don't take that class. The instructor is awful!" One woman tells a friend, "Don't go out with him. He's a drunk." An athlete says to his buddy, "The coach is really strict. If you want to go out for the team you had better be prepared."

Jack Levin and Arnold Arluke,[12] who have also studied gossip, believe that some people gossip in order to be the center of attention. To test this notion, they decided to spread some gossip on campus. They posted notices all over campus that everyone was invited to attend the wedding of Mary Ann O'Brien and Robert Goldberg on June 6 at 3:30 P.M. Both the students and the event were fictitious. Also, the researchers didn't post the flyers until June 7—a day *after* the "wedding."

A week later, they asked students how many knew about the wedding. Fifty-two percent said they knew about it—mostly from their friends who had seen the flyers. The response that surprised them the most however, was that 12 percent of the respondents *said they had been to the wedding*—many describing the bride's dress and the limo in which the couple drove away. The only way the researchers could explain this lie is that there are some people who can't stand to be left out, and so they create lies about parties they have been to, people they know, and so forth.[13]

Levin and Arluke also observed that men and women have different subjects of gossip. Women are more likely to talk about other people, particularly close friends and family members. Men are more likely to discuss acquaintances, strangers, and media celebrities—especially sports figures.[14] This would fall in line with Tannen's theory, discussed in Chapter 4, that men engage in *report*-talk while women engage in *rapport*-talk.[15]

It's important, of course, to distinguish between harmless and harmful gossip. Harmless gossip generally is about changes in others' lives: Sally is moving to Colorado; Hank has a new job; Lynn is having an operation. Harmful gossip is aimed more at character assassination—information that can cause harm to someone. Examples might be that Hank got fired from his old job because he drank too much or that you heard (but never saw) that the mechanic at the local gas station often charges customers for repairs they don't need.

Gossip is part of the human experience, and the ability to gossip and to enjoy it is often a basis of attraction between people. People who like the same kind of gossip tend to see the world and the people in it in basically the same way.

Regrettable Talk: Words We Wish We Hadn't Said

All of us, at one time or another, have said something to someone that we regretted. It may have been something that embarrassed us or the other party, it may have had the effect of hurting someone, or it may have been a secret we were not supposed to tell. Mark L. Knapp, Laura Stafford, and John A. Daly have studied these "regrettable words" with the aim of finding out: (1) if they fell into certain categories; (2) what people did once they realized the impact these words had on the other person; (3) why they said the words in the first place; (4) how the other person responded; and (5) the effect the words had on the short-term and long-term relationship.[16]

Have you ever said words you later regretted? What effect did these words have on your relationship?

The researchers discovered that 75 percent of the regrettable words fell into five categories. The most common was the blunder—forgetting someone's name or getting it wrong, or asking "How's your mother?" and hearing the reply "She died." The next category was direct attack—a generalized criticism of the other person or of his or her family or friends. The third category was negative group references and often contained racial or ethnic slurs. This was followed by a direct and specific criticism such as "You never clean house" or "You shouldn't go out with that guy." The fifth category of revealing or explaining too much included telling secrets or telling hurtful things said by others.

Seventy-seven percent of the people who said something they regretted realized it immediately. Most often they said they felt bad, guilty, or embarrassed. Some of them responded nonverbally: they winced or covered their mouths. Commonly the speaker apologized, corrected, or rephrased what he or she had said. Others discounted what they said by covering up their words or denying them.

When people were asked why they had made the remark in the first place, the most common response was, "I was stupid. I just wasn't thinking." Some said their remarks were selfish—they were intended to meet their own needs rather than those of others. Others admitted to having bad intentions: they set out deliberately to harm the other person. On a less negative side, people said they were trying to be nice and the words just slipped out. Some people said they were trying to be funny or to tease the other person and the words were taken in the wrong way.

How did the people who were the objects of the regrettable words respond? Most often they felt hurt. Many got angry or made a sarcastic reply. Some hung up the phone, walked away, or changed the subject. On the more positive side, some were able to dismiss the statement or to laugh about it. In other cases, when the speaker acknowledged the error, the listener helped to "cover" the incident by offering an explanation or justification.

One of the most interesting aspects of this study is whether regrettable words had a negative impact on the relationship. Thirty percent of the respondents said that there was a long-term negative relationship change, but 39 percent said there was no relationship change at all. Sixteen percent said that the change was positive—for example, "In the long run, I think our relationship is stronger since it happened." In looking at the entire range of regrettable messages, the researchers concluded that regrettable messages seem to be part of our interactions with others and although they might be hurtful to the other person when they occur, their effects can be overcome and the relationship has a good chance of continuing.

Self-Disclosure: Important Talk

Much of interpersonal communication is made up of small talk. We talk to our classmates about a party, we discuss the weather with a stranger, or we talk about a ballgame we saw on TV with a friend. Although this kind of talk is important to keep society functioning, if we used only small talk we would probably end up feeling frustrated. The problem with small talk is that it's

Try This Try This Try This

Probably all of us have had a conversation where we haven't been able to talk as much as we would like to. Or it might be the reverse: sometimes people complain that when they have a conversation with us, they don't have a chance to get a word in edgewise.

How does one dominate a conversation? Research has shown that dominance occurs in a number of ways. First, dominance is determined by what they call "floor management"—who gets to talk and for how long. The longer a person talks, the more he or she is perceived as dominant. Control also comes from the topic which is discussed. The dominant person is able to keep talking without relating his talk to the immediate topic. He or she also is able to move the topic into a new direction or to change topics at will.

Try this theory out by listening to a conversation between two people.

- Who talks the most?

- Who changes the subject?

- Who is free to wander away from the topic?

- Are the partners in the conversation equal or does one dominate?

Source: Mark Palmer, "Controlling Conversations," *Communication Monographs.*

not important enough. It doesn't touch on the central issue of who we are and what we need and want from life.

The Importance of Self-Disclosure

If we are going to communicate who we are to other people, we are going to have to engage in **self-disclosure**—a process in which one person tells another person something he or she would not tell just anyone. To see how this works, let's look at the case of Maria and Enrique.

One day, after work, Maria bursts into the apartment, gives a curt "hello" to her husband Enrique, and begins to fix dinner. She bangs the pots and pans, marches militantly to the refrigerator, takes out carrots and onions, and chops them up as if they are her worst enemy. Enrique, who has been married to Maria for a year, watches this all in amazement and distress. His first thought is "She's mad at me. What did I do?" However, he remembers that she gave him a loving kiss when she went out the door that morning, so that can't be it.

When Maria and Enrique sit down to dinner, Enrique gently asks her if something went wrong at work. Because he has responded to her behavior with such sympathy and concern, Maria is able to tell him that her boss asked her to do a special project and they won't be able to go away for the weekend because she has to work.

Maria is able to tell Enrique what is bothering her because they are in a close relationship. She trusts him: not only is he her husband, he is her best friend. Maria's communication to Enrique, telling him what is bothering her, is part of self-disclosure. Through this kind of disclosure she is able to check out her perceptions, her thoughts, and her feelings.

No area of communication illustrates the transactional nature of communication more than self-disclosure. Maria can tell Enrique what is bothering her because she knows from past experience that she can trust him to show concern for her problems. Enrique is secure enough in the relationship to realize that Maria is not mad at him—something else must be the cause of her behavior. Both of them know that when they talk, the other will show concern and understanding. In their conversation, they are communicating continuously and simultaneously. Enrique is wondering what Maria is thinking; Maria is sending out verbal and nonverbal signals.

We also rely on our past experience when deciding whether to engage in self-disclosure. Like Maria and Enrique, most of us will disclose things about ourselves to people we trust. Generally, we trust those people whom we predict will react to us in the way we want them to. They are not likely to tell us that we are bad or that we have done a wrong thing. For example, if you were to confess to a friend that you once flunked out of school, you would tell him this because you would expect him to react sympathetically. You can predict his reaction because you know him well and have experienced his reactions to you and to other situations. Self-disclosure, then, occurs when we discover people who believe the way we do and who react to situations and events the way we would. We trust these people enough to tell them about ourselves.[17]

The Process of Self-Disclosure

We all make choices about what to disclose and what to keep to ourselves. One way to look at how this process operates is by using a model developed by Joseph Luft and Harry Ingham. By combining their first names, they labeled their device the **Johari Window** (see Figure 6-1).[18]

The "free to self and others" area—or *open pane*—involves information about ourselves that we are willing to communicate as well as information we are unable to hide. A group of students, for example, meets for the first time in a classroom and, following the instructor's suggestion, introduce themselves. Most of them will stick to bare essentials: their name, where they come from, and their major. When people do not know one another very well, the "free to self and others" area is smaller than when they become better acquainted.

The area labeled "blind to self, seen by others"—or *blind pane*—is a kind of accidental disclosure area; there are certain things we do not know about ourselves that others know about us. For example, we may see that the man who must always have the latest model of an expensive car is really trying to hide his feelings of inadequacy and insecurity. Advertisers like to play on our blind pane. They suggest, for instance, that you do not know you have bad breath but everyone else knows.

The *hidden pane*—or self hidden from others—is a deliberate nondisclosure area; there are certain things you know about yourself that you do not want

	KNOWN TO SELF	UNKNOWN TO SELF
KNOWN TO OTHERS (Disclosure areas)	Open Pane (Free to self and others)	Blind Pane (Blind to self, seen by others)
UNKNOWN TO OTHERS (Nondisclosure areas)	Hidden Pane (Open to self, hidden from others)	Unknown Pane (Unknown to self and others)

Figure 6-1
The Johari
Window

known, so you deliberately conceal them from others. Most people hide things that might evoke disapproval from those they love and admire: "I was a teen-age shoplifter"; "I don't know how to read very well." Others keep certain areas hidden from one person but open to another: a young woman tells her best friend, but not her mother, that her grades are low because she seldom studies.

The *unknown pane* is a nondisclosure area; it provides no possibility of disclosure because it is not known to the self or to others. This pane represents all the parts of us that are not yet revealed. We might think, for example, that we are very brave, but we really don't know how we will react when we are faced with personal danger. The unknown area is most likely to be revealed when someone undergoes psychological counseling.

The disclosure and nondisclosure areas vary from one relationship to another; they also change all the time in the same relationship. Figure 6-2 shows how the Johari Window might look in a close relationship. In such a relationship, the open pane becomes much larger because a person is likely to disclose more. When disclosure increases, people not only reveal more information about themselves but also are likely to discover things about themselves that they had not known before. If you apply the Johari Window to each of your relationships, you will find that the sizes of the four panes are different in each relationship. In other words, you are likely to be more self-disclosing in some relationships than you are in others.

The Risks of Self-Disclosure

Although we may believe that self-disclosure is very important if we are going to sustain relationships, there are also risks involved.[19] There is the risk of the self-knowledge that disclosure might bring. We may suspect certain things

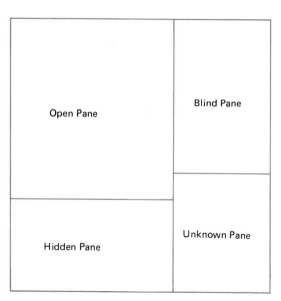

Open Pane	Blind Pane
Hidden Pane	Unknown Pane

Figure 6-2
This is what the Johari Window might look like after a relationship has had a chance to develop. With more development, the open pane is likely to grow even larger.

about ourselves but prefer that they remain in the hidden area. Research also indicates that it is very risky and inappropriate to give out too much private and personal information early in a relationship.[20] Such a revelation may stop the relationship from developing.

How much of self-disclosure is made up of secrets? How many people would you tell your secrets to?

Try This Try This Try This

*T*ake a piece of paper, divide it into four parts, and label it like this:

		(Name of a person you	
(Name of best friend)		*would like for a friend)*	
Open Pane	Hidden Pane	Open Pane	Hidden Pane

Starting with your best friend, read the following items and decide which ones you would tell him or her. Put the corresponding number for these under the open pane and for the items you wouldn't tell under the hidden pane.

 1. How I spend my free time
 2. My favorite singers and groups
 3. My major and the career I want
 4. My political affiliation and how I would vote
 5. My religious views and/or church affiliation
 6. My greatest accomplishment
 7. The most embarrassing moment of my life
 8. The thing I most regret doing
 9. My wishes and dreams for the future
10. How much money I made last year
11. How much I paid for my car
12. The lowest grade I got in college
13. How I feel about the way I look
14. The things I am most afraid of
15. The person I dislike the most
16. The worst act of dishonesty I have committed

Once you have listed these items for your best friend, go through the list again and do the same thing for the other person.

Now see if you can draw the open and hidden panes for each relationship. How do they differ from each other? In which relationship do you have the biggest open pane? Why?

Also, many people fear that if they tell something about themselves, it could be held against them. If someone has been fired from a job, he might not want to admit it to anyone because it might lead people to feel differently about him. In other cases, self-disclosure might threaten a relationship. For example, someone might not want to tell another about her struggle with alcoholism. Perhaps the greatest fear in disclosure is of negative feedback; we are afraid disclosure might mean that the other person will no longer love, accept, or want us.

Sometimes we resist hearing self-disclosure from others because it is so boring and repetitive. Let's say that a good friend is in a relationship that seems very destructive. The friend doesn't want to *do* anything about the relationship—he or she just wants to talk about it. Most of us find this kind of self-disclosure very tedious after a while.

Consider This Consider This Consider This

*M*iss Manners advises that you stay away from these topics unless you are among good friends:

Age: "That was an awfully nice young man you brought over the other night, but tell me, isn't he a little young?"

Birth Control: "Isn't this your third? Did you plan it that way?"

Children: "Shouldn't he be talking by now?"

Divorce: "And we thought you were the ideal couple. What went wrong?"

Energy: "Don't you think you keep this house too hot?"

Food: "I'm surprised to see you eating that. Didn't you tell me you were on a diet?"

Good Works: "Our development officer has figured out what a person of your income level can afford to give. Would you like to hear what it is?"

Health: "You didn't tell us what that test was you went into the hospital for. But let me just ask this: Was it benign?"

I: "I think you ought to . . ."

Source: Judith Martin, *Miss Manners' Guide to Excruciatingly Correct Behavior.*

How Should We Go About Self-Disclosure?

Disclosure should occur only in relationships that are important to you.[21] People who do not know you very well are likely to feel uncomfortable if you tell them too much about yourself too soon. Wait until you have some signs that this relationship has a possibility of developing. For example, if someone seeks you out by inviting you to parties or for coffee, this is a sign that he or she wants the relationship to develop.

For disclosure to work, both parties must do it. If one person does all the disclosing and the other party just sits back and listens, disclosure is not likely to continue.

Remember that disclosure means taking a risk. You will never know how another person will respond to your openness until you give it a try. To avoid getting hurt, try testing the water with your toe before you plunge in. One way of doing this is to talk about a subject in general terms and see how the other person reacts before you talk about your own experience with it.

Finally, examine your own motives for self-disclosure. Why do you want the other person to know this information? Will it really enhance the relationship or can it do it harm? All of us have some secrets that we should probably keep to ourselves. Sharing them may cause injury or make the other person lose trust in us. Although some secrets are a burden to keep, it may serve the interest of the relationship to do so.

SUMMARY

Interpersonal communication, or one-to-one communication, is the kind of communication we use most frequently. Interpersonal communication helps us to build relationships and find out about ourselves and others. Without relationships, we would have no sense of self.

Our psychological needs in relationships are for inclusion, control, and affection. Inclusion is the need for involvement with others. Affection is the feeling of warm emotional attachment to others, and control is the ability to have some say about our environment.

All relationships begin with attraction. Although the basis of attraction might vary greatly in different relationships, we are most attracted to people with whom we have similarities and frequent contact. Sometimes we form a relationship because we see something we can gain from it.

Relationships with others are governed by the roles we are expected to play. Roles that reflect the structure of society are more rigidly defined than roles we establish with friends. Much of the communication we have in relationships depends on the role we are playing.

We get to know one another by asking questions. These questions help us to discover a common ground with others. Other ways of establishing common ground are through small talk and gossip.

Self-disclosure is the process of communicating one's self to another person, telling another who we are and what we are feeling. For close relationships to exist, self-disclosure must take place. Self-disclosure can be understood through the Johari Window, which has four panes: open, blind, hidden, and unknown. As a relationship develops and disclosure increases, the open pane gets larger.

FURTHER READING

BEATTY, MICHAEL J. *The Romantic Dialogue: Communication in Dating and Marriage.* Englewood, CO: Morton, 1986. In this brief textbook, Beatty introduces readers to the nature of romantic love, the romantic acquaintance process, conflict, and the need for dialogue. He contrasts dialogue and monologue and ends with a brief chapter on problem solving. An interesting, basic textbook.

BHAERMAN, STEVE, AND DON McMILLAN. *Friends and Lovers: How to Meet the People You Want to Meet.* Cincinnati, OH: Writer's Digest, 1986. The authors take the position that there is too much emphasis on meeting people; we should, instead, be striving to have fun. They feel, when you are being yourself and really having fun, you radiate confidence, enthusiasm, and attractiveness.

BURNS, DAVID D. *Intimate Connections.* New York: New American Library, 1985. In this very readable book full of useful information and surveys, Burns explains cognitive behavior therapy and applies it to loneliness, shyness, and insecurity. This book will be valuable for those who suffer from low self-esteem and are worried about disapproval, rejection, or being alone.

DUCK, STEVE. *Human Relationships: An Introduction to Social Psychology.* Beverly Hills, CA: Sage, 1986. Duck focuses on personal relationships and on how they affect our daily lives and our social behavior. A well-researched and well-written examination.

GAHAGAN, JUDY. *Social Interaction and Its Management.* New York: Methuen, 1984. Gahagan is concerned about our everyday behavior with other people. She examines the nature of social interaction, the resources utilized in our engagements with others, and the ways in which these processes may be controlled and resources improved. Gahagan's book is a guide for those who want to bring their social processes under more control.

JAMES, JOHN, AND IBIS SCHLESINGER. *Are You the One for Me? How to Choose the Right Partner.* Reading, MA: Addison-Wesley, 1987. James and Schlesinger offer a method for finding out what a person is really like and deciding whether that person is right for you. They help readers decide what they want in a loving relationship and how to use their "smart dating" approach. Many exercises and surveys.

KNAPP, MARK L. *Interpersonal Communication and Human Relationships.* Boston: Allyn and Bacon, 1984. This textbook is about the way people communicate in relationships that are developing and deteriorating. Knapp answers the question of how communication behavior affects our relationships.

POGREBIN, LETTY COTTIN. *Among Friends.* New York: McGraw-Hill, 1987. Who we like, why we like them, and what we do with them is the subject of Pogrebin's book about friendship. Since Pogrebin bases much of her material on information obtained from interviews, the book has many interesting anecdotes.

REARDON, KATHLEEN K. *Interpersonal Communication: Where Minds Meet.* Belmont, CA: Wadsworth, 1987. Reardon examines the ways interpersonal communication scholars use the tools of social sciences to formulate answers to such questions as: "How do children learn to communicate?" "How do we form and maintain relationships?" "How do people interact in various settings?" and "What is competent communication?" Using theory and research, Reardon expands readers' understanding of the interpersonal communication process.

STEWART, LEA P., PAMELA J. COOPER, AND SHERYL A. FRIEDLEY. *Communication between the Sexes: Sex Differences and Sex-Role Stereotypes.* Scottsdale, AZ: Gorsuch Scarisbrick, 1990. This is a book about the influence of sex differences and sex-role stereotypes on communication. The authors identify significant sex differences and sex-role stereotypes, explain the implications and consequences, and suggest some strategies for change. Their contexts include friendship and marriage, education, the media, and the organization.

TRENHOLM, SARAH, AND ARTHUR JENSEN. *Interpersonal Communication.* Belmont, CA: Wadsworth, 1988. These authors devote Part III to relational contexts, treating interpersonal communication in the family, the way intimate relationships work, professional relationships, and the skills needed to become more competent in all contexts. Very practical approach with interesting boxed materials in each chapter drawn from many other fields.

Chapter 7

Evaluating and Improving Relationships

CHAPTER OBJECTIVES	KEY TERMS
After reading this chapter, you should be able to:	aggression

After reading this chapter, you should be able to:

1. Summarize the stages of a relationship in coming together and coming apart.

2. Tell why commitment and dialog are important in relationships.

3. Evaluate one of your own relationships in terms of its costs and rewards.

4. Describe some of the roles you are playing and question whether they are satisfying for you.

5. Explain reflective listening and the effects of "I" versus "you" messages.

6. Define avoidance and aggression, and give examples of each.

7. Identify the six kinds of defensive communication and suggest how to counter each with supportive behavior.

8. Distinguish between productive and nonproductive criticism.

9. Outline the steps of conflict resolution.

KEY TERMS

aggression
avoidance
commitment
conflict resolution
costs and rewards
criticism
defensive communication
empathy
evaluative statements
indirect aggression

*B*ill and Rich are both sophomores at the university. They are enrolled in the same political science class, and because the class is small, all the members have gotten to know one another. As the class discusses various issues, Bill discovers that Rich says many of the things Bill is thinking. Rich has also noticed Bill. One day as he is walking to the parking lot, he sees Bill getting into his car—a car that Rich admires.

Toward the end of the semester, Rich goes to the student union to get a cup of coffee. He notices Bill is sitting alone, and so he sits with him. They begin talking about their one shared experience, their political science class. Then their talk branches out into other areas. They like the same pro football team and have the same opinion of the coach. They also discover they share a fascination with cars, and Bill tells how he bought his car as an old wreck and fixed it up. Finally it's time to go. Rich has decided that he likes Bill and invites him to come along to a party that night.

Bill and Rich have had an experience that probably occurs in various forms on campuses all over the country. People get together who don't know each other very well. They talk to see if they have any common interests, and on the basis of what they discover, they decide whether to begin a relationship.

The Stages of a Relationship

As happened with Rich and Bill, every relationship begins with superficial communication; then, if the people like each other, they take steps to develop the relationship. Research seems to indicate that growth in relationships is a series of events that leads to either positive or negative commitment to the relationship.[1] Mark L. Knapp describes the ten relationship stages—five of them have to do with coming together and five of them with coming apart.[2] Let's look at these steps and see how they apply to Rich and Bill.

Coming Together

All relationships, unless they remain at the casual small-talk level, go through growth. As relationships grow, communication becomes unique to a particular relationship. How does this growth take place—or fail to take place?

STAGE ONE: INITIATING

When Rich and Bill started talking together, they began the *initiating stage.* As they conversed, they were probably assessing each other in various areas— such as clothes, physical attractiveness, and beliefs and attitudes. From all these observations each began to make judgments about the other: "He seems like a nice guy."

In this instance, the two people were interested enough in each other to begin a conversation. Two other people might have decided not to begin the initiating stage at all. On the basis of preliminary impressions, we often decide the other person isn't interesting enough or doesn't look interested enough in us to pursue the relationship any further.

In the *experimenting stage* the persons make a conscious effort to seek out common interests and experiences. They experiment by expressing their ideas, attitudes, and values and by seeing how the other person reacts. One person, for example, might feel strongly on the subject of college sports and will express an opinion to see if the other person agrees or disagrees.

If the persons find they have common interests and values, they both decide that they want to talk even more. They start going for coffee after class. They tell each other about their families and their friends. They meet once in a while outside class—to look at cars or to go to movies together. At this stage of the relationship, everything is generally pleasant, relaxed, and uncritical. Many relationships stay at this particular stage—the participants enjoy the level of the relationship but show no desire to pursue it further.

STAGE THREE: INTENSIFYING

Now the classmates have discovered that they like each other quite a lot. They spend more time with each other. This is the *intensifying stage* of their relationship. They borrow each other's CDs and spend a lot of their free time together. Not only do they enjoy each other's company, but they also begin some personal disclosure. They tell each other private things about their families and friends. And they begin to share their frustrations, imperfections, and prejudices.

Other things also happen in the relationship. They call each other by nicknames; they develop a "shorthand" way of speaking; they have jokes that no other person can understand. Their conversations begin to reveal shared assumptions and expectations. Trust becomes important. They believe that if they tell the other a secret, it will not be told to third parties. They start to make expressions of commitment: "I'm really glad we're friends." They also start some gentle challenges of each other: "Do you really believe that, or are you just saying it?" In short, they are on the way to becoming good friends.

Openness has its risks in the intensifying stage. Self- disclosure makes the relationship strong, but it also makes the participants more vulnerable to each other.

STAGE FOUR: INTEGRATING

The classmate-friends have now reached the *integrating stage*—the point at which their individual personalities are beginning to merge. People expect to see them together. If they see just one of them, they ask about the other.

The friendship has taken on a specialness. They do most things together. They go to the same parties and have a lot of the same friends. They no longer ask if they can play each other's CDs—they assume it is all right. Each of them is able to predict and explain the behavior of the other.

The integrating stage is reached only when people develop deep and important relationships. Those who reach this stage are usually best friends, couples, or parents and children.

The last coming-together stage of a relationship is the *bonding stage*. At this point, the participants make some sort of formal commitment that announces their relationship to those around them. For a couple, an announcement of their engagement or marriage would be an example of bonding. In other cases, as between friends, the bonding agreement might be less formal. Whatever form it takes, the bonding makes it more difficult for either party to break out of the relationship. Therefore it should be a step that is taken when the participants have some sort of long-term commitment to their relationship.

How do the two classmates enter into the bonding stage? As we have seen, their relationship has developed into a very strong friendship. Now, because of their commitment to each other, they have decided they want to live together, and so they take steps to rent an apartment. Their bonding involves not only living together but also signing a lease. Even though their bonding might not continue for a lifetime, as we assume the bonding of marriage partners might, their lease is a formal, binding contract that commits them to a period of time together.

ADVANCING FROM STAGE ONE TO STAGE FIVE

The five coming-together stages build on one another. Whether a relationship will move from one stage to the next depends on both participants. If one

---

Try This Try This Try This

*L*ook at an important relationship in your life that is or was with someone other than an immediate family member. (If you choose a more recent relationship, you will have a better chance of remembering the beginning stages of the relationship.) As you look at this relationship, see if you can discover the stage it is in.

1. *Initiating:* Where did you meet this person? What attracted you to him or her? Do you remember how you started a conversation with this person? What made you think you might be interested in finding out more about him or her?
2. *Experimenting:* How did you get to know this person better? What things did you do and talk about together? What made you think he or she might become more than a casual acquaintance?
3. *Intensifying:* How did you know that you could trust this person? Who was the first to use self-disclosure? How much self-disclosure has occurred by each participant in this relationship?
4. *Integrating:* Do you spend large amounts of time together? Do you have private names, a private language, and private jokes? If people see one of you, do they expect to see the other? Are you happier together than you are apart?
5. *Bonding:* Have you entered into any kind of bonding agreement that shows your commitment? What kinds of public commitments have you made?

wants to move to the next stage, it will not be possible unless the other agrees. Because most of us have only limited time and energy for intense relationships, we are willing to let most of our relationships remain at the second or third stage. The first three stages permit us to become involved in friendships and to carry out normal social activity. The fourth and fifth stages, integrating and bonding, demand much more energy and commitment—they are reserved for very special relationships.

Another point should be made about these stages. If a person is in a new relationship, he or she should not try to progress too quickly beyond stages one or two. In all relationships it is important that each participant be sensitive to feedback from the other. It is this feedback that will determine whether it is time to advance to another stage. Since stage three is the first in which there is self-disclosure, moving from stage two to stage three is particularly sensitive. If one person self-discloses too quickly, the other might feel so uncomfortable that he or she will be unwilling to go on to a new stage in the relationship.

Coming Apart

For a relationship to continue, both participants must grow and change together. If they cannot do this in ways that are satisfying to both of them, then the relationship will come apart. Although it is more satisfying to look at relationships coming together, we all know that relationships also fail. Relationships that are failing can also be described in five stages—stages that are the reverse process of coming together.

STAGE ONE: DIFFERENTIATING

The new semester has started, and our friends, who have signed a one-year lease, are living together. The first month or so goes well enough but in the second month problems begin to emerge. Bill sees the new apartment as a way of entertaining everyone he knows, and all sorts of people are starting to drop in at all hours of the day and night. The place is never cleaned up, and all the dishes are dirty. Rich has bought a very large dog, and the apartment is beginning to seem crowded.

This is the *differentiating stage*—the roommates are beginning to focus on how different they are, and much of their conversation is about their differences rather than about their similarities. Also their conversations are beginning to take on a quarrelsome tone: "I did the dishes last week. It's your turn to do them now." "Do your friends have to stay till all hours of the night? I can never get any studying done." "You should start paying more for groceries. That dog eats as much as I do."

The differences the two recognized and tolerated before become focal points for discussion and argument. "Why does Fred come over here so much? Doesn't he have a home of his own?" "Did you realize you now snore even louder than you used to?"

The most visible sign of differentiating is conflict. But differentiating can take place without conflict. It could happen that nothing specific is bothering the roommates but that they are discovering, as they mature and find new interests, that they have less and less to talk about. One, for example, might have become really interested in his subject area and have settled down to study and learn as much as possible. The other, however, might be basically interested in having a good time and unable to understand someone who wants to study so much.

STAGE TWO: CIRCUMSCRIBING

As a relationship begins to fall apart, less and less information is exchanged. Since points of conflict exist in the relationship, it seems safer to stay away from them as conversational topics to avoid a full-scale fight. Thus this is called the *circumscribing stage.*

Conversation becomes superficial. "Your mail is on your bed." "Did I get any telephone calls?" "Do you want some popcorn?" The number of interactions is decreased, the depth of discussions is reduced, and the duration of each conversation is shortened. Because communication is constricted, the relationship is constricted.

Most people who find themselves in this stage will try discussing the relationship itself and what is going wrong. At this point, the negative turn in the relationship might be resolved. In the case of the roommates, for example, Rich could decide to get rid of the dog, and Bill could take on more responsibility for doing dishes and restricting his friends' visits. In other cases, discussion about the relationship might reveal even greater differences between the participants. In such cases, discussion about the relationship leads to even more conflict, and so discussion is limited to "safe" topics.

Persons who are in this stage often cover up their relationship problems. Although they might reveal problems to very close friends, in social situations they give the appearance of being committed to each other. They create a social or public face—in essence, a mask.

STAGE THREE: STAGNATING

The *stagnating stage* is a time of inactivity. The relationship has no chance to grow, and when the participants communicate, they talk like strangers. The subject of the relationship itself is now off limits. In some cases the participants may want to talk about the relationship, but then may decide not to. Rather than try to resolve the conflict, they are more likely to take the attitude of "Why bother to talk? We'll just fight, and things will get even worse."

How long this stage lasts depends on many things. For example, Bill and Rich are uncomfortable with each other but do not feel isolated since they both have other friends. At this point, their partnership is based solely on the lease for the apartment. They both agree that when the lease is up, they will separate.

Partners in a marriage relationship, however, may feel a lot of pain during this stage. They may find it hard to separate and may hold on to the hope that they can still work things out.

STAGE FOUR: AVOIDING

The *avoiding stage* involves physical separation. The parties avoid face-to-face interaction. They are not interested in seeing each other, in building any kind of relationship, or in establishing any communication channels.

This stage is usually characterized by unfriendliness, hostility, and antagonism. Sometimes the cues are subtle: "Please don't talk long, I have an appointment." They can also be direct and forceful: "Don't call me anymore" or "I'm sorry, I just don't want to see you."

In relationships where physical separation is impossible, the participants may act as if the other person does not exist. Each one carries on his or her work in a separate room and avoids any kind of interaction. In the case of our roommates, each may plan to be sleeping or out of the apartment when the other is there.

STAGE FIVE: TERMINATING

In the *terminating stage,* the participants find a way to bring the relationship to an end. Both parties are preparing themselves for life without the other. Differences are emphasized, and communication is difficult and awkward.

In an article called "The Rhetoric of Goodbye,"[3] Knapp and his colleagues describe three distinct types of statements that commonly occur in terminating relationships. First, there are the summary statements: "Well, we certainly have tried to make a go of it" or "This isn't the end for either of us; we'll have to go on living." Second are statements that signal the likelihood of decreased access: "It might be better if we didn't see each other quite so often." Finally, there are messages that predict what the future relationship (if any) will be like: "I don't ever want to see you again" or "Just because we aren't going to live together doesn't mean we can't be friends."

It should be pointed out that some relationships cannot be entirely terminated. There are cases in which the parties have to have some contact—even though the relationship has come to a psychological end. Because Bill

---

Consider This **Consider This** *Consider This*

*W*hat are the signs that a relationship is beginning to fail? Sociologist Dr. Diane Vaughan describes the process in her book *Uncoupling.*

Dr. Vaughan says that the first person who becomes unhappy begins the process. This person typically begins by finding alternatives—often in the form of a transitional person. Although the transitional person might be a romantic interest, he or she could also be a minister, a therapist, or a good friend. When one partner begins to find satisfaction elsewhere, the couple's relationship becomes less endurable. At this point the dissatisfied person lets the other know of her or his discontent through body language and words.

Finally the time comes when the dissatisfied person lets the partner know that he or she wants to end the relationship. The other partner typically feels betrayed, hurt, and shocked—and is often unprepared.

Dr. Vaughan says that both partners suffer emotional pain and go through the same stages of disengagement—it just happens at different times for each of them.

Source: Adapted from Glenn Collins, "Drifting Apart: A Look at How Relationships End," *The New York Times.*

and Rich cannot get out of their lease, they have to find a way to live together until the lease runs out. Marriage partners who have children cannot entirely terminate their relationship if the children are going to see both parents. In this kind of situation, the parents might terminate their relationship with each other as marriage partners but decide to continue in some kind of relationship as parents to the children. In this case, it would not be unusual for them to set down a list of rules that will govern the new relationship.[4]

Essential Elements of Good Relationships

If we look at good relationships, they all have elements in common. The most important of these elements are commitment, dialog, and a careful use of criticism. Let's look at each of these elements.

Commitment

All relationships need **commitment**—a strong desire by both parties for the relationship to continue, and a willingness on the part of both parties to take responsibility for the problems that occur in the relationship. Margaret A. Farley says that although commitment is made in the present, it points to the future. It is "a relation of binding and being-bound, giving and being-claimed."[5] She also distinguishes among the different kinds of commitments.[6] An

How does a couple communicate to others that they have made a commitment to each other?

unconditional commitment is one in which you commit yourself to another—regardless of what may happen. Marriage vows are often unconditional commitments. A conditional commitment sets forth the conditions of the commitment, and it carries the implication of "only if." Examples might be "I will cook the meals during the week if you will do the cooking on the weekends" and "I will work on this project with you if you promise to commit ten hours a week to it."

Long-term relationships are usually unconditional commitments. These are commitments that spouses make to each other or that parents make to children. Although friendships may be unconditional, they are more often conditional. For example, if a friend marries, has a child, or moves away, the other friend is likely to expect less from the relationship. Work relationships are usually conditional. A boss will expect her employees to do their jobs but not to dedicate their lives and total time to those jobs.

All relationships have some kind of commitment as their foundation, but sometimes the partners in the commitment have different expectations. If these expectations are not fulfilled, the partners must work out changes or compromises if they want the relationship to continue.

Dialog

Partners in good relationships also have ongoing conversations, or dialogs, about the relationship itself. They might search together for ways of reducing conflict; they might discuss expectations they have of each other—or discuss anything else that might affect the relationship. What is important is that the partners agree to discuss the relationship periodically. Also, Deborah Tannen points out, "The belief that sitting down and talking will ensure mutual understanding and solve problems is based on the assumption that we can say what we mean, and that what we say will be understood as we mean it."[7]

Try This Try This Try This

*T*ake a look at the best relationship you have. (It can be with a friend, a boyfriend or girlfriend, a parent, a sibling, a spouse, or a child.)

1. *Commitment:* How would you describe the commitment in this relationship? Is it based on trust, loyalty, faithfulness? Do both partners in the relationship feel the commitment equally? How do they demonstrate it to each other?
2. *Dialog:* How much time do you spend talking about the relationship? Is some of the talk directed toward how the relationship could be better? Is some of it directed toward solving problems? Are both partners willing to talk about the relationship? Do both partners initiate dialog?

After answering these questions, what weaknesses and strengths have you found in your relationship? Are there any changes you would like to make?

Discussing points of conflict is particularly important if the relationship is going to continue. Most of us, however, are conditioned from early childhood to stay away from conflict. We got messages such as "Hold your tongue"; "Don't talk back to your mother"; "I don't ever want to hear you talk that way again." As adults, we have to recondition ourselves to discuss areas of conflict; withdrawing from it or avoiding it is too harmful to relationships.

For partners to continue in the relationship, they must find ways of communicating that will be mutually beneficial. Earlier, in the chapter about listening, we talked about the importance of reflective listening—listening for emotions and acknowledging the feelings of one's partner. Often conflict can be reduced when people engage in reflective listening.

Criticism in Relationships

Whether people are involved in a close relationship, such as marriage, or a more distant relationship, such as boss-employee, how criticism is handled is important to that relationship. We have all probably said at one time or another that we don't mind hearing criticism as long as it is constructive. The question, then, is what is "criticism" and what do we consider "good" criticism?

Criticism is a negative evaluation of a person for something he or she has done. Although criticism occurs with participants in a close and equal relationship, in more distant relationships it usually originates with a higher-status person and is directed toward one with lower status.[8] A teacher, for example, criticizes a student; a parent criticizes a child. If the participants are equals—for example, a couple—criticism could come from either partner.

Researchers have discovered that most targets of criticism fall into five categories: appearance (body, clothing, smell, posture, and accessories); performance (carrying out a motor skill, or an intellectual or a creative skill); personhood (personality, goodness, general ability); relationships (dealing with others); and decisions and attitudes (opinions, plans, life style). In their study, the majority of criticism was about performance, followed by relationship style, appearance, and general personhood.[9]

In studying these criticisms, researchers looked at what the recipients perceived as "good" and "bad" criticism. Some criticism was perceived as bad because of the relationship between the criticizer and the person being criticized.[10] They found that most people believed that someone who did not know them very well didn't have the right to criticize them. If they had a close relationship, people felt that if they had an argument with someone else, a good friend should side with them—not with the criticizer. Another feature of bad criticism was its inappropriateness. People were much more likely to identify criticism as "bad" if it was given in front of others rather than privately. Students, for example, felt particularly humiliated if teachers criticized them in front of their classmates.

The researchers also found that good criticism was distinguished from bad by five stylistic points. First, criticism was labeled "bad" if it contained negative language (profanity or judgmental labels such as "stupid jerk") or if it was stated harshly (by screaming or yelling). Second, criticism was better received if it was specific and gave details on how to improve. ("Your speech would be more effective if you had eye contact with the members of your audience.") Third, criticism was considered "good" if the person who offered it also offered to assist in making the change. ("Pretend I'm a member of the audience and give your speech again. Look me directly in the eyes.") Fourth, criticism was better accepted if its receiver could see how it would be in his or her best interest to change. ("If you improve your delivery, you'll get a better grade on your speech.") Fifth, good criticism places negative remarks in a broader and more positive context. ("The content of your speech is really good. All you have to do is work on the delivery.")

Good criticism, the researchers found, leads to positive consequences. When the recipients of criticism did not feel threatened, they were able to take the comments seriously and make changes. On the other hand, poorly given criticism was likely to evoke negative emotions and to be seen by the recipient as inaccurate.

Research conducted about criticism on the job has found that harsh or inept criticism in the work setting undermines work relationships, increases the likelihood of future conflicts, and prevents people from doing good work.[11]

Like the research on criticism in relationships, the best criticism on the job is that which is specific. It is also important that criticism is timely. The researchers found that people reacted angrily to criticism when the boss stored up grievances and then communicated them all at once. Finally, good criticism at work focuses on what the person has done incorrectly; it does not zero in on the person, suggesting that the poor work is a form of character deficiency.[12]

Evaluating Your Relationships

Change and Adaptation

Ideally, when a relationship faces conflict, the participants are able to change and adapt. For example, when Jane and Tom had an argument about household responsibilities, Jane pointed out that she was doing less at home because she had a part-time job. Tom agreed to help her with housework every Saturday morning and to take over all responsibilities for laundry. When Larry complained that Mariann was working so hard at her job that he never saw her, she agreed to stop working on weekends.

Rebecca Cline and Bonnie Johnson have done some valuable research that shows the importance of making careful language choices when dealing with criticism. They found that people react negatively when conversation is filled with "you" messages[13] ("You didn't empty the garbage"; "You always foul up the checkbook"; "You never change the oil in the car").

Cline and Johnson found that this kind of "you" talk made the other party feel defensive. When people used "I" messages, however ("I am afraid we will need a new car if we don't change the oil more often"), they were likely to receive a much less defensive response. The reason for this is that an "I" message takes the pressure off the other person—which makes him or her much more likely to focus on the feelings of the person who believes there is a problem. Here are some typical "I" messages: "When I am left alone at a party, I feel very shy and embarrassed"; "I can't concentrate when the room is such a mess"; "I feel uncomfortable when we have the only yard in the neighborhood where the grass isn't cut."

Not everyone can change as these two couples did. Much of our behavior is programmed into us from earliest childhood, and even if we want to change, we might not be able to. Think back on how many New Year's resolutions you have kept!

When one of the partners is unwilling or unable to change, the other must decide whether to adapt to and accept the other partner's behavior. This adaptation is most likely to come about if the person believes that it is worth adapting to the problem to continue the relationship. A frequent complaint in a marriage, for example, is that the other spouse is never willing to go anywhere. Although this may be a serious complaint, it is usually not significant enough to end the relationship. The spouse might adapt to this situation by going out or taking a vacation with a friend.

Costs and Rewards

In a relationship, the **costs and rewards** need to be weighed against each other. The *costs* are the problems in the relationship; the *rewards* are the pleasures. In a work situation, for example, you don't have much choice about your boss or the people you work with. The only way of terminating a relationship at work might be to quit your job. This is a very great cost and it must be balanced with the rewards. It might be that the job is so interesting that its rewards outweigh its costs, and so you decide not to quit. Sometimes people remain in relationships that are not entirely satisfying, but the rewards for staying in the relationship are greater than the costs of getting out.

People often stay unhappily married because the emotional and economic costs of divorce are too great. A middle-aged woman who has never worked, for example, might stay in a marriage because she has no way of supporting herself and because she can't imagine living alone. Other partners stay together for the sake of the children or because it is too much of a problem to divide property—or for any number of reasons.

If you are in a relationship that is not very satisfying, you will have to ask yourself questions about the costs and rewards of staying in it. Often the best way to do this is to make a list: on one side list the rewards, on the other the costs. This list is not one that should be made when you are feeling angry or very upset—your feelings may unbalance the list.

Once you have listed costs and rewards, take some time to evaluate the results. Again, do not make a hasty judgment. Often additional costs and rewards will occur to you, and so give your list time to develop.

Once you have evaluated your list, you are ready to make a decision about the relationship. If you are not willing to give up the rewards, then it is obvious you will want to stay in the relationship. If the costs are greater than the rewards, then your only choices are to terminate the relationship or to try to improve it.

Roles and Expectations

In successful relationships, the participants have usually worked out their roles and expectations. These roles, however, are not unchanging. A young couple, for example, might share housekeeping chores. However, if they decide to have a baby, it is important that they discuss how their roles will change once the baby is born. "Who's going to take care of the baby?" and "Who is going to get up when the baby cries?" are some of the questions the couple is going to have to answer.

Friends who are in conflict might benefit from looking at their role expectations. Let's say that whenever a man asks her out, Mary cancels her plans with her friend Beth. Beth feels hurt and angry because she believes that this behavior implies she is not as important to Mary as the man. Mary believes that male-female relationships are more important than female-female ones. Unless the two women can decide on the roles they will play in regard to each other, their friendship is in jeopardy. To take another example, if a husband expects his wife to cook dinner every night and she does not have the same expectation, then it is time to redefine their roles and expectations. Besides defining their roles, both people in a relationship have to reach mutual agreement on them. Finally, the roles and expectations that people have in a relationship must be satisfying to both parties.

Communication That Leads to Solutions

Once people have a commitment to a relationship, they can usually improve their communication within it. Better communication, including reflective listening and reevaluating when roles change, leads to better relationships.

*C*hange the following "you" messages to "I" messages:

- "You never get me a valentine."

- "You always look embarrassed when I cry."

- "You always start everything at the last minute. Why don't you try starting something on time?"

- "You don't look very good in that shirt. The stripes make you look fat."

- "If you don't retype the paper, your grade will be lower."

Reflective Listening

Chapter 3 discusses the subject of *reflective listening* in some detail. Because this kind of listening is so important to relationships, it is worthwhile to review the main points here.

Reflective listening is listening for feelings from the other person's point of view. In this kind of listening, you put aside your own feelings and try to *hear* what the other person is really saying. If your partner says, for example, "Everyone is picking on me today," you, as a reflective listener, would be sympathetic to your partner and indicate, both verbally and nonverbally, that you are ready to listen to what is bothering him or her.

The most important thing about reflective listening is that you don't try to evaluate the other person's feelings. If you respond to "Everyone is picking on me" with "You're really paranoid today," communication is likely to end. A more appropriate response might be "You really sound upset. What happened?" This response sets the stage for the other person to talk about what is bothering him or her. In reflective listening, the most important thing to remember is that people often just need a sounding board. Everyone feels happier in a relationship when the other person is a sympathetic listener.

Reevaluating When Roles Change

Sometimes relationships have to be reevaluated when the participants' roles change. Let's say, for example, that a 19-year-old marries someone who is 35. In this marriage it is likely that the younger person will depend on the older person to make decisions, to provide reassurance, and so forth. Once the 19-year-old finishes school and takes a job, it is likely that his or her self-confidence will increase and he or she will no longer depend on the spouse so much. In this situation the spouse might feel threatened by this change. In order to help this relationship the partners must discuss the roles they have been playing with a view to changing them. How can this be done?

Do you feel startled when you find someone playing a role you might not expect? Can role flexibility lead to a better relationship?

When we have been in a role for a long time, we develop habitual ways of behaving as well as assumptions about how our partner will behave. The young spouse, for example, may have let the older spouse pay the bills, advise on clothes, and make decisions about what social occasions they should attend. If, feeling newly independent, the younger spouse announces a desire to change these things, it will come as a shock to the older spouse.

The best chance for this relationship would be a renegotiation of roles. The younger spouse might say, "I'm feeling more secure now, and I would like to make my own choices about what to wear." Since this is not an unreasonable request, agreement is likely. The older spouse may see this as an opportunity to renegotiate his or her role as well, and may say something like, "Now that you're feeling more comfortable by yourself, I'd like to rejoin my Thursday evening tennis league."

It is much easier to make changes in roles when such changes are seen as being in the best interest of both partners. If one person sees the change as a loss, it will be very difficult for him or her to agree to it. The ease with which role changes are made depends also on the flexibility of the relationship. When relationships and roles are rigidly defined, change is very difficult. In many cases, the inability to change roles will lead to the end of the relationship.

Communication That Creates Problems

Avoidance

Many people who are in relationships that have problems try to dodge any discussion of the problem. Some people use silence; others change the subject if the other partner tries to begin a discussion. People who refrain from discussing relationships are often trying to avoid any kind of conflict. The dilemma of **avoidance**—refusing to deal with conflict or painful issues—is that unless the problem is discussed it probably will not go away.

If avoidance is a problem in a relationship, it might be useful to try the strategies for reflective listening (discussed earlier) and conflict resolution (discussed below). Sometimes people refuse to engage in discussion because they believe that nothing is ever resolved or that their partner will not give them a fair hearing. In such cases, discussion can often begin by calling in a third party to listen to both sides. Ideally, this should be a person who is able to listen objectively and not take sides. In the case of roommate conflict, a dorm counselor might be helpful. Partners in marriage often seek out marriage counselors.

Aggression

Aggression is a physical or verbal show of force. Some people resort to physical aggression when they are unhappy in a relationship. Unless the partners can get professional help, these relationships are usually doomed. Other people resort to verbal aggression, such as name calling or saying hurtful things. This is a very dangerous strategy because it is difficult to recover trust after your partner has said hurtful things about you. People who are tempted to use verbal aggression should be aware that such actions may destroy a relationship.

An even more subtle act, and one we are often not aware of committing, is indirect aggression. **Indirect aggression** occurs when people refuse to do anything or when they do something in such an inept way that it is hardly worth the effort. A secretary who hates making coffee for her boss might show indirect aggression by making coffee that is almost undrinkable. A child who is coerced into doing the dishes might break one every so often. A student whose parents have forced him to go to college may get even by flunking all his classes.

Why does indirect aggression occur? In all the above cases, it could have occurred because the people were forced into doing something they didn't want to do and are unable to discuss it with the person who did the forcing. Indirect aggression, then, is an avoidance technique. Often indirect aggression is not a *deliberate* act. The secretary may not set out to ruin the coffee; the child may not actually try to break the dishes; and the student may not intend to flunk out of school. In these cases, their unconscious selves may be sending a message they are not aware of.

When a partner in a relationship commits an act of indirect aggression, it is often useful for the other to bring it to his or her attention. This should

Consider This Consider This Consider This

SHOULD YOU GIVE ADVICE TO YOUR FRIENDS?

*M*ost of us are not reluctant to give advice to our friends. If asked for our opinion, we freely volunteer our thoughts on their clothes, their love life, or their life style. However, when it comes to giving advice on major life decisions, the experts advise caution.

Dr. Alan J. Klat, director of the Rockville Consultation Center, says that giving advice on major decisions can jeopardize a relationship. Whether the advice is right or wrong, many people do not want to be challenged on their views regarding what they should do about their work or their love relationships.

People seldom want the truth, according to Dr. Pierre Mornell, a psychiatrist in Mill Valley, California. They have already made up their minds, says Mornell, and they want friends to confirm their decisions.

Both experts believe that before giving advice, friends should consider the impact of the advice on the relationship. One of the best things you can do, they say, is to pledge support for whatever decision is reached.

Source: Adapted from Sharon Johnson, "Advice on Giving Advice," *The New York Times.*

be done very carefully, however, or it is likely to result in more aggression or a defensive response from the partner.

Defensive Communication

Defensive communication occurs when one partner tries to defend himself or herself against the remarks or behavior of the other. If a teacher tells a student, "This is the worst paper I have ever read," the student is likely to think (if not say), "And you are the worst teacher I have ever had." Obviously, this communication is not off to a good start.

How can we avoid defensive communication? Jack Gibb, a communication scholar, came up with six categories of defensive communication and supportive strategies to counter each of them.[14] Let's look at them.

EVALUATION VERSUS DESCRIPTION

Evaluative statements involve a judgment. If the judgment is negative, the person you are speaking to is likely to react defensively. If you tell your roommate, "It is very inconsiderate of you to slam the door when I am trying to sleep," he is likely to respond, "It's inconsiderate of you to snore every night when I am trying to sleep." Obviously such statements do not lead to solving the problem. On the other hand, a descriptive statement is much more likely to receive a favorable response. If you tell your roommate, "I had trouble sleeping last night because I heard the door slam," he is much more likely to do something about the problem. Since you have merely described the problem, the message is not nearly so threatening.

CONTROL VERSUS PROBLEM SOLVING

People are also likely to respond to you negatively if they perceive you are trying to control them. For example, if you are working on a class project with a classmate and you begin by taking charge and telling him or her what to do, it is likely you will be resented. A better approach is to engage in problem solving together. The same approach applies to close relationships. If conflict arises and you decide what should be done ("I'll take the car and you take the bicycle"), your partner is not likely to respond very positively. It is better to discuss your transportation options together.

STRATEGY VERSUS SPONTANEITY

Often strategy is little more than manipulation. Rather than openly ask people to do something, you try to manipulate them into doing it by using strategies such as making them feel guilty or ashamed. A statement that begins with "If you love me, you will..." is always a manipulative statement. A better approach is to express your honest feelings spontaneously: "I am feeling overwhelmed with all the planning I have to do for the party. Will you help me out today?"

NEUTRALITY VERSUS EMPATHY

How many times have you asked someone "Where shall we go to eat?" or "What movie should we see?" or "What do you want to do tonight?" and had the person respond, "I don't care"? This kind of neutral response indicates a lack of interest, and it is likely to make you feel defensive enough to respond, "Why do I always have to come up with the ideas?" or "If you don't care enough to make a suggestion, then we'll stay home."

On other occasions, we want and expect family members and friends to take our side. If you receive a low grade on a paper and are feeling very bad about it, you don't want your friend to say, "Maybe the teacher was right. Let's look at both sides." When feelings are high, no one wants a neutral, objective response. That can be saved for later. What is really needed in such a situation is for the other person to show **empathy**—the ability to recognize and identify with your feelings. An empathic response to a poor grade on a paper might be "You must feel bad. You really worked hard on that paper."

SUPERIORITY VERSUS EQUALITY

None of us likes people who act superior to us. Superiority may be communicated in a variety of ways. People who always take charge of situations seem to imply that they are the only ones who are qualified to do so. Others feel superior because of their role: "I am the boss and you are the employee, and don't you forget it." It's not uncommon for parents to give their children a statement of superiority: "I am your father and I will set the rules." Even if we have a position that is superior to someone else's, people will react less defensively if we do not communicate this superiority. An attitude of equality— "Let's work out this problem together"—will produce much less defensive behavior.

There are certain people who believe they are always right. Another label for these people is dogmatic. It is important that we don't confuse people who are confident and secure with people who think they are always right. Confident and secure people may hold strong opinions; they are likely, however, to make many more provisional statements—statements that permit another point of view to be expressed. For example, someone might say, "I feel strongly on this subject but I would be interested in hearing what you have to say." People who are willing to take a more provisional approach are also able to change their own position if a more reasonable position is presented.

Table 7-1 shows all the categories of defensive and supportive behavior.

Avoiding Defensive Communication: A Practical Example

Although we have discussed each of Gibb's six categories separately, in most communication several of them appear simultaneously. You can see how this works in the following dialogs.

A DEFENSIVE DIALOG

Boss: You're an hour late to work. If you're going to work here, you have to be on time. (*superiority, control*)

Employee: My car wouldn't start.

Boss: That's no reason. (*certainty, evaluation*) You should have called. (*evaluation*)

Employee: I tried but . . .

Boss: When work starts at 8:00 A.M., you must be here at 8:00 A.M. (*superiority, control*) If you can't make it, you should look for another job. (*superiority, control, certainty*) If you're late again, don't bother coming to work. (*superiority, control, strategy*)

Employee: (*sighs and remains silent*)

This dialog has left the employee feeling defensive, angry, and unable to say anything. Let's take a look at how the dialog might have gone if the boss had been more willing to listen.

TABLE 7-1
Categories of Defensive and Supportive Behavior

Defensive Climate	*Supportive Climate*
1. Evaluation	1. Description
2. Control	2. Problem solving
3. Strategy	3. Spontaneity
4. Neutrality	4. Empathy
5. Superiority	5. Equality
6. Certainty	6. Provisionalism

A SUPPORTIVE DIALOG

Boss: You're an hour late. What happened? (*description, equality*)

Employee: My car wouldn't start.

Boss: Weren't you near a phone? (*still no evaluation*)

Employee: Every time I tried to call the line was busy. I finally decided that it would be faster to walk here than to keep trying to call.

Boss: When people don't get here on time, I always worry that we're going to fall behind schedule. (*spontaneity*) Wasn't there *any* way of letting me know what happened? (*problem solving*)

Employee: Yeah. I guess I panicked. I should have asked my sister to keep trying to call to let you know what happened. If it ever happens again, that's what I'll do.

Boss: Good. Now let's get to work. There's a lot of catching up to do . . .

In this conversation, neither boss nor employee is left feeling defensive or resentful. Although the role of boss is superior to that of employee, this boss tries hard not to use his position of superior power. The result is a more equal conversation, which leads, in turn, to a better communication between the two.

Interpersonal Conflict and Its Resolution

From time to time, all of us face conflict in our interpersonal communication. Sometimes conflict can destroy a relationship; other times, if the participants can work it out, the relationship becomes stronger.

Try This Try This Try This

1. Change the following evaluative statement to a descriptive one: "You really annoy me when you expect me to exercise with you. I'm just too busy."
2. Change this controlling statement to a problem-solving one: "Tonight we eat at Joe's and then go to see a movie."
3. Change this manipulative statement to a spontaneous one: "If you really loved me, you would remember my birthday and our anniversary."
4. Change this neutral statement to an empathic one: "I know your boss irritates you, but you must remember that he has very great responsibilities."
5. Change this superior statement to an equal one: "Since I earn all the money in this household, I should decide how to spend it."
6. Change this statement of certainty to a provisional comment: "The Democrats are always right, and no one is going to persuade me they are not."

When two people are in conflict and have decided that nothing will be served by avoidance or aggression, the option left open to them is **conflict resolution**—negotiation to find a solution to the conflict.[15] Conflict arises because two individuals do not have compatible goals. Through the negotiation process, the two try to find out how they can both reach their goals. For the negotiation to be considered successful, both sides must be satisfied and feel that they have come out ahead.

Deborah Weider-Hatfield has suggested a very useful model for resolving conflict.[16] In this model, each individual looks at the conflict *intra*personally. Then the partners get together *inter*personally to work out the problem.

In the first stage, **intrapersonal evaluation, each person analyzes the problem by himself or herself.** This analysis is accomplished through a series of questions: How do I feel about this problem? How can I describe the other person's behavior? What are the facts?

In determining the facts, it is important not to confuse facts with inferences. If you have an untidy roommate, for example, a fact might be that he doesn't pick up his clothes. An inference would be that he is trying to irritate you by not hanging them up. Throughout this intrapersonal process it is important to *describe*—not judge—the other person's behavior.

In the second stage, **the parties in the conflict get together to work out an interpersonal definition of the problem.** It is important that both parties

Conflict can appear in any relationship. What is the best way to resolve it without permanently harming the relationship?

believe there is a problem and can define what it is. Partners in conflict often do not see the problem in the same light; in fact one person might not even believe there is a problem. Therefore, in this stage, it is important that each person listen carefully. To aid in listening, it is useful for each person to paraphrase what was said, to check the accuracy of what he or she has heard. The same is true for feelings. Because feelings are very intense in a conflict, it is important for each partner to express his or her own feelings and also to make sure he or she is listening accurately by also trying to paraphrase the feelings of the other. Then it is useful for each person to describe the other person's behavior. At the end of this stage both partners should agree on the facts of the problem.

In the third stage, **the partners should discuss shared goals.** Again, focusing on the problem, the individuals should ask, "What are *my* needs and desires?" and "What are *your* needs and desires?" Then they should work to see whether their needs and goals overlap. Let's look, for example, at the tidy and untidy roommates. The tidy roommate needs to have things picked up and the dishes washed. The untidy roommate hates doing housework and doesn't care if the apartment is in disorder. Thus their needs and goals in housework are incompatible. On the other hand, they like each other and like sharing an apartment. Each is also concerned that the other partner be happy. In this case, then, they have found some goals in common.

At the fourth stage, **the partners must come up with possible resolutions to the problem.** Here it is useful to create as long a list as possible. Then each individual can eliminate resolutions he or she considers impossible to live with.

In the fifth stage, **the partners move on to weighing goals against resolutions.** To see how this works, let's look again at the roommates. Since they want to live together and they want the other person to be happy, their task is to choose a resolution or resolutions that will help to reach this goal. Some compromises are inevitable at this stage. In this particular situation, the tidy roommate might agree to stop nagging, and the untidy roommate might agree to pick up everything and put it away at least once a week. These particular resolutions may not be entirely satisfactory to either partner, but they are a compromise that both hope they can live with.

Since all resolutions are easier to make than to keep, the last stage of the process is to *evaluate the resolution after some time has passed.* Does the resolution work? Does it need to be changed? Should it be discussed again at a later date? As we mentioned earlier, it is not easy to change human behavior. When partners work to resolve conflict, even when they come up with good resolutions, there is likely to be some backsliding. It therefore makes good sense to give partners a chance to live up to their resolutions. Letting time pass before both negotiators are held accountable helps achieve this goal.

Although these guidelines for resolving conflict can be useful in many situations, it must be pointed out that not all conflicts can be resolved. If partners cannot find any goals that they share, or if they cannot agree on resolutions that will enable them to meet their goals, then the conflict will probably not be resolved.

Also, although this model looks good on paper, it is much like the chair you see advertised in the local discount store; the sign says "A child can put it together in ten minutes," but when you get it home you find there are 25 nuts and bolts and 14 separate pieces, and after 2 hours' work you have something that only vaguely resembles a chair. In the same way, this model sounds simple in theory, but it will not always be easy to put into practice. Human communication is so complex, and there are so many ambiguities and subtleties in meaning, that each person in a negotiation must bring careful thought and analysis to each stage of the process. When both partners are committed to a relationship, however, there is a good chance that conflict can be worked out using this or a similar process.

Relationships That Work

Most relationships can be improved when the partners understand how to communicate with each other. Conflict occurs in all relationships; it's how it is worked out that allows the partners to find satisfaction and happiness together.

What is a relationship that works? It is one where there is intimacy and self-disclosure. When you save up the good things that have happened to you to tell to your partner, that is a good relationship. It is a relationship where you can share the good and the bad things you feel. It is a partnership where you can solve problems and feel happy that you have solved them. Most important, a relationship is the psychological space where you and your partner/friend are closest to being your truest selves. It can happen with a marriage partner, with best friends, or with a parent or child. For us to be happy, it is important that it happen with someone.

SUMMARY

Important relationships go through five stages: initiating, experimenting, intensifying, integrating, and bonding. Relationships that remain superficial might go through only the first or second stage.

Relationships that come apart also go through five stages: differentiating, circumscribing, stagnating, avoiding, and terminating. When a relationship is ending, the participants will often make statements that summarize the relationship and comments that indicate whether the relationship will continue in any form. If it is necessary for a relationship to continue in some form, the people involved might decide on a list of rules to govern it.

Good relationships need commitment and dialog. Commitment is a desire by both partners to continue the relationship and to take responsibility for problems that occur in it. Dialog occurs when the parties in the relationship have ongoing conversations about the relationship itself. An important part of dialog is to discuss conflict when it arises.

Criticism, a negative evaluation of a person for something he or she has done, must be approached very carefully. "Good" criticism should not contain negative language and should not be stated harshly. It will work best if it's specific, if the person who offers it also offers to assist in making the change, if it's given so that someone sees how it can serve his or her best interest, and if it is put in a broad and positive context.

When there is conflict in a relationship, it helps if the participants are able to change or adapt in a way to reduce conflict. If this is not possible, the partners must consider the costs and rewards of staying in the relationship. If the rewards outweigh the costs, the parties might decide to continue with the relationship—even though it is not entirely satisfying.

Several communication strategies can help improve a relationship. One of the most useful is reflective listening. In this kind of listening, you can concentrate on the other person's feelings and avoid evaluating what he or she is saying. Another strategy is for the participants to discuss roles and role expectations—especially if the two are not happy with the roles they are playing.

A relationship may also be harmed by certain communication strategies: avoidance—withdrawing or avoiding conflict; aggression—whether physical, verbal, or indirect; and defensive communication. Strategies for avoiding defensive communication include describing rather than evaluating, problem solving with a partner rather than trying to control him or her, being spontaneous rather than manipulative, using empathy rather than remaining neutral, aiming for equality rather than superiority, and being provisional rather than certain.

Using a model of conflict resolution can help reduce conflict in a relationship. The steps involve evaluating the conflict intrapersonally, defining the nature of the conflict with your partner, discussing the goals you and your partner share, deciding on possible resolutions to the problem, weighing goals against resolutions, deciding on a resolution that will reach the goal, and evaluating the resolution after some time has passed.

FURTHER READING

BRIDGES, WILLIAM. *Transitions: Making Sense of Life's Changes*. Reading, MA: Addison-Wesley, 1980. Bridges divides his book into "The Need for Change" and "The Transition Process." This is a readable, useful book on how to handle change. He helps us identify and cope with the critical changes in our lives with suggestions and advice for improving skills.

CAHN, DUDLEY D. JR. *Letting Go: A Practical Theory of Relationship Disengagement and Reengagement*. Albany, NY: State University of New York, 1987. This book takes a look at the research about relationships that fail and focuses on how poor self-concept and communication may play a part in that failure. The book is research-oriented and scholarly.

CROSBY, JOHN F. *Illusion and Disillusion: The Self in Love and Marriage*. Belmont, CA: Wadsworth, 1990, 4th ed. Crosby zeroes in on the difficulties in love and marriage and what can be done about those difficulties. This is a serious book with sophisticated case studies to support the author's analyses. A solid, scholarly piece of work that challenges, enriches, and satisfies.

FELDER, LEONARD. *A Fresh Start*. New York: New American Library, 1989. The author uses case studies and exercises to show how people turn the bad things that happen to them into opportunities for growth. Especially relevant here is how to recover from a broken relationship and how to free ourselves from unresolved conflicts.

Fisher, Bruce. *Rebuilding: When Your Relationship Ends.* San Luis Obispo, CA: Impact, 1981. This excellent and insightful book treats denial, loneliness, guilt and rejection, grief, anger, letting go, self-concept, friendships, leftovers, love, trust, sexuality, responsibility, singleness, and freedom.

Fitzpatrick, Mary Anne. *Between Husbands and Wives: Communication in Marriage.* Newbury Park, CA: Sage, 1988. The author defines five types of relationships and then shows how couples communicate with each other in each of these relationships. The book is a scholarly study with lots of statistical data.

Lerner, Harriet Goldhor. *The Dance of Anger.* New York: Harper & Row, 1985. This book, written by a psychologist, discusses the use of anger in interpersonal relationships. The author believes that anger, if used properly, can bring about positive changes in relationships. Although the book has helpful advice for everyone, it focuses on women and the kinds of anger they are likely to face.

Naifeh, Steven, and Gregory White Smith. *Why Can't Men Open Up?* New York: Crown, 1984. This book is full of practical advice and experiences that reveal ways to create intimacy in relationships. An excellent bibliography is also included.

Ray, Sondra. *Loving Relationships: The Secrets of a Great Relationship.* Berkeley, CA: Celestial Arts, 1980. Ray focuses on attracting ideal mates, creating strong relationships, preventing arguments, handling jealousy, and extending relationships. This book is easy to read, full of short chapters, and loaded with relevant examples.

Vaughan, Diane. *Uncoupling: How and Why Relationships Come Apart.* New York: Random House, 1990. Through extensive research and dozens of case histories, Vaughan explains the underlying patterns beneath every disintegrating relationship. She takes us through the process of uncoupling, from the initial secret awareness of discomfort and the display of discontent through the breakdown of cover-up, trying to patch things up, and going on. A thorough, well-documented treatment with numerous examples.

Chapter 8

The Interview

CHAPTER OBJECTIVES	KEY TERMS
After reading this chapter, you should be able to:	application letter
1. Define information interview.	closed questions
2. List some of the ways interviews are used.	employment interview
	factual information
3. Tell how interviews can enhance information gathering.	follow-up questions
	information interview
4. Construct the following kinds of questions: primary, follow-up, neutral, closed, and open-ended.	interview
	leading questions
	neutral questions
5. Describe your preparation for an information interview.	open-ended questions
	policy information
6. Write a résumé and a cover letter.	primary questions
	résumé
7. Describe your preparation for an employment interview.	
8. Identify the ways you might make an impression on the interviewer through your nonverbal behavior.	
9. Explain the role of assessment in both the information and the employment interviews.	

A member of the city council is trying to discover the feelings of her constituents on a topic of local significance. She knows a vote on the issue is coming up, and she needs guidance. In her door-to-door survey, she asks people how they feel about their neighborhood being rezoned to a commercial area. To those who are in favor of the move, she adds a follow-up question: What kinds of businesses should be permitted in this neighborhood?

A student researching a term paper on a recent court decision about federal aid to colleges and universities goes to the athletic director to ask her if the decision will affect the sports programs on campus. After talking to her, he also goes to the dean to ask whether the decision will have an impact on any of the academic programs.

A student looking for a summer job stops by a local fast-food restaurant and asks the manager if he is looking for any summer help. The manager says he will have a few jobs available and asks the student about her past job experience. After they have talked for a few minutes, the manager says he will know what is available by the end of the week and that the student should stop by and see him then.

All these examples involve an interview. Like the people in the examples, we all spend time conducting interviews and being interviewed—although we might not always label what we are doing an interview.

An **interview** is a series of questions and answers, usually exchanged between two people, which has the purpose of getting and understanding information about a particular subject or topic. Thus, when you ask a professor about a low grade you received on a paper, you are engaged in interviewing. You go in with a purpose—to find out why you received a low grade—and your conversation with the professor involves a series of questions and answers. Again, if you go to pick up your car, which has been in the garage being repaired, you are likely to have an interview with the mechanic who fixed it. You might ask what was wrong with the car, what parts had to be replaced, how long the repair is likely to last, and whether you should even keep the car.

What makes an interview different from interpersonal communication is that it is task-oriented—it has the goal of finding out specific information. You interview someone for information you need to put together a speech or you go into a job interview with the goal of presenting yourself so well that the interviewer will want to hire you.

The interview is another form of transactional communication. Because of its back-and-forth nature, communication is continuous and simultaneous. Not only are the interviewers and subjects responding verbally to each other, they are also making assessments. The person being interviewed is assessing the knowledge, poise, and preparation of the interviewer. The interviewer is thinking about what is the best way to ask a question, how to rephrase a question to get a more specific answer, or how to probe other points that have come up in the subject's comments. Roles are quite specific in interview situations. One person plays the role of information seeker and the other of information giver. During the course of the interview, questions, answers, and perceptions are determined by each person's background, education, and experience.

Interviews commonly occur in an appropriate setting. Let's say that you met a car salesman at a party and you casually mentioned you were looking for a new car. You would probably be annoyed if he asked you twenty questions about the kind of car you were looking for and then described all the cars on his lot. Since the interpersonal setting of a party is not very suitable for an interview, it would be more appropriate if he were to give you his business card and suggest you come by his office at a later time. An interview, then, is a highly structured form of interpersonal communication that takes place in a setting appropriate for serious, goal-oriented communication.

The interviews we are most likely to be involved in are information interviews and job interviews.[1] Let's begin by looking at the first.

The Information Interview

An **information interview** is an interview whose goal is to gather facts and opinions from someone with expertise and experience in a specific field; it is a useful tool when collecting information for a speech, a group discussion, or a paper. The information interview can be used to supplement the more traditional ways of research—such as getting information from books and periodicals. It may also produce information that is not available from these more traditional sources.

Information interviews help us to get the most up-to-date information. Reporters, for example, make extensive use of the information interview. They interview the mayor of the town about her plans for increasing taxes. They talk to the governor about his plans for reelection. On a campus, an interview is the most effective way of getting information from members of the college community. A student interviews the vice president for administration as to whether tuition will increase next year; another interviews a department head about the new requirements for a major.

Interviews are also very effective in getting personal reactions to events. You might read about the damage a tornado has caused in a small town, but an interview can give you a chance to discuss someone's experience with the tornado. Personal experience adds another dimension to your information; it tells you what it feels like to be in that situation.

One of the greatest advantages of the information interview is that it allows an opportunity for feedback and follow-up. If you don't understand something, the person being interviewed can explain it to you. An interview also permits you to explore interesting points of information as they arise—points you may not have been aware of beforehand. For example, if you are interviewing a member of the administration about a tuition increase, he might mention that electricity costs have gone up this year. You can explore this area: Have they gone up because the utility company has raised its rates or because of greater electricity use on campus?

The information interview is the most personal way of getting information. You can interact with the person being interviewed; you can observe nonverbal behavior; you can ask for clarification. The interview gives you a way of learning and of sharing information in a human setting.

Preparing for the Interview

Once you have chosen the subject you want to research, how do you decide whom you should interview? Basically, this depends on the kind of information you are looking for. For a class project, most interviews will focus either on **policy information** (data on how an organization should be run) or **factual information** (data dealing with who, what, where, when, and the like).

Policy Information   Every organization has people who make policy and others who carry it out. In the public schools, for example, the school board makes the policy and the principals carry it out within their own individual schools. Therefore, if the budget for music has been cut and you want to know why, you should interview a member of the school board. If, however, you want to know the impact this cut has had on individual schools, then you should interview the principal. By the same token, if you want to know why food stamps have been reduced, it would be more useful to interview someone in the state welfare office than in the local one.

In colleges and universities, policy making is usually divided into two areas: administrative and academic. The administrative area involves setting policies on when tuition has to be paid, allocation of parking spaces, food services, law enforcement, and so on. The academic area involves setting policy on such matters as curriculum, faculty, scheduling classes—anything that might influence teaching and learning. If you want to find out why the parking spaces are so limited for students, you should interview someone in the administrative area. If you wonder why so few courses are scheduled for summer school, you should talk to someone in the academic area.

Factual Information   When you are gathering material for a speech or term paper, quite often the information you need is of a factual nature. For example, you might want to know how China is controlling its population or how well women are doing at getting jobs in advertising. In such cases, you should look for the best-informed person on the subject. One of the best places to look is among the faculty on your own campus. Everyone on the faculty is an expert on some subject. If you want to do research on population control in China, for example, you might start with the sociology or political science faculty. If you do not know which instructors specialize in which areas of expertise, ask the department head.

People who work in the community are also valuable sources of information. City council members and county commissioners can tell you about the workings of local government. And don't forget city employees. The tax assessor can tell you how taxes are calculated and collected. His or her office will also have information on who owns what property. Police officials and lawyers are valuable sources of information on how the legal system works. The welfare office and the children's services offices can often provide insight into social problems in the community. Researching a medical subject? Why not talk to some local doctors? You will be surprised how many experts are available once you look around.

Anyone who is planning to conduct an interview should know something about the person being interviewed. Typical information you should have beforehand includes the proper spelling of the person's name and his or her title. If the person is well known, you might be able to discover some biographical information before the interview. *Books in Print,* for example, lists all the titles and names of authors of books recently published in the United States. *Who's Who in America* contains biographical information about prominent Americans. Don't forget to check out the specialized editions, such as *Who's Who in the South, Who's Who in American Women,* and so on. If you are going to talk to someone who works for the college or university, the public relations office is likely to have some biographical information about this person.

You should also have background information on the topic of your interview. The purpose of an interview is not to give you a crash course on a particular topic; it is to give you information that is not commonly known or new insight on an old topic. Let's say you are preparing a speech on the impact of satellites on the broadcast industry and you decide to interview the manager of the local radio station. Before you go into the interview, you should have some idea about what a satellite is and what it can do. Then, when you talk to the station manager, you can concentrate on the impact of satellites on the broadcast business. Background information can be found through library research.

As you prepare your background information, you should decide on the angle you want to take in your interview. The *angle* is the information on which you want to concentrate. If, for example, you decided to interview someone on the status of women in the Middle East, your topic would be so broad that it would be impossible to get any useful information. Women are treated very differently in Saudi Arabia than they are in Jordan. Would it be better to concentrate on just one country? Also, might you narrow the topic even more by concentrating on one aspect of women's lives, such as education,

Consider This Consider This Consider This

Many students are apprehensive about interviewing because they are afraid they might ask stupid questions. Charles Osgood, who has worked for many years in radio news, tells how he works:

I'm assuming that my curiosity is not going to be vastly different from somebody else's curiosity. I don't have a great deal of specialized knowledge about anything, and that puts me in the same boat with almost everybody. I'm talking to a general audience. So forgive me sometimes if I ask a question that the audience already knows the answer to, but if I don't know the answer, then I figure there are other people out there who don't know either.

Source: Shirley Biagi, *NewsTalk II.*

politics, or homemaking? Once you have an angle for the interview, it will be much easier to get information you can use.

Preparing for an interview gives you an advantage. If the people you are interviewing see that you have taken the time to prepare, they are much more likely to treat you as a person with whom they are willing to spend their time. If you start out with such questions as "How do you spell your name?" or "I don't know much about this topic—do you have any ideas for questions?" you are not going to inspire much confidence in your skills as an interviewer! On the other hand, if you show that you know something about the interviewee and about the topic, you are likely to find much more willingness to discuss the topic seriously.

PREPARING QUESTIONS

Primary Questions   Everyone should go into an interview with a prepared set of questions. These questions should be listed in the order you plan to ask them. **Primary questions** are those designed to cover the subject comprehensively, and they should be based on your background research. Let's say you are interviewing a sociology professor on the topic of population control in China. Some of your primary questions might be:

- Why does China need to control its population?
- What is the policy for population control?
- Who sets the policy for population control?
- How does the Chinese government explain the need for population control to the people?
- How is China able to implement its population policy?

Follow-Up Questions   Although you should always go into an interview with primary questions, these will not be the only questions you will ask. As the interview proceeds, you will think of other questions based on the answers given by your interviewee. These are called **follow-up questions,** and they are useful when you want to go into a subject in greater depth. They also enable you to pursue an area that might be new to you or to clarify something you don't understand. You learn that China's policy for population control is "one family, one child." Some of your follow-up questions might be:

- How do families feel when they are told they can have only one child?
- What happens if a family's only child dies or is physically or mentally handicapped?
- If everyone has only one child, in future generations there will be no aunts, uncles, or first cousins. What impact will this have on Chinese society?

As you can see, follow-up questions require the interviewer to listen carefully and to think about the answers. Often the answers to follow-up questions lead into such interesting areas that interviewers get information they hadn't planned on.

Open-Ended Questions   All the preceding questions about China's population policy are **open-ended questions**—ones that permit the person being inter-

Try This Try This Try This

*S*ee if you can come up with follow-up questions to the answers below from an interviewee:

- The people I hate most are drunken drivers. Ever since our family suffered such a tragic loss, I have been determined to devote my efforts to getting them off the roads.

- One of the most effective Soviet propaganda tools is "disinformation."

- People who live in tornado-prone areas should take some basic safety precautions.

- I believe that children should be more firmly disciplined. There are entirely too many unruly children in today's world.

- Hundreds of chemicals exist that are dangerous to human beings. Everyone should at least be aware of the ones that are found in every household.

- Even though our student body has not decreased, circulation of library books has decreased 25 percent this year.

viewed to expand on his or her answer. Open-ended questions lead to explanations, elaboration, and reflection. Most in-depth questions are open-ended.

Closed Questions Questions worded in ways that restrict their answers are **closed questions.** A question that can be answered with a yes or a no is a closed question. ("Do you plan to stay in this job?" "Are you going to graduate from school?") Other closed questions require only a short answer. ("Do you work better at home or in your office?" "What city would you most like to live in?")

Closed questions have some advantages. They are designed to get a lot of information quickly, and they are good for eliciting facts. Closed questions can be useful when the subject of your interview is too talkative. If he or she gives answers that are so long you don't have a chance to ask the rest of your questions, you have lost control of the interview. By interjecting a series of short, closed questions, you can regain control. If, for example, you are interviewing someone about energy costs and she begins to talk at great length about diminishing fossil fuels, you might ask: "What is the cheapest fuel?" "What is the difference between passive and active solar collectors?" "What kind of insulation should you have in the attic if you live in the Northeast or Midwest?" When you prepare your primary questions, they should be a mixture of closed and open-ended questions.

Neutral Questions versus Leading Questions Questions that do not show how the interviewer feels about the subject are **neutral questions.** Say you are a reporter interviewing the mayor about a tax increase. A neutral question might be: "Many people think this tax increase will create a hardship for people who live in the city. What do you think?"

Leading questions are those which point the interviewee in a particular direction. If you were to ask the dean "When is the college going to stop exploiting women?" you would be implying that the college *is* exploiting women. A more neutral way of phrasing this question would be "Do you think men and women have equal opportunities at this college?" or, if you want to get more specific, "Men's sports are allotted twice as much money as women's sports. Why is that?"

Leading questions often show the bias of the interviewer, and if there is a negative bias, it might arouse hostility in the person being interviewed. Sometimes, however, leading questions can be used effectively. If you were interviewing a member of the Ku Klux Klan, it might be appropriate to ask whether the Klan will ever change its racist policies. Sometimes interviewers will use a leading question to get a strong emotional reaction from the person being interviewed. When Miles Davis was interviewed by Alex Haley, Haley asked, "Linked with your musical renown is your reputation for bad temper and rudeness to your audiences. Would you like to comment?"[2] Few people could resist such a question, and Davis was no exception.

It's important to know when to ask leading questions. Since some questions can lead to hostility, especially when feelings are high, the inexperienced interviewer should leave them for the end of the interview and concentrate on neutral questions at the beginning. You should also remember that leading questions can result in explosive replies, and so you should not ask them if you are not prepared for the answers they might evoke.

Here are some examples of leading questions (LQ) rephrased as neutral questions (NQ):

LQ: Why are you so afraid of being interviewed?
NQ: Some people have noticed that you seem to be apprehensive about being interviewed. Why do you think they have this idea?
LQ: Why do you run student government like a tyrant?
NQ: Some people have called you a tyrant for the way you run the student government. What do you think you have done to make them feel that way?
LQ: Why don't you ever get anything done on time?
NQ: Do you ever have problems meeting deadlines?

Questions can be worded in many different ways. A good interview will have a variety of questions. Not only will these questions get at different kinds of information, but they will also be interesting to the person being interviewed.

SAMPLE INFORMATION INTERVIEW

In this interview, notice that the interviewer is seeking the most up-to-date information available. The interview format allows for follow-up questions. The information interview is the most personal way of getting information.

This interview was conducted by a student who was gathering material for a speech on the image of Hispanics in the United States. She decided that a good source of information would be her Cuban-born Spanish professor. (ER is the interviewer; EE is the interviewee.)

ER: Dr. Maciá, I'm doing research on the image of Hispanics in the United States for a speech in my class and I'd like to know your feelings on the subject. As a Cuban-born U.S. citizen, how do you think Hispanics are seen in the United States?

ER opens the interview by telling her subject what she wants to find out and how she is going to use the information. Her first question is a broad, primary question.

EE: As a Cuban, I can't speak for all Hispanics and my perceptions are based upon my personal experience, but I think being fluent in English helped me greatly because I haven't been subject to prejudice to any great extent.

ER: Would you say that a Hispanic with a little English is disadvantaged?

EE: Yes, and for a Spanish-speaking person, it's difficult to keep your heritage while functioning completely in American society. I feel minority females are particularly disadvantaged when they come to this country with poor education. They are treated much worse than Hispanic males.

ER: How do you feel about bilingual education in the United States?

Here the ER could have asked a follow-up question about why women are treated worse than men.

Because the subject has introduced the issue of language, ER asks a follow-up question designed to gain more information.

EE: I truly feel students in America who live in Spanish-speaking areas should learn Spanish at an early age, and that Spanish-speaking students in the U.S. should learn English early. The student in the United States learns language too late to be of real use.

ER: How do Americans perceive the Spanish language?

This is an open-ended question which allows EE to expand on her subject.

EE: I taught Spanish at the high school level for eight years and now I am teaching Spanish to college students. I've seen many different attitudes.

ER: Can you describe some of these attitudes?

This question is still about language but it is getting much more specific.

EE: At some schools, all languages were regarded in the same way. In other schools, however, French was considered to be the socially correct language, German was for the intellectuals, and Spanish was for the "bad" students because it was considered the easiest language.

ER: The media shape opinions of young people and adults to a great extent. Do you see a lack of Hispanics in advertisements?

Now the ER changes the subject and goes to another primary question.

EE: Absolutely. The Hispanics are never the object of national advertising to the extent that African-Americans are. Hispanics are difficult to generalize, hard to identify. We have a great cultural variety and I'm afraid the media would portray Hispanics too stereotypically—such as showing a Hispanic who "cannot a-speak."

ER: Only two U.S. market segments, college-aged women and Hispanics, are increasing their cigarette consumption. How do you feel about Hispanics being targeted by advertising for cigarettes?

In this question the ER shows that she has done some research.

EE: Well, smoking is a part of Latin culture, so I don't feel we are being exploited, although it is a moral dilemma for the advertiser to try to entice anyone to smoke. Smoking is still a big reality in the Hispanic world.

ER: How do you see Hispanics portrayed in TV shows?

Here is another primary question. It is stated in a neutral way.

EE: We're never chairman of the board. We are the proverbial "bad guy." Unlike African-Americans, we don't have a homogeneous identity or a cohesive heritage. We cannot be portrayed like the Cosbys.

ER: What about the portrayal of Hispanic women in the media?

EE: I went to high school with a girl who occasionally appeared on a popular TV comedy in the sixties. She played the dingbat, and she rarely spoke. She was never called by name—she had absolutely no identity. The Cuban heritage she was portraying seemed to emphasize a "floozy" identity. But since then, I think times have changed. Carmen Miranda is dead.

ER: The U.S. Census Bureau reports that the largest minority in America by 2010 will be Hispanic. I've read that can be attributed to an increased fertility rate among Hispanics. Is this a fair statement?

Again, the ER shows that she has prepared for this interview.

EE: You must understand that Hispanics are a Catholic people, and birth control is not an accepted practice.

ER: I'm glad you made that clear because my textbook made no attempt to explain it. Dr. Maciá, I'd like you to pretend you're speaking as a representative of all Hispanics for a moment. Why would you, a Hispanic, want to come to the United States?

In this question, the ER feels she should comment on the answer. Her comment shows her interest and that she is thinking about the answers. Now, she asks the EE to speculate and generalize about Hispanic people.

EE: Go live somewhere else and you will understand. There is such a high standard of convenient living in the United States—the quality of life, the cleanliness, the consumerism. America is so tempting to the foreigner because you have everything.

ER: Dr. Maciá, I'd like to thank you for taking the time to talk to me. I've learned a lot during this interview, and what you've told me will be a great help for my speech.

ER thanks her subject, and it's clear by EE's response that she has enjoyed the interview too.

EE: It's rewarding for me that you should be so motivated by Spanish culture to pursue this kind of research in your major.

Source: Rachel Hosterman conducted this interview while she was a student at Lock Haven University. Dr. Cecilia K. Maciá is an assistant professor of Spanish at Lock Haven University, Lock Haven, Pa.

TAPE OR NOTES?

Before you conduct an interview, you should decide whether you want to tape it. The main advantage of tape is that it allows you to record the interview without taking notes. If you are not tied to note taking, you are able to concentrate on listening, and you can pay more attention to the nonverbal cues you receive from the person you are interviewing. Tape also permits you to get precise quotations. This is particularly useful if the subject is controversial and you would like to get exact quotations. If you are looking only for background information, however, exact quotations might not be your goal. Note taking also has some advantages. You don't have to worry about equipment, and it is easier to review notes to find what you want than it is to go through a tape cassette.

Taping interviews also has disadvantages. Some people do not like to be taped. Albert Schweitzer, a missionary in Africa, once told a reporter he couldn't stand "those infernal taping machines." In other cases, a very controversial interviewee might not want to be pinned down to his or her exact words. A city council member who calls the mayor a fool would probably prefer not to have those words on tape. Sometimes tape recorders make people feel self-conscious, and some of the spontaneous nature of an interview can thus be lost. Another disadvantage of tape is that if you have a very long interview, you will find it time-consuming to listen to the tape and pick out the main points. Also, the mechanics on changing a tape or of remembering to turn the tape over in a long interview can be a distraction.

If you decide to tape an interview, you should follow these basic procedures:

1. When you are setting up the appointment for the interview, ask if you may tape the person's comments.

Because of the way the interviewer is sitting and because he is taking notes, what is he missing in this interview?

2. Before you go into the interview, make sure you know how to use the tape recorder.
3. Most cassette recorders have a built-in microphone. Some of these work quite well, but others will also pick up a lot of background noise. If you are going to be in a noisy place, take along a microphone that plugs into the tape recorder and can be placed close to the participants.
4. Each cassette shows its length in time. Make sure you have adequate cassettes for your interview. Cassettes have two sides. If you have a 60-minute cassette, for example, you will have to turn it over after 30 minutes.
5. Try to use a recorder with a counter. When you begin the interview, set the recorder at 000. Later, when you listen to the tape, you can jot down the place where each important segment occurs.
6. If you use a microphone, try to position it somewhere between you and the respondent. If you have to move the microphone back and forth, it can become very obtrusive. *Never* let the interviewee take the microphone out of your hand. If you do, you will lose control of the interview.
7. Let the person you are interviewing know how you are going to use the tape. He or she might react differently if you are going to use it for background information as opposed to airing the interview on the campus radio station.

If you decide to take notes instead of tape recording, it is useful to devise your own form of shorthand. After the interview is over, you should immediately write out your notes in greater detail. More than one interviewer has discovered that he or she has no idea of what some of the notes mean two or three days later. Looking at your notes immediately after the interview will

Consider This Consider This Consider This

*P*eter Rinearson, a journalist, talks about the advantages of using a tape recorder for interviewing:

In many instances, it's not until I transcribe an interview that I understand what was said. When you're taking notes, you get a sentence or two and maybe you miss a sentence. Your mind is turning back and forth between what you're writing and what you're hearing. Very often things are said during an interview that I don't have the background to understand. . . . [But] when I go back and read that transcript [from a tape recorder], suddenly it's "Where was this? I thought I knew what was going on, but now I really understand what this guy was talking about." I'll come upon this gem which was completely unperceived to me at the time the person said it. I have it because I captured it on tape, because I transcribed it and set up a system to let me get to it rapidly.

Source: Shirley Biagi, *NewsTalk I.*

also help you to fill in the gaps while the comments are still fresh in your mind.

Conducting the Interview

Whenever you conduct an interview, the most important thing you can do is to convey confidence and knowledge of your subject. Most people will feel flattered if you let them know you have been researching the subject of the interview and have taken the time to find out something about them.

People who are not accustomed to being interviewed might be feeling insecure, and so it is also important to make them feel at ease. You can best do this by thanking them for agreeing to the interview and expressing your interest in the subject you will be talking about. If you are taping the interview, try to put the recorder in an unobtrusive place so it will not make the interviewee feel self-conscious.

Once you begin asking questions and listening to answers, don't be afraid to ask for clarification. Sometimes interviewers do not do this because they are afraid of appearing ignorant. If the person you are interviewing, for example, mentions a Supreme Court case you have never heard of, you should immediately stop and ask for background information on the case.

It is important that you, as interviewer, keep control of the situation. As you ask your questions, you should set the tone for the interview and establish your authority, the course the interview will take, and your relationship to the interviewee.[3] When you are talking to people in their own area of expertise, quite often they will digress or tell you more than you want to know. If you have scheduled a half-hour interview and after the first ten minutes you are still on your first question, you are losing control of the interview and won't have time to pose all the questions you want to ask. If this happens, the only thing you can do is interrupt. This can be done with such statements as "This is really very interesting and I would like to talk more about it, but I want to ask you a few more questions."

Although we have stressed the importance of preparing questions in advance, an interview will occasionally take a completely different and more interesting direction. Let's say that you are interviewing the principal of a school about bus safety for children. During the course of the interview, she reveals that two of the bus drivers are on probation for driving violations. You should immediately follow up on this information: "What are the violations?" "What is meant by probation?" "Who made the decision to put them on probation?" One of the advantages of getting information by interview is that the discussion can always take a more interesting and provocative direction. If you stick rigidly to your prepared questions, you can miss some good opportunities.

When you are interviewing, you should watch for nonverbal cues. If the issue is sensitive, is your respondent giving you cues that he or she is dodging the questions? Is he or she avoiding eye contact? Tapping a pen nervously on the desk? Nonverbal cues can often tell you when to follow up on a subject or to steer away from it.

If you are interviewing someone who is on a tight schedule, don't run beyond the time you have scheduled. If you need more time, ask for it at the interviewee's convenience or call back on the telephone to tie up the loose ends. Occasionally, when you listen to your tape or read your notes, you will discover something you missed or something that needs clarifying. The telephone is a good way to get this information after the interview is over.

Once the interview is completed, the interviewee should be thanked. If it was a good interview, don't be afraid to say so. Even people who are frequently interviewed are pleased to hear they have been helpful. Also, let the person know how you plan to use the interview.

Analyzing the Interview

When the interview is over, you should spend some time thinking about how well you did. Your success can be measured by how the interviewee responded to you and whether you got the information you wanted.

You can tell if your questions were well worded by the way the person answered them. If he or she never quite dealt with the points you had expected, the problem may have been with the questions. If he or she asked for clarification, that is another indication your questions weren't well put.

Looking at your notes will tell you whether you were listening carefully. Are your notes confusing? Are there gaps in them? Your notes will also tell you whether you covered the subject thoroughly enough. Sometimes, after an interview is over, an interviewer thinks of all sorts of questions that should have been asked.

Finally, did you conduct the interview in a professional manner? Did you arrange the questions in a logical order beforehand? Had you researched the topic of your interview? Did you know how to run the equipment? The main measure of your professionalism is whether your interviewee took you and your questions seriously.

The Employment Interview

The **employment interview** is an interview used by an employer to determine whether someone is suitable for a job. In an employment interview you have two goals. The first is to distinguish yourself in some way from the other applicants, and the second is to make a good impression in a very short time. The key to reaching both these goals is careful preparation.

Evaluating the Job Description

Usually the first notice of a job comes from some kind of written description— a newspaper advertisement or a request filed with an organization such as a placement service. If you think the job suits your abilities and you want to get an interview, begin by making a list of the major job responsibilities and the skills you need to do the job.[4] For example, let's say you see the following job advertisement and think you want to apply.

*Administrative Assistant to Design Director/department coordinator.
Wanted for art department of weekly magazine. Varied responsibilities,
light typing, processing of all department bills. Good phone manner, organizational skills, quick thinking, some pressure. College graduate.*

In defining this position and the skills needed, your list might look like this:
Major job skills

- Light typing
- Processing of department bills
- Handling phone calls
- Organizing
- Quick thinking under pressure

In assessing the skills needed for this job, consider the following:

- Light typing means that you will not be typing all the time but you should at least know the keyboard and be able to type about 40 words per minute.
- The ad is vague about the processing of department bills, but if you are good with numbers and have some knowledge of bookkeeping, you could probably qualify in this category.
- Handling phone calls requires that you answer the telephone and make calls in a businesslike manner.
- Organizing requires that you be able to find information when it is needed and that you set priorities for the work that should be done first.
- The need for quick thinking and the presence of some pressure implies that this job is in a busy office. In this situation you may be overworked at times and may have to make decisions on your own.

Listing the job responsibilities and the skills needed is a good way for you to discover whether you qualify for a job and whether it's worth your time to apply. If you have a skill for each point in the job description and can back it up with an example (for instance, "When I was a reporter for the campus newspaper, I always had to work under pressure"), you are probably a good candidate for this position. Not only will this assessment of responsibilities and skills help you to decide whether you qualify, but it will also help you to clearly identify how to write a strong letter of application and how to perform effectively if you get an interview.

Preparing a Résumé

A **résumé** is a summary of your professional life. It is written for potential employers, and it should give an idea of your career direction, present your achievements, and cite examples of your skills. If an employer is going through a lot of resumés, he or she may spend little more than twenty or thirty seconds on each one, so it is important that you present yourself in as efficient a way as possible.

In any campus community there are many businesses that offer résumé-writing services. The experts, however, say that the resumes they put together are often more style than substance and that it's better to write your own.[5]

Robert Nesbit of the executive-search firm Korn/Ferry International says that you should follow specific rules in résumé writing:

1. Use white or off-white paper with a simple format and ample white space.
2. Try to put it all on one page.
3. Customize your résumé for each job by emphasizing work experience that is relevant to the job you're seeking.
4. Keep the language simple.
5. Don't exaggerate your experiences. If you accomplished something as a team member, say so.[6]

No standard prescribed format exists for resumes. There are, however, some components that are common to most resumes (see Figure 8.1).

Identification   The top portion of the résumé should have your name, address, and phone number. If you have a temporary and a permanent address and phone number, give both.

Career Objective   Your job objective is extremely important in your resume. If your objective is too vague, it will be meaningless ("seeking a position that will utilize academic achievements"). On the other hand, if you are too specific, you might limit yourself too much. Often, when people are considering several different positions, they will write resumes with different job objectives. Then they can match the job objective with the position for which they are applying.

Education   Your highest degree should be listed first. Begin with the name of the college, followed by the degree, major, and date of graduation. If you are looking for a position where your major might not be relevant, list the job-related courses you have taken. Don't list your grade-point average unless it's above a 3.0.

You don't have to limit yourself to formal degrees in this section. Depending on their relationship to the job you are seeking, you can also list certificates, minors, workshops, honors programs, or study abroad.

Experience   In this section, you should list only the positions that directly relate to your career goals. Usually the most recent job information is listed first. However, if you have had experience that ties in directly with the job you are seeking, you should put that at the top. In addition to jobs you have held, experience may include student teaching, internships, management trainee positions, or significant volunteer experiences. For each position you should list your job title, the organization, its location, and the dates you worked there. After listing these, you should write a job description that includes the skills you used, your responsibilities, and any outstanding results ("increased past sales by 22 percent").

If you haven't had very much professional experience, you should also include summer and part-time jobs.

References   Many students have their references in the placement service on their campus. If this is true in your case, give the name, address, and telephone number of the service. If you don't have a file with a placement service, put "References Furnished Upon Request" at the bottom of your resume.

When you have accomplishments that don't fit into the basic sections of your resume, you can add additional categories. Here are some possibilities:

Special Skills and Interests   High-level skills such as fluency in another language, knowledge of computers, artistic ability, or a pilot's license should be listed in this category. Cite anything that could make you more desirable for this position.

Activities   Extracurricular activities, community involvement, or membership in professional organizations should be included if they are relevant to the job you seek. If you have held a leadership position in any of these activities, mention that too.

Honors and Awards   Include this category if you have received *several* awards. Typical awards and achievements might include appearing on the dean's list or being awarded a scholarship, special recognition on campus, or membership in an honorary society. If you do not have enough of these to justify a separate heading, include them in your education or experience section.

While you are putting your résumé together, you should keep some pointers in mind. Experiment with your headings and text to see what works and looks best. Proofread and check for spelling and grammar.

Once you have completed the first draft of your resume, take a critical look at it and consider these points:

- Have you overused the word "I"?
- Are you absolutely sure of your grammar and spelling?
- Have you been consistent with your use of capital letters and underlining?
- Does your résumé have enough white space to avoid looking crowded?

Once you are satisfied with your résumé's basic format, ask someone with professional experience to read and critique it. Remember that this résumé is going to be advertising *you*. If it's effective, it should open some doors for interviews. (See Figure 8-1.)

The Letter of Application

When you send your résumé to an employer, it should be accompanied by a letter of application, also called a cover letter. This **application letter** introduces you to the employer, tells why you are writing, and emphasizes the contributions you can make to the job. Like the résumé, the application

Figure 8-1
Sample Résumé

CAROLYN WAGNER
P.O. BOX A92
SHERMAN, ME 04777
(207) 555–1609

PROFESSIONAL OBJECTIVE

A challenging office administrator position leading to increased responsibility, advancement, and growth.

EDUCATION

Bachelor of Science Degree in Business Administration, May 1991.
Major: Management Minor: Office Information Management
University of Maine at Machias   GPA: 3.5

RELEVANT COURSEWORK

Administrative Office Management	Business Communication
Business, Professional,	Human Behavior In Organizations
Technical Writing	Public Speaking
Personnel Management	

WORK EXPERIENCE

Job Start Assistant. Resource Development Department, WHCA, Milbridge, ME

January 1990-May 1990. Assisted director with implementation of the Job Start Program, responded to inquiries about the program, consulted with clients personally to provide business technical assistance, compiled a handbook for Business Support Groups, and performed business operation skills such as bookkeeping, marketing, and data management. Used organizational, oral, and written communication skills.

Management Aid. Division of Health Engineering, Maine Human Services, Augusta, ME

May 1989-August 1989. Interviewed engineers to determine a more efficient way of handling the permit process via computer. Used Wang Word Processor and D Base to facilitate the office tasks of generating form letters, permits, and certificates.

Supervisor: Information Management Center, University of Maine/Machias, Machias, ME

September 1988-May 1989. Trained and supervised word processing operators, delegated daily assigments, assisted the operators with various questions and problems, and edited all work processed in the center. (This position was a promotion from word processor in the previous semesters.)

Clerk Typist. Dental Health Programs, University College, Bangor, ME

September 1986-May 1987. Organized the filing system, typed and filed confidential information, utilized PSF:File for data entry, and performed other office-related duties.

COMPUTER EXPERIENCE

Microsoft, Multimate, PFS: File, Wang, and general knowledge of D Base and spreadsheets.

ACTIVITIES

Dormitory Council	Honors Program	Kappa Eta Academic Sorority
Peer Advisor	Special Olympics	Yearbook Staff (Sales)

REFERENCES AVAILABLE UPON REQUEST

letter should sell you to the interviewer and interest him or her in interviewing you.

The application letter usually has three paragraphs. In the first, you should tell why you are writing, name the position you are applying for, and tell how you learned of the opening.

The second paragraph should tell the employer why you are interested in the position, the organization, and its products or services. In this part of the letter it is very important to let the employer know why you are the right person by pointing out how your experience and education tie into the job being advertised. Your résumé gives the details of your background: it's up to your application letter to point out the connection between your background and the employer's needs.

In your closing paragraph, request an appointment for an interview to discuss your qualifications. You may want to give the best times you can be reached by telephone. End the letter by showing appreciation for the employer's time.

The letter should be error-free and neatly typed in business-letter format. Address it to a specific individual with his or her correct title.[7]

The Interview

The big day comes when an employer calls you to schedule an interview. Of all the application letters and résumés the company has received, yours has stood out enough for the employer to want to see you. However, it's likely that he or she is going to interview several other people too. During your interview you are going to have to sell yourself as the best candidate for the position.

Again, you have some work to do.

PREPARING FOR THE INTERVIEW

In preparing for an employment interview, you should find out about the company and what it does. Research findings show that applicants who do their homework about potential employers ask better questions and feel more confident during interviews.[8]

How do you go about this research? Let's say, for example, you are looking at a job in an advertising agency. Are you aware of any of the work it has done? Have you seen its ads or heard its commercials? What are its major accounts? How big is the agency? These are some of the things you might find out before you go to the interview. The interviewer is going to be more impressed by an applicant who can talk about one of the company's ad campaigns than by an applicant who is unfamiliar with any of its work.

Many companies are public—meaning that their stock can be bought by the public. Every public company is required to issue an annual shareholders' report, which can provide valuable information—particularly about profits and losses. If the company is a local one, it has probably been the subject of articles in the local newspaper. The Chamber of Commerce or the Better Business Bureau can also give you information about local businesses. If the company is national, it may have been written about in magazines such as

How can you tell
that this is an
interesting and
lively interview?

Business Week or *Fortune* and in the *Wall Street Journal*. Most businesses are
also covered by trade publications—magazines that concentrate on a particular
line of business. In advertising, for example, the trade publication is called
Advertising Age, and it is likely to be available in your college library. Such
magazines concentrate on trends, and they are an excellent way of finding
out what important things are happening in a particular line of business.
Professional groups—doctors, lawyers, and teachers—also have specialized
magazines that discuss important occupational issues.

INTERVIEW QUESTIONS

Most employment interviews follow a predictable line of questioning. Here
are some kinds of questions you are likely to be asked in a job interview.
Before you go to the interview, you should think about how you would answer
them.

Job Expectations The interviewer will want to find out if what you are
looking for in a job is compatible with the job the company has to offer. To
this end, you will be asked what you want in a job, what kind of job you are
looking for, and whether you would be content in this particular job. The best
way to prepare for these kinds of questions is to study the job description
carefully and see whether your qualifications and expectations match the job

description. Sometimes people go into a job interview thinking they can redefine the job to meet their own needs. For example, if you wanted a job as a copywriter at an advertising agency but the agency had only a secretarial job, taking the job might help get your foot in the door, but it would be unrealistic to think that you are immediately going to be able to write copy. You should also be realistic about how quickly you can advance. If you start as a clerk, you will probably have a long wait before you can become a manager. The job interview is a good time to find out if your expectations are realistic.

Academic Background   The interviewer will want to know whether you have had enough education to do the job. To find this out, he will ask you questions about the schools you attended, the degrees you have, and the grades you got. This is a good time to mention extracurricular activities that might be pertinent to the job. If you are a social work major, for example, and spent time teaching jail inmates to read and write, this is part of your education too.

Knowledge of the Organization   All interviewers will be impressed if you know something about their organization. They assume that if you are interested enough in the job, you will have taken the trouble to find out something about the employer. Sometimes you will be asked a direct question: "Why do you want to work for this company?" An answer might be "I know several people who work here, and they like the company very much" or "I am impressed by your management training program." Even if you are asked no direct questions, you should be prepared to ask some questions yourself about the company or organization. An example might be "Do you have a training program for new employees?" or "I know that you have some excellent computer hardware. Do you have any plans to get into software?"

Work Experience   The interviewer will want to know about other jobs you have had and whether anything in your past work experience might relate to the present job. Even though your past work experience might not be directly related to the job at hand, you should not necessarily assume it is irrelevant. Let's say that you are applying for a job as manager of a local store and your only job experience has been taking junior high students on canoe trips every summer. Although this summer job might not be directly relevant, it would

Try This Try This Try This

After you have finished the final draft of your résumé and have conducted research on the organizations that interest you, try a mock interview with a friend—preferably one who has had some interviewing experience. Give your friend a copy of your résumé beforehand and ask him or her to play the recruiter or employer. Ask for good, tough questions and for a critique after the interview is over. This is a good opportunity for you to think on your feet and to find out how you can improve.

certainly show that you are a responsible person—a characteristic an employer will be looking for in a manager. You should also consider whether any volunteer experience might be relevant to the job. Someone who has served as chairperson for the annual heart fund drive, for example, has a good deal of administrative and management experience that might be useful in many jobs.

Career Goals   Most interviewers will be interested in knowing your short- and long-term goals in relation to the job. Short-term goals concern what you want to do in the next year or so. Long-term goals are directed to a lifetime plan. Typical questions about long-term goals might be "Where do you see yourself ten years from now?" "What kind of career do you want with a company?" Interviewers ask these kinds of questions to discover whether you are thinking about your future, to gauge your ambition, and to see whether you will fit into the company's long-term goals. If you are interviewing for a management trainee position in a bank, for example, the interviewer will try to find out whether you can foresee a long-term career with the bank and whether the bank is justified in putting you in its training program.

Strengths and Weaknesses   Most interviewers will want to find out whether hiring you will enhance the organization. To this end you might be asked directly "What do you see as your greatest strength?" or "What is your greatest

---

Consider This **Consider This** *Consider This*

H O W   T O   D R E S S   F O R   A N   I N T E R V I E W

Your primary goal in dressing for an interview is to feel great about the way you look while projecting an image that matches the requirements of the job and the company.

Go for perfection. Wear professionally pressed clothing in natural fabrics. . . . Don't make a fashion statement. Conservative is the password. Dark blue, gray, and muted plaids helped President Bush get elected—and you're just interviewing for a job.

Redefine cleanliness. Soak in the tub. Polish your glasses and frames.

The interview is not the time to make a personal statement of nonconformity or disagreement with society's concept of professional image.

It's against both federal and moral laws to discriminate based on appearance, but I ask you, how many bankers have full beards? How many female computer representatives wear heavy high-fashion makeup? How many McDonald's employees have three earrings in one ear? Image is important to all companies.

Remember, if you look good, you'll feel good, and that will only help in the job-search process. . . .

Source: John L. LaFevre, "Interviewing: The Inside Story from a College Recruiter," *CPC Annual.*

weakness?" Before you go into an interview, you should think about both of these points in relation to the job being offered. Even if you are not asked directly about your strengths, you should be prepared to sell yourself on your good points during the interview. If on your last job you reorganized a department and improved its efficiency by 50 percent, now is the time to mention it. You should be cautious when replying to questions about weaknesses. You don't want your answers to ruin the possibility of getting a job. The best approach to a weakness is to admit you have it but are working hard to overcome it. For example, "I am not a very fast computer programmer, but I am very good on detail and I expect I will pick up more speed as I get more experience" or "I am not always as well organized as I could be, but I am getting better at setting priorities."

The above kinds of questions will probably make up the bulk of the interview. Since these questions are so often asked, you should think about how you will answer them. The most important thing to remember is that every interview is different: even if the questions are the same, the answers might be different. Your success will depend on how well you can answer in relation to the job being offered.

BEING INTERVIEWED

Once you have researched the company, prepared your résumé, and thought about the questions you are likely to be asked, you are ready for your interview.

Research suggests that the first few minutes of an interview are the most important, for it is then that many interviewers establish their biases and make their decisions.[9] Thus it is important that you make a good impression right from the start. Much of the good impression you convey is nonverbal: being on time, being dressed appropriately, and giving a firm handshake. It will also help if you can appear confident—even though you might not be

---

Consider This Consider This Consider This

*C*ompared to the successful applicants, the unsuccessful applicants used less of the time available to them. Although each interview was scheduled to last 30 minutes, the unsuccessful interviews averaged only 25 minutes of the allotted time. By contrast, interviews of the successful applicants averaged 29.5 minutes. In addition to securing more interview time, the successful applicants spoke a greater percentage of the available period than their unsuccessful counterparts. Only 37% of the words in unsuccessful interviews were spoken by the applicants, while successful applicants talked 55% of the total time. The latter also controlled the interviews to a greater extent, having initiated 56% of their comments whereas the unsuccessful applicants initiated only 36%. Thus, the successful interviewees behaved as active participants in the interviews; the unsuccessful interviewees behaved more as passive respondents.

Source: Lois J. Einhorn, "An Inner View of the Job Interview: An Investigation of Successful Communicative Behaviors," *Communication Education.*

feeling that way. Before you go into an interview, it would be useful to review the material in Chapter 5, "Nonverbal Communication." You are going to be evaluated on your personality as well as your skills for the job. When William N. Yeomans asked managers from several companies what they looked for in a candidate for a job, they mentioned personal characteristics, such as appearance, enthusiasm, tact, and honesty. Although they mentioned job-related characteristics such as work experience, leadership, and communication skills, no one listed "a demonstrated ability to do the job."[10] This would indicate that a personality that fits the job is even more important than specific job skills.

SAMPLE EMPLOYMENT INTERVIEW

Like many other structured forms of communication, the employment interview has an opening, a body, and a closing. Let's look at some of the things you should do in an interview and apply them to an interview situation. In the following example, Pam Harris is being interviewed by John Lopez, the general manager of a radio station, for the job of radio news reporter.

THE OPENING

(Pam Harris is shown into Lopez's office by the secretary.)

JL: Hi. I'm John Lopez. You must be Pam. Come on in and have a seat.

PH: It's good to meet you. I've heard you a lot on the air and it's nice to see you in person. You have an attractive facility here. I hear that you have just moved into the building.

JL: Yes, we're finally getting settled down. I think it is going to work out well for us. We have a lot more space.

Notice that the beginning of this interview is mostly small talk. The purpose of small talk is to set up a friendly atmosphere and to enable both participants to feel comfortable. In this case, Harris takes the lead in suggesting a subject for small talk—the new building. By talking about this, she also suggests she knows something about the station.

THE BODY

JL: Do you know anything about our operation here?

PH: Well, I know that you operate on 5,000 watts and cover a two-county area. You seem to have a lot of news coverage. I have heard a lot of local news on your station.

JL: Yes, we have a lot of pride in our local news. We have two full-time reporters, and with this job we will be adding a third. What experience have you had?

Much of the body of the interview will concentrate on Harris's experience and what she knows. When she gets a question about what she knows about the station, she is able to answer because she has prepared for this interview.

PH: I've worked as a stringer on the radio station in my hometown. While I was in college, I covered local radio news for the campus radio station, and in my senior year I was the radio news director. I have also done some reporting for the campus newspaper and television station, but I prefer radio.

JL: Most people like television better. Why do you prefer radio?

PH: Radio is more exciting. If you have an important story, you can get it on the air right away. Newspapers are too slow, and television news often waits for videotape.

JL: I agree. I always feel proud when we beat the newspaper on a story. What kind of technical experience have you had?

PH: I can run a simple radio board, and I know how to run cassette and cart machines. I don't feel intimidated by equipment. I like to figure out how it works.

JL: Have you had any experience with reel-to-reel recorders?

PH: Not very much. I have used them once or twice, but most of my experience has been with cassette machines.

JL: Do you know how to splice tape?

PH: I did it once, so I understand how it works; but I would need more experience before I got very efficient.

JL: Have you done any mixing?

PH: I'm not sure. Could you be a little more specific? (Lopez explains mixing.) No, I haven't had any experience with mixing. We had only very simple equipment.

JL: What do you think are your greatest strengths in working in radio?

PH: I seem to have a strong sense for a news story. While I was news director for the radio station, we scooped the local media several times.

Answers to questions in an interview should be thorough but to the point. When Harris is asked about her experience, she gives some details about her radio experience since that is what the job is all about. She briefly mentions her newspaper and television experience—just to show she has had additional reporting experience.

Honesty is important. Harris admits to limited experience with tape recorders and splicing. On the other hand, she says she is not apprehensive about working with unfamiliar equipment. Since the employment interview attempts to find an applicant whose experience and education will meet the needs of the job, some applicants will discover that they are not qualified.

Notice that Harris asks for clarification when she doesn't understand the question. Most interviewers do not expect you to know everything. You often appear in a better light if you admit what you do not know.

When Harris is asked about her strengths, she answers with something that is really important for a reporter—her sense of news.

JL: What do you think your weaknesses are?

PH: I am not as fast as I would like to be. I've been picking up speed as a writer, but I'm still pretty slow with some of the technical stuff. I'm sure I'll get a lot faster when I work with it every day.

> When she mentions her weaknesses, she expresses confidence that it is only a temporary problem that will be overcome with more experience.

JL: I guess we've pretty much covered all the facts. If we were to hire you, what would be your goals on this job?

PH: My main goal is to learn to cover stories faster and more efficiently. Once I have learned this, I would like to be a radio news director. Some day I would like to work in news in a big city.

> Lopez is trying to find out how Harris will fit into the organization and to get some sense of her long-range plans. Most interviewers would not hire someone who was going to leave the organization in a short time. On the other hand, the interviewer might have a job that is basically for a beginner and might not want to hire someone who plans to stay in it forever.

THE CLOSING

JL: I think I've covered everything I need to know. Do you have any questions?

PH: Yes. I have a few questions about the station. (Harris asks the following questions, and Lopez responds to them: Do you have any research on your audience for news?
Are most of your newscasts sponsored? How well do you compare with other stations in the ratings?)

> Note that Lopez asks Harris if she has any questions. Every interviewer is likely to do this. This is the time to ask some questions about the company or organization. In this interview, Harris asks some business-related questions—showing that she knows that news is just one part of a station's business.

JL: Thanks for coming in. I will be making my decision by Monday. I will call you then.

PH: Thank you for the interview. I'm glad I have had a chance to meet you and visit the station. I'll look forward to hearing from you.

> At the end of the interview, the interviewer often mentions what will happen next. In this case, Lopez lets Harris know when he is going to be making his decision. If the interviewer does not raise this issue, the person being interviewed should. Like the opening of the interview, the closing will probably end with small talk.

The Follow-up Letter

After every interview, you should write a follow-up letter. This letter shows your interest in the organization and helps to keep your name in the employer's mind.

Follow-up letters are generally short and to the point. To follow the standard five-step format, you should (1) thank the employer for the interview, (2) state your interest in one or two specific aspects of the position or the company discussed in the interview, (3) supply any additional information that was requested during the interview, (4) express your continuing interest in the position, and (5) thank the interviewer for the interview.

SUMMARY

An interview is a series of questions and answers, usually between two people, which has the purpose of getting and understanding information about a particular subject.

Interviews can be used for a wide variety of purposes, including speeches, group projects, and research papers. Careful preparation is essential. The person conducting the interview should gather background information—both about the person being interviewed and about the topic. Questions should be prepared beforehand, and the interviewer should strike a balance between informational and thought-provoking questions.

Before the interview, the interviewer should decide whether she is going to use tape or take notes. Tape offers the advantage of greater accuracy, and it frees the interviewer from note taking. The disadvantages of tape are that it is time-consuming to listen to after the interview has been completed and that some interviewees will react differently if they are being taped.

Gaining employment usually involves a several-step process. You begin by evaluating the job description; then you write an application letter and a résumé that are tailored to the position. Before going to an employment interview, it's important that you research the organization that is offering the job.

During the employment interview you should be prepared to talk about all the following: your job expectations, your academic and work background, your knowledge of the organization, your career goals and your strengths and weaknesses as a potential employee. After the interview is over, you should write a follow-up letter indicating that you are still interested in working for the organization. The letter should also thank the interviewer for the interview.

FURTHER READING

BEATTY, RICHARD H. *The Five-Minute Interview: A New and Powerful Approach to Interviewing*. New York: Wiley, 1986. Although the title suggests that the interview advocated here lasts but five minutes, the author's position is that this is how long the *decisive* part of the interview lasts. Five minutes puts the job interviewee in proper control—"to position yourself as the one applicant who can take the company where it wants to go." This is a step-by-step, how-to approach.

BOLLES, RICHARD NELSON. *What Color Is Your Parachute?* Berkeley, CA: Ten Speed Press, 1991. (First edition, 1972; published annually.) This is a complete guide to the job hunt. Although more than about just interviewing, the job hunt *is* more than just interviewing! Bolles includes an interview checklist and a complete discussion of salary negotiation. In this practical book, Bolles supports the theme that those who get hired are often those who know the most about how to get hired. Job hunting is more than winning interviews.

BRADY, JOHN. *The Craft of Interviewing*. New York: Random House, 1977. Brady covers all aspects of the interview process—getting the interview, doing research, handling the subject face-to-face, hurdling hazards, getting tough, taking notes, taping, concluding the interview, verifying it, and writing it up. Designed especially for journalists, but useful for everyone.

DONAGHY, WILLIAM C. *The Interview: Skills and Applications*. Glenview, IL: Scott, Foresman, 1984. Donaghy solidly grounds his book in current interviewing theory, but he emphasizes the acquisition of skills and the practical application of those skills in a variety of interviewing situations. He includes numerous exercises and activities in this very thorough textbook.

DOWNS, CAL W., G. PAUL SMEYAK, AND ERNEST MARTIN. *Professional Interviewing*. New York: Harper & Row, 1980. What are some of the most important decisions that need to be made in conducting interviews? The authors of this work provide some basic behavioral research findings useful in making decisions. This is a very thorough, skills-oriented textbook.

HUNT, GARY T., AND WILLIAM F. EADIE. *Interviewing: A Communication Approach*. New York: Holt, Rinehart and Winston, 1987. A basic textbook on interviewing that covers fundamental communication skills such as planning, managing, and interpreting, and then covers types of interviews, such as informational, employment, persuasive, and helping. A straightforward, no-nonsense textbook.

MEDLEY, H. ANTHONY. *Sweaty Palms: The Neglected Art of Being Interviewed*. Berkeley, CA: Ten Speed Press, 1984. How do you conduct yourself in an interview? What do you do? How can you prepare? What will the interviewer ask? What should you say? What should you ask? What should you wear? This book helps interviewees overcome the fear of the unknown.

SINCOFF, MICHAEL Z., AND ROBERT S. GOYER. *Interviewing*. New York: Macmillan, 1984. This textbook is designed for the beginning student as well as the working manager of people. The authors begin with a systematic description of the process that is intended to result in communication, including the generation, transmission, and perception of messages and the evocation of desired meaning. They deal with both the event and the process of interviewing.

STEWART, CHARLES J., AND WILLIAM B. CASH, JR. *Interviewing: Principles and Practices*, 6th ed. Dubuque, IA: Brown, 1991. This is a complete, research-based textbook that includes information on both the general and specific aspects of interviewing. The authors offer a readable approach to preparing and structuring interviews.

Communicating in Groups

Chapter 9

Small Groups

CHAPTER OBJECTIVES	KEY TERMS
After reading this chapter, you should be able to:	brainstorming
	cohesiveness
1. Describe the situations in which group decision making is superior to individual decision making.	commitment
	conflict
	consensus
2. List the characteristics of a small group.	groupthink
	norms
3. Tell the difference between norms and rules.	questions of fact
	questions of policy
4. Explain how the physical setting will help a group to function better.	questions of value
	rules
5. Explain how a group becomes cohesive.	small group
	substantive conflict
6. List and explain the steps in group problem solving.	
7. Explain how conflict can have some value for a group.	

*A*n issue of a city newspaper announces the following coming events:

- **WORK FOR HUMAN RIGHTS.** Attend an Amnesty International meeting. March 11, 7 P.M., at St. Paul's Church.

- **WORLD TRAVELERS ANONYMOUS.** Addicted to travel? Meet others. Monthly traveler's slide show/meeting. Friday, March 15, 7 P.M., Lakeview Library.

- **THE EXCHANGE**, a support group for women in business, will meet at 6:00 P.M., Tuesday, March 11, at the Women's Business Development Center.

A campus paper announces upcoming events:

- The **RECREATION CLUB** will meet Monday at 4 P.M. in Zimmerli, Room 27.

- Members of the **NEWMAN CLUB** will meet in the Newman Center at 7 P.M., Wednesday, to plan a retreat.

If people from another planet were to land on U.S. soil and pick up a newspaper, they might think that Americans spend most of their time in meetings. They wouldn't be far from wrong. All over town and all over campus people are meeting for business, political, educational, religious, social, and personal reasons. Regardless of the purpose of these meetings, they have something in common. They all bring together **small groups**—gatherings of three to thirteen members who meet to do a job or solve a problem.

Small groups are essential in helping society function efficiently, and many of us spend several hours each week communicating in such groups. We might take part in a seminar discussion, talk with a group of coworkers about improving job conditions, or discuss with family members how to make the household run more efficiently. Many of us belong to service or professional groups. Many of these groups are involved both with completing tasks and with social life.

Whatever groups we belong to, we want them to function efficiently. But participation should also be pleasurable; we want to meet, get on with the job, and then spend some time socializing with other group members.

This chapter and the next one discuss how groups work. In this chapter, we note the characteristics of small groups and how such groups go about solving a problem.[1] In the next chapter, we concentrate on how one can effectively lead or participate in a group.

Why Discuss?

When a group has a job to do, its main form of communication is discussion. Group members meet to exchange information and ideas in an effort to better understand a particular issue or situation. A band boosters group discusses how to raise money for band uniforms; the tenants' committee discusses ways

Try This Try This Try This

*L*ist all the groups you are a part of right now. Then answer the following questions about each group:

1. Is the purpose of the group mostly social, or does it meet because it has a job to do?
2. What do you have in common with the other group members?
3. If you were to drop out of this group, how would your life change? Do you think the group would continue to influence you?
4. How would your life be different if you didn't belong to any group?

of improving the apartment complex; the social committee discusses security arrangements for an upcoming concert.

Not all people like discussion Many find it time-consuming and boring. What, then, is the value of discussion?

In a democratic society, one of the first assumptions is that no one person will make the decisions for everyone. Discussion is a way for everyone to participate and be heard. It is a forum where ideas are proposed and then modified in response to group feedback.

Group decision making is often superior to individual decision making. Those who study small groups have found that people who work in groups accomplish more than people who work alone.[2] Other research has found that students learn better in classroom discussion groups. When exam times come, they will do better and find the task more enjoyable if they join a study group.

Often a group can do a job more efficiently than an individual. The study group is a good example: each member of the group, rather than outline every chapter, can outline one and share it with other members. Or take the case of the band boosters, the group that is trying to earn money for new high school band uniforms. This is clearly a group project; no individual can do the job as well. First the group talks about how to raise the money. Then individual members help in the fund-raising efforts. If this were left to one individual, it would be an overwhelming job.

If you have worked in a group, you probably have discovered that motivation increases when everyone works together.[3] If five roommates decide to redecorate their apartment, it is much more fun if everyone pitches in and helps. Also, the five roommates are likely to come up with more ideas about how to do things than if only one person takes on the project. People are also likely to be more motivated when others are depending on them.[4] If one roommate, for example, has to strip the windowsills before the others can paint, he or she is likely to get the job done so that the others can go ahead with what they have to do.

When people work in groups, they have opportunities to ask questions when an idea or issue is not clear. In addition to learning faster, group members are able to absorb more information.[5] Not only does more information become available, but group members can help decide which information is important.

We can see how this works in a practical situation. Let's say that the state has a new recycling law that says all individuals and organizations must recycle aluminum, glass, and paper. Your university appoints ten people to a group to work out the details of how this will be done. The group is made up of hall directors, students, faculty, and buildings and grounds staff. When the group meets, its members agree that recycling will work best if people on campus don't have to expend very much effort. They decide that the most effective way to organize recycling is to provide places on every floor of every campus building where people can put things for recycling. Because nobody knows how many collection areas this will require, the group members decide to split up. Faculty will scout the floors and best collection sites in all the classroom buildings, the hall directors will look at the dorms, and the students will check out all the remaining buildings. The staff from buildings and grounds is assigned to find a centralized location for the collection of all recycled materials. Because the members of the committee split up the jobs, no one is responsible for too much work. When they meet again, they will have enough information for the group to work toward the next phase.

When you see how effectively a group can solve a problem, it's no surprise that groups are so important. In one study of 200 top- and mid-level managers in eight different organizations, the researchers found that senior managers spent an average of 23 hours a week in meetings and midlevel managers 11 hours.[6] If a quarter to a half of each work week is devoted to meetings, it's important that we all learn how to work in groups.

Characteristics of Small Groups

All small groups have common characteristics. They reflect the culture in which they occur; they have **norms**—expectations that group members have of how other members will behave; they have **rules**—formal and structured directions for behavior. Let's look at each of these.

Cultural Values

When Americans think they should solve a problem at work or in the community, their first instinct is to form a group. Once the group begins to

---

Try This Try This Try This

*H*ere is an exercise that will let you see how decisions are made on your own campus. Interview all the instructors you have this semester to find out how many meetings they attended on campus over the past week, how long each meeting ran, and what the purpose was of each meeting. From their replies, what can you conclude about how decisions are made at your college?

function, everyone plays a more or less equal role. If someone wants to talk, he or she is given a chance. If everyone in the group cannot agree on a solution, then the group takes a vote and the majority will decide.

This kind of group-forming and group-operating behavior is so natural that we don't think twice about it: it is part of our culture. We should not assume, however, that other cultures work the same way. When one of our authors asked a Polish friend why the Poles didn't organize child care cooperatives, her friend replied, "In Poland, we never work in groups."

Most societies have some dominant kind of problem-solving mechanism, but it may differ greatly from culture to culture. In many countries men are much more likely than women to make decisions about the workplace and the community. In many of these same countries, one must be an elder member of the group before he or she can participate in decision making.

Seventy percent of the world lives in a collectivist society—a society where loyalties are to the family or, more broadly, to the clan, the tribe, or the caste.[7] In these groups problem solving and decision making is most likely to occur within the family or the clan. If a group were formed that included members from different clans or families, the way the members of each particular group worked to solve a problem would depend on how they perceived the solution would affect their families or clans.

Americans who join a group in another country cannot assume that the group will function in the same way that an American group does. In a campus setting, if American students work with international students, they should also be sensitive to the different ways the group work may be perceived. In some cases it might be appropriate to explain how American groups work.

Group Norms

Norms are the expectations group members have of how other members will behave, think, and participate. These norms are informal—they are not written down. Members assume that others understand the norms and will follow them.

A college seminar is a good example of how norms operate. At the beginning of the semester, the instructor does not have to tell class members how to behave. She assumes that students will attend each session, speak in turn, buy the textbook, and generally act in a polite and responsible manner—in other words, that they will follow the norms of behavior for a seminar.

In familiar settings, we take group norms for granted. But if we join a group where the norms are not so obvious, we might just sit back and listen until we figure out what the group norms are. For example, a new person appointed to a board of directors will probably try to get a sense of how the group operates before he participates.

Norms are important because they give a group some structure. If members know how to behave, the group will function more efficiently. Also, outsiders can look at the group's norms to see whether they want to join the group. If, for example, you feel comfortable only in informal settings, you will probably not want to join a group that has numerous rituals and ceremonies.

Some groups are not very specific about their norms. It is assumed that because you join the group, you believe in its norms. You show that you believe in the group by attending meetings from time to time. Often a task-oriented group's main norm is to get the job done.

Group Rules

Unlike norms, **rules** are formal and structured directions for behavior. In many cases, groups follow rules such as those in *Robert's Rules of Order*. These rules tell what jobs members should do, how meetings should be conducted, how motions should be introduced, and so on. The rules help a meeting to progress and ensure that everyone can be heard but that no one person will monopolize the floor. Quite often a group will appoint a parliamentarian to see that the rules are properly interpreted and followed.

Small-Group Effectiveness

Why do some groups succeed and others fail? Why do some come up with creative solutions for problems while others flounder for answers? Why do some groups have members who get along and other groups have members who are always fighting?

Research shows that effective small groups have certain common characteristics: they have a sense of solidarity, they are able to focus on their task, and they have a task that is appropriate for their particular group.[8]

Solidarity can come from sharing common interests (doll collecting, skiing), from knowing each other at work, or from sharing some social time together before and after group meetings.

Focus comes from a leader or member who tries to keep the group directed toward its subject. This is the person who says, "That's an interesting point, but our problem is to . . . ."

Appropriateness occurs when a group and its task are well-matched. For example, a student group cannot solve the problem of a deficit in the university budget. However, it might be able to solve a problem like screening strangers who enter dormitories or finding a better way to publicize elections for student senators.

In addition to having solidarity, focus, and task appropriateness, a truly effective group must be of a workable size, must meet in appropriate surroundings with suitable seating arrangements, and must inspire its members to feel cohesiveness and commitment.

Workable Size

A group works best when all its members can communicate and interact with one another. For a group to be effective, it should have anywhere from three to thirteen members. Research indicates that an ideal size for a group is five members.

If a group consists of too many members, it cannot work effectively to solve problems or do the job at hand. In such cases, it should be broken up into smaller groups—each with a job to do. The student government, for example, is usually broken down into committees: the Social Committee, the Food Advisory Committee, the Constitutional Revision Committee, and so on. The committees then study the issues and make recommendations to the larger body, the student government.

A group may be too large if all members do not have an opportunity to speak or if all members do not participate in group decisions or actions. When this occurs, it is time to break the group into still smaller units. With the student Social Committee, for example, some members could check out the availability of certain musical groups, while other members could conduct a poll to see which musicians the students would like to have on campus.

Groups can also be too small. When there is a lot of information to gather or when the task requires specialized skill or knowledge from its members, it is important to have enough members to do the job. For example, if a department sets up a computer lab, it is going to have to make many decisions. Some people might be assigned to decide the best kinds of computers for the lab; some might look for a place where the lab could be put; others might be assigned to find the best software packages. If there are enough members to investigate each of these areas, no single person will have too much to do.

An Appropriate Meeting Place

The place where a group meets will often influence the general atmosphere of the meeting. A group that meets in a classroom or a conference room will probably be more formal than a group that meets in someone's room or apartment.

The meeting place can be chosen on the basis of who the group members are and what they want to accomplish. Members who know each other well might want to meet in someone's home; when members do not know each other well or if the group wants to continue to attract new participants, it would be better off meeting in a public place.

Sometimes the meeting place will be determined by what the group wants to accomplish. The local government study group, for example, has to meet in City Hall so that members of the public can attend. The literacy council meets in the public library because it stores its materials there.

Suitable Seating Arrangements

Seating of group members should not be left to chance, with each member choosing a chair. Donald C. Stone, a professor of public service, believes that seating is important if people are going to pay attention at meetings.[9] For small groups, Stone recommends seating people where they can all see one another's faces. A circular table would serve this function, as would classroom desks or small tables placed in a circle. For larger groups, Stone recommends a U-shaped arrangement of tables. In this arrangement people should sit only on the *outside* of the U. Otherwise, they will have their backs to one another.

Stone also makes recommendations about chairs. The perfect chair, he says, is one that has a little padding on the seat. If the chairs have hard seats,

Does the seating
arrangement tell
you the probable
leader in this
group?

people will not be comfortable in them for very long; if they're too soft, group members might be tempted to doze off.

Cohesiveness and Commitment

As a positive force, **cohesiveness** is the feeling of attraction that group members have toward one another.[10] It is the group's ability to stick together, to work together as a group, and to help one another as group members. **Commitment** is the willingness of members to work together to complete the group's task. When members are committed, the group is likely to be cohesive. There are few more powerful and satisfactory feelings than the feeling of belonging to a group and of being loyal to that group.

Although cohesiveness is often a matter of group chemistry, an effective group leader can help cohesiveness to develop when the group meets for the first few times. A good leader will make certain that all members are introduced and, if appropriate, are given a chance to say something about themselves. Cohesiveness will also be helped if members have a chance to do a little socializing before and after the meeting. Finally, during the discussion, a good leader will try to draw out the quieter members. The more everyone participates, the better the chance for group unity to develop.

Groupthink

Cohesive groups often show signs of unity. For example, the campus radio station staff wears T-shirts with the station logo. They show mutual support by filling in for each other on broadcasting shifts, and they help newcomers learn their jobs. Many of the group members form lasting friendships and spend free time together.

Sometimes a group can become too cohesive—so much so that it isn't open to new ideas or it will not let new members participate. Irving Janis says that these groups suffer from **groupthink**—a group dysfunction in which the preservation of harmony becomes more important than the critical examination of ideas.[11] When groupthink takes over, certain conditions are present.[12] The group ignores or discounts negative information ("Even if there is not enough money in the church budget for a new organ, we will come up with it somehow."). Members might ignore the ethical consequences of their decisions ("Let's not take this issue to the department. They'll just argue about it."). The group stereotypes members of other groups or people who do not belong to their own group (The coaches at the university say, "The Athletic Policy Committee is made up of people who could never get on a team."). If a group member tries to introduce an idea that goes against groupthink, the group uses peer pressure ("Are you for us or against us?").

Ideally, cohesiveness should be a positive force that helps group members work together. This cohesiveness, however, should permit a free flow of new ideas and the opportunity for any group member to challenge ideas that are not working or might not work in the future.

Discussion in Groups

Most groups that work efficiently use some kind of structure to discuss a problem. Many structures work equally well: what is important is that the structure helps the group to focus on the problem. Many groups use a sequence of steps that is similar to the one you see in Figure 9-1. Let's look at each of these steps in some detail.

Choosing a Topic

If you are in a class, you are often required to pick a topic your group can discuss. How do you choose a topic? How do you find a subject that all group members will find interesting enough to work on?

Your first approach might be to look at your own school. Are there any problems or improvements your group might like to tackle? How's the housing? Does registration run smoothly? Does the bookstore have fair prices? Is the library open at convenient times? Any of these questions might lead to an interesting discussion.

Take a look at the community. Are there any problems there? How do students get along with the local townspeople? Are students good neighbors? Do the banks cash out-of-town checks without adding a service charge? Do the local merchants realize how important students are to the economy of the town? Are there issues in the city council or county commissioner's office that might affect the school?

If your group is interested in attacking a broader social issue, the supply is almost limitless. Nuclear weapons, abortion, and federal spending are all issues that have been hotly debated through the years and will continue to be debated in the future. Discussing one of these topics in your group might be a good way for everyone to become informed about an important issue.

When a group cannot find a topic that all members consider interesting, it should try brainstorming. In **brainstorming** all members of the group throw out ideas—however far out they might seem. The goal of brainstorming is for the group to be as creative as possible. No one should make judgments about the ideas during the brainstorming session. If members fear that their ideas might be condemned, they will be less willing to share some of their wilder thoughts.

Once the group runs out of ideas, it should stop brainstorming and take a look at the topics it has generated. Sometimes one idea is so good that everyone says, "That's it." More commonly, however, the group will have to

Figure 9-1
Solving a Problem

1. Choose a Topic   2. Identify the Problem   3. Analyze the Problem   4. Find and Evaluate Solutions   5. Choose a Solution

evaluate the ideas. Each topic should be assessed in terms of whether all members are willing to work on it and whether it can be narrowed enough to permit comprehensive research. For example, taking on the problems of the country's landfills (garbage dumps) is too big a job. However, the group might be able to research and discuss the problems with the local landfill.

Identifying the Problem

Once the group has a topic, it should work toward identifying a specific problem. At this point, much of the work focuses on narrowing the problem so that it can be covered thoroughly. For example, let's say the group wants to work on the subject of recycling. Since there is an enormous amount of material on this subject, members will have to decide which aspect of recycling they want to work with. Someone in the group who has taken a chemistry class mentions the problem of throwing out household products that contain dangerous chemicals. After some discussion, the group decides that this is an interesting problem they would like to try to solve.

The most important thing the group can do in this stage is to identify a problem that is manageable. One of the biggest mistakes groups make is choosing a problem that is so broad that it cannot be adequately covered.

Analyzing the Problem

THE FIRST QUESTIONS

Groups can take several approaches to analyzing problems. Sometimes it is useful to know what has caused the problem; other times it's enough to

How often do you work in small groups at your job? What kinds of problems do you solve with these groups?

acknowledge that the problem exists. For example, a group that wants to raise money to send poor children to summer camp doesn't need to explore why these children cannot afford to pay their own way. However, a group interested in looking at mental health on campus might find it useful to see how many students are using the counseling center.

Before making a final choice of topics, a group might want to find out how extensive the problem is and how many people are affected by it. For instance, students might object when the library cuts out its Saturday morning hours. However, if the group finds that only five to ten students studied in the library for the past three Saturday mornings, they should conclude that the problem isn't worth their time.

The group should also ask whether anyone is trying to solve the problem now or has tried to solve it in the past. For example, if the group wants to solve the problem of inadequate parking on campus, it can be sure that somewhere, sometime, someone else has worked on this problem. Sometimes the group can add to the work that other people have already done; other times the group might have to look for a new problem if it can't come up with new insights.

Once the group has gone through this initial analysis, it should decide whether to proceed or to find a new topic. If it decides to proceed, it's ready to begin defining terms.

DEFINING TERMS

The group should define any terms related to their problem that might be vague or ambiguous. For example, a classroom group decided that the campus mailroom took too long to deliver mail. Since individual members in the group defined "too long" in various ways, the group had to arrive at a precise meaning for the term. After some discussion they agreed that *too long* was anything over 24 hours. A community group that wanted to start a program to teach illiterate persons how to read and write first had to define *illiterate*. Did it apply only to people who could not read or write? What about a person

---

Try This Try This Try This

*H*ere is a list of possible discussion topics. Which words and phrases need defining?

1. Should parents who send their children to private schools receive tuition tax credits?
2. Should welfare mothers receive federal money for abortions?
3. Should the government limit nuclear weapons?
4. Should the government prohibit broadcasters from showing violent programs on television?
5. Should affirmative action guidelines be allowed to discriminate against men?
6. Should the solid waste authority make use of the country's landfill?

who could do some reading and writing but not enough to function in ordinary society? From a practical point of view, was this person also illiterate?

SEEKING OUT INFORMATION

To understand a problem fully, a group will need to seek outside information. The kind of information will vary depending on the problem or task. To get information, individual members may each investigate a different aspect of the problem. First they might decide to interview people who have had experience with the problem. For example, if they were trying to find out why library hours had been cut, one group member could interview the director of the library and others could interview students or faculty to see if they are affected by the reduced hours.

Many subjects require research that extends beyond personal experience. The group that is discussing the problem of harmful household products being dumped in landfills would find it useful to interview an expert, such as a chemistry professor. Groups can also find background information on their subjects in the library. Chapter 12 has many suggestions on library research.

A group will work more efficiently if every member prepares for each meeting. Then when the group meets, all members will be ready for discussion and able to move on to the next task.

DECIDING ON THE WORDING OF THE FINAL QUESTION

Once the problem is analyzed, the next step is to phrase it as a question. A well-worded question should summarize the group's problem; it should be simply and clearly worded; it should focus on a single central idea. It should use neutral terminology and present a specific problem for the group to solve. Depending on the topic, it should take the form of a question of fact, a question of value, or a question of policy.

Questions of fact deal with what is true and what is false. Examples of these questions might be: "What is the most efficient fuel for heating a house: wood, coal, gas, or oil?" "Does alcohol consumption harm a fetus?" "How can our group invest its money to get the highest interest rate?"

Questions of value are questions of whether something is good or bad, desirable or undesirable. Examples are: "Are student foreign exchange programs desirable?" "Is it a good idea to permit freshmen to have cars on campus?" "Are coed dorms desirable?"

Questions of policy are about actions that might be taken in the future. Such questions are often asked in institutional settings, such as schools, businesses, or organizations, and they usually include the word "should": "Should all students be required to take two years of a foreign language?" "Should the company ban smoking in common work areas?" "Should the college build a new football stadium?"

Note that many questions of value also involve policy, and vice versa. For example, "Should the college build a new football stadium?" is a question of policy, but it also has a question of value built into it: "Is a new football stadium desirable?"

When a group is engaged in fact finding, it is most likely to use questions of fact. If some students, for example, are curious about how much money is spent on college athletics, some of their fact-finding questions might be: "What percentage of the student activity fee is spent on athletics?" "What percentage of the total college budget is spent on athletics?" "What percentage of salaries paid at the college goes to coaches?" These and other fact-finding questions will help them to gather information about how much money is budgeted for athletics.

When a group is going to make recommendations, it will use questions of value or questions of policy. A group considering the parking problem on campus might ask: "Should freshmen be permitted to bring cars on campus?" "Should faculty and staff be given the first choice of parking spots?" "Should everyone be required to pay for parking stickers?" Research into these questions will help the group move to the point where it can make recommendations.

Finding and Evaluating Solutions

Most problems do not have a single easy solution. Sometimes there are a numer of alternatives, and the way a group looks at these alternatives is an important factor in the group's effectiveness. Not only must a group suggest alternatives that are realistic and acceptable, but it must also look at both the negative and the positive consequences of all the alternatives.

Other times a group has difficulty finding appropriate solutions. If members cannot come up with good solutions when they work together, they may find it helpful to work separately for awhile, with each member coming up with two or three solutions to present at the next meeting. Some research has shown that when people work alone, they often come up with more innovative ideas than they would in a group.[13]

Sometimes a group can think of several solutions, but some will have to be discarded because they are impractical. In a group that wanted to teach adults to read and write, for example, someone suggested that unemployed elementary school teachers should be hired to teach illiterate adults. Although everyone agreed this was a good idea, no one could find a way to get the money to pay the teachers.

To see if their solutions are practical, the group should list each one along with its advantages and disadvantages. Some of the questions a group can ask about proposed solutions include: Will the solution solve the problem? Is it practical? Is permission necessary to put the solution into effect? Who will implement the solution? How much money will it cost? How much time will it take? If a solution doesn't pass such scrutiny, the group will have to keep working until it finds one that does.

Ideally the group should work toward **consensus**—the point at which all group members agree. If this is impossible, they will have to choose their solutions by the majority vote. Some groups decide on a solution too quickly because they want to get the task done. This is a mistake: a group is only as good as its solution.

Conflict in Groups

When individuals meet in a group to solve a problem, there's no guarantee of agreement. **Conflict**—differing and incompatible ideas among group members—might arise at any stage of discussion: in defining the problem, in deciding how to go about solving it, or in choosing the solution.

Group conflict generally occurs for one of several reasons. The first, and perhaps the easiest to solve, is conflict about procedure. How often should the group meet? Should it use parliamentary procedure? What form should the minutes take?

To keep such conflict from occurring, the group should discuss and resolve issues of procedure at its first meeting. If it does so, it is not likely to face further conflict in this area.

The second source of conflict is the desire of individual members for power. Research has found that in business and corporate settings a group often becomes a focal point for power struggles.[14] However, power struggles are not so common in classroom groups. If one person wants power, the problem is often solved by making him or her chair. If this doesn't solve the problem and members continue their power struggle, the group will probably not work very efficiently.

The third source of conflict, and one of the greatest in classroom groups, is that some members often work harder than others. When a lot of work must be done and some do very little, the harder workers feel anger and hostility—especially if the group is working for a grade. Like power struggles, this kind of conflict is difficult to resolve. Since few students are willing to tell the instructor about such inequality, their only hope is to confront the group members who are not working and use peer pressure to persuade them to change. If this approach doesn't work, it might console them to know that most instructors have a good idea of who does their work and who doesn't.

Although these three kinds of conflicts can interfere with group work, not all conflict is harmful. The fourth kind of conflict, conflict about substantive issues, can be rewarding. Let's look at this area more closely.

The Value of Substantive Conflict

Substantive conflict occurs when people have different reactions to an idea. It is likely to occur when any important and controversial idea is being discussed. As in all exchanges of ideas, people's opinions and perceptions are influenced by their upbringing, education, and experience. These perceptions cause them to react differently to ideas and can create conflict in a group. For example, a classroom group is assigned the question of whether a physician should be able to help a suffering patient commit suicide. Even though group members may not have read anything on this subject, when they hear the discussion question, they are still likely to have opinions based on their perceptions. Ricardo, 18 years old and a devout Catholic, is shocked by the possibility. He thinks, "What's there to discuss? Everyone should be against this idea." However, Mary, another group member, who is 40 years old and has returned to school, has another reaction. She thinks, "I wish someone had helped my mother to die. She went through terrible suffering the last weeks of her life."

Although two group members start out strongly disagreeing, they will not necessarily continue to do so. When the group members begin their research, they read current cases and report their findings to the group: one member finds a news story of a retired physician who rigged up a machine which enabled a woman who was suffering from cancer but who was not his patient to kill herself. Another student discovers the case of a doctor who told his patient how many barbiturates she would need to kill herself. The doctor had been treating this patient for many years and knew that her disease would not respond to treatment.

As the group discovers this information, Mary and Ricardo find that because they have more information, their opinions are beginning to shift. Mary realizes that a physician-aided suicide may take different forms, some less preferable than others. Ricardo is also adjusting his point of view. Mary has told the group about her mother's suffering, and Ricardo, finding himself very moved by her account, begins to question his previous position.

However this group resolves its question, the conflicts of substance between Mary and Ricardo have had a good effect on the group—especially since both have been willing to hear new information and listen to different points of view. By the time the group completes the project, it will have a better understanding of the ideas and can make a better decision. Also, because the group has worked together to learn, and the learning has been rewarding, the group has become more cohesive.

SUMMARY

A small group is made up of people who get together to solve a problem. Groups can often solve problems better than individuals because they generate more ideas and the work can be divided among the members.

Two characteristics of small groups are that they have norms and rules and that they vary from one culture to another. Small groups are often more characteristic of a democracy than of other forms of government.

For a small group to be effective, it must have a common goal, a workable size (usually from three to thirteen members), an appropriate meeting place, and suitable seating arrangements. Groups that work effectively are cohesive. However, when group members start to think too much alike, there is a danger of groupthink.

Groups that meet together to solve problems should use a problem-solving sequence to structure their work. A common sequence is that the group chooses a topic, identifies the problem, analyzes the problem, finds and evaluates solutions, and chooses the best solution.

Although conflict in a group may be disruptive, it may work in the group's favor. Substantive conflict can help group members to see other points of view and motivate them to seek additional information.

FURTHER READING

BEEBE, STEVEN A., AND JOHN T. MASTERSON. *Communicating in Small Groups: Principles and Practices*, 3d ed. Glenview, IL: Scott, Foresman, 1990. This well-written, documented, and illustrated textbook covers the essentials of small-group processes and problem solving. The text includes chapters on theory, group formation, relating in groups, group climate, leadership, and problem solving.

BRILHART, JOHN K. *Effective Group Discussion,* 5th ed. Dubuque, IA: Brown, 1986. An excellent, comprehensive textbook on small groups and group discussion. The text contains a balance between empirically grounded theories of the dynamics of small-group communication and specific practical procedures and techniques for improving the functioning of groups. Written for the beginning student.

CATHCART, ROBERT S., AND LARRY A. SAMOVAR. *Small Group Communication: A Reader,* 5th ed. Dubuque, IA: Brown, 1988. This is a classic anthology full of interesting, stimulating, and comprehensive readings in the field of small-group communication. A varied array of topics and authors makes this both a flexible and broad approach to undergraduate study in this area.

FISHER, B. AUBREY. *Small Group Decision Making,* 3d ed. New York: McGraw-Hill, 1989. Fisher emphasizes both decision making and communication. The book is intended for university students studying group discussion. This is a very thorough, well-constructed, well-researched approach to small-group decision making.

GOODALL, H. LLOYD, JR. *Small Group Communication in Organizations.* Dubuque, IA: Brown, 1985. This textbook is divided into eleven chapters. The first five are devoted to basic skills, the sixth details the processes and tools of observing and evaluating, the seventh and eighth investigate decision making. Chapters 9 through 11 propose ways for improving communication in groups. Numerous exercises and references make this a valuable resource.

HARE, PAUL A. *Creativity in Small Groups.* Beverly Hills, CA: Sage, 1982. Hare develops various perspectives on social interaction, examines group processes and structures, and summarizes his analysis of individual and group creativity with a flow chart of the steps involved in the process of creative problem solving.

JANIS, IRVING LESTER. *Groupthink: Psychological Studies of Policy Decisions and Fiascoes.* Boston: Houghton Mifflin, 1983. Although Janis focuses on foreign relations, his thesis concerns the psychological effects that groups have on individual and group thinking. Numerous case studies are provided. This is an insightful, contemporary volume full of discussion applications.

JOHNSON, DAVID W., AND FRANK P. JOHNSON. *Joining Together: Group Theory and Group Skills,* 3d ed. Englewood Cliffs, NJ: Prentice-Hall, 1989. This 510-page paperback provides the theory and experiences necessary to develop an understanding of group processes and effective group skills. The authors stress an experiential approach to learning by including brief, clear theoretical explanations followed by exercises—more than eighty that supplement and illustrate the ideas discussed.

NEWMAN, PAMELA J., AND ALFRED F. LYNCH. *Behind Closed Doors: A Guide to Successful Meetings.* Englewood Cliffs, NJ: Prentice-Hall, 1983. The authors provide a guide for organizing and conducting business meetings. They cover how to prepare for a meeting, plan an agenda, conduct a meeting, and evaluate its success. This is a practical, readable book full of helpful advice.

TUBBS, STEWART L. *A Systems Approach to Small Group Interaction,* 3d ed. New York: Random House, 1987. Tubbs emphasizes traditional problem-solving methods as well as interpersonal relations and personal growth. As the pioneer of the systems approach in groups textbooks, this book is widely known and respected for its combination of theory and research blended effectively with skill development.

WILSON, GERALD L., AND MICHAEL S. HANNA. *Groups in Context,* 2d ed. New York: McGraw-Hill, 1989. The authors provide a comprehensive and up-to-date introduction to group discussion. They effectively combine theory, research, and practical guidelines; however, the unique perspective of this volume is the application of group discussion to a wide variety of career, community, and social contexts. A useful textbook.

Chapter 10

Leader and Participant Responsibilities

CHAPTER OBJECTIVES	KEY TERMS
After reading this chapter, you should be able to:	agenda

After reading this chapter, you should be able to:

1. Define the ways in which a leader can influence followers.

2. Tell what is meant by an interactionalist approach to leadership.

3. Distinguish among democratic, authoritarian, and laissez-faire leaders.

4. List the procedures that should be established at the beginning of a group meeting.

5. Explain how a leader can help a group to progress.

6. Distinguish among task, maintenance, and negative roles, and give examples of each.

7. Explain the ways in which conflict can be managed in a group.

8. Tell some ways in which group members can evaluate group sessions.

KEY TERMS

agenda
authoritarian leader
coercive power
democratic leader
expert power
interactionist approach
laissez-faire leader
leader
leadership style
maintenance roles
organizational power
referent power
reward power
task roles

Most Americans spend a good deal of time in meetings. A faculty member at your school might go to four or five meetings a week. In business, the average manager spends 35 to 55 percent of time in meetings. Reaching the top level of management does not reduce one's meetings: senior managers spend almost half of their work time in meetings.[1] The end of the work day, however, does not mean the meetings are over. If you are on the board of such community groups as the YMCA, the literacy council, or the public library, you can count on filling after-work hours with even more meetings.

Yet if you were to ask people what they disliked most about their jobs or community activities, they would probably mention the number and quality of the meetings. William N. Yeomans compiled a list of what people dislike about meetings[2] that probably reflects some of your own feelings:

- People don't know what the meeting was called for.
- No one is clear about what is to be accomplished.
- There is no agenda or timetable.
- Meetings run too long.
- Meetings are boring.
- People tell "war stories."
- There are too many items to be covered.
- No one wants to talk about the real problems.
- Some participants are not interested, should not be there.
- There are too many distractions, interruptions.
- The leader has already decided on a course of action. The meeting is only a rubber stamp.
- People attack one another.

The problems Yeomans lists are common to all groups. The extent to which a group suffers from any or all of these problems depends on how much control is kept over its meetings. Some of this control is exerted by group leaders. They are responsible for keeping the meeting on track, for sticking to the agenda, and for not permitting certain people to monopolize the group.

The leader, however, is not the only one at fault when a group functions poorly. Many group participants sit back and observe an ineffective and boring meeting without doing anything to make the meeting move faster or more efficiently. A group can function only as well as the combination of its leaders and its participants. What, then, are the responsibilities of the people who make up a group? Before answering this question, let's begin with leaders, how they come to lead, and what their styles of leadership are, and then move on to participants and the role they play in groups.

What Is a Leader?

If we were asked to make a list of all the leaders in our lives, most of us could probably come up with at least a hundred. Some of the people on our list would hold recognized leadership positions: the president of the United States,

Consider This Consider This Consider This

Skilled leaders—in business, politics or virtually any field—share traits that elevate them above the majority of managers. While most managers concern themselves with doing things right, leaders focus on doing the right thing.

In the past few years, I have studied 90 top leaders. At first, I was struck by their pluralism and diversity, but when I looked more closely I found that they have much in common:

They all have a compelling vision, a dream about their work. They are highly conscious at all times of what they want. They are the most results-oriented people I ever encountered. I discovered this in a funny way. Among those I interviewed was a conductor. When I asked one of his musicians what made this man remarkable, he replied, "He doesn't waste our time." And when I began observing this conductor rehearsing, he always seemed to know precisely what he wanted.

*Source: "*A Conversation with Warren Bennis: Effective Leadership—The Exception, Not the Rule," *U.S. News & World Report.*

a state senator, the principal of our elementary school. Others would not have formal leadership positions, but would be leaders because a group acknowledges them as such: the kid who organizes a summer softball team, the student who takes charge of a group project in the classroom, the friend who always comes up with the best idea for what to do on Friday night. The characteristic that all these leaders have in common is that they exert some kind of influence. A **leader,** then, is a person who influences the behavior of one or more people.

Why is one person more influential than another? Why are some people leaders and others followers? Where do leaders get their power to influence others? What kind of power do they have?

How Leaders Influence Followers

Some leaders influence their followers through the sheer force of their personalities. Others wield influence because they are in a position of power in an organization and the people they lead are their subordinates. Most often, however, leadership is a combination of factors. Researchers have identified five sources of influence for leaders: reward power, coercive power, organizational power, expert power, and referent power.[3]

REWARD POWER

A leader can have influence if he or she can reward the followers; this is known as **reward power.** In an organization, reward can come from such forms as promotions or pay raises. If the leader is liked and admired, he or she can reward followers by praising them, giving them approval, recognizing them, or giving them attention. On the campus newspaper staff, for example, the editor rewards her subordinates by giving them good stories to cover and praising the stories they write.

COERCIVE POWER

Coercive power is punishment. In an organization the leader could punish followers by demoting them or refusing to raise their pay or, more drastically, by firing them. Leaders can also exercise coercive power by criticizing their followers or refusing to pay attention to them. The editor of the paper, for example, doesn't assign interesting stories to reporters she considers second-rate. When they write stories, she often edits them so much that they barely resemble the original.

ORGANIZATIONAL POWER

A leader is influential because he or she is "the boss." The people who report to the leader must comply because of the organizational structure and its rules. This constitutes **organizational power.** In the military, for example, the lower ranks must always defer to the higher ranks; ability and personality are not factors.

EXPERT POWER

Expert power denotes the influence and power an expert has because he or she knows more than anyone else. For example, when a group studies the problem of certain athletes not graduating from college, the group member with the most influence is the one who has done some research and perhaps has studied an NCAA report on this subject.

REFERENT POWER

Leaders with **referent power** enjoy influence because of their personality. Members look up to them, want their approval, and try to emulate them. For example, a student who writes a humor column for the campus newspaper is greatly admired. Because of this widespread admiration, many students defer to her judgments on a variety of subjects.

Figure 10-1 shows when these five sources of influence come from organizations or from personality and where they overlap.

How People Become Leaders

What makes a person a leader? Why do some people always take on leadership roles, regardless of the situation they are in? Why do people rise to leadership positions in organizations? Robert A. Baron and Paul B. Paulus, writers on organizational theory, believe leaders arise because of their personality traits and the situations in which they find themselves. These two factors work together in what they call an **interactionist approach** to leadership.[4] Let's look at these elements in more detail.

PERSONALITY

We have all heard the term *born leader,* and we all know individuals who fit this description. Most people like and admire them. They take charge of situations, they are the people that others turn to, and they are the ones who

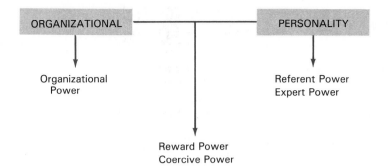

Figure 10-1
**Sources of
Influence**

come up with the most creative solutions. They can cut through the discussion to identify the essence of the problem, and they show the ways in which the group can make a decision. All these traits are internal—they are found in the personality of the leader.

SITUATION

In many situations people emerge as leaders because they have the competence and the skill to solve the problem. The person who emerges as leader is the one who is best able to meet a specific group's needs. These characteristics are external in that they depend on the situation and on the kind of skill or expertise needed to solve the problem. For example, if a group of students is assigned to make a videotape and only one student knows how to run a video camera, he or she will be the leader—at least until everyone else has learned.

THE INTERACTIONIST APPROACH

Although there are times when someone might become a leader solely on the basis of outstanding personality or skills, most often people become leaders when their personalities or skills are appropriate for a *particular* circumstance. This describes the **interactionist approach** to leadership. Since various circumstances demand different personalities or different skills, the person who becomes leader is the one who best meets the needs of a particular situation. This means that leadership is not limited to a small group of individuals; anyone can become a leader who meets a group's needs at a given time.[5] Let's look at an ideal situation to see how the interactionist approach works.

The International Students Association meets for the first time in the fall and decides to set an agenda of programs and activities. The club decides that its three priorities are to recruit more members, plan a sightseeing trip to Washington, D.C., and present a panel on world peace. The executive committee gets together and figures out which people in the organization will be best to work on each project. They all agree that Ranjan would be their best recruiter. Although he is not very organized, everyone likes him, and he is usually good at persuasion. Ranjan, then, is chosen to lead this particular activity because of his personality. The committee appoints Ming to head the group that will plan the trip to Washington, D.C., because she has been to Washington several times and knows the city well. Ming, then, is chosen

Consider This **Consider This** *Consider This*

IS IT LONELY AT THE TOP

*O*ne cliché in America is that it's lonely at the top—that our top leaders are so busy leading that they don't have time for friends and family. When researchers set out to study this alleged loneliness, however, they discovered that it didn't exist. Where it was really lonely was at the bottom.

The researchers believe that life isn't lonely at the top because people at the top have such strong relationships at work that they compensate for the time spent away from their families.

Why is this image of lonely high-level leaders so prevalent? The researchers speculate that people of high status must act as though they are sacrificing in order to justify the benefits they receive. The people who really might be suffering, according to the researchers, are the spouses and children, who see little of the top leaders.

Source: Adapted from "Is It Lonely at the Top? Career Success and Personal Relationships," *Journal of Communication.*

because of her knowledge and skills. Luis is chosen to organize the panel on world peace and contact speakers. On previous work with the association, Luis has always done an outstanding job when he handled such activities. He is goal-oriented, and he presents himself in a very professional way. He is therefore the right choice for a job that requires both personality and competence. Although leaders do not always emerge in such a clear-cut way in real life, this example shows how the interactionist theory of leadership works to create three different leaders.

Leadership Styles

The amount of control a leader exerts over a group is called **leadership style.** Styles can range from the leader who tells the participants exactly what to do, to the leader who depends on participants to point the way. No one leadership style is the best in all situations: how a leader acts should depend on the job to be done. We can see how this works in three different leadership styles: authoritarian, democratic, and laissez-faire.

The Authoritarian Leader

The **authoritarian leader** holds the greatest control over a group. He or she takes charge by deciding what should be talked about and who should talk. This leader approves some ideas, and discards others. Most of the discussion in the group is directed to the leader for approval.

Although this style of leadership does not sound very desirable, there are situations where it can work quite well. Authoritarian leaders often gain their position because they are the only group member with expertise. Sometimes a group starts out with an authoritarian leader, but later the group operates more democratically. For example, members of a committee are meeting for the first time in the academic year, and only one person has served on the committee before. In the beginning, this member may have to be more authoritarian, but group members will begin to play greater roles as they gain experience.

An authoritarian leader is often best when a group must do a job very quickly. For example, a group is meeting to write a grant proposal that is due in two days. One person takes charge of the project and appoints other members to do various tasks. This is the most efficient way to get the job done in the available time.

Authoritarian leaders will be ineffective if group members are equal in experience, knowledge, or status. Such members are likely to resent an authoritarian leader and will not cooperate.

The Democratic Leader

One who lets all points of view be heard is a **democratic leader**. Rather than decide things personally, he or she will throw out ideas and let the group react to them. Ideally, such a leader keeps the discussion on track but makes a real attempt to let all members be heard. The group is never told what to do, though the leader may suggest a direction it can take. Leadership in a democratic group is often functional: it may vary with the task and may even move from one individual to another when the group finds doing so would be appropriate. All members have a chance to contribute, and information can move among them as well as back and forth to the leader.

Do your think that gestures play a role in keeping attention in a group?

Democratic groups work best when members are equal in status and experience and when there is sufficient time to solve the problem. Due to its open nature, a democratic group provides more opportunity for originality and creativity than does an authoritarian group. Since members share in the decision making, there is also greater motivation. Because members identify with the group, they are more interested in helping the group achieve its goal.

The Laissez-faire Leader

The **laissez-faire leader** does very little actual leading. He or she might call the group together, but that's about it. Such a leader neither suggests any direction nor imposes any order on the group. In some groups there is a reluctance to name one person as leader. Support groups, such as groups for people with cancer or for people who were abused as children, might feel uncomfortable with an acknowledged leader since the members attend for the purpose of helping one another. As members of the group they want to be able to respond to a particular member's problem rather than be tied to a schedule or topic. However, these groups could fall into a pattern where the discussion is so unstructured that they don't provide very much help to anyone.

Leading the Group

The role of a group leader is to help the group get the job done. To do this the leader must have a certain sense of detachment. He or she needs to look at the group from a different perspective than other members—the perspective of "Is the group functioning as well as it should?" "Is the group making progress?" "What can I do to make the group work better?" Leaders can help groups work better when they establish procedures, help the group to keep moving, raise questions, focus on answers, delegate responsibility, and encourage social interaction.

Every small-group meeting should be conducted according to a plan that organizes the group's work. This plan, called the group's *procedures*, specifies how the group should operate.

If the group is meeting for the first time, the person who has convened the group should ask it to elect a leader. If the members do not know one another, it is a good idea for all participants to introduce themselves before a leader is chosen. If appropriate, the convener might also ask members to tell why they joined the group and what they would like the group to accomplish.

Many groups function more efficiently if someone volunteers or is elected to act as secretary. This person keeps a record of what goes on at every meeting. This record can take the shape of formal minutes that are read at the next meeting or a simple list of topics the group has discussed that members can refer to when necessary. At all meetings, if group members make motions to pass resolutions, each resolution should be recorded exactly as the member worded it, along with the tally of votes for and against it.

After the members have been introduced and someone agrees to take notes, the leader can briefly state what the group's work will be for that meeting. Once the work has been outlined, the discussion is ready to begin.

Many groups structure their time with an **agenda**—a list of all the items that will be discussed during the meeting. In the previous chapter we discussed the problem-solving sequence. This is an excellent sequence for a group with a single problem to solve. Many groups, however, have a variety of matters to handle during a meeting. These groups are more likely to use an agenda that begins with the reading of the minutes from the last meeting and proceeds

---

Consider This Consider This Consider This

*T*hink of vehicular traffic. When there is light traffic at an intersection, stop signs are adequate; when traffic is heavy in all directions, a great deal of skill is required to time your entry into (or across) the traffic flow, and accidents are more likely to happen. Some kind of signaling system, traffic lights or a policeman, ensures safety and also increases the rate of flow through the intersection. You heave a sigh of relief when you discover a policeman at a busy intersection and don't have to poke the front part of your car into cross traffic and pray that the other cars will stop.

The same is true of a meeting. If you know someone is concerned with seeing that everyone is heard, that no one is attacked, and that individuals can signal for entry into the conversational flow, you are relieved of a great deal of unnecessary tension. You can devote more of your energy to listening to others and thinking about what you want to contribute.

Source: Michael Doyle and David Straus, *The New Interaction Method: How to Make Meetings Work.*

to announcements, old business, committee reports, and new business. Figure 10-2 shows a typical agenda.

Throughout the meeting, the leader should give everyone a chance to participate. If the leader conducts the first meeting and includes everyone, it is a sign to all members that everyone's opinion is welcome.

Helping the Group to Progress

Groups cannot move ahead when members spend too much time dealing with trivia or with only a single aspect of a problem. An effective small-group leader will move the group toward the next topic when a sufficient amount of information has been presented, when information is being repeated, or when the discussion becomes too trivial. The leader might say "I think we are beginning to repeat ourselves. Let's move along to the next issue."

Helping the group move along requires some assertiveness on the part of the leader. Leaders must be willing to interject themselves and enforce the group's agenda. This requires some discretion and diplomacy because group

Figure 10-2
An Agenda

COMMUNITY NURSING SERVICE OF CLINTON COUNTY, INC.

BOARD MEETING AGENDA
March 19, 1991

A. Approval of February 19, 1991, minutes
B. Treasurer's report and payment of listing of bills
C. Nursing report
D. Committee reports
    1. Personnel Committee
    2. United Way
E. Correspondence
    1. Blue Cross
F. Executive Director's report
G. Old business
    1. Public meeting
H. New business

members do not like to be bossed. A leader might say, for example, "Excuse me for interrupting you, Deb, but I wonder if we might hear what some of the others are thinking."

Summarizing is one good way to help the group progress. It alerts the group to where it has been, what it has accomplished, where it is now, and where it is going. A final summary and a statement of goals for the next meeting is also a good way to close each group meeting. "Today we had a disagreement over whether we should lease our equipment to outsiders or permit only our own students to use it. At our next meeting, I think we should work to resolve this issue."

Raising Questions

One of the ways a leader can be most helpful is to raise pertinent questions. Sometimes, during discussion, it is easy for a group to lose sight of its original goal. A group of students, for example, might be discussing vandalism of classrooms and get diverted to the subject of unfriendly law enforcement officials. If the group leader says "Is this directly related to the problem of classroom vandals?" the group will realize that it is not and will get back on the subject.

Sometimes a group will try to discuss a subject but will lack sufficient information. A group discussing faculty and student parking might realize that it doesn't know how many parking places are assigned to each group. The leader may ask someone to find this information. If it is not known, he or she may ask members to count the spaces in the various lots.

Information that the group receives must be evaluated. Some information may be insignificant, irrelevant, or invalid. Appropriate questions for the leader to ask include: How recent is the information? Who is the source? Might the source be biased? Facts and opinions should be scrutinized carefully for possible errors or misinterpretation.

Focusing on Answers

To accomplish its task, a group needs answers. If the function of the group is to solve a problem, members need to keep their attention on possible solutions. An effective group leader will focus members' attention on the need for answers and will support members who work toward answers.

Focusing on answers involves evaluating alternatives by considering their advantages and disadvantages. A useful leadership role is played by members who ask such questions as: What consequences are likely to occur? What are the costs going to be? What barriers have to be overcome? How serious are the barriers?

Sometimes solutions call for a plan of action. If your group decided that the only solution to its problem is to demonstrate against the administration, members would be faced with making plans for that demonstration. How are you going to publicize your grievances, get recruits, and carry out the protest? Effective leadership helps a group plan carefully for the action it has decided to take.

Delegating Responsibility

Many people do not want to become leaders because they think that leadership involves too much time and trouble. These people often see a leader as the one who does all the work. This should not be true in any group. A good leader should be able to delegate responsibility to the group's members. If a group is going to do research, for example, the leader could assign some members to go to the library, some to interview experts, and others to coordinate and present the information to the group.

Some leaders do not delegate because they believe they are the only ones who can do the job right. If you are one of these people, you should consider taking a risk and letting some of the other people do some of the work. You might be surprised how well they do it.

Encouraging Social Interaction

Social interaction occurs in a group when people feel recognized and accepted, unthreatened, and valued by other members. The more friendliness, mutual trust, respect, and warmth exhibited, the more likely the members are to find pleasure in the group and to work hard to accomplish the group's goals. The

---

Try This Try This Try This

*H*ere is some expert advice on how to make meetings work.

1. Determine whether the meeting is required. Can the business of the meeting be better handled by memo or telephone?
2. Get the right people to attend. Include only those people who are responsible for the business of the meeting and who will carry out the decisions that result.
3. Decide what the meeting will be about and stick to it. Even if interesting diversions occur, get the meeting back to the subject.
4. Prepare for the meeting. Do your homework, read any material, including the minutes that have been distributed beforehand. Have some idea of how you are going to react to this material when you come to the meeting.
5. If you are the leader, don't express your opinion too early. In many situations, particularly if you're the boss, everyone will go along with what they think you want.
6. Stick to the schedule. Start and end the meeting on time, and don't let a group member move an agenda item ahead because he or she has to leave early.
7. Review the results of the meeting before you adjourn, and set guidelines for acting on them. When the group has decided to take some sort of action, make sure there is a plan in place.

Source: Adapted from Diane Cole, "Meetings That Make Sense," *Psychology Today.*

use of first names and the use of such words as *we, us,* and *our* will help group members feel a sense of belonging. The group leader can also strengthen social interaction by encouraging shy members to speak, by complimenting worthwhile contributions, and by praising the overall accomplishments of the group. Group leaders should also plan to leave a little time before and after a meeting so members can socialize.

Participating in Group Discussion

Roles in Discussion

Groups, like individuals, can be defined as mature or immature. Often an immature group is a new one. It is overly dependent on its leader and, in the beginning, is often passive and unorganized. As the group matures, it is able to function independently of its leader and its members become actively involved and capable of organizing their discussions.[6]

Although most groups have a specified leader, the leader does not have total responsibility for giving the discussion a direction or for moving the group along. In most groups, an individual member may temporarily take over the leadership from time to time. For example, a member who temporarily leads a group may have more information or experience in a certain area than the usual leader.

Individual group members continue to play the same roles in groups as they do in any other communication. A person who likes to take charge is likely to want the role of group leader. A person who is shy is going to be as hesitant in a group as in any other kind of communication. In addition to the

How is this group leader encouraging participation?

roles we play in life, however, some roles are specific to small-group communication. Kenneth Benne and Paul Sheats, in a classic study, have pointed out that group members play task and/or maintenance roles.[7]

TASK ROLES

Task roles are those that help get the job done. Persons who play these roles help the group come up with new ideas, aid in collecting and organizing information, and analyze the information that exists. Task roles are not limited to any one individual; they may be interchanged among the members as the group goes about its job. Following are some of the common task roles.

Initiators-Expediters   Members who act as *initiators-expediters*—by suggesting new ideas, goals, solutions, and approaches—are often the most creative and energetic of the group. When the group gets bogged down, they are likely to make such statements as "What if we tried . . ." or "I wonder if . . . would solve our problem."

Initiators-expediters often can suggest a new direction or can prevent the group from losing sight of its objectives. They are not afraid to jump in and give assistance when the group is in trouble. Often they are the ones who hold the light so others can see the path.

Information Givers and Seekers   Individual members may both seek information and give it. Since lots of information will lead to better discussion, many members will play these roles. *Information givers* are often the best-informed members of the group. They might have had more experience with the subject or even be experts on it.

The more complex the subject, the greater the group's need for *information seekers*. These are people who are willing to go out and research the subject. They might agree to interview experts, or they might go to the library to do research. If the group has very little information on a subject, it might be necessary for several members to play the role of information seeker.

The roles of information giving and seeking are the most important in any group. The information the group gets provides the foundation for the

---

Consider This **Consider This** *Consider This*

*T*he winning football team is the one that seems able, at will, to break away for that critical score. It's perfectly put together to do its job, to force its will upon its opponents. But is that really what a championship team is, a single force that overcomes its competitors? No. Like any organized group, it's a blending of a number of individual talents, kicking just a little bit better, blocking a little bit better, passing better, running the ball better. When all these talents are put together, that complex unit called the "team" wins.

Source: Frank Snell, *How to Win the Meeting.*

entire discussion. The more group members who play these roles, the better the quality of group discussion.

Critics-Analyzers *Critics-analyzers* are those who look at the good and bad points in the information the group has gathered. These people see the points that need more elaboration, and they discover information that has been left out.

The critic-analyzer is able to look at the total picture and see how everything fits together. People who play this role usually have an excellent sense of organization. Often they can help keep the group on track: "We have mentioned this point twice. Maybe we need to discuss it in more depth." "Maybe we should go back and look at this information again. Something seems to be missing."

MAINTENANCE ROLES

People who play **maintenance roles** focus on the emotional tone of the meeting. Since no one wants to spend his or her entire time being logical, gathering information, and doing the job, it is important that some emotional needs be met. People who play maintenance roles meet these needs by encouraging, harmonizing, regulating, and observing.

Encouragers *Encouragers* praise and commend contributions and group achievements: "You really did a good job of gathering this information. Now we can dig in and work."

The best encouragers are active listeners. They help in rephrasing points to achieve greater clarity. They do not make negative judgments about other members or their opinions. Encouragers make people feel good about themselves and their contributions.

Harmonizers-Compromisers Those who help to resolve conflict in the group, who settle arguments and disagreements through mediation, are the *harmonizers-compromisers*. People who play this role are skillful at discovering solutions acceptable to everyone. Harmonizers-compromisers are especially effective when they remind group members that group goals are more important than individual needs: "I know you would like the library to be open on Sunday morning, but we have to find the times that are best for everybody."

Regulators As their name implies, *regulators* help regulate group discussion by gently reminding members of the agenda or of the point they were discussing when they digressed: "We seem to be wandering a little. Now, we were discussing . . ."

Good regulators also find ways to give everyone a chance to speak: "Jane, you haven't said anything. Do you have any feelings on this subject?" Sometimes the regulator has to stop someone who has been talking too much: "Jerry, you have made several interesting points. Let's see what some of the others think of them." A regulator who is too authoritarian, however, might find that others resent him or her. In this role, it is important that statements or questions be tactfully worded.

Observers *Observers* aid in the group's cohesiveness. They are sensitive to the needs of each member: "I think we have ignored the point that John just made. Maybe we should take some time to discuss it."

Managing Group Conflict

As we said in Chapter 9, conflict within a group can have positive effects. However, there are times when it can slow a group down or even bring it to a screeching halt. When conflict arises, the group leader has to step in and try to help group members resolve it. The approach the leader takes should depend on the seriousness of the conflict. Galanes and Brilhart, who have written about groups, suggest some ways of managing conflict.[8]

Avoidance

Sometimes groups argue over points that are so minor that they are not worth the time. If the leader sees this happening, she should suggest that the issue doesn't seem very important and that the group should move to another topic. For example, when one group disagreed about the time its banquet should begin, the leader pointed out that there was little difference between 6:30 P.M. and 7 P.M. and that it would be more productive to choose the earlier time and move on.

Accommodation

This occurs when people on one side of an issue give in to the other side. If a leader sees this as a possibility, she should attempt to find out how strongly people feel about the sides they have taken. If it is not really important to one side, the leader might suggest that they give in. For example, when a group was planning a children's day, members argued over whether they should spend money for a clown or for pony rides. The side that favored pony rides decided that children would also enjoy a clown, and so they were willing to give in.

Competition

Competition can cause considerable harm to a group. It occurs when one side cares more about winning than it does about other member's feelings. When a leader sees competition rising, he should try to deflect it before members get entrenched in their positions. Sometimes individual members feel competitive with one another, and they use the group sessions to work out their feelings. If this is happening, the leader might point out to each member privately that the conflict is keeping the group from working together.

Try This Try This Try This

WHAT IS YOUR ROLE IN A GROUP?

*W*hich statements best describe you when you are working in a group? (Make a note of the numbers that apply.)

1. I feel frustrated when the group wanders off the subject and I try to get it back on track.
2. I usually do research before the group meets and come prepared to participate.
3. I often encourage people to say something if they haven't been talking.
4. I often rephrase points to make them clearer.
5. I often have a solution to a group problem that no one else has thought of.
6. I am often able to see how all the pieces fit together.
7. I usually can sense when someone is feeling uncomfortable in the group.

If you answered 1, 2, 5, and 6, you probably play a task role. You play a maintenance role if you answered 3, 4, and 7. If you answered some from each category, you probably play both roles.

Collaboration

In collaboration, people who are in conflict try to work together to meet the other person's needs as well as their own. Collaborators do not attack one another; instead they try to understand opposing points of view and work hard to stay away from anything that might harm the relationship. For example, a faculty committee was asked to choose one curriculum proposal to send to the state for funding. Since they received two—one for a women's studies minor and the other for a leadership minor, they had to make a choice. Both proposals were well thought out and clearly written, but members of the committee were divided as to which proposal they favored. After many hours of discussion, they decided to choose the women's studies proposal, but they saw many points in the leadership proposal that could make the women studies proposal even stronger. By combining the two proposals, they had a true collaboration.

Compromise

In compromise, each side has to give up something in order to get what it wants. This involves a kind of bargaining in which each side makes an offer of what it will sacrifice. Compromise will work only when each side believes that what it gets is fair and that it has gained at least a partial victory. For example, a fraternity was planning its annual banquet and dance. One side favored holding it at the Elks hall and making it a formal party, whereas the other side wanted to hold it at a rustic lodge and make it a casual party. The group finally compromised: the party would be held at the Elks, but it would be informal.

Evaluating Group Performance

Since you are learning how groups work, toward the end of each meeting your group should evaluate its performance. The first and most important question your group should ask is whether it made progress toward finishing its job or solving its problem. Your instructor may have evaluation forms to help you answer this question. Another way of evaluating group work is for each member to take one minute to write down what the group has accomplished during its session and then compare notes with other members.

If the group has not made progress during its session, it is useful to answer the following questions: Did members stick to the topic? Did everyone come prepared with the material the group needed? Was everyone able to participate and contribute? Did the atmosphere encourage members to try to understand other members' points of view? Was time used efficiently? Was the leader skillful in helping members to participate and voice their opinions? If the group answers "no" to any of these questions, then it will have an idea of where it needs to make improvements.

The group should also consider whether the process of group work has been rewarding. Do members feel good about what they accomplished? Were they satisfied with the roles they played? Would they like to work with this group again?

Successful work in groups can be rewarding and even exhilarating. Group work gives you a chance to play an active role in your own learning. Therefore,

---

Try This **Try This** *Try This*

*T*hink about the last time you were a member of a problem-solving group, then use these questions to rate your performance. Use 5 for always, 4 for frequently, 3 for occasionally, 2 for seldom, 1 for never.

_____1. I showed initiative by asking questions and by making contributions that were related to the goals of the group.

_____2. I tried to listen to opinions that were different from mine and tried to understand other points of view.

_____3. Whenever I thought something was important, I spoke up.

_____4. I was patient when others spoke—even though some group members were slow in expressing themselves.

_____5. I tried to concentrate on what I thought was important for the group rather than on what I wanted.

How do you rank as a group member? Are there any places where you can improve?

when you have an opportunity to work in a group, make your best effort. Even work in a classroom setting prepares you for the workplace and for participation in the life of your community.

SUMMARY

A leader is a person who influences the behavior of one or more people. Leaders gain influence through five kinds of power: reward, coercive, organizational, expert, and referent.

One theory of leadership is that people become leaders because of their personality and the situations in which they find themselves. These two factors work together in an interactionist approach.

Leaders tend to fall into three categories: authoritarian, democratic, and laissez-faire. An authoritarian leader takes charge of a group—a style that is most successful when the group has little information or experience. A democratic leader gives everyone a chance to participate in decision making. This style of leadership works best when members are equal in status, education, and experience and when there is sufficient time to solve the problem. The laissez-faire leader does little leading. This kind of leadership works best in self-help groups.

A group leader has six responsibilities: to establish procedures, to keep the group moving, to raise questions, to focus on answers, to delegate responsibility, and to encourage social interaction.

Participants in group discussion play a variety of roles. Members in task roles focus on getting the job done; members in maintenance roles are concerned with the emotional tone of the group.

One important task of a leader is to manage conflict in a group. He or she should determine how serious the conflict is and take one of the following approaches: avoidance, accommodation, competition, collaboration, or compromise.

When a group has completed its job for the day, it should evaluate its performance. The evaluation should focus on whether the group is making progress in solving the problem and whether its members have a sense of interpersonal satisfaction from working together.

FURTHER READING

BENNIS, WARREN, AND BURT NANUS. *Leaders: The Strategies for Taking Charge.* New York: Harper & Row, 1985. The authors offer a study of the qualities of today's great leaders. They provide four strategies: (1) attention through vision, (2) meaning through communication, (3) trust through positioning, and (4) the deployment of self. The concept of empowerment is discussed too—the role reciprocity plays in leading others. This is an excellent, readable, anecdotal book full of experience, insight, and innovation.

BURNS, JAMES MACGREGOR. *Leadership,* New York: Harper & Row, 1979. Burns presents a theory of leadership as involving reciprocity between ordinary people (followers) and political and ideological leaders. According to Burns, leadership thrives on conflict and demands no consensus. Through creative scholarship, the author analyzes and synthesizes the central role leadership has played throughout history.

CRAGAN, JOHN F., AND DAVID W. WRIGHT. *Communication in Small Group Discussion: An Integrated Approach*, 2d ed. St. Paul, MN: West, 1986. This basic textbook is divided into three major parts: (1) theoretical considerations, (2) discussion principles and practices, and (3) applications to settings and situations. This is a practical approach that uses research, case studies, and examples.

DEVILLE, JARD. *The Psychology of Leadership: Managing Resources and Relationships*. New York: New American Library, 1984. DeVille discusses the patterns that affect performance as well as the ways to manage different personalities. How do you manage logically? Objectively? Inspirationally? Supportively? He concludes by offering a balanced management style and offers suggestions for building a community of achievers.

FIEDLER, FRED E., AND MARTIN M. CHEMERS. *Improving Leadership Effectiveness: The Leader Match Concept*, 2d ed. New York: Wiley (A Wiley Press Book), 1984. The authors present an interactive, self-diagnostic approach to management development. They show readers how to identify their leadership style and match it with the situation that best brings out their abilities. This training guide is practical, step by step, interesting, and valuable.

LAWSON, LESLIE GRIFFIN, FRANKLYN D. DONANT, AND JOHN D. LAWSON. *Lead On! The Complete Handbook for Group Leaders*. San Luis Obispo, CA: Impact, 1982. This is a 162-page handbook that is skills-oriented. Twenty-four key leadership skills are presented informally and straightforwardly. The book is divided into four parts: tuning up, getting started, getting results, and starting anew. There are twenty-four-brief chapters and many suggestions for further study.

LEIDER, RICHARD J. *The Power of Purpose*. New York: Fawcett Gold Medal, 1985. This is a hands-on workbook to help people realize their expectations. There are self-assessment questionnaires, checklists, and exercises designed to help readers identify their talents, create an appropriate work environment, and take the risks that help them get what they want. Leider discusses the birth of purpose, living on purpose, working on purpose, tapping the power of purpose, living at risk, and the purpose connection.

RATLIFFE, SHARON A., AND ERNEST STECH. Skokie II: National Textbook Company, 1989. This *manual* is intended for use by small groups that must accomplish tasks. The authors place their emphasis on the interdependence of effort for the purpose of task accomplishment. Readers will increase their understanding and mastery of the concepts and strategies which, in turn, will increase their ability to work more effectively in groups. This book is participant-oriented.

WILLIAMSON, JOHN N., ED. *The Leader-Manager*. New York: Wiley, 1986. This collection of readings includes material on change, leadership, growth, mission, goals, feedback, rewards, and support. The volume offers a new lens through which to view the management of people. The focus is the importance of leadership.

WOOD, JULIA T., GERALD M. PHILLIPS, AND DOUGLAS J. PEDERSEN. *Group Discussion: A Practical Guide to Participation and Leadership*. New York: Harper & Row, 1986. The authors "hope to help people become effective participants and leaders in whatever groups they serve" (p. xi). Their book covers topics that include a basic understanding of groups, participating and leading, conflict, and the six phases of the standard agenda. Their final chapter covers presentational speaking and report writing.

Communicating in Public

Chapter 11

Getting Started

CHAPTER OBJECTIVES	KEY TERMS
After reading this chapter, you should be able to:	audience analysis
1. Choose a topic for a speech.	central idea
	demographic analysis
2. Assess whether the topic is appropriate for you, the audience, and the speech occasion.	general purpose
	informative speech
3. Narrow the topic to make it manageable.	personal inventory
4. State a general purpose for your speech.	persuasive speech
5. State a specific purpose for your speech.	specific purpose
6. State a central idea for your speech.	
7. Distinguish between an informative and a persuasive speech.	
8. Make some inferences about your audience's knowledge, attitudes, and interests.	

Hyung Suk is the director of the Korean Cultural Center. The center gets a lot of its funding through United Way. This year the board of directors would like to add programs for children, but to do this the center will need more money from United Way. The board asks Hyung Suk to put together a presentation to show how the additional money would be used.

Cheryl is a high school music teacher. After several years of experience she is convinced that band competitions are bad for the school program. She believes that when the school band is involved in competition, the students play the same pieces again and again, which limits the new material they could learn. She convinces the principal of her point of view, but he tells her that she must present her case to the school board. Cheryl spends several days gathering and organizing the information she will present to the board.

Bill's best friend is getting married on Saturday. The custom among his friends is to toast the bride and groom with short speeches about each of them. Bill has been asked to speak about the groom. Since the occasion is a wedding reception, he knows his remarks should be short, light, and humorous.

Francisco is president of the Young Democrats club on campus. One of the Democrats from the state legislature has agreed to speak to the club, and Francisco is going to introduce him. Francisco begins his research by collecting details about the senator's career.

Sharon is president of the local branch of the Electrical Worker's Union. For several months the executive committee has been negotiating with management about a cost-of-living pay raise. The committee now realizes that management is not going to come through and that the union will have to ask members for a vote to strike. Sharon will speak to her local branch to explain why a strike vote is necessary.

Kelly is the editor of the school literary magazine. Over the past few years the magazine has been getting fewer and fewer contributions. Kelly knows that many students write poetry and short stories but that they often don't think of submitting them to the magazine. She asks her instructor in her American Literature class if she can speak to her class about contributing to the magazine. He agrees, and she organizes a short presentation for the class.

All these people are in a position where they are going to give a speech. Their speeches are not going to be given in large auditoriums before vast audiences; they are part of the routine of school and work. People give speeches like this every day. They make presentations (to committees or boards of directors), hold workshops (for community members or professionals), or conduct seminars (for people who want to learn something). Whatever the purpose, all these forms of speaking have a speaker and an audience.

Public speaking involves the same elements as other forms of communication: senders-receivers, a message, a channel, and feedback. The speaker is the main sender-receiver, although audience members will also respond as sender-receivers by providing nonverbal feedback or asking questions. The message in public speaking is the most structured of all communication. The speaker works on the message beforehand, carefully planning what he or she will say. Usually the channel is the voice and gestures, but some speakers enhance the channel by using graphics such as posters or slides. Feedback to a speech usually comes from the entire audience rather than from one or a few individuals. Typical feedback would be applause or laughter from the audience.

Public speaking has some of the characteristics of transactional communication, although its transactional nature differs from that of interpersonal and small-group communication. When an audience is small and the speaker can see everyone, continuous and simultaneous communication between the speaker and the audience can exist. However, when an audience is very large, it's difficult to say that all the communication between the speaker and the audience is continuous and simultaneous. Let's say, for example, that several instructors on campus require their classes to go to hear a speech. The auditorium, which holds 500 people, is packed. One group of students sits in the back, in the shadows. This group has no intention of listening to the speaker. Because the auditorium is very large, the speaker isn't aware of them and is unable to say something that will engage their attention. In this situation there is probably little communication between the speaker and these members of the audience.

The transactional elements of past, present, and future usually apply to public speaking. Some people go to hear a speaker because they have past experience in the subject and want to learn more. How they react to the speech and the speaker may depend on how the speaker and the topic tie into their past experience or whether it is of value to them in the future. For example, in a speech class, students will look forward to hearing some student speeches because, in the past, these have been interesting.

Consider This Consider This Consider This

*R*ex Kelly, general manager of Corporate Communications for the Mississippi Power Company, asks and answers the question of why speakers make speeches:

Why do politicians go out on the campaign trail? Surely they would experience less wear and tear if they just mailed everybody 8 by 10 glossies and a copy of their platform.

Why do preachers preach? And why are television evangelists so remarkably successful? I know for a fact that the Christian message is readily available in printed form. What is it about the way they present their message?

And finally, with records, television, and movies, why will perfectly intelligent people pay $25 to $200 to go see an entertainer 'in person'?

All of these questions have the same answer. THERE IS AN ELEMENTAL POWER IN HAVING A LIVING BREATHING HUMAN BEING—RIGHT HERE, RIGHT NOW—INTERACTING WITH OTHER HUMAN BEINGS.

And when that living, breathing human being is a skilled communicator, he or she possesses real power. The power to change the way people feel, to change the way they think, and even to change the way they act.

Source: Rex Kelly, "Speakers and the Bottom Line," *Vital Speeches.*

The transactional element of roles is also present in public speaking. Steve Allen, who because of his career as a comedian and an actor has often been asked to give speeches, offers an interesting perspective on the role of the speaker:

> *I learned very early in my experience as a speaker—as distinguished from an entertainer—that if there were five hundred individuals present, they were perceiving not one Steve Allen at the lectern, but five hundred separate me's.*
>
> *To give just a few illustrations:*
>
> *A young woman, to whose father I might bear a physical resemblance, might perceive me primarily as a male, to some degree physically attractive.*
>
> *An elderly conservative Republican gentlemen in the front row might perceive me primarily as a notorious Democrat or liberal.*
>
> *A tailor in the audience might perceive me as someone attired unfashionably.*
>
> *A fan of my television comedy program might perceive me as too stuffy and serious on this particular occasion.*
>
> *A poorly educated person might perceive me as someone who uses too many big words.*
>
> *One of my sons might perceive me as just "Dad."*
>
> *My wife might perceive me as having put on a bit too much weight recently.*[1]

Selecting a Topic

Most of the people in the examples at the beginning of the chapter did not have to select a topic for a speech—the topic grew out of the work they were doing. On other occasions people are asked to speak on their area of expertise, but the specific topic is left up to them. The Lions Club asks Professor Cooper, an energy expert, to give a speech, and the professor chooses the subject of how to turn a front porch into a passive energy collector. Hank Jones, the county agricultural extension agent, is asked to speak to the garden club and decides to talk about the pruning and trimming of bushes.

Since you are in a speech communication course, you will have to make several speeches during the course of the term, and the choice of topic will probably be left up to you. Choosing the topic is one of the most difficult parts of making a speech; so let's take a look at how to go about it.

The most important consideration in choosing a topic is to find a subject that interests you. If the subject is one that you like, you are going to be more motivated to research it and your presentation will be more lively. How do you find a subject that is interesting and that would also lead to an effective speech? Let's look at some areas that you should investigate.

The first place to look for a topic is within yourself. You can begin by making a **personal inventory**, which involves appraising your own resources. What are you interested in? Would your interest make a good speech? Sometimes a hobby will lead to a good speech. A hobby can make you an expert about any number of subjects—rap musicians, computer games, or Elvis memorabilia.

Another area you might examine is how you spend your free time. If you listen to music or play an instrument, you might have the basis for a speech. Are you interested in nutrition, or do you like to cook? Maybe you can tell your audience something about food that they would find interesting.

Have you done anything unusual? One student gave a speech on how to teach a cat to do tricks—something most cats are reluctant to do. Have you been to any unusual places, or have you done something unusual—such as foraging for food in the woods?

Sometimes people have unique skills. Do you have the ability to make old cars run? Are you familiar with laser technology and how it works? Are you particularly good at entertaining children? Do you have any innovative ways of studying you can share with others?

Often the books, magazines, and newspapers you read will offer possibilities for speech topics. Hundreds of thousands of articles are published in magazines and newspapers every year. Most of these articles are about what people are currently interested in and could lead to ideas for speech topics. To get some idea of the range of topics covered, take a look at the *Readers' Guide to Periodical Literature*. Here you will find hundreds of different subjects to choose from.

What newspapers and magazines do you read? What sections do you turn to first? Are there issues in these sections that might result in good speeches? For example, if you always read the sports section, you know that scores and accounts of games are unlikely to provide material for speeches. Well-written sports pages, however, also include stories on important issues in sports. Typical examples: "What percentage of college athletes graduate?" "How should we define 'amateur'?" "Should the Olympics be held only in Greece to keep politics out of sports?"

Newspapers and magazines are also the best source of information for what is going on in your city or state, the nation, and the world. Even though you might not ordinarily pay attention to this kind of news, take an hour or so some day to leaf through a big-city newspaper or a news magazine such as *Time* or *Newsweek*. What subjects catch your attention? What's going on in the community or in the nation that might affect you and the people you know? For example, what is the local zoning board up to? Do you know that this is the board that decides how many people can live in a single dwelling? This is certainly an issue that affects students, who often need to save money by living with four or five others.

What is the state legislature up to? If you are attending a college or university supported by state money, this is an important question, since your state legislature will decide how much money your college will get and even how much tuition you will be paying. The federal government also makes many decisions that affect us all (nuclear power plants and defense spending) and many that affect college students in particular (draft registration and student loans).

Your college library probably subscribes to hundreds of magazines. Take a look at some you are not familiar with. Magazines such as *Science Digest, Psychology Today*, and *Consumer Reports* cover dozens of subjects that could make good speech topics.

Sometimes the books you read can inspire speech topics. Generally, nonfiction books (which deal with facts and true stories) offer better speech topics than do works of fiction. Every year in this country, thousands of nonfiction books are published on subjects ranging from dieting to nuclear physics. If you were to look at the card catalog entries on a computer screen in the library, you would probably find dozens of book titles that would suggest good ideas for speech topics.

Whenever you seek a speech topic, remember that you will do best with material you know something about. While you are making a personal inventory, your emphasis should be on discovering interests and skills that you have and would like to share with others. Figure 11-1 diagrams the various sources where speech topics might be sought.

Brainstorming

In Chapter 9, we discussed brainstorming in groups. You can also brainstorm all by yourself. As we noted earlier, *brainstorming* is a technique of free

Figure 11-1
Finding a Topic

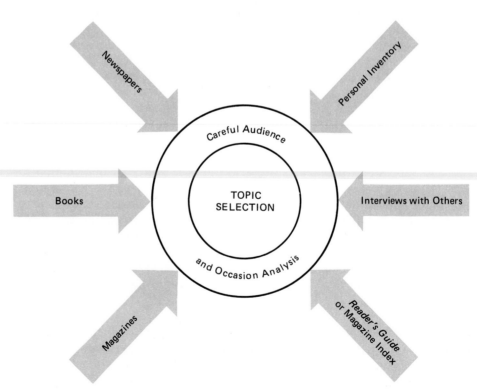

*B*egin your own personal inventory by completing the following statements.

1. In my spare time I . . .
2. If I sit down to read, I'll usually read . . .
3. When I'm with my friends we often talk about . . .
4. The leaders and celebrities I most admire are . . .
5. Campus issues important to me are . . .
6. Social issues that most affect me and my friends are . . .
7. If I could change the world in one way, I would . . .

Once you have completed the statements, ask yourself if any of your answers could lead to a speech topic.

association. You take a subject—cars, for example—and think of everything that might possibly be related to this subject. The goal of brainstorming is quantity—to come up with as many ideas as possible.[2]

When you are ready to brainstorm, it is a good idea to sit in a comfortable chair and relax with a paper and pencil by your side. Once you are comfortable, think about something you are interested in (maybe from your personal inventory) and write down everything that comes into your mind. Don't try to edit any of your ideas—in fact, don't even think about them. Work quickly and make your list as long as possible. After you have finished with one topic, try other areas that might seem promising. Some possibilities might include your major, your reading interests, school-related subjects, and so forth.

Let's say, for example, that we were going to brainstorm on the subject "cars." Our list might look something like this:

Antique

Cost of gas

Mileage

Safety

Front-wheel drive

After you have come up with a brainstorming list on a subject, you should go back and look at it with a more critical eye. If a topic doesn't look as though it will work, or if it is an aspect of the subject you are not really interested in, eliminate it from your list. In our list of car topics, for example, we might decide that we don't know anything about antique cars, and so we eliminate it from the list. Gas or mileage could provide a topic, but both would involve researching OPEC and politics in the Middle East—subjects that would get away from cars. Front-wheel drive does not seem meaty enough for a speech, and so we eliminate it too. Now we are left with safety. Since safety is a broad concept, we brainstorm a little more to see what could come under this heading, and we come up with:

> Restraint systems (seat belts and airbags)
> Safety records on large versus compact cars
> Car color as a safety factor

These three aspects of safety could all be covered in a speech about car safety. Sometimes when you brainstorm, however, you might find that your list does not yield anything you want to talk about. In this case, take another subject and brainstorm again. It might take two or three brainstorming sessions before you find a topic you really like. Once you find a topic (or topics), you need to test to see if it (they) will work in a speech.

Testing the Topic

When choosing among possible topics, you should consider three questions: (1) Is the topic appropriate for your audience? (2) Is it appropriate for you? (3) Is it appropriate for the speech occasion?

What would be some of the ways this state trooper could adapt her presentation of a safety program to these children, as opposed to an audience of adults?

Appropriate for the Audience?

To determine whether a topic is appropriate for an audience, you have to ask whether you can speak about it on a level the audience can understand. Does the subject require specialized or technical knowledge? Can you talk about this subject in a language everyone will understand? Can you make this topic interesting for your audience? Does the audience have enough background to understand the subject? Answers to these questions will help you decide whether the topic will be appropriate.

Appropriate for You?

A topic is appropriate for you if it meets this test: Can you get involved in it, and is it interesting enough to motivate you to do the necessary research? A student majoring in air traffic control would probably have a high interest in air disasters—especially those caused by mistakes on the part of traffic controllers. A student studying restaurant administration would probably find it interesting to research the causes of food poisoning. Someone with a collection of African coins would be motivated to learn even more about the subject.

To give a good speech you are also going to have to speak with confidence and expertise. Do you know enough about the subject? Can you learn enough about it to give a speech? There is nothing worse than getting up before an audience and realizing that you don't know what you are talking about!

Appropriate for the Occasion?

The first consideration here is whether you are giving the right kind of speech for the occasion. An after-dinner speech, for example, should have a light touch and not be too long, since it will occur when members of the audience have just eaten and are not feeling at their most alert. On the other hand, if you are giving a speech at a seminar, this will be an opportunity to speak on a more complex topic. In a classroom setting, you will probably be given only a limited time to speak; so you have to decide whether you can cover your topic adequately in the time you have.

If you are speaking at a special occasion, you should tie at least some of the speech into the occasion itself. If the speech is for some kind of ritual occasion such as a graduation or bar mitzvah, certain conventions are expected of the speaker. At a graduation, for example, a speaker typically has some words about the future for graduates. At a bar mitzvah, a Jewish ceremony initiating a boy into religious adulthood, it would be appropriate to praise the young man and his parents.

Another consideration is whether you can fit the speech into the time limits of the occasion. Usually a speaker is given some idea of how long to speak. In a speech class, this is always true. You must consider whether you can cover your topic or whether you need to narrow it down so you can cover it adequately within the time allowed.

For many of us, making a final decision about a topic is difficult—especially when we are faced with several good options. When you are deciding on a

Consider This Consider This Consider This

*I*nforming yourself about the audience—how many people there'll be, how educated they are, what occupations and interests they represent, how much do they already know about the subject, what appeals to them, what offends them, and so forth—all this and more are crucial to . . . an effective speech.

Yet time after time, I've seen speakers give the wrong speech for an audience. I've even written a few like that. The speech may have been patronizing, offensive or, worse, irrelevant to the audience. And it's usually because the speaker and the writer just didn't do their homework.

Along that line, I've heard speeches which didn't fit the occasion. I've heard speakers deliver a speech that belonged in a lecture hall, rather than a union hall—or deliver a tedious, solemn policy address at graduation ceremonies in which the graduates and families just want to hit the exits and have a good time.

Again, homework is the key. You have to find out and think through what the event is all about.

Source: Robert B. Rackleff, "The Art of Speech Writing," *Vital Speeches.*

topic for your speech class, however, it is important that you choose a single topic well ahead of the date the speech is due. If you don't do this, you will waste a lot of time doing unfocused and unusable research on several topics. If you have several topics that seem equally appropriate and you just can't make up your mind, put all the topics in a hat and draw one out. Now that you have one topic, stick with it!

Narrowing the Topic

A common mistake made by beginning speakers is trying to cover a topic that is too broad. If you wanted to talk about a social issue, such as crime, racial equality, or educational reform, you would discover so much relevant material that you would not even be able to read it all, let alone cover it in a single speech. If you tried to cover the entire topic, your treatment would have to be so superficial that your speech would not be very meaningful. Let's say you wanted to speak on the subject of education. One could probably divide education into 100 or more different subsections. Do you want to talk about elementary schools or high schools? Special education? Bilingual education? If you choose elementary education, there are still many possibilities. Do you want to talk about how children learn? About curriculum? About educational games? About interactive learning?

Narrowing a topic is the process of finding the specific aspect of a subject that will best meet the time restraints and other demands of the speaking situation. Let's see how three different students narrowed their subjects for speeches.

Baljit, a student from India, has been taking a health class and becomes interested in the issue of health in third-world countries. She is particularly interested in infant mortality since two of her cousins back home had babies who became seriously ill.

She decides to see what she can find on the topic and goes to the library to use a computer data base to see what is available. After Baljit types "infant mortality" and "third world" the computer comes up with hundreds of entries. Baljit realizes that the topic is much too large and that she will have to narrow it. As she looks at the titles of some of the articles, she realizes that several are about infant formula. Since she knows several young women in her country who use infant formula rather than breast-feed their babies, she decides to pursue this subject.

When she types "infant formula" and "third world" into the computer, she still finds the subject is too broad—there are more than forty articles on the subject. Since she wants to stay with the topic of infant formula and cannot narrow it down any more on the computer, she decides to look at some of the articles to see if she can tighten her focus even more.

After looking at several articles, Baljit finds that the following issues are addressed:

- Infant formula is safe for babies only if it is mixed with the correct amount of pure water.
- The manufacturers of infant formula consider the third world to be a lucrative market for their product.
- Manufacturers of infant formula are using advertising that manipulates third-world mothers into thinking that formula is better for their babies.
- Infant formula is safer than breast milk if the mother has AIDS.
- Poor women often dilute infant formula to make it last longer.

All these subjects sound interesting to Baljit, but she realizes that she can't cover them comprehensively enough in a 5-minute speech. She decides not to deal with the manufacturers of infant formula and their advertising campaigns and to concentrate instead on health issues. Once she has narrowed down the subject to how infant formula affects health, she finds seven articles that are relevant and uses the material from them as research for her speech.

Jeff knows that he wants to talk about some aspect of football. He uses brainstorming to narrow down his topic. He writes "Football" at the top of the page and lists everything he can think of under this heading. His final list looks like this:

FOOTBALL

College
Professional
Ethical aspects
Organization and administration
Injuries
Photography
Rules
Super Bowl
Televising of

Although this list might not cover every aspect of football, it covers Jeff's main interests. He now studies this list and looks for something he can talk about. Since he is a photographer and always takes his camera to football games, he decides that "Photography" is the aspect that interests him most. His speech topic will be "How to Take Good Action Photographs." He has narrowed his subject in a way that will enable him to present information that will be useful and interesting to his audience.

Sherri, a mother of two preschool children, has returned to school to get her degree. Because she has had so many problems in arranging for baby-sitters, she knows she wants to give her speech on some aspect of child care for preschool children. She goes to the library and finds several articles about child care. Some focus on psychological problems; others discuss families where both parents work; yet others deal with professional standards in child care institutions. Sherri finds these articles interesting but decides that she wants to focus on practical information that will help others who face her problem. Finally she asks herself, "What would be the ideal child care arrangement for my family?" Her answer to the question becomes the topic of her persuasive speech: "Colleges Should Provide Child Care for Student Parents."

By starting with a subject they found interesting, Baljit, Jeff, and Sherri were able to work with it and narrow it in a way that would make it manageable for a speech. Now they are ready to start thinking about the purpose for which they will be giving the speech.

Selecting a Purpose

Whenever you give a speech you should have a good idea of your purpose or reason for speaking. Having this purpose in mind beforehand is very much like planning a trip: if you know where you're going, you are able to plan the route ahead of time. In the same way, having a purpose for your speech will help you to look for materials, organize and outline your speech, and adapt your speech to the needs and interests of your audience.

There are three stages in working out the purpose for your speech: (1) selecting the general purpose, (2) selecting the specific purpose, and (3) stating the central idea.

The General Purpose

When you are asked to state a **general purpose** for your speech, you should tell whether you intend to inform or to persuade. **Informative speeches** generally concentrate on explaining—telling how something works, what something means, or how to do something. A speaker who gives an informative speech usually tries to give his or her audience information without taking sides. For example, if a speaker is giving an informative speech about using animals for research, he will not state whether he is for or against it; he will let members of the audience make up their minds. When the subject is controversial, the informative speaker will present all sides of the issue. In an informative speech about running for fitness, for example, you could give the advantages (physical fitness and feeling good) and the possible disadvantages (shin splints and other injuries).

In a **persuasive speech** the speaker takes a particular position and tries to get the audience to accept and support that position. For example, a speaker tries to persuade her audience that it should oppose the nuclear freeze movement. Someone else tries to persuade the audience to support making ice hockey a varsity sport or to sign a petition against chemical dump sites in the community. In a persuasive speech, the speaker concentrates on looking for the best information available to support his or her point of view.

Often the same subject could lead to either an informative *or* a persuasive speech—depending on your wording of the topic and your approach. Say your subject is the ethics of abortion. If you choose as your topic "The Ethical Issues of Abortion" and cover the ethics on both sides of the issue, the wording of your topic and your approach are appropriate for an informative speech. But if your topic is "Abortion: The Wrong Choice," you clearly have a persuasive speech, because you have made up your mind and are in favor of one particular side of the issue. Here are some other subjects that are phrased first as informative (*I*) and then as persuasive (*P*) topics:

I: Hispanic Increase in U.S. Population
P: Hispanics Must Work to Elect Their Own Candidates

I: Educational Games for Children
P: Motivate Your Child to Learn with a Game

I: The Coupon Craze in the Supermarket
P: Use Coupons to Take Dollars off Your Supermarket Bill

Sometimes it's difficult to fit a speech firmly into an informative or a persuasive slot. In a persuasive speech, informative material often plays an important role. If you are speaking in favor of political candidates, it is natural to use information about their background and voting record. In an informative speech, even when you try to present both sides, one side might seem more persuasive than the other to some audience members.

Consider This **Consider This** *Consider This*

*I*f you are going to make a speech, whether it is within your home, at your workplace, or in a public forum, you have a certain responsibility. Well-mannered people who are present at the time are going to feel that they have to listen to you—you are therefore obligated to say something worth hearing. Never mind whether you are being paid money for your speech or not; you are *always* being paid in your listeners' time. They could be doing something else instead of listening to you. You owe them.

Source: Suzette Haden Elgin, *More on the Gentle Art of Verbal Self-Defense.*

Try This Try This Try This

*H*ere is a list of speech topics and purposes. Which word should go in the blank, inform or persuade?

1. To inform/persuade the audience that they should vote for the Democrats.
2. To inform/persuade the audience to learn one new vocabulary word each week.
3. To inform/persuade the audience of the amount of fat found in fast food.
4. To inform/persuade the audience how soybean products are often used as meat substitutes.
5. To inform/persuade the audience that vinyl records are superior to CDs.
6. To inform/persuade the audience of money-making opportunities in college.
7. To inform/persuade the audience to go abroad during one semester of college.
8. To inform/persuade the audience to do an intership in college.
9. To inform/persuade the audience that flea collars are bad for the health of pets.
10. To inform/persuade the audience about the job market in service industries.

Answers: 1. *P*   2. *P*   3. *I*   4. *I*   5. *P*   6. *I*   7. *P*   8. *P*   9. *I*   10. *I*

The Specific Purpose

After you have decided whether the general purpose of your speech is to inform or to persuade, you must then decide on a **specific purpose**. The statement of your specific purpose will help you focus on precisely what you want to accomplish—that is, it will help you define exactly what you are going to inform or to persuade your audience about. In deciding your specific purpose, you should follow four guidelines.

1. *State your purpose clearly and completely.* Examples of a specific purpose statement would be:

   To inform my audience how a record gets on a top-40 chart.

   To explain to audience members how to make titles for home videos.

   To persuade audience members to look for bargains in school supplies in discount stores.

   To persuade audience members to use computer-generated charts and graphs in their research papers.

2. *State your purpose in terms of the effect you want to have on your audience.* What information do you want to give to your audience, or

what do you want them to think or do when the speech is over? In an informative speech the main effect you seek is to have your audience remember the information. For example:

To inform my audience about how to calculate the amount of fat they are eating each day.

To inform my audience about how to cut the cost of a wedding.

In a persuasive speech, however, the effect you might want is for audience members to take direct action:

To persuade my audience to walk to campus if they live less than a mile away.

To persuade my audience to contribute to the fund to restore the bell.

3. *Limit your purpose statement to one idea.* Keeping your purpose statement limited to one idea will help you to narrow your topic and keep it specific. Notice that each of the above examples has only one idea. If the first example had been "To inform my audience how a record gets on a top-40 chart and how to become a disk jockey," the speaker would have had two topics to cover rather than one and the speech would have lacked focus.

4. *Use specific language in your purpose statement.* The more precise your language, the clearer the ideas will be in your mind. For example, "To persuade my audience against nuclear power" is too vague. Do you mean nuclear missiles? Or nuclear power plants? You could rephrase your purpose like this:

To persuade my audience that stockpiling nuclear arms is likely to lead to a war that will destroy the world.

or

To inform my audience about the risks of nuclear-produced electric power.

Once you have determined your statement of purpose, you should subject it to some tests. Does it meet the assignment? You might discover, for example, that your opinions on a subject are so strong that you are unable to talk about it without favoring one side over the other. This means your subject is better for a persuasive speech than for an informative one. If you have been assigned an informative speech, then you should keep this subject for a later time.

Another important test is to ask whether you can accomplish your purpose within the time limits of the speech. If your speech purpose is too broad to fit in the allotted time, you will have to either narrow the topic further or find a new topic. One speaker discovered, for example, that her purpose, "To inform my audience about physical fitness," was too broad; too many issues were involved. She rephrased her purpose: "To inform audience members how low-impact aerobics can improve their health."

The Central Idea

Whereas the specific purpose expresses what we want to accomplish when we give the speech, the **central idea** statement (also called the *thesis statement*) establishes the main thrust of the speech. Everything in the speech relates to the central idea. In an informative speech the central idea contains the information you want the audience to remember; in a persuasive speech, it tells audience members what you want them to do.

The difference between a specific purpose and a central idea statement is illustrated in the following examples. Notice that the central idea explains the *why* or the *how* of the specific purpose.

Specific Purpose: To persuade my audience to eat less salt.
Central Idea: Excess levels of salt in the body can lead to heart problems, depression, and irritability.

Specific Purpose: To inform my audience of what safety features to look for when buying a car.
Central Idea: When you buy a car, look for three safety features: color, weight, and restraint systems.

Specific Purpose: To inform my audience of the dangers inherent in "selling" political candidates through television commercials.
Central Idea: When we base our choice of candidates on television commercials, we put greater emphasis on the image of the candidate than on the issues he or she stands for.

The central idea should be stated in a full sentence, contain one idea, and use precise language. Sometimes it is not possible to come up with a central idea statement until you have finished organizing and outlining the speech. When you start working on your speech, you should have a tentative central purpose in mind; when you have finished organizing and outlining the speech you can refine it.

Joe decided on a speech topic and a specific purpose right away. His parents had just finished building a new house, and many of the materials that were used in the construction had been recycled. Joe decided to give a speech with the specific purpose "To inform my audience how recycled materials can be used in building houses." Joe knew his central idea would contain information about the kinds of recycled materials that could be used, but the specific concepts did not emerge until he had a rough outline:

   I. *The United States builds a million houses each year, and many of the materials traditionally used are in short supply.*
  II. *Waste paper products can be used to replace wood that is not visible.*
 III. *Shredded tires, plastic, melted scrap steel, and iron can be used throughout the house.*

Once Joe had completed his outline, he knew his central idea would be: "The United States can save many of its scarce resources by building houses from recycled materials."

Margaret Hernandez is the director of an organization called Citizens for a Better Environment (CBE). The organization has decided that its priority for the year is to conduct a campaign to get people to avoid buying products with excessive packaging or with packaging that is difficult to recycle. Since much of the campaign will consist of educating the public, Ms. Hernandez has scheduled several speeches throughout the community. She will speak to all kinds of audiences: on Monday to sixth graders in a middle school, on Wednesday to senior citizens, on Thursday to a college class, and on Friday to landfill managers in a statewide meeting.

In her speeches Ms. Hernandez always talks about packaging. However, she does not make the same speech to every audience. Instead, she adapts her material to make it appropriate for each particular group. Before she makes the speech to sixth graders, she finds out from their teacher that they have started a unit on recycling in their social studies class, and so they have some knowledge of the need to recycle. Ms. Hernandez decides to talk about two product packages that sixth graders are likely to know about: peanut butter and catsup. In this speech she discusses how difficult it is to recycle plastic and points out that they can help the recycling effort by urging their parents to buy these products in glass containers.

When Ms. Hernandez goes to speak to senior citizens, she assumes that many of them eat frozen dinners that can be heated in the oven or microwave. She brings in one brand of dinner that has three layers of packaging and uses this as a starting point to talk about the problems of packaging. She takes a similar approach with the college students. This time, however, she uses a package of microwave popcorn, a popular item in the dormitory. She asks students to imagine how large the trash pile would be if, in one week's time, half the students in the dorm made microwave popcorn in throw-away containers. Before she leaves, she gives the students a handout on how to make popcorn in containers that can be reused.

When Ms. Hernandez prepares to talk to the landfill managers, she knows that her speech should take a different direction. Since they run the landfills throughout the state, they are well aware of the problems of too much trash and garbage. Ms. Hernandez decides that her focus with this group will be on public education. Because there are only two branches of Citizens for a Better Environment, she tells them how to set up similar organizations in their own communities. She also recommends some activities they can engage in to educate the public.

The Role of the Speaker

In all of the above examples, Ms. Hernandez was playing the role of the speaker. Whenever you play this role, the audience has certain expectations of you. When an audience comes to hear you, it expects that you will be knowledgeable about your topic and that you will present what you know in an interesting way. Ms. Hernandez is a competent speaker not only because she knows her subject but also because she knows her audiences.

What Ms. Hernandez has done is to use audience analysis to adapt her subject matter to the specific characteristics of each group. **Audience analysis** is the process of finding out what the members of the audience already know about the subject, what they might be interested in, what their attitudes and beliefs are, and what kinds of people make up the audience. In your role as speaker you should consider audience analysis as one of the most important parts of your preparation.

Audience Knowledge

One important aspect of audience analysis is to take into account how much the audience is likely to know about a subject. In a practical sense, we can make only an educated guess about our audience's knowledge. We can assume that if we are talking to a lay audience and we pick a topic related to a specialized field of knowledge (electronics, radar, nuclear medicine, behavioral psychology), we will have to explain and define a lot of basic terminology before we can go into the subject in any depth. For example, when Sam spoke to his class about the fat in one's diet, he had to explain such terms as "saturated," "polyunsaturated," and "hydrogenated" before he could talk about anything else.

On some subjects we can assume that audiences have a base of general knowledge. If we are speaking on vitamins, we can assume most people know that vitamins are good for us and even that vitamin C is particularly good when people have colds. But a general knowledge about other vitamins should not be taken for granted.

Speakers should realize that although people have general information about many subjects, they usually don't know the specifics. Most people know, for example, that the Constitution guarantees us the right to free speech. Yet if you were to ask them what free speech means, they would probably be a little fuzzy on a definition or on what is encompassed by the term. Would they know, for example, that the courts regard ringing a bell or burning a flag as a form of free speech?

To give another example, when speaking to a college audience about her recent trip to mainland China, Ming assumed that most of her listeners would know approximately where China is located and that most of them would know that China is ruled by a Communist government. She figured, however, that most of them would not know much about such important Chinese ideas as communal farming or the Cultural Revolution, and so she took some time to explain them. Once she had given this background information, her speech and slides about what she had seen and done made much more sense.

In a college speech class, you can get some idea of how much your audience knows about your subject by asking your friends and classmates what they know. If you have been asked to speak before a group you belong to, you can ask a couple of members what they know about the subject. If they don't know very much, you can assume that your audience won't either and that you will have to start by giving basic information. Often the program chairperson who is responsible for finding speakers will be able to give you some information about audience members' level of knowledge and also about what is likely to interest them.

Audience Interest

Some subjects seem to be inherently interesting. Books on the best-seller list usually are about diet, exercise, and money. If you look at the topics covered by popular magazines, you will discover that self-help or self-improvement is the category of articles that appears most often. However, most of us do not want to be limited to speaking about physical fitness, diet, and self-help. Instead, we have to find a way to make other subjects appealing to our listeners.

One way to interest an audience in a topic is to point out that it has importance and relevance to them. Jan, an English major and a tutor in the Writing Center, wants to give a speech on the importance of writing skills. She knows that most students would like to improve their grades, but she also knows that most of them do not want to listen to a lecture on English composition. She decides to call her speech "Five Tips for Better Grades on Papers" and concentrates on giving specific and practical advice.

Another way to attract an audience's interest is to get it involved in the subject. Judy wants to persuade her audience that the school district should allocate more money to teach children with learning disabilities. She starts her speech with figures on the link between learning disabilities and juvenile delinquency and goes on to tell the stories of two disabled children who were so frustrated by their inability to learn that they dropped out of school and began to get into trouble with the law. Even though her audience might not have had an interest in the subject to begin with, her examples are so compelling that she creates an interest.

Since you will be speaking on a subject that interests you, it might be useful to spend some time thinking about why you find this area so intriguing. What things about it caught your attention in the first place? If you can re-create your own enthusiasm for a subject, you will have a better chance of exciting your audience's interest too.

How successful has this speaker been in appealing to audience interest? How should the speaker respond to this feedback?

Audience Attitudes and Beliefs

When planning your speech, you also need to consider your audience's attitudes and beliefs about your subject. Often you will be speaking before an audience that shares your beliefs—as when you speak before your club or your church group. The Sierra Club (a conservation group) will appreciate a speech on how to preserve the desert. Animal lovers will support a proposal to establish a local animal shelter. Fellow employees will be interested in a speech about improving working conditions. College students will favor a proposal requiring instructors to state their grading policies at the beginning of the semester. These subjects tie into the attitudes and beliefs of the audience members.

But sometimes your audience may not have any particular attitudes or beliefs about your subject. They may not have enough information to make up their minds, or they may not care enough to have an opinion. The latter will be especially difficult to deal with. If you want to appeal to an indifferent audience, you will have to try especially hard to make your listeners feel that the speech has relevance and importance to them. Bob, for example, wanted to speak to his class about the importance of voting in the student government election. He knew that most of his listeners believed that voting was a good idea but that when election day came, few of them would actually vote. In order to motivate them, he began his speech by pointing out that student government controls three areas of high interest to students: concerts, athletics, and food service.

Sometimes your own beliefs run contrary to those of your audience, and your speech may be met with hostility. If you think your audience may be opposed to your ideas on a subject, you have to plan your speech very carefully. Deb, for example, knew that her classmates would be opposed to the idea of a tuition increase. Yet by researching her topic carefully and presenting reasons for an increase, she was able to show that an increase was necessary. Her audience might not have been happy about the increase, but they had a better understanding of the reasons for it. In his speech, John set out to persuade members of his speech class that the college should drop its entire football program. Since football is a part of college life, he expected his audience to be hostile to the idea. John, however, was able to show that

---

Try This Try This Try This

*A*ssume that you are going to speak to three different audiences: a college speech class, a group of senior citizens, and a group of eighth graders. Take one of these topics and adapt it to each of these audiences with reference to the members' level of knowledge about the subject, their interest in the subject, and their attitudes toward it.

- Chewing Tobacco Is Harmful to Your Health

- The Government Should Regulate Commercials on TV

- Everyone Should Have a Daily Exercise Program

attendance at games was declining, that football consumed an enormous portion of the athletic budget, and that the money could be better used if it were applied to intramural programs that would benefit all students. Not all of his classmates were persuaded but after the speech was over, several of them told John that his ideas were worth considering.

Since people's attitudes and beliefs will affect how your speech is received, it is absolutely essential that they be considered when your speech is in the planning stage. Important clues to people's attitudes and beliefs can be discovered through audience demographics—to which we now turn.

Audience Demographics

Even if you have no specific information about your audience's knowledge of, interest in, and attitudes toward your subject, certain factual information about the audience members can tell you a great deal. **Demographic analysis** reveals data about the characteristics of a group of people, including such things as age, sex, education, occupation, race/nationality/ethnic origin, geographic location, and group affiliation.

When we work with demographic information, we generalize about the *entire audience*; our generalizations might not be true of individual members. For example, based on demographic data we have gathered, we might generalize that the age of our speech class audience is between 18 and 27— even though one member is in his fifties. In the same way, we can make generalizations about the class's educational level or about its racial composition. And on the basis of such generalizations, we can make some predictions about what might interest the people in this audience and what they might be knowledgeable about. Let's consider each of the demographic characteristics in turn.

AGE

As a speaker you need to have a sense of the age range of your audience because interests differ with age. College-age people are usually interested in school, future jobs, music, and interpersonal relationships. Young parents are often interested in subjects that might affect their children, such as school bus safety and school board policy. People in middle age tend to be focused on their jobs, and older adults tend to be interested in issues related to leisure activities and health. However, not all subjects are age-related. Computers, elections, and world and national news, for example, have interest for most age groups because they affect everyone.

Sometimes the same subject can be of interest to various age groups if it is adapted to each group's particular concerns. Take the subject of nutrition. If you were speaking to an elementary school audience, you would probably not go into detail about vitamins and minerals because you would have problems keeping the attention of the children. Instead, you might use puppets (one who eats junk food and the other who eats good food) or put your speech into a story with characters the children could identify with. If you talked about nutrition to pregnant mothers, you could adapt your speech to the needs of the fetus, assuming that every mother-to-be has a high interest in having a healthy baby. When you speak to older adults, you could talk about their particular nutritional needs, such as the importance of calcium to avoid bone injuries.

GENDER

The gender of audience members can also be important. In a speech that's open to the public, you will probably have both males and females in your audience. If you have either an all-male or all-female audience, it will probably be because you are talking to a club or organization whose members are all of one sex. The topic of your speech will then be influenced more by the organization itself than by the sex of its members. For example, the American Association of University Women (AAUW) has long been interested in education. If you were speaking to this group, its interest in education would be more important than the fact that the group is all female.

EDUCATION

The audience's level of education is important to a speaker because it gives some idea of the group's knowledge and experience. We can assume that the more education people have, the more specialized their knowledge. Lawyers, doctors, and Ph.D's all have specialized knowledge; however, they might have little information about subjects other than their own. Your main consideration when you prepare a speech is whether your audience has the same knowledge you have or whether you will have to start with the basics. For example, if you are a psychology major, don't assume that your speech class will know what the terms *paranoid* and *schizophrenic* mean. Even though people use these terms loosely, they often do not know the proper scientific definitions.

OCCUPATION

The occupation of audience members may influence how you approach some topics. Sometimes occupation indicates an area of specialized knowledge: paramedics and nurses know about the human body; lawyers know about human rights; social workers know about social problems. Occupation can also indicate interest in a subject. Most professional groups would probably be interested in a speech about ethics in their profession. Factory workers might be interested in the workings of a union or how to form one. If you are speaking to an occupational group, see if you can adapt your speech to that audience's job interests.

RACE/NATIONALITY/ETHNIC ORIGIN

Politicians are the people most likely to have whole audiences made up of a single race or ethnic group. To identify with these groups, they eat knishes in Jewish neighborhoods, burritos with Mexicans, and soul food with African-Americans. When they speak to one of these groups, they try to identify with their goals and aspirations.

If you are speaking to a group with diverse backgrounds, you should be particularly careful in your use of language. If your audience includes foreign students, they may have problems understanding slang and colloquial expressions. If you are in a class with different ethnic groups, some groups might not understand experiences that are typical of your own group. For example, not everyone has gone to summer camp and not everyone has eaten kim chi.

You should always be careful in any speech not to offend the feelings of others. Stereotypes of any group, or jokes that hold an ethnic group up to ridicule, are always inappropriate.

GEOGRAPHIC LOCATION

Your audience's geographic location may affect the content and approach of your speech. If the federal government is giving money to improve airport runways, find out if some of this money is coming to the local airport. If the nation has been hit with a crime wave (or a heat wave), has this been a problem in your local area? If you have a chance to speak in a town or city other than your own, the audience will be pleased if you know something about its area. Ralph Nader, the consumer advocate, always does some geographical research before he speaks. When he spoke on the environment to upstate New Yorkers, he mentioned specific environmental problems in their own area.

GROUP AFFILIATION

Knowing the clubs, organizations, or associations that audience members belong to can be useful because people usually identify with the goals and interests of their organizations. If you speak to a group, you should be aware of what it stands for and adapt your speech accordingly.

If you speak to the local historical society, its members will expect you to speak on a subject that has some historic angle. The campus journalism society will be interested in a speech dealing with the theory (e.g., freedom of the press) or practice (e.g., using video display terminals) of journalism.

Try This Try This Try This

*L*ooking at your speech class, what demographic information can you come up with?

- *Age:* What is the age range? What is the average age?

- *Sex:* How many females? How many males?

- *Education:* What is the level of education? Mainly freshmen and sophomores or juniors and seniors?

- *Occupation:* Do your classmates work? What kinds of jobs?

- *Race/nationality/ethnic origin:* What races, nationalities, and ethnic groups are represented in the class? What parts of the country or the world do they come from? Is everyone a native English speaker?

- *Group affiliation:* What groups do your classmates belong to? Can you determine any attitudes and beliefs they might hold from their group affiliations?

Some groups have particular issues or themes for the year, and they look for speakers who can tie their speeches into these themes.

Analyzing the Occasion

When planning your speech, as well as doing audience analysis, you need to consider the occasion. Factors to take into account when analyzing the occasion include the length of the speech, the time of day, and the location of the speech.

Length of the Speech

Always stick to the time limit set for the speech. If you are giving a speech in class, you will probably be told the amount of time you can speak. If you are asked to give a speech to a group or organization, you should ask how long you will be expected to speak. When the audience has an expectation of the length of your speech, it will get restless if you go on too long or be disappointed if you run short. If your speech topic is too complicated to be covered in the allotted time, you should narrow your topic or find another subject to speak on.

More than one speaker hasn't known when to stop. Mortimer J. Adler has written about the time he was giving lectures on philosophy to college students. Student interest in the subject was great, but not great enough to sit through each of Adler's two-hour lectures! When Adler returned the next year to deliver another series of lectures, the students hid alarm clocks in the lecture hall. After an hour, all of the alarms went off. At the second lecture, a student pulled the main switch after an hour and blacked out the lecture hall. Adler got the message; he cut his remaining lectures to a listenable length.[3]

Time of Day

The time of day should also be a consideration when choosing your topic. In a classroom setting, students seem to be less alert in the early morning and late afternoon. If you are in a class that meets at one of these times, you have to pay special attention to the appeal of your presentation. An interesting topic or a topic handled in an interesting manner can get the attention of even a sluggish audience. Probably most public speeches occur at night. Since people are usually somewhat tired, the speaker has to take special care to find material that will hold the audience's attention.

Physical Setting of the Speech

The place where the speech will be given might also be a consideration. If you are not familiar with the room, you might want to take a look at it before you speak. Is the lectern where you want it? Are the chairs arranged the way you want them? Is there a public address system? Do you need one? It is easier to make changes before the audience arrives.

Comfort should also be considered in a location. Many a politician has given a speech from the courtyard steps, where there was no place for the audience to sit. If you are in a location where the audience cannot be comfortable, be prepared to give a short speech and get to the point before you lose your audience.

SUMMARY

Whenever you are scheduled to make a speech, it is important to find a topic that interests you. Two techniques will help you discover topics: making a personal inventory, which means taking a careful look at what interests you, and brainstorming, which is a method of generating ideas through free association.

Once you have an idea for a topic, you should test whether the topic is appropriate for the audience, whether it is appropriate for you, and whether it is appropriate for the occasion.

Whatever you plan to speak on, you should narrow the topic so that it can be adequately covered within the time set for your speech. Narrowing the topic means taking some specific aspect of the subject and speaking about that.

Every speech should have a general purpose, a specific purpose, and a central idea. The general purpose relates to whether the speech is informative or persuasive. The specific purpose focuses on what you want to inform or persuade your audience about. The central idea captures the main idea of the speech—the idea you want your audience to retain after the speech.

Audience analysis is the process of finding out what the audience knows about the subject, what it might be interested in, what its attitudes and beliefs are, and what kinds of people are likely to be present. Useful demographic information about an audience includes age, gender, education, occupation, race, nationality/ethnic origin, geographic location, and group affiliation.

In analyzing the speech occasion, the speaker should consider the length of the speech, the time of day, and the physical setting where it will take place.

FURTHER READING

ADLER, MORTIMER J. *How to Speak, How to Listen.* New York: Macmillan, 1983. Written from a layman's perspective, this book discusses the sales talk, lectures and discussion, conversation as well as question-and-answer sessions. The book is full of examples and practical suggestions. Adler is a philosopher and tends to emphasize matters of content and substance.

ALLEN, STEVE. *How to Make a Speech.* New York: McGraw-Hill, 1988. This engaging, entertaining how-to book is simple and specific. Allen brings his many years of radio and television work as both comedian and actor as well as his forty years at the lectern to bear on this work. An enjoyable book to read. Allen's background is entertainment, and the focus of this work tends to be presentational skills.

DETZ, JOAN. *How to Write and Give a Speech.* New York: St. Martin's Press, 1984. Detz is a corporate speechwriter who gives practical advice on focusing the topic, assessing the audience, organizing material, simplifying and sharpening language, making humor work, handling tough question-and-answer sessions, delivering speeches with style, and getting good media coverage. A fast-paced, confidence-building book. Detz's background is business, and she writes a practical guide for business executives.

EHNINGER, DOUGLAS, BRUCE E. GRONBECK, RAY E. MCKERROW, AND ALAN H. MONROE. *Principles and Types of Speech Communication*, 10th ed. Glenview, IL: Scott, Foresman, 1986 (and Gronbeck, Ehninger, and Monroe, *Principles of Speech Communication*, 10th brief ed., 1988). These are excellent textbooks that offer readers a comprehensive introduction to the nature of public speaking.

HENNESSY, BERNARD. *Public Opinion*, 5th ed. Monterey, CA: Brooks/Cole, 1985. The author includes several sections on conducting polls and administering questionnaires. A useful source for those interested in techniques for gaining information about their audience.

LUCAS, STEPHEN E. *The Art of Public Speaking*, 4th ed. New York: Random House, 1992. In this textbook, the classical and contemporary theories of rhetoric are applied to the practical skills of public speaking. Major aspects of speech preparation and presentation are discussed in an interesting and lively manner.

MCCROSKEY, JAMES C. *An Introduction to Rhetorical Communication*, 5th ed. Englewood Cliffs, NJ: Prentice-Hall, 1986. A textbook that offers a useful blend of the theories of rhetorical communication based on traditional rhetoric and contemporary social science research. A fine textbook for increasing our understanding of the process of rhetorical communication.

RUBIN, REBECCA B., ALAN M. RUBIN, AND LINDA J. PIELE. *Communication Research: Strategies and Sources*, 2d ed. Belmont, CA: Wadsworth, 1989. These authors provide a valuable reference guide for the entire research process. In addition to a comprehensive analysis of research sources, they provide step-by-step advice on the actual development of the research effort.

WELLS, GORDON. *How to Communicate*, 2d ed. New York: McGraw-Hill, 1988. This is a lively guide to style, clarity, and precision written by a former journalist who is a member of one of the world's largest public relations firms. After a 43-page preamble on style, there is a glossary—a cross-referenced index of words, rules, subjects, and phrases. A useful resource. As a journalist, Einstein's primary focus is on language and style.

Chapter 12

Finding Speech Material

CHAPTER OBJECTIVES	KEY TERMS
After reading this chapter, you should be able to:	abstract
	catalog
1. Include some of your own experiences as part of your speech.	comparison
	contrast
2. Gather speech information by interviewing.	data base
	definition
3. Research your speech in the library.	example
	periodicals
4. Use the various reference tools in the library.	polls
	statistics
5. Recognize the various kinds of supporting materials.	study
	supporting material
6. Use the supporting materials that are most appropriate for your topic and your audience.	testimony
	vertical file

Karen was desperate. She had to give a speech and she hadn't found a topic yet. As she sat with her friends in the student union, she said, "Come on, you guys. Help me find a topic for my speech." One of them, who was reading his horoscope, said, "What about astrology? Everyone's interested in that." Karen said, "That's a great idea. Students are always talking about their signs." Karen didn't have much time to prepare a speech, but she knew that she should start in the library. She checked out the card catalog under "Astrology" and found a few book titles. But once she had located the books in the stacks, she realized she didn't have time to read them. However, she did find two magazine articles that were useful.

Later that night when she put together her speech, she found she didn't have much material at all. When it was organized and she tried it out, she found it was only three minutes long—and that was only when she paused a lot. However, it was too late to do anything about it. When she gave the speech the next day, Karen's audience listened closely at first but soon lost attention. Since it was clear she had little information, they asked no questions. The speech was barely mediocre, and Karen felt embarrassed about the whole experience.

In another speech class a second student, Tim, was planning to give a speech on the same subject. Tim was an astronomy major, and he had read in one of his textbooks that astrology was an early form of astronomy. Tim thought this might be a good speech topic, so he went to the library to see what he could find. He found several books and articles on the subject and was able to put together lots of note cards of information. As he was reading, he also discovered that astrological signs are now being charted by computer. He decided to organize his speech around the history of astrology—beginning with the days it was considered a science and ending with computers.

The audience listened to Tim's speech with obvious interest. It was clear that he had done some research and knew quite a lot about his subject. After the speech was over, several people asked him questions, and at the end of class someone even asked where to go to get a computer horoscope. By doing his research and carefully planning his speech, Tim had come across as a *credible*—that is, believable—speaker.

No doubt you would like to have the same reaction from your class that Tim had. You would like to be thought of as credible, as knowing your subject. The key to having this happen lies in the research you do for your speech. The more diligent you are about finding relevant material and adapting it to your audience, the more successful you are going to be when you give your speech.

Researching Your Topic: Where to Look

Once you have decided on the topic and specific purpose of your speech, it is time to begin looking for useful information. The three most common sources you can draw on for relevant material are your own personal experience and observation, interviews, and the library. Let's look at each of these.

If you have chosen a topic in which you have a strong interest, the first thing you should ask yourself is whether you have had any direct experience with the subject. Your own experience can provide some of the most interesting and valuable material. For example, when Dan spoke to his speech class on the subject "Preventing Fires in Your Home," he drew heavily on his experiences as a volunteer firefighter. Not only did he describe the tragedy of a family being burned out of its home, but he also gave some facts and figures on the causes of home fires that he had learned during his training period.

When Kelly spoke of the danger of drunk drivers, she too gave facts and figures: how many innocent victims are killed each year by drunks on the road. Then she stunned her classmates by telling them that her own sister was one of those victims. Because Kelly spoke out of personal experience, her example became much more vivid and real than if she had used only statistics from a book or an article.

Sometimes we do not put enough value on personal experience; we think that if it happened to us, it can't be important. However, relating our own experiences to the subject of our speech can often provide the most interesting material of all.

Interviewing

Interviews can be an excellent source of speech material. Because you can talk directly to decision makers, interviews are one of the best ways of gathering material on campus-related topics such as why three people are put in dorm rooms intended for two or what energy-saving devices are used on campus. Interviews are also a good way of getting up-to-date information from experts. For example, if a war breaks out in the Middle East, you can interview the person on campus who is most knowledgeable in this area. Another advantage of interviewing is that if the subject is complicated, you can ask questions about points you don't understand. Chapter 8 deals with the subject of interviewing, and if you are considering gathering material through an interview, you might find it helpful to look at that chapter again.

Consider This **Consider This** *Consider This*

*I*t is natural enough for beginners to feel disconcerted—lost and lonely—in a strange library. You can quickly overcome this feeling by making up your mind to learn your library. Regardless of size, all libraries have common features that the experienced researcher looks for at once. After you have conquered a few of these strongholds you will realize that to master one library is to master them all.

Source: Jacques Barzun and Henry F. Graff, *The Modern Researcher.*

Using the Library

The library can be one of the richest sources of material. Any library—whether large or small—has millions of pieces of information. Fortunately for users, all libraries organize their information in essentially the same way, and so once you learn how to use one library, you can use this skill in *any* library. The goal of this section is to help you make the most of your campus (or public) library to find information that will be useful in preparing speeches.

THE LIBRARY CATALOG

The library **catalog** consists of information about all the material in the library and identifies where it can be found. In practically every college or university, the catalog is either printed on small cards housed in a many-drawered cabinet or on a central computer to which you can gain access through a terminal. Both systems use call numbers. Although call numbers organize library materials by subject, to the library user their main use is to help locate the book. All call numbers that begin with "PN," for example, will be located in the same general area.

Since card and computer catalogs are somewhat different, we would like to discuss each one here.

The Card Catalog Entries are organized in three ways: by author, by title, and by subject. If you want a particular book and you know who wrote it, you can look it up by author. If you know only the title, you can look it up by title. If you don't know any authors or titles but are interested in a particular subject, you can look in the subject catalog. Figure 12-1 shows the same book—classified by author, title, and subject. Note that in the upper left corner of each card the call number is given.

The catalog entries not only tell you where to find the material, but also give you some general information about it so you can decide whether it will be useful. Always check the date of the materials. On some subjects, the date when the material was published is not very important. However, in other subjects you will want to have the most timely information.

The Computer Catalog In many ways the computer catalog duplicates the card catalog: it has call numbers and entries arranged by author, subject, and title. The main difference in the computer catalog is that it almost always gives you more information. Let's look at this in greater detail.

When you sit in front of a computer screen, remember that entries start with the general and, with each new screen, move to the more specific. As you can see in Figure 12-2, if you type in "biological rhythms," the computer responds with all the material in that category. If you want to look at a single entry, such as the book by Shirley Moore, you type in "12," and the screen for her book comes up. Note that at the bottom of the entry, the screen not only gives the call number, but also tells exactly where the book is located in the library. In addition, the computer will tell you whether the book is available. As you can see on the third card in Figure 12-2, one copy of a particular book about Freud is available for circulation. Other information

```
        Rovin, Jeff.
ref.
P       The encyclopedia of monsters/Jeff Rovin.—New York :
96      Facts on File, c1989. ix, 390 p. : ill. ; 28 cm.
.M6     Includes index.
R68     ISBN 0–8160–1824–3
1989


        1. Monsters in mass media—
        Dictionaries. 2. Popular culture—
        Dictionaries. I. Title
```

```
        The encyclopedia of monsters
ref.
P       Rovin, Jeff.
96
.M6     The encyclopedia of monsters/Jeff Rovin.—New York :
R68     Facts on File, c1989. ix, 390 p. : ill. ; 28 cm.
1989    ISBN 0–8160–1824–3


        1. Monsters in mass media—
        Dictionaries. 2. Popular culture—
        Dictionaries.
```

```
        MONSTERS IN MASS MEDIA—DICTIONARIES.
ref.                                              1989
P       Rovin, Jeff.
96
.M6     The encyclopedia of monsters/Jeff Rovin.—New York :
R68     Facts on File, c1989. ix, 390 p. : ill. ; 28 cm.
1989    ISBN 0–8160–1824–3


        1. Monsters in mass media—
        Dictionaries. 2. Popular culture—
        Dictionaries.
```

Figure 12-1
**Card Catalog: The
Same Book
Classified by
Author, Title, and
Subject**

```
Biological rhythms (82 citations)
[1]  Advances in climatic physiology. [1st ed.]. [1972].
[2]  An analysis of biorhythms and their effect on athletic injuries.
     / Klug, Gary A. 1973.
[3]  Analysis of periodicity of arrhythmias in patients with acute
     myocardial infarctions. / Nail, Lillian M. 1974.
[4]  Analysis of selected physiological variables and selected
     biological rhythms in the performance of track and field
     competitors. / Hall, Larry T. 1976.
[5]  Aspects of human efficiency: diurnal rhythm and loss of sleep.
     1972.
[6]  Avian breeding cycles. /  Murton, R.K. 1977.
[7]  Bio rhythms [slide]. c1981.
[8]  Bioclocks [slide]. 1976.
[9]  Biological and biochemical oscillators. 1973.
[10] Biological clocks. / Brady, John. 1979.
[11] Biological clocks. / Cloudsley-Thompson, J. L. c1980.
[12] Biological clocks and patterns. / Moore, Shirley. [1967].
[13] Biological clocks and shift work scheduling. / United States.
     Congress. House. Committee on Science and Technology.
     Subcommittee on Investigations and Oversight. 1983.
—  —  —  —  —  —  —  —  —  —  —  —  —  —  —  —   —Lib All
>>> 1
>>>
To see more citations, press [NEXT] or [PREV].
```

```
Biological rhythms
Moore, Shirley.
     Biological clocks and patterns. New York, Criterion Books, [1967].
     133 p. illus. 22 cm.
     Bibliography: p. 117-127.
     1. Biological rhythms. 2. Biological control systems.
Call#: QH527.M65
     East Pattee Second Floor
—  —  —  —  —  —  —  —  —  —  —  —  —  —  —  —   —Lib All
>>> 12                                                    12 of 82
>>>
```

```
The scientific credibility of Freud's theories and therapy. / Fisher,
     Seymour. c1977.
BF173.F85F55
—Central Pattee Level 2
     Blue—
Now in Reserve Reading
     Room
     1 Available
—  —  —  —  —  —  —  —  —  —  —  —  —  —  —  —   —Lib All
>>> st
>>>
```

Figure 12-2
Screens from the
Computer Catalog

on the status of the book could tell you that the book is lost, that it is checked out (and when it will be back), or that it's in the reserve room.

Perhaps the greatest advantage of a computer catalog is that it's very easy to browse when you are using it. If you have several subjects in mind, you can easily check out the computer to see what is available. You can also browse through the library's shelves without ever leaving your chair since most systems have a "shelf" command, which will show you all the items with a particular call number—items that would be shelved in the same section of the library.

If your library has its collection on computer, take some time to check the instruction manual to see how to use it best. Usually it's easy to search for books by author, title, and subject, but the computer can do much more than that. The more you know about the computer, the more sophisticated and efficient your search will be.

LOOKING FOR ARTICLES

Periodicals—the inclusive name for magazines, journals, and newspapers— have the latest available information on a subject, and are often used as source material for speeches. If you want to know, for example, what the American president said to the Soviet premier yesterday, the newspaper is your best source, for it will have the latest information. Magazine articles typically cover such subjects as the latest trends in a variety of popular subjects; academic journals cover the latest research.

The card or computer catalog will tell you which periodicals are held in the library, including those on microfilm. The catalog, however, does not list the articles for these periodicals. To find them, you must either check the periodical indexes in book form or use a computer designed for searching periodicals. Let's look at the indexes first.

Since hundreds of thousands of magazines and journal articles are published every month, you will need an index to find the particular articles you need. Your library is likely to have several such indexes, and, like the catalog, their entries are classified by author, title, and subject. When you are searching for articles in periodical indexes, you should identify the general category and then look for an index that is likely to cover that subject. For example, if you want to research preschools, the *Education Index* is likely to have articles on that subject. If you are looking for articles about preschools in mass-circulated magazines, *The Reader's Guide to Periodical Literature* would be a good place to start.

Some other common indexes found in libraries are: *Social Science Index, Applied Science and Technology Index, Index to Periodical Articles by and about Blacks, Books in English: Authors, Subjects, Titles, Business Periodicals Index, Monthly Catalog of United States Government Publications,* and *Consumer Index.*

Many periodicals sections of libraries have computers designed to search for articles in periodicals and journals. These computers have access to a **data base**—a collection of information that can be read on a computer screen. Data bases commonly found in periodical rooms are ERIC, an index to periodicals in education, and InfoTrac, an index of general interest and academic periodicals.

To use these computers, you type in the name of the subject you wish to search. The computer will respond with all the relevant articles. Some data bases also have **abstracts**—summaries of the articles. Abstracts will tell you enough about an article for you to decide whether it is worthwhile to locate the entire thing.

Your search will be more successful if your entry is very specific. The computer finds what you are looking for by matching the words you type with the same words in its data base. For example, let's say you want to make a speech about how to protect your house from fire. If you type in only "fire," you could get hundreds of entries. However, if you type in "house fires," the computer will list only those titles that have both "house" and "fire" in them.

Whether you use indexes or a computer to search for articles, the actual periodical might not be available in your campus library. Thus when you are researching, make a longer list of possible sources than you will actually use because you might be able to locate only a fraction of them.

Since libraries are always short of space, many of them have material (especially periodicals) on microfilm or microfiche. Microfilm and microfiche differ only in the method by which pages are put on the film. *Microfilm* presents data on a roll, with one page following another. In *microfiche*, a large number of pages are put on the same piece of film, which looks like a small note card. The machines needed to read each one are different. Don't let the machines intimidate you. Someone in the library will show you how to use them.

Newspapers   Most libraries have the local newspaper, papers from around the state, and a few of the important big-city newspapers. The big-city papers deal comprehensively with international and national issues, while the local papers cover information of importance to the particular area. Practically every college has *The New York Times*. This paper is particularly useful for research, since it publishes an index of many of the articles it carries. *The New York Times* is also one of the few newspapers to carry partial or full texts of such documents as Supreme Court decisions, legislation, and speeches (especially presidential ones).

What kinds of publications are on microfilm in your university library?

If you don't see the newspaper you want on the newspaper rack, check the card catalog. Some libraries store newspapers and magazines on microfilm to save space.

FINDING REFERENCE WORKS

Every library has a reference section which contains materials that do not circulate. The reference works found in this section are factual materials that cover every subject you can think of. If you don't know very much about a subject, the reference section is a good place to begin.

Encyclopedias Encyclopedias are an important part of any library's reference collection, and most libraries have several different sets. Encyclopedias contain short articles written by experts, and they are a very good way to get basic information on a subject you don't know much about. They work best as a starting point. Once you have the basic knowledge, you can do further research in other sources. Most encyclopedias are arranged in alphabetical order by subject. Some of the best known are *The American Academic Encyclopedia, The Encyclopaedia Britannica, World Book Encyclopedia, Collier's Encyclopedia,* and *The Encyclopedia Americana.*

Almanacs Almanacs are compilations of factual material. Although they do not contain in-depth material on which to base a speech, they are very useful for checking out facts. If you want to know who won the World Series in 1964 or how many people were executed in 1981 or how much the federal government spends on defense, you'll find it in an almanac. Some of the most popular almanacs are *The World Almanac, Information USA, Reader's Digest Almanac, Guinness Book of Records,* and *Information Please.*

Biographical Sources Biographical information can be useful in many contexts and is particularly useful if you are going to introduce or speak about someone with an established reputation. Several biographical sources are available, of which the *Who's Who* series is the best known. There are the broad, general editions—*Who's Who in the World, Who's Who in America*—and there are the more specific ones: *Who's Who in Finance and Industry . . . of American Women . . . in American Politics . . . in Government,* and *. . . in Science*—to name just a few. The entries, listed alphabetically by last name, typically list birth date, names of spouse and children, school attended, and accomplishments. Other biographical sources include *Current Biography, Dictionary of National* [English] *Biography, Dictionary of American Biography, New York Times Biographical Service,* and *The Biography Index.*

Figure 12-3 shows entries for Stephen King, the novelist, from two biographical sources.

Government Documents Documents pertaining to city, state, and federal government are an important part of the collection in most libraries. Many of these documents describe how government is run. If you are doing a speech on any aspect of government policy, it would be useful to check out this information. Typical city (or county) information will cover such subjects as

KING, Stephen (Edwin) 1947–
(Steve King; pseudonyms: Richard Bachman, John Swithen)

PERSONAL: Born September 21, 1947, in Portland, Me.; son of Donald (a merchant sailor) and Nellie Ruth (Pillsbury) King; married Tabitha Jane Spruce (a novelist), January 2, 1971; children: Naomi Rachel, Joseph Hill, Owen Phillip. *Education:* University of Maine at Orono, B.Sc., 1970. *Politics:* Democrat.
ADRESSES: Home—Bangor and Center Lovell, Me. *Office*—P.O. Box 1186, Bangor, Me. 04001. *Agent*—Arthur Greene, 101 Park Ave., New York, N.Y. 10178.
CAREER: Writer. Has worked as a janitor, a laborer in an industrial laundry, and in a knitting mill. Hampden Academy (high school), Hampden, Me., English teacher, 1971–73; University of Maine, Orono, writer in residence 1978–79. Owner, Philtrum Press, a publishing house, and WZON–AM, a rock 'n' roll radio station, both in Bangor, Me. Has made cameo appearances in films ''Knightriders,'' as Steven King, 1980, ''Creepshow,'' 1982, ''Maximum Overdrive,'' 1986, and ''Pet Sematary,'' 1989; has also appeared in American Express credit card television commercial. Served as judge for 1977 World Fantasy Awards, 1978. Participated in radio honor panel with George A. Romero, Peter Straub, and Ira Levin, moderated by Dick Cavett on WNET in New York, October 30–31, 1980.
MEMBER: Authors Guild, Authors League of America.
AWARDS, HONORS: Carrie named to *School Library Journal's* Book List, 1975; World Fantasy Award nominations, 1976, for '*Salem's Lot,* 1979, for *The Stand* and *Night Shift,* 1980, for *The Dead Zone,* 1981, for ''The Mist,'' and 1983, for ''The Breathing Method: A Winter's Tale'' in *Different Seasons;* Hugo Award nomination from World Science Fiction Society, and Nebula Award nomination from Science Fiction Writers of America, both 1978, both for *The Shining;* Balrog Awards, second place in best novel category for *The Stand,* and second place in best collection category for *Night Shift,* both 1979; *The Long Walk* was named to the American Library Association's list of best books for young adults, 1979; World Fantasy Award, 1980, for contributions to the field, and 1982, for story ''Do the Dead Sing?''; Career Alumni Award, University of Maine at Orono, 1981; *Firestarter* was named to the American Library Association's list of best books for young adults, 1981; Nebula Award nomination, Science Fiction Writers of America, 1981, for story ''The Way Station''; special British Fantasy Award for outstanding contribution to the genre, British Fantasy Society, 1982 for . . .

Contemporary Authors, New Revision Series, 1990

KING, STEPHEN EDWIN, novelist; b. Portland, Maine, Sept. 21, 1947; s. Donald and Nellie Ruth (Pillsbury) K.; m. Tabitha Jane Spruce, Jan. 2, 1971; children: Naomi Rachel, Joseph Hillstrom, Owen Phillip. B.S., U. Maine, 1970. Tchr. English Hampden (Maine) Acad., 1971–73; writer in residence U. Maine at Orono, 1978–79. Novels include Carrie, 1974, Salem's Lot, 1975, The Shining, 1976, The Stand, 1978, Firestarter, 1980, Danse Macabre, 1981, Cujo, 1981, Different Seasons, 1982, The Dark Tower: The Gunslinger, 1982, Christine, 1983, Pet Sematary, 1983, The Talisman, Cycle of the Werewolf, 1985, Skeleton Crew, 1986, The Eyes of the Dragon, 1987, Misery, 1987, The Dark Tower: The Drawing of the Three, 1987, The Tommyknockers, 1987, The Dark Half, 1989, The Stand, 1990; short story collection Night Shift, 1978; author numerous other short stories; (as Richard Bachman) Rage, 1977, The Long Walk, 1979, Roadwork, 1981. The Running Man, 1982, Thinner, 1984; author numerous short story screenplays. Mem. Author's Guild Am., Screen Artists Guild, Screen Writers of Am., Writer's Guild. Democrat.

Who's Who in America, 1991

Figure 12-3
Biographical Sources

budget allocations, social service agencies, maps, and surveys. Many state governments publish yearly almanacs, which contain such information as the number of people in the state, the longest river, per-capita income, and so on. Most states also publish information about state law and state tax structure. Often libraries also carry tourist and promotional information about the state. Since state and local governments differ in how they publish and organize information, ask the reference librarian for help if you want to use this material.

The United States government is the biggest publisher in America. To find out what it is publishing, check the *Monthly Catalog of United States Government Publications.* This is an index to articles about various federal departments.

Here are some of the departments covered:

Agricultural Cooperative Service

Census Bureau

Centers for Disease Control

Civil Rights Commission

Congress

Education Department

Environmental Protection Agency

Fish and Wildlife Service

Indian Affairs Bureau

Justice Department

National Center for Health Statistics

National Portrait Gallery

State Department

Supreme Court

Since federal government publications are so extensive, few libraries carry all the articles listed in the *Monthly Catalog.* If your library does not have the material, you have two choices: you can write away for the material (the catalog tells how to do this) or you can ask your librarian for the location of the nearest federal depository library. A federal depository library is a regular library, but it is also one in which the federal government has chosen to put all of the documents it publishes. There are 1350 federal depository libraries in the United States, so there is probably one not very far from where you live. (Your own library might be one.)

The Vertical File If you need more information on a subject, or if you need a subject for a speech, see if your library has a vertical file. Most libraries receive hundreds of publications from consumer groups, business, industry, and the consumer divisions of state and federal government. To make these available, libraries file them alphabetically by subject matter in filing cabinets called the **vertical file**. If you opened a drawer of your library's vertical file, you might find the following subjects:

Silicon

Silicosis

Silk

Silk screen printing

Silos & silage

Silver

Silver plating

Silverware

Singapore

Singing

Single people

Sinkholes

Sinus disease

Sisal

Skateboards

Skeletons

Skibobbing

Skiing

Skin

Miscellaneous Material   In addition to the reference material already discussed, every library has a miscellaneous collection of material of interest to its patrons. For example, many libraries have telephone books from around the country, annual reports from corporations, historical and genealogical information that is used for researching a family tree, and books about local history.

USING INTERLIBRARY LOAN

When your own library doesn't have a book or an article you need, it can usually obtain it from some other library. Since each library has a specific procedure for requesting books through interlibrary loan, check with one of the librarians. You will have to plan ahead if you want to use this service. A photocopy of a magazine article will take about ten days; a book might take longer.

USING THE LIBRARY STAFF

Whatever the size of a library, its librarians are its single greatest resource. All their education and experience has been devoted to finding and organizing information, and because of this training they are able to help you find anything you want to know. Although you should be able to do most of your

---

Consider This **Consider This** *Consider This*

A good Reference Librarian can be your best assistant in preparing your speeches. If you give speeches fairly often, it would be worth your time to go to your library and meet the Reference Librarian in person. Generally, he or she is someone who enjoys digging out obscure bits of information. Such specialists get a kick out of finding out the real name of that famous movie star, or the cost of our first aircraft carrier, or how high in the sky those satellites are that relay our TV programs.

Source: Leon Fletcher, *How to Speak Like a Pro.*

library work on your own, you should not be afraid to ask for help when you need it.

291

Finding Speech Material

TAKING NOTES

Since library research is time-consuming, there is no sense in having to do it twice. Careful note taking will help you use your time efficiently. Make sure to copy source information completely and accurately. This will help you if you should need to find the material again. Also, if you are asked about any of the sources you have used, you can tell someone where to find them.

Whether it is for footnotes, end notes, or bibliographies, make certain you copy the author's full name correctly. In addition, for a book, copy the title of the book, place of publication, name of publisher, publication date, and page numbers you have used; for an article, copy the title of the article, title of periodical, volume numbers, date, and page numbers of the article. Figure 12-4 shows sample note cards.

Supporting Material: What to Look for

Once you have learned where to look for information, your next project is to find supporting material for your speech. **Supporting material** is information that backs up your main point and provides the main content of the speech. To find effective material you need to return to the specific purpose of your speech. Let's say you are interested in art and you want to speak on how to visit a museum, and your specific purpose statement is "to inform the audience about how they can enjoy their visit to an art museum." Now you have to find supporting material that will help you achieve your goal of informing the audience about museums.

Before you begin to look for such material, you should think about what might work in your speech and make some notes about what to look for. Your notes might look something like this:

How many museums are located in this area?	Look for names and locations.
What kinds of collections exist?	Identify the different types of collections, e.g., modern, historical.
What guide books are available at each museum?	Collect some sample guides.

By thinking out the speech beforehand, you save yourself time because you won't need to read everything about museums. You will have a good idea of what you are looking for and can pass over information that does not serve your purpose. Sometimes you might find some interesting material you hadn't thought about. If it fits into your speech, use it.

Every speech you put together should have supporting material for the main content of your speech. Some of the material you will find through library research; other material can come from your personal experience or from interviews.

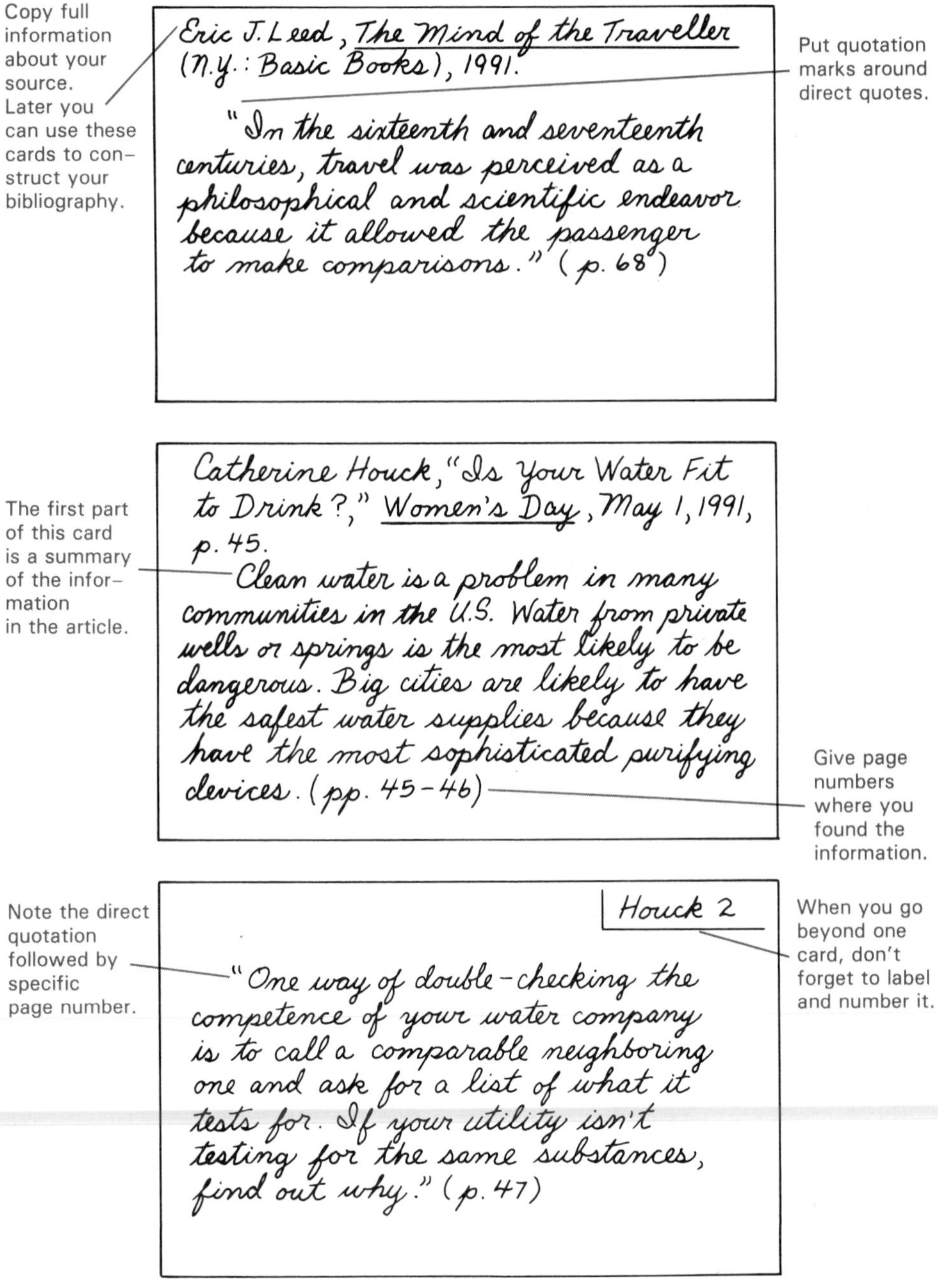

Copy full information about your source. Later you can use these cards to construct your bibliography.

Eric J. Leed, *The Mind of the Traveller* (N.Y.: Basic Books), 1991.

"In the sixteenth and seventeenth centuries, travel was perceived as a philosophical and scientific endeavor because it allowed the passenger to make comparisons." (p. 68)

Put quotation marks around direct quotes.

The first part of this card is a summary of the information in the article.

Catherine Houck, "Is Your Water Fit to Drink?," *Women's Day*, May 1, 1991, p. 45.
Clean water is a problem in many communities in the U.S. Water from private wells or springs is the most likely to be dangerous. Big cities are likely to have the safest water supplies because they have the most sophisticated purifying devices. (pp. 45-46)

Give page numbers where you found the information.

Note the direct quotation followed by specific page number.

Houck 2

"One way of double-checking the competence of your water company is to call a comparable neighboring one and ask for a list of what it tests for. If your utility isn't testing for the same substances, find out why." (p. 47)

When you go beyond one card, don't forget to label and number it.

Figure 12-4
Taking Notes: Sample Note Cards

In the sections that follow, we are going to discuss some types of supporting material. Each time you prepare a speech, you should decide which type will work best for your particular speech.

Comparison

Comparisons point out the similarities between two or more things. For example, a student who spoke about the way to cut wedding costs said:

Think of your wedding reception as a very big party. Like a party, the reception should have tasty food, interesting entertainment, and time for the guests to mingle and talk to each other.

Comparisons can often be used as a way to help your audience imagine something that is outside its experience. For example, this student wanted her audience to imagine what it was like to snorkel in the ocean. She used several comparisons:

Imagine swimming in a giant aquarium and you are only as big as the smallest fish. One of the rocks you see is as big as a two-story house. The coral all around you is larger than a fully grown oak tree.

Sometimes a comparison can show us a new way of looking at something. We have often heard the United States referred to as a "melting pot" of different races and nationalities. Wanting to use the same concept but not the same cliché, the Rev. Jesse Jackson found a new comparison:

America is not like a blanket—one piece of unbroken cloth, the same color, the same texture, the same size. It is more like a quilt—many patches, many pieces, many colors and many sizes, all woven and held together by a common thread.[1]

Contrast

Contrasts point out the differences between two or more things. A contrast might tell how baseball is different from softball or how an all-terrain bike is different from a standard ten-speed. One student who was speaking on the subject of keeping a diary made this contrast:

Men's and women's diaries are very different from each other. In most cases, men's diaries concentrate on their public life; women, on their private life. Men seldom write of wives and children; women have numerous entries about their families. Most important, women write of their feelings; men write of their deeds.

It can be effective to contrast the familiar with the unfamiliar. This student, just back from an exchange program in Poland, informs her class of the difference between an American (familiar) and a Polish (unfamiliar) university education.

Unlike American students, high-school students in Poland have no guarantee of admission to a college or university. After leaving high school, the Polish student takes a stringent examination which involves weeks and weeks of study. Even though the students study hard, only a small percentage will be admitted.

Once the students are admitted to the university, they spend 30 to 35 hours in class each week whereas American students seldom spend more than 18 hours a week in class. In Poland textbooks are not common. If a student is studying biology, for example, the teacher will prepare a list of acceptable books which are available in the library. The student then submits a request for the book in the library and has to wait two or three days for it.

Definition

A **definition** is a brief explanation of what a word or phrase means. It should be used whenever you suspect that some people in your audience might not know what you are talking about. After you define something, it also might be appropriate to give an example. This student gives a definition followed by an example in his speech about the kinds of fat found in food:

Saturated fat *is usually solid or semisolid at room temperature and primarily comes from animal sources. Examples are cream, lard, and butter.* Polyunsaturated fats *are liquid at room temperature and come from vegetable sources. Examples are oils that come from corn, soybean, safflower, sunflower, sesame, and cottonseed.*

Monounsaturated fats *can be found in solid or liquid foods. They are found in peanuts, olives, peanut oil, and olive oil.*

An **example** is a short illustration that clarifies a point. Commonly used in speeches, examples can come from personal experience, from research, or from imagination.

PERSONAL EXPERIENCE

Often you will choose a topic for a speech because you have some personal involvement in it. Ask yourself whether you can provide any examples from your own experience. Nothing beats "I know what I'm talking about because I've been there," as you can see in this speech against drinking and driving:

> *Three years ago, I was a senior in high school. One night my best friend Jeff called and asked if I wanted to go out to the lake and have a few beers. Since I had planned to see my grandmother, who was in the hospital, I told him I couldn't go but to give me a rain check.*
>
> *There was no next time. That night Jeff and three of my other friends were killed in an accident. According to the police report, they hit a tree while going 75 miles an hour. All of them had alcohol in their blood.*

Not all personal examples will be so dramatic. Another student uses a commonplace experience to make her point in a speech about how college students are affected by inflation:

> *Last year, when I bought a spiral-bound, five-subject notebook at the college bookstore, it cost $3.00. This year when I bought the same note-book, it cost me $3.25, or 25 cents more. That's how inflation affects us.*

Research   Often if you have not had personal experience with a topic, you can use the examples you find in your research. When you do this, however, be sure to cite your source. A common way of doing this is to say, "In the latest issue of *Newsweek* . . . ," or "according to a January 1992 issue of *Popular Science* . . . ." A student who was giving a speech on why the hair dye industry should be regulated used this example that she found during her research:

> *A current issue of* In Health *tells about a woman who was dying her hair. As soon as she applied the dye, her vision blurred, her face swelled, and she began to feel dizzy. Suddenly, she couldn't breathe and passed out. Fortunately her son was in the house and called the paramedics. It turned out that she had had an allergic reaction.*

Hypothetical Examples   Sometimes speakers use hypothetical examples—examples that are made up—to illustrate a point. A speaker should always tell the audience if an example is hypothetical. When this student spoke about the need to use infant seats, he involved his audience in his example. The words "imagine yourself" cue the audience that the example is hypothetical:

> *Imagine yourself in this situation. You are taking your 2-year-old son out for an ice cream cone. You don't bother to strap him in his seat because*

the ice cream shop is less than a mile away. As you are traveling about 25 miles an hour, a car pulls out in front of you. As you slam on your brakes, your son is still moving at 25 mph—right into the windshield.

Statistics

Statistics—which are facts in numerical form—have many uses in a speech. Being factual material, they are a convincing form of evidence. Quite often, a speaker who uses statistics is seen as someone who has done his or her homework.

Sometimes statistics can support your speech in a way no other information can. Bob, for example, wanted to speak about religion and the college student. He ran across a survey in the newspaper, *The Chronicle of Higher Education*, which reported that 83 percent of freshmen attend a religious service. The poll also found that 32 percent were Roman Catholic and that the largest Protestant affiliation was the Baptists with 18 percent. Twenty-nine percent of the freshmen identified themselves as born-again Christians.[2] With this data, Bob could show that there was considerable interest in religion—at least among the freshmen.

Statistics are easy to find. Many books contain nothing but statistics, such as the *Statistical Abstract of the United States*. Many state governments also publish books about statistics within their jurisdictions. Often you don't have to make a special search for statistics; the sources you use for your speech will have figures you can use.

RULES FOR USING STATISTICS

Use the Best Possible Sources   If you see the headline "Peanut Butter Causes Half of All Heart Attacks," it will be much more believable if it comes from *The New York Times* than from one of the tabloid newspapers by the checkout stand in your local supermarket. Pick your statistics from well-respected sources.

Make Sure the Information Is Up to Date   Figures on military spending in 1973 are useless—unless you want to compare them with the figures for the current year.

Use Statistics That Show Trends   We can often tell what is happening to an institution or even a country if we have information from one year to another. For example, one student wanted to show how attitudes toward euthanasia were changing in this country. She cited a poll that had been taken in three different decades:

> *This question was asked in a poll of Americans: "When a person has a disease that cannot be cured, do you think doctors should be allowed by law to end a patient's life by some painless means if the patient and his family request it?" In 1947, 37 percent of those asked said yes. By 1973 slightly over half agreed, and by last year, 63 percent said yes.*[3]

For the angle this photograph has been taken, imagine yourself in the back row. Can you see and read the speaker's chart?

Use Concrete Images When your numbers are large and possibly hard to comprehend, using concrete images is helpful. For example, one student spoke about the problem of increasing amounts of garbage. Since she knew that audience members would have difficulty imagining figures such as a million tons, she used a visual image that she found to convey the information:

> *There is enough [garbage] to fill the New Orleans Superdome from floor to ceiling twice a day including weekends and holidays. In eight years there will be enough national garbage to fill the same stadium three times a day.*[4]

Testimony

When you cite **testimony**, you use another person's statements or actions to give authority to what you are saying. Experts are the best sources of testimony. Suppose you are planning to speak about NCAA violations and you get some of the information from the athletic director of your school. When you use this information in your speech, tell your audience where it came from. Because the information is from an expert, your speech will have more authority and be more convincing.

Testimony can also be used to show that people who are prominent and admired believe and support your ideas. For example if you are going to persuade your audience to take up swimming for fitness, it might be useful to mention some famous athletes who swim to stay fit. If you want people to sign your petition to build a new city park, mention other citizens who are also supporting this park.

Consider This **Consider This** *Consider This*

I spend a great deal of time researching quotes. I use *Bartlett's Quotations*—
but not the way most writers use it. When I find a new quotation, I check
Bartlett's, and often discard it if it's in there. My reasoning is that I don't
need quotations which are available to everybody else. . . .

I look for quotations which are authoritative, which may be startling
(because of who said what), which are short and powerful, which may be
funny or ironic, and which can inspire. I want something which audiences
find memorable and striking. As a measure of how an audience can respond
to such quotations, twice I've heard audiences interrupt a speech of mine to
applaud a quotation. I was astounded.

Again, like humor, quotations are a lot of trouble. But using a really
good one effectively pays off handsomely.

Source: Robert B. Rackleff, "The Art of Speech Writing," *Vital Speeches.*

Testimony can be made up of direct quotations. You can quote what
public figures or celebrities are saying, or you can quote historic figures by
using books of quotations found in the reference section of the library.

Try to use quotations that are short and to the point. If they are too
lengthy, your speech could end up sounding like everyone but yourself. If you
have quotations that are long and wordy, put them into your own words.
Whether you quote or paraphrase, you should give credit to your source.

Polls

Polls are surveys of people's attitudes, beliefs, and behavior. Quite often polls
are conducted on controversial subjects. If you want to know how the American
public feels about abortion, nuclear arms control, or environmental issues,
you will probably be able to find a poll.

National polls also can provide useful information as to what particular
segments of the population think or know about an issue. For example, Table
12-1 shows the results of a Gallup poll. This poll would be a very good piece
of supporting material for a speech about American's political knowledge.
Notice how the poll is broken into demographic categories such as sex, age,
region, and so forth. Since all this information would be too overwhelming
for a speech, you only use some of it. For example, if you were giving a speech
to your classmates you might want to mention only the responses of 18- to
29-year-olds.

When your statistics come from a survey, you should look to see how
many and what kind of people were questioned. For example, if you discovered
survey results saying that 30 percent of the American public eats with
chopsticks, you might find the statistic fairly startling and you might be
tempted to use it—until you note that the survey included only 100 people
and that many of them were Chinese immigrants.

TABLE 12-1
Knowledge of Own Representative

QUESTION: Do you happen to know if your Representative in Congress is a Republican or Democrat? Could you please tell me the name of your Representative in Congress—that is, your U.S. congressman?

National	Republican or Democrat?				Representative's Name?		
	Republican 36%	Democrat 36%	Don't Know Which 28%	No Opinion* ●	Gave a Name 56%	Could Not Name/ No Opinion 43%	No. of Interviews 1012
Sex							
Male	40	40	20	●	65	35	507
Female	33	32	35	●	49	51	505
Age							
18–29 years	33	25	42	●	35	65	190
30–49 years	38	38	24	●	61	39	447
50 & older	37	42	21	●	65	35	366
Region							
East	36	40	24	●	55	45	248
Midwest	33	38	28	1	57	43	257
South	34	39	27	●	56	44	300
West	44	26	30	●	58	42	206
Race							
White	37	37	26	●	59	41	899
Black	30	36	34	●	40	60	60
Other	35	35	30	●	40	60	50
Education							
College grads.	40	44	16	●	71	29	300
College inc.	37	39	24	●	57	43	218
High school grads.	40	31	29	●	53	47	387
Not H.S. grads	22	36	41	1	47	53	103
Politics							
Republicans	51	26	23	●	58	42	342
Democrats	25	48	27	●	57	43	328
Independents	35	36	29	●	57	43	323
Registered Voter							
Yes	39	40	21	●	61	39	825
No	26	24	50	●	38	62	187
Ideology							
Liberal	34	36	30	●	55	45	326
Moderate	36	42	22	●	71	29	101
Conservative	42	34	24	●	58	42	476
Income							
$50,000 & over	44	39	17	●	68	32	234
$30,000–49,999	39	38	22	1	59	41	258
$20,000–29,999	35	35	30	●	53	47	175
Under $20,000	32	35	33	●	50	50	272

(Continued on next page)

TABLE 12-1 *Continued*
Knowledge of Own Representative

QUESTION: Do you happen to know if your Representative in Congress is a Republican or Democrat?
Could you please tell me the name of your Representative in Congress—that is, your U.S. congressman?

National	Republican or Democrat?				Representative's Name?		
	Republican **36%**	**Democrat** **36%**	**Don't Know Which** **28%**	**No Opinion*** ●	**Gave a Name** **56%**	**Could Not Name/ No Opinion** **43%**	**No. of Interviews** **1012**
Employment Status							
Full time	40	37	23	●	59	41	568
Part time	32	35	33	●	49	51	113
Unemployed	33	26	41	●	44	56	119
Retired	34	42	23	1	64	36	200
Religion							
Protestant	38	36	26	●	59	41	574
Catholic	34	36	30	●	50	50	246
None	30	38	31	1	58	42	102

● Less than 0.5%; *includes "other party."
Source: The Gallup Poll Monthly, November 1990.

Studies

As the term implies, a **study** is an in-depth investigation of a subject. The subject might be anything—from how white rats run mazes to how newspapers present political news. Studies are found in popular magazines, newspapers, and academic journals. If you are interested in finding what research has been done in a particular field, check the indexes for such periodicals. For example, Table 12-2, based on a study by the U.S. Bureau of the Census and the U.S. Bureau of Labor Statistics, is a gold mine of information about women in the work force, the jobs they are doing, how much they are getting paid, and the progress they have made over a 10-year period.

Adapting Supporting Material to Your Audience

Because each kind of supporting material may work better with some audiences than with others, you should keep your audience constantly in mind as you build your speech.[5]

Consider, for example, a speech about videocassette recorders (VCRs). If you were going to speak to a group of potential customers, you would give some technical information from a magazine such as *Consumer Reports* about various VCR brands: what the various options are—such as the number of shows that can be recorded—whether four heads are better than two, and so on. If you were speaking to parents, you might want to talk about some of

TABLE 12-2
Women in the Work Force

A Decade of Change: Proportion of female workers in selected occupations, 1975 and 1985

	1975	*1985*
Architect	4.3%	11.3%
Bartender	35.2	47.9
Bus driver	37.7	49.2
Dentist	1.8	6.5
Elementary school teacher	85.4	84.0
Lawyer, judge	7.1	18.2
Mail carrier	8.7	17.2
Registered nurse	97.0	95.1
Waiter/waitress	91.1	84.0
Welder	4.4	4.8

Education and Earnings: Yearly earnings by sex and educational attainment of full-time, year-round workers, 1984 (in dollars)

Educational Attainment	*Women's Earnings*	*Men's Earnings*
Fewer than 8 years	$ 9,828	$14,624
1–3 years of high school	11,843	19,120
High school graduate	14,569	23,269
1–3 years of college	17,007	25,831
College graduate	20,257	31,487
1 or more years postgraduate	25,076	36,836

Source: Adapted from *The New York Times,* June 26, 1987, based on U.S. Bureau of the Census and U.S. Bureau of Labor Statistics.

the best videos for children. In this case you might want to quote some experts on the subject. For an audience of school teachers, a discussion of how videos can be used in the classroom would be appropriate, and your supporting material could include statistics on how videos enhance learning.

You also need to consider the attitudes of the audience toward your topic. If your audience is suspicious of you or your message, you will probably do best with facts and figures and with quotations and testimony from people your audience respects. Citing *evidence* in the form of statistics and facts will give you a better chance of persuading them to accept your point of view.

Finally, you should consider what kind of supporting material will hold your audience's attention. If you are speaking to a young and potentially restless audience, examples and narratives will probably hold its attention best.

Since audience members often come from a variety of backgrounds, no one form of supporting material will work uniformly well. If you have an adult audience with different levels of knowledge and different attitudes, you

Try This Try This Try This

*U*sing a topic that you have chosen for a speech, try to develop some ideas for supporting material by answering the following questions:

- *Definitions:* Are there any words or phrases that need defining?

- *Explanations:* What kinds of explanation does your topic need? Is there any material that is so technical or specialized that your audience might not understand it?

- *Comparison and Contrast:* Is there anything your subject can be compared with to make it more understandable? Is there something the audience might be familiar with that would provide a basis for comparison? What about a contrast? Can you show how your subject is different from something in order to explain it?

- *Examples:* What examples can you draw from your own life to help your audience understand the topic? Can you use any examples from your research? Would a hypothetical example be appropriate?

- *Statistics:* Are there any statistics available on your topic? If you used them would they make your speech better?

- *Testimony:* Will testimony be useful in this speech? Are there any people you can quote that might help you to prove your point? Are there any experts you can quote?

- *Polls and Studies:* Have any polls or studies been done on your subject? Can you fit them into your speech? Can you explain them in such a way that they will be interesting to the audience?

should use a variety of supporting material. In the following extract, the speaker begins with a statistic and then goes on to give an example:

> *A California study of 3,000 divorced couples found that one year after the divorce, the woman's income had dropped 73 percent while the man's had increased 43 percent.*
>
> *Karen Jackson is one of these women. Last year she was living with her three children in a comfortable middle-class neighborhood. Now she is living in a slum and needs food stamps to feed her children.*

Presenting a variety of supporting material is like offering a variety of fruit in a fruit bowl. Some people will like the grapes and others will like the peaches, but everyone will be pleased to find something appealing.

SUMMARY

When you are putting together material for your speech, you should consider drawing on three areas: your own experience, interviews with others, and research in the library. Depending on the topic, one of these sources might provide better information than the others.

Library material is organized into three categories: books, periodicals, and reference works. Book titles, authors, and subjects can all be found in the card or computer catalog. Magazine and journal articles can be located through periodical indexes. Reference material includes encyclopedias, almanacs, biographical yearbooks, government documents, and vertical files.

Supporting material forms the main content of every speech. Supporting material includes the following: comparisons, which are similarities between two or more things; contrasts, which point out differences; definitions, which give the meaning of words or phrases; examples, which illustrate points; statistics, which are facts in numerical form; testimony, in which the statements or actions of others are used to give authority to the speech; polls, which indicate what a selected number of people think, feel, or know about a subject; and studies, which are in-depth investigations.

When choosing supporting material for a speech, you should consider which kinds will be appropriate for the audience. To make this choice, consider the audience's level of knowledge about and attitude toward your topic, and ask which material will best hold the audience's attention.

FURTHER READING

BARZUN, JACQUES, AND HENRY F. GRAFF. *The Modern Researcher*, 4th ed. New York: Harcourt Brace Jovanovich, 1985. This is an outstanding book full of useful ideas for serious researchers. The section on research includes chapters entitled "Finding the Facts," "Verification," and "Handling Ideas." For those looking for suggestions to help improve their writing, the section entitled "Writing" is also superb. A fine book.

BRADLEY, BERT E. *Fundamentals of Speech Communication*. 6th ed. Dubuque, IA: Brown, 1991. Bradley includes chapters entitled "The Criticism of Speeches," "Understanding and Adapting to Attitudes of the Listeners," "Selecting the Subject and Purposes," and "Developing Content" that are especially relevant here. There is no doubt why this textbook has continued to a sixth edition; it is a solid book with a strong emphasis on substance.

MILLS, GLEN E. *Putting a Message Together*, 2d ed. Indianapolis: Bobbs-Merrill, 1972. Mills's book examines the preparation of messages and the role played by messages in communication. He places his analysis within the context of principles, theories, and motives of communication. This is a knowledgeable, witty, succinct book designed for the specialist.

PARTNOW, ELAINE. *The Best of Quotable Woman: From Eve to the Present*. New York: Facts on File, Inc., 1991. In most of the standard books of quotations, men dominate. This book is made up of quotations by women.

POULTON, HELEN J., AND MARGUERITE S. HOWLAND. *The Historian's Handbook: A Descriptive Guide to Reference Works*. Norman, OK: University of Oklahoma, 1972. This is a book designed to introduce students to the wide variety of research material available. Poulton surveys the major reference works and the important titles. Valuable key for unlocking the library's many secrets.

RICO, GABRIELE LUSSER. *Writing the Natural Way*. Los Angeles: J. P. Tarcher, 1983. Although designed for writers, Rico provides specific techniques to develop readers' natural expressive powers. Filled with quotes, writing samples, and inspiring images, this book emphasizes uninhibited self-expression, spontaneity, and creativity.

RUBIN, REBECCA, ALAN M. RUBIN, AND LINDA J. PIELE. *Communication Research: Strategies and Sources.* 2d ed. Belmont, CA: Wadsworth, 1990. The usefulness of this volume is its emphasis on information sources. How to search the communication literature, write and organize research papers, design the research project, computer search on-line bibliographic data bases, and discover other relevant material is covered. Great aid for beginning researchers.

TUCKER, RAYMOND, RICHARD L. WEAVER II, AND CYNTHIA BERRYMAN-FINK. *Research in Speech Communication.* Englewood Cliffs, NJ: Prentice-Hall, 1981. We list this book especially for its Chapter 3, "Documentary or Library Research." In this chapter the authors discuss types of library research, procedures in library research, suggestions for the library researcher as well as values and limitations of library research. It is a practical approach designed for all researchers and writers.

WILSON, JOHN F., AND CARROL C. ARNOLD. *Public Speaking as a Liberal Art.* 6th ed. Boston: Allyn and Bacon, 1990. The authors approach public speaking as an art and discuss some general problems—rhetorical invention, style, delivery, and the like. Chapters 4 to 6, on invention, are cogent and especially relevant here.

Chapter 13

Organizing and Outlining the Speech

CHAPTER OBJECTIVES	KEY TERMS
After reading this chapter, you should be able to:	bibliography
1. Organize and outline your speech.	body (of speech)
2. Identify the six patterns of organization for a speech and choose the best one for your purpose.	cause-and-effect order conclusion (of speech) full-sentence outline
3. Explain the function of an introduction and be able to write one.	introduction (of speech) key-word outline
4. Explain the function of a conclusion and be able to write one.	main point minor point motivated sequence
5. Explain the function of transitions and be able to write them.	outline problem-solution order
6. Use both full-sentence and key-word formats to outline a speech.	spatial order time order topical order
7. Write a bibliography for your speech.	transition

K elly got up early because she had a lot to do. After she had eaten breakfast, she compiled the grocery list. As she put together her list, she had a mental picture of the store's layout so she could organize her list according to the aisles. Before she left the house she wrote a note to her 12-year-old son: "If you don't mow the lawn today, don't plan on getting your allowance."

As Kelly set out to do her errands, she tried to plan the most efficient route through the city traffic. She decided to pick up some prescriptions (even though she didn't need them yet) because the supermarket was next to the drugstore. She also dropped off some shoes to be repaired, since the shoe repair shop was located in the next block.

While driving to the supermarket, she mentally went over the list of what she still had to do. In the afternoon she had to clean up the house because company was coming for dinner that night. Was there anything she had to do for dinner? The salad greens were washed, she had made a pie yesterday, and her husband was picking up the fish. As she reviewed the list, she remembered she had to buy sweet corn.

Once Kelly's errands were done and she had solved all her immediate problems, she started thinking about the speech course she was taking at the nearby community college. She reminded herself that some time during the weekend she had to work on an outline for her speech. She wasn't looking forward to it. The last time she had outlined something had been when she was in high school, and she remembered the experience as difficult and unpleasant.

What Kelly didn't realize was that the skills she needed for organizing and outlining her speech were the same skills she had been using all morning. When she reviewed what she had to do, she set priorities—which things had to be done right away and which could wait. She organized her grocery list by the way the store was laid out. She planned her errands (supermarket, drugstore, and shoe repair) by geographical area. Although Kelly did not plan it that way, her errand list resembled an outline:

Shoe Repair
Drugstore
   Prescriptions
   Cotton balls
Supermarket
   Oranges
   Sweet corn
   Flour
   Baking soda
   Sour cream
   Eggs

As you can see, then, organizing and outlining are not mysterious processes used only in academic settings. They are among the skills that we all know and use regularly. Let's see how we can apply these skills to the job at hand—organizing and outlining a speech.

When you are putting a speech together, you must organize it so it will make sense both to you and to your audience.[1] As you organize it, you should follow the principles of organization discussed below.

Relate Points to Your Specific Purpose and Central Idea

The points you make in your speech should relate directly to your specific purpose and central idea. In this speech titled "Checking Out Charities," notice that all the main points do this.

Specific Purpose: To inform my classmates about the need to check out charities before giving them money.

Central Idea: Contributors can ensure that their money is well spent if they take some easy steps to check out a charity.

Main Ideas:
I. Find out the purpose of the charity.
II. Ask what the charity has accomplished.
III. Ask about the charity's method of collecting money.
IV. Find out how the charity uses its contributions.

Distinguish between Main and Minor Points

When organizing your speech, you should distinguish between main points and minor points. If you do this, the speech will flow more naturally and will seem logical to your listeners. The **main points** are all the broad, general ideas and information that support your central idea; the **minor points** are the specific ideas and information that support the main points. Say that the purpose of your speech is to persuade your audience to learn to use a computer word-processing program to write their research papers. The central idea of your speech is that they can write better and more efficiently by using a computer. Your main point would have this broad, general idea: "Computers help you to write faster, revise more easily, and produce a better-looking paper." Your minor points will be any ones that explain the main point in

---

Consider This Consider This Consider This

*T*here remains much merit in the old advice to the public speaker: Tell them what you're going to say; say it; and tell them what you've said. [To do this] it may help you to resort to numbering your points: *The Supreme Court erred in three ways. First, it distorted the statute; second, it trampled upon the Constitution; third, it trespassed upon the power of Congress.* You would then go on to expand upon these offenses, taking them in the same order.

Source: James J. Kilpatrick, *The Writer's Art.*

Try This Try This Try This

*F*or each of the following sets of sentences, identify the main point with an *M* and the minor or supporting point(s) with an *S*.

_____1. There are thousands of different kinds of dolls.

_____2. Nesting dolls is the term for dolls that fit inside each other.

_____3. Baby dolls resemble infants.

_____1. Don't wear anything that glitters.

_____2. Don't wear all-black or all-white clothing.

_____3. If you are appearing on television, be careful what you wear.

_____1. The amount of agricultural land under cultivation does not support the population.

_____2. Famine can occur for many reasons.

_____3. Population exceeds the food sources.

_____4. Unusual weather, such as drought, occurs.

In each of the next sets there are *two* main points. Find them and match them with the correct minor points.

_____1. Certain signs indicate that your pet is too fat.

_____2. Cut back food by one third.

_____3. It tires easily after a little exercise.

_____4. Put your pet on a diet.

_____5. Use low-calorie fillers such as rice or cottage cheese.

_____6. It looks fat (or everybody calls it butterball).[2]

_____1. Some studies indicate that people who drink coffee in large amounts are more prone to heart disease.

_____2. Caffeine can cause birth defects such as cleft palate and bone abnormalities.

_____3. Decaffeinated coffee is a good alternative to coffee with caffeine.

_____4. If you want to break the caffeine habit, do it by a cup or two a day.

_____5. People who drink large quantities of coffee may be endangering their health.

_____6. You can break the coffee-caffeine habit.

Answers: The main points are:
• There are thousands of different kinds of dolls.
• If you are appearing on television, be careful what you wear.
• Famine can occur for many reasons.
• Certain signs indicate that your pet is too fat.
• Put your pet on a diet.
• People who drink large quantities of coffee may be endangering their health.
• You can break the coffee-caffeine habit.

more specific terms. Examples might be: (1) most people can type about 33 percent faster on a computer; (2) a computer enables you to revise any section of a paper without retyping it; (3) a computer printer produces a professionally typed paper. All these minor points help to explain the ways in which the computer is more efficient for writing purposes.

If you have difficulty distinguishing between major and minor points, write each of the points you want to make on a separate index card. Then spread all the cards out in front of you and organize them by main points, with minor points coming under them. If one arrangement doesn't work, try another. This is the advantage of having each point on a separate card.

Phrase All Points in Full Sentences

If you write all your points in full sentences, it will help you think out your ideas more fully. Once your ideas are set out in this detailed way, you will be able to discover problems in the organization that might need more work.

Give All Points a Parallel Structure

Parallel structure means that each of your points will begin with the same grammatical form. For example, on a speech about ways to lose weight, this speaker started each suggestion with a verb:

- Exercise at least three times a week.
- Stop eating snacks—especially after the evening meal.
- Count your daily calories.

Patterns of Organization

Once you have researched your speech, have decided on a specific purpose, and have listed the main points, you are ready to choose an organizational pattern. This organizational pattern will mainly affect the **body**—the main part of the speech. (Introductions and conclusions are discussed later in the chapter.)

The body of the speech is made up of your main points. Most classroom speeches should not have more than four or five main points, and many of them will have no more than two or three. Your choice of how many main points to use will depend on your topic. If you want to cover a topic in depth, you will use fewer main points. If you want to give a broad, general view, you might want to use four or five main points.

There are many ways to arrange the main points in your speech. Your choice will depend on what best suits your material. In this section we will discuss six possible arrangements: time order, spatial order, cause and effect, problem-solution, motivated sequence, and topical order.

Time Order

Time order, or chronological order, is used to show development over time. This pattern works particularly well when you want to use a historical approach. For example, in a speech about the development of the circus, the speaker arranged her main points in chronological order:

Specific Purpose: To inform my audience about the development of the circus.

Central Idea: The circus went through four major stages of development.

Main Points: I. The circus began in Rome thousands of years ago.
II. The modern circus developed in England during the 1700s.
III. The earliest circus in America was established in 1792.
IV. The golden age of the American circus began in the late 1800s.

Time order is often used to explain a process. The process could be anything from how to wrap a gift to how to apply for a student loan. This student used time order for describing the process of making a pot:

Specific Purpose: To inform my audience of how a pot is made.

Central Idea: Making a pot involves four steps: wedging, shaping, glazing, and baking.

Main Points: I. In the first step the potter gets the air bubbles out of the clay in a process called wedging.
II. In the second step the potter shapes the pot on the potter's wheel.
III. In the third step the potter glazes (puts a color finish on) the pot.
IV. In the fourth step the potter bakes the pot in a kiln.

Spatial Order

When you use **spatial order,** you refer to a physical or geographical layout to help your audience see how the parts make up the whole. To help your audience visualize your subject, you explain it by going from left to right or from top to bottom, or in any direction that best suits your subject.

For example, a student decides that spatial order is the best way to explain the use of solar heating elements in building a new house. He then organizes his speech around the different parts of the house: the roof, the windows, the walls, and the floors. He could have proceeded outside to inside, but he chose top to bottom:

Specific Purpose: To inform my audience about several ways in which solar heating elements can be built into a house.

Central Idea: Solar heating elements can be built into a house in the roof, windows, walls, and floors.

Main Points: I. Solar panels built into the roof will gather the sun's heat.
　　　　　　 II. Banks of south-facing windows can bring solar heat into the house.
　　　　　　III. Solar storage units built into the walls will absorb heat on sunny days and release it into the house at night.
　　　　　　IV. Floors made of concrete or stone can be placed to absorb solar heat and release it into the house.

Spatial order works particularly well when the speech focuses on a chart or diagram. When using the visual aid, the speaker naturally moves from top to bottom or from left to right. For example, when a student decided to speak on the topic "Who Makes Decisions on Campus," she used a spatial order and worked from top to bottom on a flow chart showing who the administrators were and what they were responsible for:

Specific Purpose: To inform my audience about who makes decisions on campus.

Central Idea: Campus business is divided into two branches: the administrative branch and the academic branch.

Main Points: I. The president is the chief administrative officer of the college and the main spokesperson for the college in the community.
　　　　　　 II. The academic vice president is responsible for everything that concerns classes, such as curriculum and faculty.

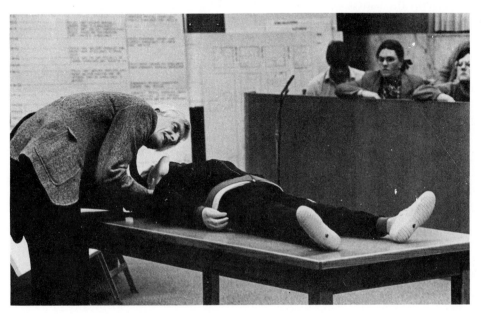

What order would the speaker be likely to use in organizing his speech on CPR?

III. The administrative vice president is responsible for all nonclass activity, such as law enforcement, revenues, and payroll.

Cause-and-Effect Order

A speaker who uses **cause-and-effect order** divides a speech into two major parts: cause (why something is happening) and effect (what impact it is having). Here is how a speaker used a cause-and-effect arrangement to talk about the problem of dust mites:

> *Specific Purpose:* To inform my audience about dust mites.
>
> *Central Idea:* Dust mites may cause allergic reactions and even lead to asthma.
>
> *Main Points:* I. Dust mites, microscopic organisms that live in bedding, stuffed furniture, and carpets, may be a serious problem in well-insulated homes with wall-to-wall carpet.
>
> II. Many people are allergic to the fecal pellets of dust mites.
>
> III. Children who live in homes with a high concentration of dust mites are more likely to develop asthma in their early teens.

You do not always have to start with the cause and end with the effect. In this speech about dust mites, the order could have been reversed: the speaker could have begun with examples of the effects of dust mites and then could have continued with the causes. If you are using a cause-and-effect order, begin with the aspect most likely to capture the audience's attention.

Problem-Solution Order

Like speakers who use a cause-and-effect arrangement, a speaker who uses a problem-solution order also divides a speech into two sections. In this case, one part deals with the problem and the other deals with the solution. For example:

> *Specific Purpose:* To inform my audience how to protect themselves from shopping-mall crime.
>
> *Central Idea:* You can protect yourself from shopping-mall crime by parking close to elevators, sending parcels home, accompanying small children at all times, and carrying as little cash as possible.
>
> *Main Points:* I. Shopping malls attract muggers, car thieves, child molesters, drug peddlers, and pickpockets.
>
> II. Shoppers can take several precautions to protect themselves from shopping-mall crime.

Here is another example:

Specific Purpose: To persuade my audience that American schools need to teach students more about the Third World.

Central Idea: Americans must know about the Third World because what happens in these countries affects all of our lives.

Main Points: I. Most Americans have negative impressions of the Third World from the mass media.
II. Most Americans are ignorant of the impact that the Third World has on American trade.
III. Most Americans do not know how the Third World influences political decision making among the super powers.
IV. American teachers and curriculum planners must add material about the Third World to the school curriculum.
V. Textbook publishers should add Third-World material—especially to textbooks in the social sciences.

Motivated Sequence *Persuasive*

The **motivated sequence**, developed by Professor Alan H. Monroe in the 1930s,[3] is also a problem-solving pattern of arrangement. The sequence is designed to persuade listeners to accept a point of view and then motivate them to take action. The full pattern has five steps:

1. *Attention:* The speaker calls attention to the topic or situation.
2. *Need:* The speaker develops the need for a change and explains related audience needs. This is the problem-development portion of the speech.
3. *Satisfaction:* The speaker presents his or her solution and shows how it meets (satisfies) the needs mentioned.
4. *Visualization:* The speaker shows what will result when the solution is put into effect.
5. *Action:* The speaker indicates what kind of action is necessary to bring about the desired change.

Any persuasive problem-solving speech can be adapted to the motivated sequence. Notice how this speaker uses the pattern:

Specific Purpose: To persuade my audience that they should order carefully when they eat in Chinese restaurants.

Central Idea: Unless you make careful choices in ordering food in Chinese restaurants, the food is very bad for your health.

Main Points: I. *[Attention]* Where would you eat a meal with a third of a cup of fat, three times the recom-

mended daily amount of sodium, and 700 calories
of fat in a single dish? The answer: in the Chinese
restaurant in your hometown.
  II. *[Need]* Chinese restaurant cooking has been
      adapted to American tastes: a stir-fry recipe might
      use a third of a cup of oil, soy sauce is loaded
      with salt, and the popular sweet-and-sour recipes
      are double-fried and served in a sauce made with
      fat, sugar, and cornstarch.
 III. *[Satisfaction]* If you want to eat a healthy meal,
      choose a clear broth as your appetizer and a dish
      that is steamed or grilled for your entrée.
  IV. *[Visualization]* Chinese food can be healthy and
      satisfying if you make the right choices.
   V. *[Action]* Before you go into a Chinese restaurant,
      look at the menu on the window outside. If all the
      food is fried or stir-fried, choose another restau-
      rant.[4]

Topical Order

When your speech does not fit into any of the patterns described so far, you
will probably use a topical pattern of organization. You can use a **topical
order** whenever your subject can be grouped logically into subtopics. Here
are some examples: four ways to save money for college, good dogs for house
pets (group by breed), traveling by bicycle (group by places you could travel
to or by helpful hints), or three reasons to give up eating meat.

In the next sample, a student uses a topical order to explain how to
bargain in a retail store. Topical order is the only choice for this speech. Time
order won't work because there are no steps to follow, nor is there a physical
or geographical pattern that would permit spatial order. Because there is no
problem, neither the problem-solution nor the motivated sequence would
apply. Topical order works because the speaker wants to talk about five
things—all related to the central idea of bargaining:

Specific Purpose: To inform my audience how to bargain for goods in
retail stores.

Central Idea: If Americans would try to bargain for goods in retail
stores, they would often save a considerable amount of
money.

Main Ideas: I. Do your homework by checking out the prices at
               competing stores to see what the product is selling
               for.
           II. Bargain with someone who has been authorized
               to cut prices—usually a manager.
          III. Bargain in private by going to the store when
               there will be fewer customers.

IV. If you can't get the item for the right price, be willing to walk away.

V. Bargain for a special price if you want more than one item.[5]

In a persuasive speech on the advantages of arranged marriages, an Indian student used a topical order to show why such marriages worked better:

Specific Purpose: To persuade my audience that the Indian system of arranging marriages is better than the American system of finding one's own mate.

Central Idea: Indian marriages are highly stable and are based on logical rather than emotional considerations.

I. The Indian divorce rate is much lower than the American rate.

II. Parents can make a better choice of suitable mates for their children because they go about the task logically rather than emotionally.

III. When parents arrange marriages, their children are free from the stresses of courtship and decision making.

IV. When parents arrange marriages for their children, love is not confused with infatuation.

V. In most Indian marriages, love develops as the relationship matures.

The Speech Introduction

The **introduction** is the opening statement of your speech. It gives the audience members their first impression of you, it introduces them to the topic, and it motivates them to listen. The introduction is very important: if

---

Try This Try This Try This

*W*hich organizational pattern might you use for each of the following speech topics?

1. Overcoming the problem of adult illiteracy
2. Reading a road map—what those red and blue lines really mean
3. Three ways to fight the flu
4. Building an inexpensive bookcase for your room
5. Industrial pollution: a problem for the future

Answers: 1. problem-solution or motivated sequence 2. spatial order 3. topical order
4. time order. 5. cause-and-effect order

you don't hook audience members in the beginning, you might not ever get their attention.

Stating Your Purpose and Main Points

In most situations, a speaker will use the introduction to tell what he or she is going to talk about. When a speaker does this, the audience can turn its attention to the topic and begin to concentrate. Although you do not have to mention the topic in your very first words, you shouldn't wait too long. By the time you reach the end of your introduction, your audience should know what you intend to accomplish and the central idea of your speech. By including this information in your introduction, you are providing a signpost about the direction you will be taking. For example:

> *The physical abuse of children is a serious problem in this country, and today I want to talk about how bad the problem is and some of the things we can do about it.*

In your introduction, you might also want to preview your main points. Not only does this give members of the audience a sense of your direction, but it also helps them to follow your speech more easily. The student speaking on the physical abuse of children previewed her main points this way:

> *Since this problem covers such a broad area, I would like to limit my talk to three areas: parental abuse of children, social agencies that deal with abuse, and what the ordinary citizen can do when he or she suspects a child is being abused.*

Getting Attention

In addition to telling your audience what you are going to talk about, your introduction should arouse attention and interest. Gaining attention is not just a matter of getting audience members to listen to your first words—they would probably do that anyway. It is rather a matter of creating interest in your subject. You want your audience members to think "This really sounds like an interesting subject" or "I am going to enjoy listening to this speech."

Certain techniques are proven to be attention getters. Let's look at them and at the functions they serve. Note that sometimes a speaker might use more than one of these techniques.

USE SOME HUMOR

Research shows that speeches with some humor produce a more favorable reaction to the speaker.[6] Often a speaker will use humor in his or her introduction. This is how a speaker began her speech for Senior Recognition Day:

> *Greetings to you, seniors, who invited me to address you today and who soon will be able to decide whether that was a mistake. Greetings to you,*

*colleagues, and to you, freshmen, and most special greetings to anyone
who came even though you were not required to.*[7]

USE AN EXAMPLE

Short examples often work quite well in introductions. They can be personal
examples, or they could have happened to someone else. A student used this
example to spark interest in her speech.

*Gilbert is 42 years old. He has three children, ages 17, 10, and 4. Gilbert
never read to his two oldest children or helped them with their schoolwork.
If they asked for help with reading, Gilbert's reply was, "Ask your mother."
Last week everything changed. Gilbert read* The Cat in the Hat *to his 4-
year-old. It was the first time Gilbert had ever read to one of his children.
In fact, it was the first time Gilbert had read anything aloud at all.*

*Gilbert had been illiterate. For the past four months he has been
learning to read through a program in the literacy council. I am Gilbert's
teacher.*

REFER TO THE OCCASION

If you are asked to speak for a special occasion or if a special occasion falls
on the day you are speaking, make a reference to it, as in the following:

*I am very honored to have been asked to give a speech for Founder's Day.
This occasion has a special meaning for me because, one hundred years
ago, when this college began, my great-grandmother was in its first class.*

SHOW THE IMPORTANCE OF THE SUBJECT

Showing the audience that the subject is important to their own lives is a
good way of getting and keeping attention. Not only does this student let his
listeners know how important the subject is to them, but he also keeps their
attention by building suspense:

*I would like to speak on a topic that affects all of us. It raises the price of
every product we buy. It often makes us feel inadequate because we are
not beautiful enough, thin enough, or young enough. It makes us go in
debt because we buy things we cannot afford. It comes uninvited into our
homes, and it interrupts us every ten minutes or so. What is this thing
that has such a negative influence on our lives? It's television advertising.*

USE STARTLING INFORMATION

Using information that startles or surprises your audience is a good device
for gaining attention. This speaker tells us about U.S. economic growth by
citing statistics on familiar things:

*Consider what has happened in the United States during the decade of the
1980s alone:*

- *The percentage of households with cable television went from 19 percent
to 51 percent.*

- *The percentages of households with VCRs went from 1 percent to 58 percent.*
- *The number of personal computers in use went from 2 million to 38 million.*
- *The percentage of elementary and secondary schools with microcomputers rose from 18 percent to 96 percent.*[8]

USE QUESTIONS

Questions get audience members involved right away because they will mentally answer the questions as you ask them. Sometimes questions can be used to build suspense. Here's how one student began her speech about buying a secondhand car:

> *How do you shop for a secondhand car? Do you look for a particular model, or do you go in to see what's available? Is there any kind of research you can do before you go to the car lot? Is there any way of knowing what a particular car is worth? Are secondhand cars ever under warranty by the dealer? These are some of the questions many of us ask when we go to buy a secondhand car. Today, I am going to try to give you some answers.*

USE PERSONAL EXAMPLES

Don't be afraid to refer to your own life when you can tie examples from it into your subject. Personal examples make a speech stronger because they are a way of showing that you know what you're talking about. This speaker used an example from his own experience to begin a speech about dropping out of school:

> *Seven years ago I was a teen-age dropout. I went away to college because my parents wanted me to. I moved into a dorm, made lots of friends, and began to have a wonderful time—a time that was so wonderful that I only occasionally went to class or studied for an exam. The college, realizing that freshmen take time to adjust, put me on probation for the first year. In the second year, however, I had to settle down.*
> *I tried to study, but I didn't have any idea of what I was studying for. I didn't have a major and I had no idea of what I wanted to do with my life. Finally I asked myself, "What am I doing here?" I could come up with no answer. So after finishing the first semester of my sophomore year, I dropped out of school. It was the second-best decision I ever made. The first-best was to come back to school—at the grand old age of 24.*

Sometimes examples from your life help tell your audience why you are qualified to speak on your subject. If the audience thinks you have some experience or expertise, you will have more credibility as a speaker:

> *Today I am here to persuade you never to take up smoking. You might think it is a case of the pot calling the kettle black. You have all seen me smoke at every possible opportunity. All I can say is that if I had one*

*wish, I would like to be a nonsmoker. Why do I want to give it up? Let
me tell you what you might not know. Every morning I cough for half an
hour when I get out of bed. I have thrown away countless clothes because
I have burned tiny holes in them with cigarette sparks. The windows of
my house and car are covered with a greasy yellow film from smoke.
Worst of all, my favorite cat won't sit in my lap because she hates smoke.*

*Why haven't I given it up? Because it is a powerful addiction that is
very hard to break.*

USE A QUOTATION

Sometimes you can find a good quotation that will get your speech off to a
good start. A well-chosen quotation may also give credibility to your speech.
When a journalism student spoke to her class about what goes into television
reporting, she quoted Bill Whittaker, a correspondent for CBS:

*I think most people think it's glamorous and exciting and fast-paced and
fun. And it is. But what they fail to realize is how demanding it is, how
much it requires of you. CBS can call you at any hour of the day or night
and ask you to get out of your bed, catch a plane and fly to Nowhere,
U.S.A., and stand in the mud and rain and talk about a flood.*[9]

Additional Tips for Introductions

When writing an introduction to a speech, remember these points as well:

1. Although you might want to build curiosity about your speech topic,
   don't draw out the suspense for too long. The audience will get annoyed
   if it has to wait to find out what you're going to talk about.
2. Keep your introduction short. The body of your speech contains the
   main content, and you shouldn't wait too long to get there.
3. In planning your speech be sure to adapt the topic to the occasion and
   to the audience. Before you start to speak, ask yourself whether there

---

Try This Try This Try This

What kinds of introductions do you think would work well for the
following speech situations?

- You are asked to give the annual Lincoln Day speech at the local high
  school. You will be speaking on Lincoln's Birthday.

- You are speaking about child abuse to a group of local social workers
  who work with delinquent girls. You want to stress the point that children who have been abused might grow up to abuse their own children.

- You are going to speak about the value of water aerobics. As you plan
  your speech you remember how difficult it was for you to discipline
  yourself and how many times you were tempted to give it up.

is anything in the situation that you did not anticipate and need to adapt to. For example, did someone introduce you in a particularly flattering way? Do you want to acknowledge this? Did your audience brave bad weather to come and hear you talk? Do you want to thank them?

The Speech Conclusion

A good **conclusion** should tie a speech together and give the audience the feeling that the speech is complete. It should not introduce any new ideas.

If you have not had very much experience in public speaking, it is especially important that you plan your conclusion carefully. No feeling is worse than knowing that you have said all you have to say but do not know how to stop. If you plan your conclusion, this won't happen to you.

As with introductions, certain kinds of conclusions are used time and time again. When you are working on your conclusion, consider one of these. Note that even though the conclusions are of different types, they all have an inspirational quality. They make the audience feel that the speech was terrific and that they would like to hear this speaker again.

Summarize Your Main Ideas

If you want your audience to remember your main points, it helps to go back and summarize them in the conclusion of your speech. The student whose

How might organizing your speech with the aid of a computer help to ensure that your conclusion will be effective?

topic was "Five Tips for Improving Term Papers" concluded her speech this way:

> *Let me briefly summarize what you should do whenever you write a term paper. Use interviews as well as books, show enthusiasm about the subject, paraphrase quotations, don't pad your paper, and have your paper typed by a good typist. If you follow these hints you are certain to do better in the next paper you write.*

Use a Quotation

If you can find a quotation that fits your subject, the conclusion is a good place to use it. A quotation gives added authority to what you have said, and it can often help sum up your main ideas. In his speech to persuade the audience not to make political choices on the basis of television commercials, this student used a closing quotation to reinforce his point:

> *An executive in the television industry once wrote, "Television programming is designed to be understood by and to appeal to the average 12-year-old." If that is the opinion that television executives have of the typical American, I would suggest that we fight back. There is only one way to do that. Turn off the television set.*

Inspire Your Audience to Action

When you give a speech, especially a persuasive one, your goal is often to inspire an audience to some course of action. If this has been the goal of your speech, you can use your conclusion to tell audience members precisely what they should do. In the following example, a student has been trying to persuade members of her audience to join campus organizations. Notice how she motivates them to take this action:

> *We often hear that college is not part of "real life." Real life, however, is made up of clubs and organizations—all of which function to make decisions about our community, our lives, and even the course of democracy. This campus has 159 different clubs and organizations. If you are not a member of one of them, I encourage you to join today. If you join one of them, you become part of campus life. If you start working with an organization, you are preparing yourself for life in the "real world." On the table by the door there are lists of all of these organizations along with their telephone numbers. Please pick up a list on your way out. I'm sure you will find that at least one organization has something for you.*

Additional Tips for Conclusions

1. Work on your conclusion until you feel you can deliver it without notes. If you feel confident about your conclusion, you will feel more confident about your speech.

2. If you tell your audience you are going to conclude, do it! Don't set up the expectation that you are finished and then go on talking for several more minutes.
3. Don't let the words "thank you" take the place of a conclusion.
4. Give your conclusion and leave the speaking area. If you don't do this, you will ruin the impact of your conclusion and perhaps even your entire speech.

Speech Transitions

The final element to work into your speech is **transitions**—comments that lead from one point to another to tell your audience where you have been and where you are going. Transitions are a means of smoothing the flow from one point to another. For example, if you are going to show how alcohol and tobacco combine to become more powerful than either acting alone, you might say:

> *We all know, then, that cigarette smoking is hazardous to our health and we all know that alcohol abuse can kill, but do you know what can happen when the two are combined? Let me show you how these two substances act synergistically—each one making the other more powerful and dangerous than either would be alone.*

Now you are set to speak about their combined effect.

Tips for Transitions

In writing transitions, you should pay attention to these points:

1. Use a transition to introduce main heads and to indicate their order: "First . . . Second . . . Third . . . "; "The first matter we shall discuss . . ."; "In the first place . . ."; "The first step . . ."; "Let us first consider . . ."; and the like.
2. Write out your transitions and include them in your speech outline. A transition that is written out and rehearsed is more likely to be used.
3. If in doubt about whether to use a transition, *use it*. Since a speech is a one-time event, listeners cannot go back. Anything you can do to make the job of listening easier and more accurate should be done.

Preparing an Outline

An outline is a way of organizing material so you can see all the parts and how they relate to the whole. Outlining your speech will help you organize your thoughts and discover where your presentation might present problems in structure.

Your speech will be organized into an introduction, a body, and a conclusion (with transitions connecting them). Since the introduction and the conclusion deal with so few points, they are usually not outlined. (However, some speakers like to write out the introduction and conclusion and include them as part of the outline.)

MAIN AND SUPPORTING POINTS

The outline sets forth the major portion of the speech—the body—and shows the content's organization into main and supporting (minor) points. Remember that the broad, general statements are the main points and the minor points contain the more specific information that elaborates on and supports the main points.

STANDARD SYMBOLS AND INDENTATION

All outlines use the same system of symbols. The main points are numbered with Roman numerals (I, II, III) and capital letters (A, B, C). Minor, more specific, points are numbered with Arabic numerals (1, 2, 3) and lowercase letters (a, b, c). The most important material is always closest to the left-hand margin; as material gets less important, it moves to the right. Note, then, that the outline format moves information from the general to the more specific through the use of numbers, letters, and indentation.

I. Vegetables
   A. Root Vegetables
      1. Carrots
      2. Potatoes
      3. Parsnips
   B. Leafy Vegetables
      1. Spinach
      2. Collard greens
      3. Lettuce

Another thing you should note about the outline format is that there should always be at least two points of the same level. That is, you can't have just an A and no B; you can't have just a 1 and no 2. The only exception to this is that in a one-point speech, you would have only one main point.

Full-Sentence and Key-Word Outlines

There are two major types of outlines: full-sentence and key-word. **A full-sentence outline** is a complete map of what the speech will look like. All the ideas are stated in full sentences. In a full-sentence outline it is easy to spot problem areas and weaknesses in the structure, support, and flow of ideas. This type of outline is very useful as you plan and develop your speech.

Key-word outlines give only the important words and phrases; their main function is to remind the speaker of his or her ideas when delivering the speech. Sometimes speakers will add statistics or quotations to key-word outlines when such information is too long or too complicated to memorize. Some speakers prepare a full-sentence outline on the left and a key-word outline on the right, as in the following example. The key-word outline enables the speaker to avoid having to look at his or her notes all the time.

Produce should be carefully washed before you eat it.	Wash produce
Breads without preservatives should be refrigerated.	Refrigerate bread
Meat should not be eaten raw.	No raw meat

The main points (whether presented in full sentences or by key words) are sometimes put on cards—one to a card. We will discuss the reasons for this in the next chapter.

The Bibliography

At the end of your outline you should have a **bibliography** of all the material you have used in preparing your speech. This bibliography should include everything you have read (books, newspapers, magazines) and all the people you have interviewed. Figure 13-1 shows how items should be listed in a bibliography. At the end of this chapter, following the sample outline, you will find a sample bibliography.

SAMPLE OUTLINE

To help you do your own outline, here is a sample speech done in outline form. Note that the speech follows a topical pattern of organization. The topical outline works well for this particular speech because all the main points are illustrations of the central idea. The speech outline appears on the left, our commentary on the right.

Title

Drug Testing and Employment

Specific Purpose

To inform the audience about drug testing in the workplace.

Central Idea

Drug testing of job applicants and employees is widespread in business and government.

By stating your specific purpose and central idea you will be able to stay on track while you are doing your outline. Whenever you add a new main point, ask yourself whether it ties in directly with your purpose and central idea.

Bibliographies should have items stated in a specific way. Since books, magazines, and interviews are the most common sources for speeches, an example is given of how each should appear in the bibliography.
Items in the bibliography should be listed alphabetically by author.

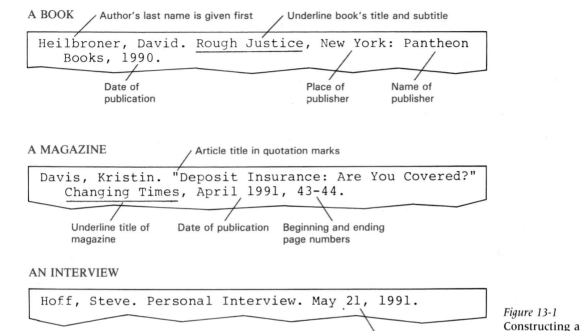

A BOOK · Author's last name is given first · Underline book's title and subtitle

> Heilbroner, David. Rough Justice, New York: Pantheon
> Books, 1990.

Date of publication · Place of publisher · Name of publisher

A MAGAZINE · Article title in quotation marks

> Davis, Kristin. "Deposit Insurance: Are You Covered?"
> Changing Times, April 1991, 43-44.

Underline title of magazine · Date of publication · Beginning and ending page numbers

AN INTERVIEW

> Hoff, Steve. Personal Interview. May 21, 1991.

Date of interview

Figure 13-1
Constructing a
Bibliography

Introduction

In the past few years we have seen vivid examples of how drug use has brought a major change in many people's careers. A candidate for the governorship of Pennsylvania may have lost an election because he admitted that he had smoked marijuana in his youth. A Supreme Court nominee withdrew his name from consideration after he admitted to occasionally having smoked marijuana in the 1960s and 1970s. Even new college graduates are being affected: if they have recently used any drug, it is likely to show up in a medical test conducted by a potential employer.

These examples are particularly dramatic because they involve people in high places.

Transition

Since drug testing is so prevalent and is expected to grow, it is clear that people

This transition gives the audience an idea of where the speaker is going.

who use drugs are going to have problems in getting jobs.

Body

I. Employers are becoming increasingly concerned about drug use by employees.
   A. The Research Triangle Institute estimates that drug and alcohol abuse costs employers at least $33 billion a year.
   B. In a survey of managers, 95 percent say that drug use is a problem in their organization.
   C. In this same survey, 42 percent say they are testing for drug use, 38 percent are considering it, and 12 percent plan to begin testing within the next year.

The speaker develops the first main point under Roman numeral I. Note that this point is stated as a full sentence.

Subpoints **A**, **B**, and **C**, are also stated as full sentences. However, items below this level—those with Arabic numbers—do not have to be stated in full sentences.

Transition

A positive test will mean being rejected for a job, being fired from a job, or being required to undergo some sort of rehabilitation.

II. Urine samples are a reliable and hard-to-beat way of detecting drugs.
   A. According to a study by the American Association for Clinical Chemistry, labs show a 99.2 percent accuracy rate on their tests.
   B. Robert Fogerson of Pharm Chem Laboratories says the tests are hard to beat: "These tests were developed many years ago to detect drugs and alcohol in hard-core addicts. The people taking tests now have not even approached the level of deviousness that we've seen.
   C. A manager at International Paper says, "Our nurse is tough. She knows all of the tricks that people use to hide evidence of drug use in their urine."

The second main point is stated in a full sentence, as are subheads **A**, **B**, **C**.

The speaker uses two people who have expertise to give the speech more authority.

Transition

One question you might rightfully ask is whether employers have a right to test you for drugs.

III. Drug testing is legal in the United States.
    A. Former President Ronald Reagan issued an Executive Order for mandatory testing of federal employees.
    B. The U.S. Supreme Court has ruled that drug testing is constitutional when the occupation is one where drug use might endanger public safety.
    C. There are certain to be other court cases that will challenge the right to test applicants and employees.
    D. Many employees have seen evidence of drug use at work.
        1. 41 percent of employees in a Massachusetts poll
        2. 30 percent of employees in a nationwide poll

This transition moves the speech from discussion of the controversy to practical information that will be useful to the audience.

Transitions

Whether all drug testing is legal remains to be seen. However, one important question is whether it has worked.

IV. Studies have shown that drug use in the workplace is on the decline.
    A. SmithKline, a drug-testing facility, noted recently that 11 percent of 1.9 million workers and applicants tested positive—down 12.7 percent from the year before.
    B. Several national and regional studies of drug abuse have noted the same trend.

Conclusion

Experimenting with drugs is not worth it: A would-be governor and a would-be Supreme Court justice can tell you that. Don't do something now that can cause

The speaker ties the conclusion to the introduction by referring to the original example. This helps to unify the speech.

problems for you later. The increasing trend to test for drugs will affect you. If you're not using them, don't start. If you're using them, quit. It's foolish to jeopardize your working future.

Bibliography

Articles

————, "Gains in the Drug War," *Telegram & Gazette,* Worcester, Mass., Feb. 20, 1991, p. A10.

Goetz, K., "High on the Job: A Growing Problem?" *Psychology Today,* May 1987, p. 16.

Greenhouse, Linda, "Nominee for Supreme Court Says He Used Marijuana and Regrets It." *The New York Times,* Nov. 6, 1987, pp. 1A, 17A.

Lewis, Diane E., "Gallup Finds 95% Majority in State Favors Drug Testing," *The Boston Globe,* Boston, Mass., April 25, 1991 (no page given).

————, "Reagan Administration Drug Testing Program: Pro and Con," *Congressional Digest,* May 1987.

Interview: Manager, International Paper Company (Lock Haven Plant, Lock Haven, Pa.), May 16, 1991.

This bibliography lists all the sources the speaker used in preparing the speech. If she (or anyone else) wants to check her information, the bibliography tells where to look.

SUMMARY

The principles of organization include selecting information that relates to the specific purpose and central idea; distinguishing among the introduction, body, and conclusion of the speech; distinguishing between main and minor points; and phrasing all points in full sentences with parallel structure.

Six patterns of organization work well for organizing speeches; time order, using a chronological sequence; spatial order, moving from left to right, top to bottom, or in any direction that will make the subject clear; cause-and-effect order, showing why something is happening and what impact it is having; problem-solution, explaining a problem and giving a solution; motivated sequence, following the steps of attention, need, satisfaction, visualization, and action; and topical order, arranging the speech into subtopics.

The purpose of the introduction is to set the tone for the speech, introduce the topic, and get the audience's attention. Some attention-getting devices are using humor, giving personal examples, referring to the occasion, showing the importance of the subject, telling startling information, asking questions, and using quotations.

The speech conclusion should signal the audience that the speech is over and should tie all the ideas together. In their conclusions, speakers often summarize main ideas, use quotations, and inspire the audience to take further action.

Speech transitions help an audience follow where a speaker is going. They introduce main heads and may be written into the speech outline.

An outline is a way of organizing material to highlight all the parts and how they relate to the whole. In most cases, the body of the speech is what is outlined—the introduction and conclusion are handled separately.

The outline shows the organization into main and minor points through the use of standard symbols and indentation. Many speakers like to construct two outlines: a full-sentence outline for organizing the speech and a key-word outline to summarize the main ideas and to function as notes during delivery of the speech.

Your outline should be followed by a bibliography—a list of all of the material from other sources that you have used in your speech. All the items should be stated in a standard bibliographical form.

FURTHER READING

BOYD, STEPHEN D., AND MARY ANN RENZ. *Organization and Outlining: A Workbook for Students in a Basic Speech Course.* Indianapolis, IN: Bobbs-Merrill, 1985. This workbook can be used by individuals without direction. It helps develop proficiency by systematically providing principles, frequent examples, sample exercises, and possible answers. It begins by discussing points of focus of speeches and ends with the complete outline.

BRICKMAN, GAYLE F., AND LYNNE E. FULLER. *Organizing for Impact: A Practical Guide for the Public Speaker.* Dubuque, IA: Kendall/Hunt, 1986. The authors provide a systematic approach for putting together a presentation: analyze your audience, brainstorm for a topic, funnel the topic to a suitable length, derive pertinent, clear main points, then use their "Branching Sheet" to make certain that all main components are in place. A practical, useful book full of specific suggestions and guidelines.

DEWEY, JOHN. *How We Think.* Boston, MA: Heath, 1933. For those who are looking for some of the theoretical underpinnings of organization, this book is invaluable. The section on "Analysis of Reflective Thinking" is especially succinct and instructive. This is an insightful resource despite its age.

HAYNES, JUDY L. *Organizing a Speech: A Programmed Guide,* 2d ed. Englewood Cliffs, NJ: Prentice-Hall, 1981. Haynes begins her book with a review of the elements of outlines. She then discusses the structuring and sequencing of ideas, as well as the finishing touches. She offers a step-by-step method for acquiring the essential skills.

NOONAN, PEGGY. *What I Saw at the Revolution.* New York: Random House, 1990. Noonan writes about what it was like to be a speechwriter for a U.S. president. She wrote speeches for both Ronald Reagan and George Bush. Chapter 5 is particularly interesting since it describes all the writing and revisions of a speech before it is actually delivered.

RICO, GABRIELE LUSSER. *Writing the Natural Way: Using Right-Brain Techniques to Release Your Expressive Powers.* New York: J. P. Tarcher, 1983. For those who find organizing difficult, Rico's chapters on "Clustering: Doorway to Your Design Mind," "Discovering Design: The Trial Web," and "Recurrences: The Unifying Thread" are especially relevant and valuable. A creative outlet for outlining ideas.

ROBBINS, LARRY M. *The Business of Writing and Speaking: A Managerial Communication Manual*. New York: McGraw-Hill, 1985. The author integrates basic skills, intellectual inquiry, and specific topics of communication. The first section deals with the general principles of communication and the principles that underlie effective writing and speaking. Robbins even includes a chapter on developing logical arguments. This is a solid book on effective preparation and organization.

WHITMAN, RICHARD F., AND JOHN H. TIMMIS. "The influence of Verbal Organizational Structure and Verbal Organizing Skills on Select Measures of Learning." *Human Communication Research*, 1 (Summer 1975): 293–301. An excellent article that describes the various effects of organization.

Chapter 14

Delivering the Speech

CHAPTER OBJECTIVES	KEY TERMS
After reading this chapter, you should be able to:	articulation
1. Show attentiveness to your audience.	diagram
	enunciation
2. Achieve a conversational quality in your speech.	extemporaneous speaking
	flip chart
3. Distinguish among the four types of delivery.	graph
	impromptu speaking
4. Use body movement, eye contact, and gestures to enhance your speech.	inflection
	monotone
5. Identify the elements that affect how you sound, and adjust them to improve your delivery.	organizational chart
	pace
	poster
6. Use visual aids to increase your audience's attention and understanding.	pronunciation
	table
7. Employ several techniques to control your nervousness.	visual aids
8. Outline the steps to follow in practicing your speech.	

G inny DeVries had been out of college for two years. She had majored in social work and was now working for the Department of Social Services. Most of her work involved finding foster homes for problem children and helping the children adjust to their new families. Ginny loved her work, and when the Social Work Club at her alma mater asked her to speak she was excited by the opportunity. She decided to speak on the subject "Foster Care for Problem Kids," and she hoped to inspire some of the future social work graduates to choose the area of foster care for their own careers.

In preparing her speech, Ginny gathered facts and figures about foster care in the state. She prepared two charts: one a list of characteristics that make up a good foster home, the other a graph showing the percentage of children who stay out of trouble once they have been in a foster home. In addition to her factual and statistical material, she had a large number of examples and anecdotes based on her own experience. She organized all this material into a full-sentence outline—choosing items she thought would be particularly interesting to her audience.

Ginny had not done any public speaking since her speech class in college, but she remembered that it had been very helpful to practice her speech beforehand. Once it was organized, she gave the speech in her living room—pretending it was filled with an audience. On the first run-through she discovered it was 20 minutes long, whereas she had been asked to speak for only 15 minutes. She worked to cut it back and also added a couple of transitions to make the speech run more smoothly. When she had finished her editing and revising, she tried giving the speech again—this time in front of a mirror. She found her speech was the right length and the transitions worked very well, but she wasn't using enough gestures. She made notes on the margins of her note cards to move around a little more and use more gestures. This she would practice in her next run-through. Feeling satisfied with her progress, she went to bed.

The next morning she woke up with a new idea for the introduction. She made a few notes and then went off to work. During her lunch hour, she shut her office door and ran through the speech again. As she was giving it, she made an effort to add gestures and to move around. The speech went so smoothly that she felt confident and went back to her work.

That evening, on her way to give the speech, she was feeling a little nervous, but she told herself that she was in good shape: the speech was well prepared and she knew she could deliver it well.

When she arrived in the room where she was to give the speech, she was still feeling a little apprehensive, and so she took the remaining time to look over her note cards again.

When she stood up to speak, she started with a humorous anecdote, thus winning the complete attention of the audience. Ginny felt that she was off to a strong start and that this was going to be a good speech. As she spoke, she remembered to look around the room—particularly toward the back row and corners. She also looked at individual audience members. When she was two-thirds through the speech, she noticed some restlessness, and so she added an anecdote. Immediately she had the audience's attention again.

When the speech was over, the chairperson asked if there were any questions. With barely a pause, several hands went up. Ginny answered dozens of questions—all of them dealing with different aspects of her work. The questions went on for so long that the chairperson had to call a halt—campus security had come to lock up the room. As the audience left the room, the chairperson told Ginny that this was the best speech the Social Work Club had heard all year. She added, "We'll be sure to invite you back next year." As Ginny drove home, she felt very good about herself. She thought, "I would like to do this again. It was a lot of work but it really paid off."

Characteristics of Good Delivery

A good speech can bring even more satisfaction to the speaker than it does to the audience. There is nothing quite like the experience of communicating your ideas, having them understood, and having an entire audience respond to you in a positive way. Yet speaking to an audience does not come naturally; it is a skill you have to learn. By now you have begun to master the skill of finding material and putting your speech together, and so it is time to shift focus to delivering your speech.

Attentiveness

You might wonder how a speaker could be inattentive to his or her own speech. Yet it's quite possible to be present and functioning as a body while not being there in spirit. When Deb's friend complimented her on the speech she had given in speech class, Deb replied: "You know, it's almost like I wasn't there at all. I don't remember looking at anyone and I barely remember what I said."

Not being attentive to your own speech is really a matter of internal noise: you are so overcome with the mechanics and anxiety of giving a speech that you forget this is basically a human encounter between a speaker and listeners.

Attentiveness means focusing on the moment. It means saying to yourself that you have come to tell your listeners something important and that you are going to do your very best to communicate with them. It is also a matter of being aware of and responding to your listeners' needs. To ensure that you will be attentive to your audience, you can do several things:

1. *Pick a topic that is important to you.* If you are speaking on something of great interest and importance to you, it is likely that you will communicate your interest and enthusiasm to your audience. Also, if you can get involved in your subject, you are likely to feel less anxiety about giving your speech.
2. *Do all the work necessary to prepare the best speech possible.* If you work on your speech—organize and practice it—you will be much more confident about it and will feel less anxious when the time comes to give it. Then you will be able to concentrate on delivering your speech.
3. *Individualize your audience members.* Try to think of your audience as individual human beings rather than as a mass of people. As you give

the speech, think: "I am going to talk to Kathy, who sits in the second row. Kevin always looks like he is going to sleep. I am going to give a speech that will wake him up."

4. *Focus on the audience rather than on yourself.* As you speak, look for audience feedback and try to respond to it. The more you focus on the audience members and their needs, the less likely you are to feel anxiety.

Ginny followed these four guidelines when she gave her speech. She selected a topic, "Foster Care for Problem Kids," that was important to her; she did the work necessary to prepare the best speech she could; she looked at individual audience members; and she focused on the audience rather than on herself. At one point, noting some restlessness in her audience, she even added an unplanned anecdote to her speech.

Conversational Quality

Some of our models for public speaking come from orators who address huge audiences. Their voices rise and fall dramatically, their gestures are large and expansive, their voices big and booming. Although this might be an effective speaking technique for some occasions, such as political rallies and religious revivals, it is usually most effective to use a conversational quality in public speaking.

When you use a conversational quality you talk to your audience in much the same way you talk when you are having a conversation with another person.[1] The value of a conversational tone in public speaking is that it gives the impression that the speaker is talking *with* the audience rather than *at* it. Notice how this speaker uses conversational language and the word *you* to involve his audience:

> *Have you ever felt embarrassed—I mean really embarrassed—where you never wanted to show your face in public again? Has your face ever turned red when lots of people were watching you? I would guess that you have had this experience once or twice in your life—I know I have. But— have you ever wondered what happens to us physically and psychologically when we are embarrassed?*

How do you achieve a conversational tone in speaking? The most useful way, right from the planning stage, is to imagine giving your speech to one person or to a small group of people. Have a mental picture of this person or persons, and try to talk directly to them in a normal, conversational manner. This will help you to achieve the right tone.

However, a conversational tone doesn't mean being casual. A speech occasion is more formal than most conversations. Even though you're aiming for a conversational tone, you shouldn't allow long pauses or use such conversational fillers as "O.K." or "you know." You should also avoid some of the slang and "in" jokes or expressions you would use in casual conversation.

Try This Try This Try This

*T*he following information has been written in a rather formal style. Using the guidelines for conversational speechmaking, try to adapt it for oral delivery in a conversational style:

I am not a very funny person although I think I have a reasonable sense of humor. I do enjoy laughing and laughter; however, I have a very difficult time remembering jokes. When I try to tell them to other people—my friends, for example—either I get the information out of sequence or I forget the punch line. I really find the best kind of humor is that which flows directly and naturally from the situations in which I find myself. More than anything else, I have found, having a sense of humor involves my willingness to laugh at myself and at life. I think all of us take life, and even ourselves, too seriously. We need to loosen up a bit and just enjoy life for all of its richness, pleasure, and especially—fun!

Here are a few additional hints on how to achieve a conversational quality:

* When you give your speech, imagine you are giving it to someone you know.
* Use contractions such as don't, can't, isn't, and weren't.
* Use words everyone will understand.
* Use an outline rather than writing out your speech word for word.

Types of Delivery

Recall a particularly good speech you have heard. Do you remember how it was delivered? From notes? From a manuscript? From memory? Was the speaker making a few brief, off-the-cuff remarks?

Speakers have four methods of delivery: making impromptu remarks, reading from a manuscript, memorizing the speech, and delivering extemporaneously.

Impromptu Speaking

Impromptu speaking is the giving of a speech on the spur of the moment. Usually there is little or no time for preparation. Sometimes your instructor might ask you to give an impromptu speech in class. Other times you might be asked to give a toast or offer a prayer at a gathering, or you may make a few remarks at a meeting.

If you are asked to give an impromptu speech, the most important thing is not to panic. Your main goal is to think of a topic and organize it quickly in your head before you start to speak.

In finding a topic, look around you and at the occasion. Is there anything you can refer to? Formal occasions always occur for a reason. They often honor someone or something, and the person or thing being honored can provide a focus for your speech: "I am delighted to be at this yearly meeting of documentary film makers. Documentary film making is one of the noblest professions. . . ." Other times you might want to refer to the place or the people: "I am happy to be here in Akron again. The last time I was here . . ." or "I am very touched by the warm reception you have all given me. . . ."

In impromptu speaking it's essential to keep your remarks brief. No one expects you to speak for more than a minute or two. The audience knows that you are in a tight spot, and it doesn't expect a long and well-polished speech.

Speaking from a Manuscript

Speaking from a manuscript involves writing out the entire speech and reading it to the audience. When you read a speech you can get a clear idea of how long it is, and so manuscript speaking is a good method when exact timing is necessary. Because a manuscript also offers preplanned wording, political leaders often favor this method when they speak on sensitive issues and want control over what they say. When Jane, for example, decided to run for president of the student government, she prepared a five-minute speech in manuscript form for her appearance on the campus television station with the other candidates. Jane knew that having a manuscript would help her stay within her time limit and would also help her say exactly what she wanted to say. However, she also knew that she had to be very familiar with the manuscript so she could break away from it to establish eye contact.

When using a manuscript, speakers find that it is difficult to sound spontaneous; if listeners think they are being read to, they are more likely to lose interest. Experienced speakers who use manuscripts are often so skilled at delivery that the audience is not aware the speech is being read. Beginning speakers, however, have difficulty making a manuscript speech sound spontaneous and natural.

Feedback is another problem in speaking from a manuscript. If the audience becomes bored and inattentive, it is difficult to respond and modify the speech; the speaker is bound to the manuscript. A manuscript also confines a speaker to the lectern—because that's where the manuscript is.

Try This Try This Try This

*T*ake the following information that has been written in an academic or formal style and rephrase it to make it more easily understood in a speech.

1. Although there is a formal mechanism for centralized reporting of drug incidents of this nature, compliance is voluntary and, therefore, somewhat sporadic. Thus it is not very surprising that accurate data concerning the true frequency of occurrence is not available.
2. These results also identify features of the reticent's communication style that can be easily remediated.
3. Police say they will not impose any limitations on the number of participants in the future.
4. Although quite a bit of anecdotal evidence suggests that illiterates compensate for their inability to record information in written form through the development of an extraordinary memory, this was not apparent in the study.
5. A group needs some heterogeneity to ensure differing viewpoints and experiences. But a too-diverse group runs the risk of failing to achieve necessary cohesiveness.

Speaking from Memory

Speaking from memory involves writing out the entire speech and then committing it to memory word for word. It has the same advantages for speakers as the manuscript method: exact wording can be planned, phrases and sentences can be crafted, and potential problems in language can be eliminated. Also, a memorized speech can be adapted to a set, inflexible time limit. Jess, who was running against Jane in the student election, decided to memorize his speech. He decided this was a good idea because he wanted exact wording but he also wanted the freedom to move around. Feedback was not a problem to Jess because he was speaking to a television audience. In other situations, however, responding to feedback can be a problem because it is difficult for the speaker to get away from what he or she has memorized.

A memorized speech can create considerable pressure. Not only does the speaker have to spend hours memorizing the speech, but he or she is also likely to worry about forgetting it. In addition, making a memorized speech sound natural and spontaneous requires considerable acting talent.

Extemporaneous Speaking

When using the **extemporaneous speaking** method, a speaker delivers a speech from notes. The speaker might commit the main ideas of the speech to memory—possibly also the introduction and conclusion—but will rely on notes to remember most of the speech.

The extemporaneous method has several advantages. It permits flexibility so that a speaker can adjust to the feedback of listeners. For example, if a speaker sees that several audience members do not understand something, he or she can stop and explain. If the audience looks bored, the speaker can try moving around or using a visual aid earlier than planned. The extemporaneous method is the one method of delivery that comes closest to good conversation because a speaker can be natural and responsive to the audience.

One disadvantage of the extemporaneous method is that the speaker may stumble over or grope for words. However, much of this problem can be overcome by rehearsing the speech beforehand. Sometimes speakers want to use exact words or phrases. Although in extemporaneous speaking the speech as a whole is not memorized, there is nothing wrong with memorizing a particularly important sentence—or having it written down and reading it from a note card.

For the beginning speaker, the extemporaneous method is the best type of delivery. In addition to eliminating heavy burdens for the speaker (writing out and/or memorizing the speech), it enables a natural and spontaneous style of speaking. It also makes the listeners a central element in the speech, for the speaker is able to respond to them at all times.

How You Look

Appearance

As you rise from your chair and walk to the lectern to give your speech, the audience's first impression of you will come from how you look. Audience members will notice how you are dressed, whether you walk to the lectern with confidence, and whether you look interested in giving this speech.

On days when you are going to make a speech it is a good idea to look your best. Not only does looking good give the audience a positive impression of you, but it also gives you a psychological boost.

Try to stay away from clothing that might distract from your speech. For example, avoid T-shirts with writing on them. The message itself may be distracting, and audience members will divert their attention by trying to read or to guess what your T-shirt says if some of it is hidden by the lectern. Also, avoid accessories you might be tempted to play with. Scarves or jewelry worn around the neck can be troublesome in this regard.

When you are giving a speech in public, wear what the audience would expect you to wear. If it's a formal occasion, wear dress-up clothing; if it's informal, wear what you think everyone else will wear. If you don't know this, ask the person who has invited you to speak.

Body Movement

Movement usually causes a response. Blinking-turn signals on a car attract more attention than tail lights; most of us prefer motion pictures to still photos; the most interesting commercials show the products working. By the same token, a speaker who uses some movement is likely to attract more attention than a speaker who stands absolutely still.[2] Of course, this does not mean that all movement is good. To be effective, your movement should be carefully coordinated with your speech. For example, if you want to stress

Consider This Consider This Consider This

*R*osalynn Carter writes of her fear of giving speeches. This fear surfaced when her husband was governor of Georgia and she was often asked to speak. She writes how she overcame her fear when she discovered the extemporaneous speech:

I went to the luncheon at a downtown hotel armed with my card with six or eight words on it. I tried to appear nonchalant, as though I did this every day with great ease. I carried on a conversation with my hostesses in a conscious effort to keep the speech out of my mind. I even ate my lunch. Finally I was introduced. I stood up to speak and looked out over the crowd and pretended they were all tourists. Suddenly they all looked like tourists—all strangers, all looking at me, just as they did at the mansion—and while I was enjoying the thought because that made it easier, I began to talk about the Governor's Mansion . . . and it was easy. They were listening attentively, and when I got through they wanted to hear more. So I answered questions with no problem, no problem at all.

The speech over, I said my good-byes, walked calmly from the room, then ran to find a telephone. I couldn't wait to tell Jimmy. I called him at his office: "I did it! I did it!" And Madeline, my secretary, still remembers that day when I got back for a big dinner party that evening when my car drove up, the door opened, and I burst in, saying, "I did it! I did it!"

I had done it. It was a wonderful feeling and quite a breakthrough for me. Although I have never gotten completely over my nervousness, I have been making speeches regularly ever since.

Source: Rosalynn Carter. *First Lady from Plains.*

your most important point, you might indicate this nonverbally by moving closer to your audience. If you want to create intimacy between you and your audience as you are telling a personal story, you could sit on the edge of the desk for a brief period.

Avoid movement that might be distracting. Probably you have seen a speaker (or teacher) who paces back and forth in front of the room. This movement is not motivated by anything other than habit or nervousness: as a result, it's ineffective.

Speakers cannot move around very much if they depend too heavily on their notes. If you must constantly return to the lectern to consult your notes, you will not be able to move very far. The better you know your speech, the more you will be able to experiment with movement.

When you are planning how to deliver your speech, you should consider whether to include deliberate body movements. If you leave these movements to chance, you might not move at all or might move in a way that distracts your listeners. For example, when Susan planned her speech about abused children, she decided to stay behind the lectern when she talked about policy, but to move in front of the lectern when she talked about individual children. So that she wouldn't forget, she wrote reminders about moving on her note cards.

When might infor-
mal communication
be more effective
than formal
communication?

Eye Contact

In our culture, it is considered extremely important to look into the eyes of the person we are talking to. If we don't, we are at risk of being considered dishonest or of having something to hide. Public speaking is no exception. Speakers are expected to scan the audience and to look directly into the eyes of individual audience members.[3]

Eye contact is also an important way of gauging audience reaction to your speech. For example, as a student explained how to get coupon refunds, she noticed that some of her audience members were confused. Because she had been making eye contact with her audience, she was able to identify the problem as soon as it occurred and take steps to remedy it.

Ideally, a speaker should look into the eyes of audience members 90 percent of the time. If audience members know a speaker is looking at them, they are much more likely to pay attention. Also, a speaker should look at all members of the audience—not just at those in some parts of the room. When you are speaking, work out a plan for eye contact. For example, you could start in the front row, go to the back, and then cut across the room in two diagonals. This way you would look at the entire audience.

Although the idea of this much eye contact may be scary to you, it can have positive benefits. Every audience will include members who look sympathetic and interested in what you are saying. Once you realize you are getting a positive response, you will begin to feel much more confident.

Facial Expressions

Facial expressions are the most difficult movements to change. Since we seldom have a chance to see our own faces while we are communicating, it is difficult to know what we are expressing. Generally, however, this is an area of movement that you don't have to worry about *unless you get some negative reaction*. For example, if someone remarks that you look bored to death while you were giving a speech, this is an area you should work on for your next speech.

Gestures

When we speak, most of our gestures are made up of hand and arm movements. We usually use gestures to express or emphasize ideas or emotions. Most of us are too stiff when we speak and could benefit by using more gestures. The best way to add more gestures to your speech is to practice in front of a mirror. Always aim for gestures that look spontaneous and that feel natural to you.

Posture

Posture is a matter of how we walk and stand. It can give the audience all sorts of messages. If you drag your feet or slouch, you could be communicating that you are lazy, sick, tired, or depressed—none of which you would want to communicate when giving a speech.

It should also be remembered that the way you sit in your seat, rise and walk to the lectern, and return to your seat after the speech can leave as much of an impression as the posture you use during your speech.

When giving a speech, we usually don't have a very good idea of our eye contact, facial expressions, or general body movement. Because we don't have a very good sense of how we look to others, a speech class is a great opportunity to get some feedback. Try to listen to critical remarks from your instructor and classmates without feeling defensive. If you can learn from your mistakes, you will improve every time you give a speech.

How You Sound

When members of a speech class have a chance to see themselves on videotape, most of them react more negatively to how they sound than to how they look. Very few people really like their own voice.

Our voice reveals things about us that might be far more important than the words we speak.[4] How loud, how fast, how clear and distinct the message— all are part of the information we send about ourselves.

The voice is also a powerful instrument of communication. Because it is so flexible, you can vary it to get the effect you want. You can speak in a loud voice and then drop to a mere whisper. You can go through basic information quickly and then slow down to make a new and important point. You can even use your voice to bring about a change of character. Notice how many different voices your favorite actress or comedian uses.

We have some idea of how we look to other people because we can see ourselves in a mirror. However, very few of us have any idea of how we sound, and once we find out, most of us would like to make some changes. When members of a speech communication class were asked to identify the things they most disliked about their voice, the most common complaints were poor articulation, speaking too fast, not sounding confident, and not having enough expression.

Volume

Many students who thought that they did not sound confident enough attributed this fault to not speaking loudly enough. As one student wrote, "I sound as soft as a mouse." Her comment reflects the perception in our society that a weak and hard-to-hear voice implies the speaker has little confidence. You don't want people to think that about you! In a public speaking situation, you have to speak loudly enough so that people in the back row can hear you. Because your voice-producing mechanism is so close to your ears, you probably think you are speaking louder than you really are. This means that you probably need to speak in a louder voice than you feel comfortable with.

Always check out the back row to see if people can hear you there. Generally you can tell if they are straining to hear you, and often they will give you some nonverbal sign (e.g., leaning forward) that you need to speak louder. If the place in which you are speaking is unusually large, you could even ask if people in the back can hear. If people have to strain to hear you, they probably will not make the effort unless you have something extraordinary to say.

Using a Microphone

If you are speaking in a large auditorium or in a room with poor acoustics, there might be a microphone at the lectern. The rules for using microphones are simple: make sure it is turned on, don't blow into it to see if it's working (it could ruin it), adjust it to your height, and stand 8 to 12 inches away from it while you speak.

Pace

Like volume, pace is easy to vary. **Pace** refers to how fast or how slowly you speak. If you speak too fast, you may be difficult to understand. If you speak too slowly, you risk losing the attention of your audience. If audience attention seems to be drifting away, try picking up your pace. Usually you don't know that you have been going too fast until someone tells you so after your speech is over. If you are told this, guard against the mistake in the future: in your next speech write reminders on your note cards to slow down.

Ideally a speaker varies his or her pace. Speaking fast and then slowing down helps keep the attention of the audience. Also, don't forget the benefits of pausing. Making a pause before or after a dramatic moment is a highly effective technique. The next time you are watching a comedian on television, notice how he or she uses pauses.

Pitch and Inflection

As we noted in Chapter 5, pitch is the range of tones used in speaking. **Inflection** is a related concept. It refers to the change in pitch used to emphasize certain words and phrases. The person who never varies his or her speaking voice is said to speak in a **monotone.**

Sometimes a person's voice might not seem very interesting because of lack of inflection. If you listen to professional newscasters or sportscasters, you will discover that they use a lot of inflection. By emphasizing certain words and phrases, they help direct the listeners' attention to what is important. Emphasis can also bring about subtle changes in meaning. Try reading the following sentence emphasizing a different word each time you read it. You should be able to read it in at least eight different ways.

You mean I have to be there at seven tomorrow?

Try This Try This Try This

*Y*ou can practice correct articulation by saying each of the following tongue twisters three times, rapidly.

1. She sells seashells on the seashore.
2. Rubber baby buggy bumpers.
3. The little lowland lubber was a lively lad, lucky, liberal, and likable.
4. The theme is there for them.
5. Betty battled bottles for thirty days.
6. Fanny Finch fried five floundering fish for Frances Fawlie's father.
7. While we waited for the whistle on the wharf, we whittled vigorously on the white weatherboards.
8. Meaninglessly meandering Melina managed to master Monday's memory work.
9. We apprehensively battled with the bragging apprentices, but they broke away from our blows and beat a poor retreat.
10. Grass grew green on the graves in Grace Gray's grandfather's graveyard.

Source: Adapted from Glenn R. Capp, G. Richard Capp, and Carol C. Capp, *Basic Oral Communication.*

The best way to get inflection in your voice is to stress certain words deliberately—even to the point of exaggeration. Try taping something in your normal voice and then in your "exaggerated" voice. You might be surprised to find that the exaggerated voice is more interesting.

Enunciation

Enunciation is made up of articulation and pronunciation. **Articulation** is the ability to pronounce the letters in a word correctly; **pronunciation** is the ability to pronounce the whole word. Not only does good enunciation enable people to understand us, but it is also the mark of an educated person. Most of our articulation problems go back to the people from whom we learned our language. If our parents, teachers, or peers pronounced words incorrectly, we probably will too.

Try This Try This Try This

*B*elow is a list of paired words that sound somewhat alike. Read them so that they can be told apart.

accept	except
access	excess
adapt	adopt
amplitude	aptitude
are	our
Arthur	author
ascent	accent
axe	ask
comprise	compromise
consecrate	confiscate
consolation	consultation
disillusion	dissolution
immorality	immortality
line	lion
martial	marital
Mongol	mongrel
pictures	pitchers
statue	statute
vocation	vacation
wandered	wondered

Source: John P. Moncur and Harrison M. Karr, *Developing Your Speaking Voice.*

Three common causes of articulation problems are sound substitution, omission of sounds, and slurring. Sound substitution is very common. Many people say "dere," "dem," and "dose" for "there," "them," and "those." In this case a *d* is substituted for the more difficult *th* sound. The substitution of a *d* for a *t* in the middle of a word is widespread in American English. If you need any proof try pronouncing these words as you usually do: "water," "butter," "thirty," "bottle." Unless you have very good articulation, you probably said: "wader," "budder," "thirdy," and "boddle."

Some people believe they have a speech defect that makes them unable to produce certain sounds. This can be easily checked. For example, if you always say "dere" for "there," make a special effort to make the *th* sound. If you are able to make it, you have a bad habit, not a speech defect.

We also commonly omit sounds. For example, we sometimes say "libary" for "library." And we frequently omit sounds that occur at the ends of words, saying "goin" for "going" and "doin" for "doing."

Slurring is caused by running words together. We use such phrases as "Yawanna go?" and "I'll meecha there." Slurring, as with other articulation problems, is usually a matter of bad speech habits, and it can be overcome with some effort and practice.

Once you are aware of a particular articulation habit, you can try to change it. Changing a habit is not easy, since the habit has probably been a part of your behavior for many years. Sometimes it helps to drill, using lists of words that give you trouble. It also helps to have a friend remind you when you mispronounce a word. Once you become accustomed to looking for the problem, you will catch yourself more often. If you have several articulation problems, do not try to solve them all at once. Work on one sound at a time; when you can handle that sound, then attempt another one.

Pronunciation is a matter of saying words correctly. Most of us have a bigger reading vocabulary than speaking vocabulary, but we don't know how to pronounce many of the words we read. If you are in doubt about how to pronounce a word, check it in the dictionary.

Using Visual Aids

Visual aids are devices such as charts, graphs, and slides that help illustrate the key points in a speech. Visual aids serve three functions: they help hold the attention of the listeners, they provide information in the visual channel, and they help the audience remember what you've said. A study has shown that if members of an audience are given only verbal information, after three days they will remember a mere 10 percent of what they were told; if they are shown material without verbal communication, they will remember 35 percent. However, if both verbal and visual information are provided, they will remember 65 percent after three days. Just because you have a visual aid, however, does not mean that your audience will automatically give you its attention. A poorly designed or inappropriate visual aid will not keep an audience's attention.

How much does retention
improve when the speaker uses a
visual aid?

Types of Visual Aids

Your visual material should help make your topic lively and interesting to the audience. There are numerous types of visual aids to choose from. In making your choice, ask yourself which kind of visual material would best illustrate your topic and appeal to your listeners.

THE CHALKBOARD

Since a chalkboard exists in every classroom, it is the most accessible visual aid. It works particularly well if you write key words or phrases while you are talking. You can also use it to draw very simple diagrams.

When you use the chalkboard, it's important that you write quickly to avoid having your back to the audience any longer than necessary. Once you have the word or diagram on the board, turn around, stand next to it, and as you explain, point to it with your hand. Make sure that your writing is large and dark enough for the entire audience to read.

THE ACTUAL OBJECT

Sometimes it is useful to use the thing you are talking about as a visual aid. An audience likes to see what you are talking about—especially if the object is not familiar to them. One student brought a violin and viola to class to demonstrate the differences in the sounds and the looks of the two instruments.

Consider This Consider This Consider This

*A*round 10,000 B.C., during the last period of Paleolithic culture, humans drew leaping bison on the walls of a cave near Altamira, Spain. Today, historians wonder why. Possibly there was some early religious significance. Or maybe prehistoric persons painted merely for their own enjoyment. Well, as long as opinions are being ventured, I'll advance one of my own. Perhaps it was a training session, and the prehistoric presenter had found that the use of visuals added an entirely new dimension to explanatory grunts.

Farfetched? It seems as good an explanation as the others. Why not? Almost 12,000 years later, training experts would be laboring over drawings of their own—curves and bar charts that can increase comprehension and retention by as much as 500 percent.

Source: Terry C. Smith, *Making Successful Presentations: A Self-Teaching Guide.*

Another, explaining how to make minor adjustments on one's car, brought a carburetor. Still another borrowed a skeleton from the biology department to illustrate a speech on osteoporosis, a bone disease.

MODELS

A model is a replica of an actual object that is used when the object itself is too large to be displayed (e.g., a building), too small to be seen (e.g., a cell),

Is this speaker's presentation going to be more effective because she is using a visual aid? Why or why not?

or inaccessible to the eye (e.g., the human heart). A model can be a very effective visual aid because it shows exactly how something looks. It is better than a picture because it is three-dimensional. For example, a student who was discussing airplanes used in warfare brought in models or planes he had constructed.

POSTERS, DIAGRAMS, AND CHARTS

A **poster** consists of lettering or pictures, or both. The purpose of a poster is to enhance the speaker's subject. For example, when speaking about the design of cars, a student used a poster showing pictures of one make of car to show how its style had changed over a 15-year period. A poster may also be used to emphasize the key words or thoughts in a speech. A student who spoke on how to save money on clothes used a poster to list the following points:

1. Decide on a basic color.
2. Buy basics at one store.
3. Buy accessories at sales.

Not only did the poster provide the audience with a way to remember the points, but it also gave, in visual form, the general outline of the speech.

A **diagram** may range from a simple organizational chart to a complex rendering of a three-dimensional object. Diagrams are particularly valuable in showing how something works. For example, in a speech about storing toxic wastes, a student uses the diagram in Figure 14-1 to show how waste can be stored in a salt cavern. Including a drawing of the Empire State

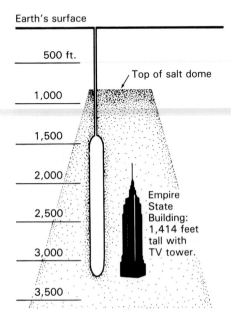

Earth's surface

500 ft.

Top of salt dome

1,000

1,500

2,000

Empire State Building: 1,414 feet tall with TV tower.

2,500

3,000

3,500

Figure 14-1
One Cavern's Size

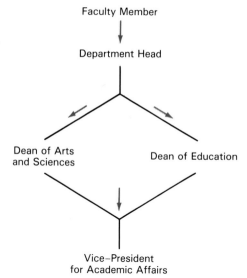

Figure 14-2
Organizational Chart

Building is particularly useful because it gives the viewer an idea of the depth of the mine.

An **organizational chart** shows the relationships among the elements of an organization, such as the departments of a company, the branches of federal or state government, or the committees of the student government. For example, note how a speaker used the organizational chart in Figure 14-2 to show how the academic side of a university is organized and how a student wishing to express dissatisfaction should approach people in a specific order.

A *flip chart* is a series of pictures, words, diagrams, and so forth. It's called a flip chart because it is made up of several pages that you "flip" through. A flip chart is best used when you have a complicated subject which needs several illustrations or when you want to emphasize several points in your speech.

TABLES AND GRAPHS

These visual aids are easy to prepare and can be used to condense a lot of information into a useful, understandable form. Perhaps most important, anyone can make them because no special skills are required.

Tables are columns of figures arranged in an order that enables the viewer to easily pick out the information needed. For example, when a student spoke about the need for more female professors, he used Table 14-1 as his visual aid.

Graphs are statistical material presented in a visual form that help viewers see similarities, differences, relationships, or trends. There are three commonly used graphs: bar, pie, and line. If you want to see the variety of graphs available, look in any issue of *USA Today*.

TABLE 14-1
Number and Percent of Faculty by Gender 1981–1990

	Male		Female		Total	
Fall	*N*	*%*	*N*	*%*	*N*	*%*
1981	129	75.9	41	24.1	170	100.0
1982	129	75.9	41	24.1	170	100.0
1983	132	76.3	41	23.7	173	100.0
1984	129	75.9	41	24.1	170	100.0
1985	135	75.0	45	25.0	180	100.0
1986	137	77.0	41	23.0	178	100.0
1987	134	74.4	46	25.6	180	100.0
1988	134	72.0	52	28.0	186	100.0
1989	133	66.5	67	33.5	200	100.0
1990	138	65.7	72	34.3	210	100.0

Source: Lou Fabian, Lock Haven University, Lock Haven, Pennsylvania, 1991.

Both bar and pie graphs are used to show how information is broken up proportionately. For example, a student used the bar graph in Figure 14-3 to illustrate grade inflation and to show that a "C" is no longer the average grade. In Figure 14-4 another student used the pie graph to show the various kinds

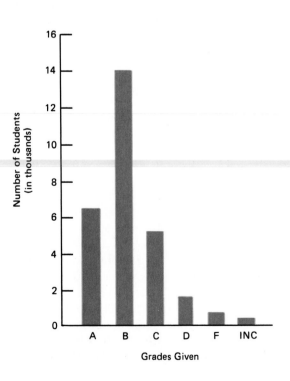

Figure 14-3
Bar Graph: Grading of Students in One University

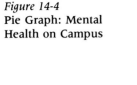

Figure 14-4
Pie Graph: Mental
Health on Campus

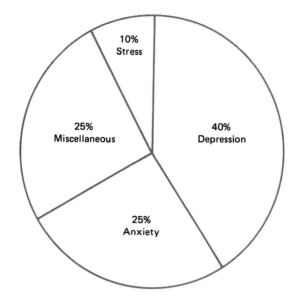

of mental health problems on campus. Note that in both of these graphs, the point the student is making is immediately apparent.

A line graph is particularly useful in showing trends over a period of time or in making comparisons. For example, a student who was trying to persuade his audience that the university should provide additional parking used the line graph in Figure 14-5 to show how the number of commuting students had increased.

COMPUTER GRAPHICS

If you do not draw or letter well but have access to a computer, consider computer graphics. There are several software programs that offer a variety of drawings and typefaces. Figure 14-6 shows a very simple poster that was made with computer graphics. If your printer software doesn't make the pictures or letters large enough, many copy machines have an enlargement feature. For optimum clarity, make sure that your printer has a fresh, dark ribbon.

PROJECTED MATERIAL

Videos, slides, and other projected material are useful visual aids. When you are using projected material, remember that it should enhance, not replace, your speech.

If you decide to use a video, you have two choices: you can use one made by other people or you can make your own. If you are making a long speech, a preprogrammed video can be a very good visual reinforcement of what you are saying. A student who gave a speech on how applicants are propagandized

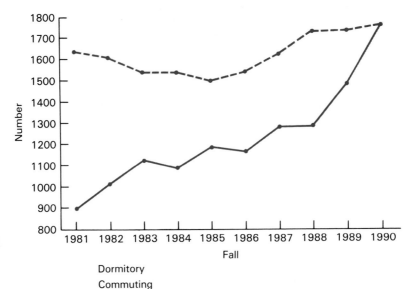

Figure 14-5
Line Graph:
Comparing
Resident and
Commuter
Student
Populations

by college admission tapes followed her speech with the college's own admissions video. The students were amazed and appalled at the difference between their perception of the college and the tape's portrayal of it.

If you have access to your own video camera, you can make your own tape and customize it to match your subject and your audience. One student made a videotape illustrating four basic karate moves for his speech. Because video is so easy to work with, he was able to stop the tape, talk about the move, then go on to the next one. Another student, speaking about a dangerous intersection on the campus, made a short video of students trying to cross the street. Her video was an effective way of persuading her audience of the need for a traffic light.

You may have slides you could use in a speech, or you may have access to a set of slides that have been commercially produced. Since you are giving a speech rather than a slide show, however, you should limit the number of slides you use. One student who had traveled to China decided to limit her slides to those of the Great Wall. She figured this single site would be of greatest interest to her audience.

Overhead projectors are a very easy way of showing visual material. With an overhead, a page from a book can be projected and enlarged on a movie screen—which is much less complicated than copying from the book onto a chart. With an overhead projector you can also draw your information on an ordinary sized piece of paper since it will appear enlarged on the screen.

HANDOUTS

When material is complex or when there is a lot of it, audience members may need a handout. For example, a student who spoke about the calories in fast

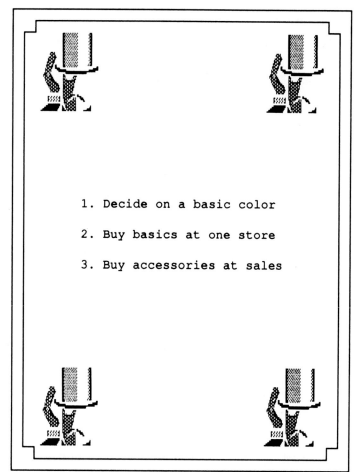

Figure 14-6
Poster Showing Computer Graphics

food gave audience members a handout showing caloric values of specific foods. Other times a handout is useful to reinforce the points you are making in your speech. A student who spoke about ten ways to save energy made a handout of her main points and distributed it at the end of her speech.

If you use handouts, choose the best time to pass them out. If you distribute your handouts too early, the audience will read them and ignore you. Also, most people dislike having a handout read to them. If your handout repeats the points you are making, give it out when your speech is over.

YOU AS A VISUAL AID

Often you can be the best visual aid—especially if you want to show your audience how to do something. For example, if you're telling audience members how to improve their tennis stroke, bring your racket and demonstrate. If you want to tell your audience that it can save money on clothes by using accessories, bring the accessories along, put them on, and show everyone how they look.

Rules for Using Visual Aids

You want a visual aid that will really work for you. The wrong one could detract from your speech and make it much less effective.

When you are considering a visual aid, keep the following rules in mind:

1. *Use the visual aid to supplement, not replace, the speech.* The visual aid should not become the whole show. It should be a useful addition to support the speech.
2. *Choose visual aids for points that need more explanation.* Look over your speech and decide which details could be better explained by a visual aid. Is there a particular statistic you want to stress? Will something be more easily understood if your audience can see it? Will it help your speech to show your main points visually?
3. *Show the visual aid only when you are ready for it.* Put the visual in an inconspicuous place; then, when you are ready to use it, take it out. When you are finished with it, put it away. You don't want it to compete with you for attention.
4. *Make sure everyone can read the visual aid.* When making a chart, use a dark marker with a thick tip so you can draw bold lines that will show up. If you have any doubts, check your visual aid beforehand. Set it up in the front of the room and stand in the farthest corner to see if you can read it. If you can't read it easily, fix it so you can.
5. *Before your speech, check the room to see if your visual aid can be easily displayed.* If you are using projection equipment, find the electrical outlets and see if the room has blackout curtains. If you are hanging a chart, decide how to hang it. Are you going to need tape or thumbtacks?
6. *Practice with your visual aid before the speech.* If you are using some sort of chart, stand next to it and point to it with your right or left hand rather than standing in front of it with your back to the audience. Practice using any kind of equipment until you can operate it quickly and easily. If you are using something complicated, such as projection equipment, consider having a classmate run it for you. If you do this, practice with him or her. When practicing with your visual aid, check to see how much time it takes. If it is going to take too much time, decide how you will cut back.
7. *Talk to the audience, not to the visual aid.* You may need to look at your visual aids occasionally, but remember to maintain eye contact with the audience.
8. *Maintain control of the speech situation.* Since visual aids can distract audience attention away from you, keep them simple.

Controlling Nervousness

In studies of what makes people anxious, public speaking always ranks right up there at the top. Public speaking makes people nervous, no matter how famous or how experienced they are. Winston Churchill, who became one of the most famous statesmen and orators of the twentieth century, fainted dead

Try This Try This Try This

*T*he next time you use a visual aid, subject it to the following check:

1. Does the visual help to make the speech better?
2. Can everybody see it?
3. Is it short and simple? Did I use color, dark lines, and heavy letters?
4. Do I need anything to mount the visual aid?
5. Will I need a pointer?
6. Is there a place to put the visual aid before and after it is needed?
7. Do I know how much of the speech time using the visual will take?

away the first time he gave a speech.[5] Willard Scott, a television weather announcer, says, "Each day, as soon as I get out of bed, when I know that I've got to go on the air, I have a panic attack in the form of anticipation."[6]

Speaker anxiety has been well-documented. While most people have a normal heart rate of 70 beats a minute, as a person anticipates giving a speech, the rate may increase from 95 to 140. And once he or she begins speaking, it can jump from 110 to 190. As the person proceeds with the speech, however, the heart rate begins to drop.[7]

No matter how nervous a speaker might be, there is some comfort. Studies have shown that most audience members *do not realize that a speaker is nervous.* Even observers who are trained to look for anxiety cues usually do not see them in a speaker.[8] This means that if your palms sweat, your knees shake, or your mouth is dry, you are probably the only one who knows it.

A good deal of research has been done on the subject of anxiety. Researchers have found that about 10 percent of college students have an intense fear of public speaking and will even go as far as to drop a public speaking course they need in order to graduate. The other 90 percent have fears they can overcome; they are nervous but it doesn't impair their ability to make a speech.[9] Although people who are phobic often need professional help to conquer their speaking phobia, people who have normal anxiety can usually find at least one strategy that helps them deal with their nervousness by themselves.

Unfortunately there is no single sure-fire formula that reduces every person's anxiety before a speech. However, some strategies work for many people and are thus worth trying to see if they will work for you:

1. Accept that you are nervous, but don't focus on it.
2. Practice some positive self-talk. Whenever a negative idea appears ("I'll never get through this speech"), replace it with a positive one ("I'm feeling nervous but that won't stop me from doing a good job.")
3. Anticipate and prepare for situations that could cause you last-minute anxiety. For example, if you think you will have difficulty in getting through your introduction, write it out on a note card. Then if you need it, it's there. Or, if you think that you might get lost or forget your

words, prepare a handout. Then if you get lost, you can pass out the handout while you're gathering your thoughts.

4. Practice your speech beforehand. Don't just go over it in your mind; stand up and say it aloud as many times as you need to remember your main points.

5. Focus on your audience rather than yourself. Think about really communicating with them about your subject.

6. If your anxiety is very high, ask your instructor if you can speak first. Sometimes anxiety increases if you sit and wait to speak.

7. Give yourself a reward after your speech and congratulate yourself for having succeeded.

Practicing Your Speech

Practice will help you give a better speech. You may hesitate to practice systematically—probably because you feel silly talking to an empty room. Yet if you go into a store to buy a new piece of clothing, you probably spend a lot of time in the dressing room looking at it from all angles. By practicing, you are doing the same thing with a speech. You are trying it on to see if it fits; if it doesn't, you will have time to make the necessary alterations.

How can you practice delivery so you will feel comfortable with the content and language of your speech and yet not get so locked in that your words sound memorized or mechanical? Here is a plan that seems to work well for most speakers.

Preparing Your Speech

Before you give your speech in a practice session, you should do the following:

1. Prepare the content thoroughly. Your speech will be no better than the effort you've put into it. Do you have a clear statement of purpose? Do the materials you have collected support this statement of purpose? Have you done enough research to provide support for each of your main points?

2. Organize your content into a full-sentence outline. Have you made the proper distinction between main idea and supporting points? Does your outline flow clearly and logically? Are you quite clear about what you are going to say in your introduction and conclusion? Is your conclusion worded in such a way that you can end the speech and sit down without feeling awkward?

3. From your full-sentence outline, prepare a key-word or short-phrase outline that you can use while you rehearse and also while you give your speech. Put your key-word outline on a series of 3 × 5 cards. Can you follow the speech from this outline? Have you written out phrases or quotations that you want to quote precisely? Can you read the cards easily?

"**Y**ou are one of the best speakers I've ever heard," a man told me in Portland, Ore. "You're a natural, but the reason you're good is that you believe what you're saying."

I doubt that I'm a natural. While in college I received a D in public speaking and for years I was reluctant even to ask a question at a medical meeting because I would get heart palpitations when I did. But I do believe in what I'm saying. And I believe with the passion that comes from the belief that I alone possess the truth. When I work myself up to that pitch, the audience comes to believe it as well.

Until recent years I shared the common dread of public speaking. Now lecturing is what I do best. Losing the fear won the battle. My concern became the message, not myself. When I shifted the focus to what I could do for my audience I no longer worried about being stupid or foolish or boring. And gradually I learned how to make them laugh and think and even cry so they would take my thoughts into their hearts and heads.

Source: Dr. George Sheehan, Toledo *Blade*.

Trying Out Your Speech

During the tryout session, emphasis should be on the content of the speech and whether it is working the way you imagined it in your head. (There is often a big difference between the way we imagine something will sound and the way it really sounds.) In this session you want to actually say the words— stopping to clear up imprecise language, maybe adding a transition, trying out the conclusion. In this practice session, it will take you a while to get through the speech because you will be making corrections as you go along.

Practicing Actual Delivery

The next stage is to actually deliver the speech. As you practice your delivery, try to imagine an audience.

1. Stand against one wall and look over your "audience." Remember to establish eye contact with people in all parts of the room.
2. Check your starting time. In this practice session you want to find out how long your speech is.
3. Deliver the speech all the way through without stopping. As you are speaking, remember to look at your "audience."
4. When the speech is over, check your ending time.
5. Now analyze your performance: Did any parts of the speech give you difficulty? Did the speech seem clearly organized? Check your outline. In giving the speech, did you leave anything out? Was your outline

clear and easy to follow? How about time? Did you need to add or delete any material to make the speech the proper length?

6. Make the necessary changes and practice the speech again.

You should practice delivering the speech until you feel comfortable with it. As you practice, try to use wording that sounds natural to you. Every time you speak, your wording should be a little bit different—otherwise your speech will sound mechanical. Also, as you practice, you should become less and less dependent on your notes. Try to consult them as little as possible.

If you think you will need a lot of practice to feel comfortable with your speech, it is better not to rehearse it all at one time. Put the speech away for a few hours or even overnight. The next time you approach it, you may be surprised to find fresh ideas or ways of solving problems that hadn't occurred to you before.

Evaluating and Trying Again

Many speakers feel their work is done after they speak the final words of their conclusion. However, some of the most valuable work begins after the speech is over. This is the time to ask whether you reached your goal and to discover what effect you had on your audience.

Here are some questions you can ask yourself:

1. Did I follow the plan for my speech? Did I stick to my outline and cover the material I wanted to cover? Did I keep my central idea in mind?
2. Was my speech completed in the time allotted for it? If it was too long, did I go too slowly or have too much material? If it was too short, did I have enough material or did I talk too fast?
3. Did I pay attention to my audience? Do I have a sense of how they responded to my speech? If audience members started losing attention, did I do anything to try to reengage them?
4. Did I make eye contact with the audience? Was I conscious of using appropriate gestures to make certain points?
5. Did I have a well-defined conclusion? Did I communicate to my audience that the speech was finished?
6. The next time I speak, what things should I change?

Your answers to these questions should help you improve every time you get up to speak. Remember, the goal of your speech communication class is to make you an effective communicator. Take advantage of the opportunity.

SUMMARY

Good delivery in a speech involves attentiveness—focusing and paying attention to giving the speech. It also involves achieving a conversational quality in your speech.

The four ways of delivering a speech are speaking impromptu, with very little preparation; speaking from a manuscript; speaking from memory; and speaking extemporaneously, from notes. For the beginner, extemporaneous speaking is the best type of delivery because it permits the speaker to depend on notes and still sound spontaneous.

All speakers should be aware of how they look and what they can do to look better. Speakers should concentrate on what they wear and on their body movement, eye contact, gestures, and posture so that they appear at their very best.

How the speaker sounds is also an important consideration in public speaking. Speakers should pay special attention to volume, pace, pitch and inflection, and enunciation. If they find they have a problem with one of these areas, they should work to improve it.

All speakers should consider using visual aids in their speeches. Visuals help to hold attention and to clarify information. Common visual aids include the actual object, models, chalk boards, posters, diagrams, charts, tables, graphs, computer graphics, videos, and handouts. When using visual aids, make sure that they can be easily read and that they enhance the speech rather than take it over.

Practically everyone is nervous about giving a speech. Most people, however, can overcome their nervousness. Some ways of handling speech anxiety are to acknowledge that the anxiety exists, practice positive self-talk, anticipate difficult situations that could arise, practice the speech beforehand, focus on the audience while speaking, and reward yourself once it's over.

The final step in getting ready to deliver a speech is to practice it. Your practice should include rehearsing delivery of the speech, imagining an actual audience, checking the speech for clarity and organization, and checking its length.

Your skill in speaking will grow if you evaluate each speech when it is over. Ask whether you stuck to your outline, stayed within the time limits, paid attention to the audience, made eye contact, and offered a well-defined conclusion.

FURTHER READING

BEHNKE, RALPH R., CHRIS R. SAWYER, AND PAUL E. KING. "The Communication of Public Speaking Anxiety." *Communication Education*, 36 (April 1987): 138–141. What is the relationship between speakers' self-reported speech state of anxiety and audience perceptions of that anxiety? Untrained audiences are not proficient at detecting it. When detected, they perceive the levels to be lower than reported by the speakers themselves. Anxiety is *not* communicated well to audiences.

CRANNELL, KENNETH C. *Voice and Articulation*, 2d ed. Belmont, CA: Wadsworth, 1990. Crannell has written a book designed to help readers speak clearly and skillfully. It is fairly evenly divided between learning and doing. Many interesting and varied exercises are included. Crannell does not advocate standardized speech; rather, he encourages readers to retain unique cultural aspects of their speech, while making their speech and voice more flexible and effective.

GARNER, ALAN. *Conversationally Speaking*, rev. ed. New York: McGraw-Hill, 1989. Garner identifies several specific skills vital for social effectiveness. These skills build self-confidence and can be transferred naturally to public-speaking situations. Garner clearly identifies the conversational quality useful in delivery.

HAHNER, JEFFREY, MARTIN A. SOKOLOFF, SANDRA L. SALISCH, AND GEOFFREY D. NEEDLER. *Speaking Clearly: Improving Voice and Diction*, 3d ed. New York: Random House, 1989. This is a drill book for increasing effectiveness in voice and diction. The authors treat "dealing with nervousness," "the speech process," "the sounds of American English," "diction: the consonants," "diction: the vowels and dipthongs," "voice production," and "vocal expressiveness." This is an excellent, well-constructed textbook, and the chapter on dealing with nervousness is very helpful.

LEATHERS, DALE G. *Successful Nonverbal Communication: Principles and Applications*. New York: Macmillan, 1986. This book offers valuable insights relevant to this chapter's sections entitled "How You Look" and "How You Sound." Besides chapters on personal appearance and vocal communication, Leathers has excellent material on selling yourself nonverbally, impression formation, and management.

NEISSER, ULRIC. *Memory Observed: Remembering in Natural Contexts*. San Francisco: W. H. Freeman, 1982. Neisser provides a sophisticated, research-oriented consideration of memory. He offers many useful insights for public speakers, especially for those who must make a speech from memory.

NELSON, ROBERT B. *Louder & Funnier: A Practical Guide for Overcoming Stagefright*. St. Paul, MN: Pragmatic Publications, 1985. Nelson first explains the nature of stage fright, then the reasons why we fear, and provides his model for overcoming it. In addition, he offers other methods for overcoming stage fright and controlling its symptoms. He includes a separate chapter entitled "Overcoming Stagefright During Delivery."

Chapter 15

The Informative Speech

CHAPTER OBJECTIVES	KEY TERMS
After reading this chapter, you should be able to: 1. Get the attention of listeners. 2. Increase listener understanding. 3. Aid listener retention. 4. Use specific strategies in informative speeches.	anecdote comparison composition etymology example function informative speech rhetorical question

Mike is studying to be a dietician. Since he works in the college cafeteria to help pay for his education, when he is assigned to give an informative speech he decides to explain how the college food service plans and readies meals. In preparation for the speech, he interviews the head dietician at the college, finds several books on diet and nutrition in the library, and even writes a letter to the American Dietetic Association for more information.

Since Susan is taking a course in robotics, her informative speech is about how robots are being used to build television sets. Like Mike, she looks for books and articles in the library. She also arranges to spend some time observing robots at work on the assembly line at a local factory. Although Susan's presentation will deal mostly with the technical aspects of robotics, she is also interested in the human problem. Before she leaves the factory, she interviews the union president and asks whether robots are a threat to jobs.

Before Scott decided to go back to school he was a truck driver who had driven over half a million miles without an accident or a ticket. He decided that "Safe Driving Tips" would be a good subject for a speech since he had seen so many drivers do foolish things on the road. To add to what he knew from his own experience, Scott also visited the local office of the automobile association and sent a letter to the National Safety Council requesting information about accidents and their causes.

Lori is a student worker in the audiovisual department of the university. Now that fall classes are starting, she is going to hold several training sessions for the students who run movie projectors. She knows she is going to have to do a thorough job, for once the projectionists start showing films all over the campus, she is not going to be there to help them. As she plans the training sessions, she makes a list of steps that must be followed to load a film in the projector. Once she has figured out the steps, she will have the list duplicated so that each projectionist can have a copy.

Mike, Susan, Scott, and Lori all have something in common: they are preparing information. Like a majority of people in the United States, much of what they do is concerned with producing, processing, and distributing information.

The need for high-quality information demands skill in our ability to produce and deliver it. Although some of this information is delivered in written form, much of it is oral: the teacher before the class, the radio or television reporter broadcasting to an audience, the professional sharing ideas with colleagues, the employer explaining policies to employees—all of them need oral skills to convey information.

The **informative speech**—one that defines, clarifies, instructs, and explains—is a common phenomenon in our society. If we are going to prosper in the information society, the ability to give an informative speech is a necessary skill.

Goals of an Informative Speaker

With so much information available, it is surprising that listeners don't buckle under from information overload. When listeners are so swamped with information, we face a serious problem as speakers. We have to ask ourselves: "How can I, as an informative speaker, make *my* information stand out?"

Getting Attention

The first goal of a speaker is to get the attention of the audience members. In most public speaking situations there are many distractions: people come in late, the air conditioner fan turns on and off, a fly buzzes around the room, the microphone gives off feedback.

Once you have attention, there is no assurance that you will keep it. Attention spans are short. You have probably noticed that as you listen to a speech or lecture, your attention wanders—even when you are very interested in the message. Since this pattern of wandering attention is characteristic of most listeners, as a speaker you have to work to get attention back again.

The best way to get and keep attention is to create a strong desire to listen to your material. Ask yourself whether your material is *relevant*. Does it apply to the people in your audience? If it doesn't, how can it be adapted to them?

If the audience perceives the information as *new*, it is more likely to pay attention. New doesn't necessarily mean a subject no one has ever heard about—it might be a matter of a new perspective or a new angle. Certain topics are going to provoke a "ho hum" reaction from the audience. You don't want your audience to think "Not another speech about jogging . . . or losing weight . . . or stopping smoking." When one student chose to speak on physical fitness, he wanted to give a new perspective to an old topic. He ran across an article that said too much running might be dangerous and decided to base his speech on some of the dangers of exercise. He used material from the article to plan an introduction which would get the attention of the audience. He began:

> *David Nieman, an administrator in public health, knew that it was important to exercise. His own form of exercise was distance running. However, he noticed that soon after he ran in a marathon, he would catch a cold or get the flu. He began to question other runners and found that they had the same problem. Finally, in a survey of 2,300 runners who had run the Los Angeles Marathon, he found a surprising result: the more these runners trained, the more likely they were to get sick. After looking at these results Nieman began to question whether strenuous exercise was good for your health.*[1]

Although audience members knew this speaker was going to speak on physical fitness, most of them did not expect such a speech to begin by questioning the value of exercise.

Increasing Understanding

Since the goal of an informative speech is to give the audience new or indepth information on a subject, it is particularly important that a speaker put together a speech that audience members will understand. Several things will help understanding: language choice, organization, and illustrations and examples.

LANGUAGE CHOICE

In our highly technological world, many of us speak a specialized language that is understood only by people in the same field. Because we are so accustomed to this language, we often don't realize that other people don't know what we are talking about. If you are giving a speech that uses technical or specialized vocabulary, you must take the time to define your terms, or consider whether you can avoid technical terms altogether.

ORGANIZATION

Organization not only helps you put your speech together but also helps listeners understand what you are talking about. A good organizational pattern will show how ideas relate to one another and will help listeners move from one idea to another. Recent research has found, in addition, that listeners give higher ratings to better-organized speeches.[2]

ILLUSTRATIONS AND EXAMPLES

Probably the greatest key to understanding is an ample supply of illustrations and examples. If you are going to explain a principle that might be unfamiliar to your audience, use an example to show what it is or how it works. For example, a student who was explaining three basic body types held up pictures to illustrate each type. When he held up a picture of a thin, lightly muscled person, the meaning of the term *ectomorph* was immediately clear.

Helping Retention

An important goal of informative speaking is to have your listeners remember what you said once the speech is over. Listeners are more likely to remember speeches in which they felt some kind of emotional involvement. This involvement might range from sympathy when they hear about an adult who can't read to high personal interest in a speech about how to get a better job. For the speaker, then, the goal is to involve the listeners by speaking about subjects which they can identify with or which have an impact on their lives.

When you want people to remember certain points, it is useful to give these points special emphasis. Sometimes this can be done with verbal cues: "This is my most important point" or "If you remember only one thing I said today, remember this." Sometimes you can use a cue after a point: "Now let me show you how important what I just said can be to you." A point can be emphasized, too, by repeating it, by changing your rate of speech, or by pausing just before you say it.[3]

Strategies for Informative Speeches

There are different types of strategies for presenting material in informative speeches. Each type requires a special skill. Sometimes all of these types can be found in a single speech; usually at least two will be used.

A **definition**—an explanation of the meaning of a word or phrase—can often make a critical difference in whether your audience understands your speech. Sometimes it's sufficient to give a dictionary definition; other times a speaker must expand by using his or her own words. For example, in defining public relations this speaker says:

> *As I see it, public relations is defined in terms of public opinion and behavior.*[4]

Another speaker took the traditional definition of *designer* and contrasted it with an updated version:

> *One hundred years ago, a "designer" was an individual craftsman or artist who applied his or her skills to a plan for fabricating a specific object, be it a warship, a dress, a quilt, or a chair. In many cases, the designer actually made the object he or she designed. Today's industrial designer is a bit more distant from the production process. He or she deals with the most advanced realms of high technology, often as part of a vast industrial complex which produces products for millions of homes and businesses.*[5]

This speaker defined what he meant by "media environment" by contrasting what people wanted in different decades:

> *In the '50s, we liked Ike, suburbia, and lots of kids. Back then, TV was really special—since only 10 percent of people had television. In the '60s, we simultaneously broke all society's rules and TV's sound barrier . . . television penetration hit 90 percent! In the '70s, we sang Me, Me, Me, and in the '80s we negotiated for more, more, more. But the grab it, snatch it, and "take it all" extremism of the '80s has given way to the time-crunching '90s.*
>
> *Consumers today are stuck between a clock and a hard place . . . and the '90s will be governed by demand for convenience and speed in virtually everything that touches our lives. Faster food, faster news, faster mail, fax, fax, fax.*[6]

Definition can also go beyond explaining words or phrases. Four useful ways to define concepts in a speech are by etymology, example, comparison, and function.

ETYMOLOGY

Etymology, the study of the origin and development of words, can be used as a basis for definition. For example, when discussing romantic love and the intense feelings that occur, one speaker pointed out that the word *ecstasy*, which is a common label for emotions during the time of romantic love, is derived from a Greek word meaning "deranged"—a state beyond all reason and self-control.[7] She went on to show that the word *deranged* accurately describes the state of mind that exists early in romantic relationships. The *Oxford English Dictionary* provides the best source for word etymologies.

EXAMPLE

An **example** is something that is used to illustrate a point. When using an example, a speaker often either points to an actual thing or points out something verbally. This speaker defines a *feminist* by giving a series of examples of what a feminist believes in.

> *What is a feminist? Someone male or female who believes the world cannot work well as long as there are separate and unequal distinctions based on sex; someone who believes that issues like poverty disproportionately affecting women and children today are as significant as the issues of wealth and weapons which at this point in our history disproportionately involve men. Feminists are women and men who are tired of caricatured distinctions between the sexes which reinforce prototypes of macho strong men and passive female dependency. Feminists know that these stereotypes keep us from fulfilling our own potential and from recognizing others. And feminists know that until we utilize the creative capacity of half the human race which has been excluded from decision making, the world can never be whole.*[8]

COMPARISON

Comparisons point out the similarities between two or more things. This speaker compared two schools of thought regarding our future:

How does showing the actual object make this speech more meaningful?

There is a school of thought that believes "the more things change, the more they stay the same." There is another school across the street that regards the dynamism of cultural and technological change as a very real force in shaping human destiny.

   I got my diploma from that second school. I admit that I am addicted to the future. I see change not only as inevitable, but desirable.[9]

The speaker's entire speech is based on defining change as desirable. He establishes the desirability of change at the outset through comparison, then develops his speech from there.

FUNCTION

With certain topics it's useful to define by **function**—showing how a thing performs or how it can be used. Speakers may stress an object's usefulness, advantage, benefits, convenience, or service. Here is how a speaker explained a new method of stripping paint without harming the environment:

But now, the Navy can strip paint with a technique called "media blasting." It works basically by shooting thousands of tiny plastic pellets at an object, and the pellets chip off the paint. The technique eliminates all liquid and gas wastes. So instead of having maybe 30 barrels of liquid waste, all you have is about 4 barrels of tiny paint chips and plastic beads.[10]

Describing

Many times your audience will be able to visualize what you are talking about if you describe it by creating a picture for them. This speaker, for example, created a vivid picture in his speech about garbage.

In just a few years, the most widely viewed artwork in the world may not be the Mona Lisa, or the Statue of Liberty. . . . No, it just might be a landfill in Kearny, New Jersey.

   The state recently closed the landfill, and now it's considering one artist's idea to beautify this one-hundred-foot high mountain of buried

Try This Try This Try This

*F*or each of the following ideas, decide which kinds of definitions would work in a speech: etymology, function, example, or comparison.

love	*in loco parentis*
inflation	unbeatable bargain
educational opportunity	intimate relationship
a movie beyond comparison	alcoholic
low-impact aerobics	job skills

*garbage. The artist wants to turn the dump into an enormous celestial
calendar and call it "Sky Mound." . . . It will have steel posts, earthen
mounds, a plume of burning methane, and radiating gravel paths aligned
with the seasonal movements of the sun, the moon, and the stars.*[11]

SIZE OR QUANTITY

Notice how this speaker compares the size of an early computer with things
that are familiar to us.

*The machine we are looking at here is the Eniac, the world's first success-
ful high speed electronic digital computer. The Eniac weighed 60,000 lbs.
It covered 1,600 square feet of floor space. It was about as big as a single-
family home. It had inside it, 17,000 pickle-sized vacuum tubes, the kind
you used to find in old-fashioned radios.*[12]

SHAPE

In a speech on "Bigfoot" one college student used a description in his quotation
from an article in *Science Digest*. Notice the emphasis on shape:

*What people usually report is something seven to eight feet tall with an
extremely heavy build—about eight hundred pounds—and covered with a
fairly dense coat of brown or black hair two to four inches long. Its face
has less hair or is naked; it looks somewhat like a gorilla's face, but much
longer. Its shoulders are large and high, so that the mouth and chin are
below shoulder level, which is a very apelike characteristic. But it walks on
two legs in a human manner, with the walking hinge, the hip joint, about
mid-height.*[13]

The student emphasized shape with words like "extremely heavy build," a face
that looks longer than a gorilla's face, shoulders that are "large and high,"
and its "human manner" of walking.

WEIGHT

Since people have a hard time visualizing large numbers, speakers need to
relate them to something from the listeners' own experience. One speaker was
trying to impress her listeners with how much a million was. She said that a
class in Des Moines, Iowa, collected 1 million bottle caps. According to the
speaker, these caps weighed 2½ tons: "They were put into 200 bags and the
bags were so heavy it required a moving van to take them away."

COLOR

Color is an obvious component of description and serves quickly to call up
mental pictures. In this speech the speaker makes a vivid use of color when
discussing race:

*In truth God made no black or white people but a flower garden of
beautiful persons of colors ranging from cream to oven-burnt brown. No
person is white; were he truly white and void of melanin or pigmentation,
the ultra-violet radiations from the sun would burn him up. No one is*

black either; were one black, he would be a perfect receptor of the sun's radiations—and his body temperature would rise rapidly to over 106 degrees, into a fever so severe that he too would burn up.[14]

COMPOSITION

Composition, a description of the makeup of a thing, can be a useful part of description. Sometimes an analysis of composition can help an audience understand an abstract concept. To describe a *global village*—a term that has been used a lot but seldom explained—a speaker used demographic figures for the world's population to create a representative global village of 1000 people:

According to the World Development Forum, if you lived in a representative global village of 1000,

- *564 citizens would be Asian*
- *210 Europeans*
- *86 Africans*
- *80 South Americans*
- *60 North Americans*
- *300 Christians*
- *175 Moslems*
- *128 Hindus*
- *55 Buddhists*
- *47 Animists*
- *85 smaller religious groups*
- *210 without religion or atheists*

Of this group:

- *60 would control half the total income*
- *500 would be hungry*
- *600 would live in shantytowns*
- *700 would be illiterate*[15]

FIT

You can often describe something by the way parts belong together or the relationship among parts. A mental picture emerges when listeners can fit all the parts into a proper relationship.

Say you are speaking about the campus newspaper and you want to explain how all the parts fit together. You talk about the responsibilities of the editor, then of the jobs of the features, news, and sports editors and what their relationship is to the editor. Next you talk about the roles of the business manager and advertising department and the relationship these people have to the editor. If you discuss how all these people fit into the overall structure, your audience will have a good idea of how the newspaper works.

Explaining

Almost everything that we know how to do was explained to us at one time or another. We were not born knowing how to do such things as cook or play volleyball—someone told us how to do them. Many of the questions we ask are requests for explanations. What does this concept mean? How does this work? How do I get there? Explaining, then, is the process of making something clear.

The most common form of explaining is when you teach someone to do something. Usually this is a matter of breaking the process down into steps. For example, in this speech on how to make a toasted cheese sandwich with an iron, the speaker used the following steps:

1. Gather what you need: bread, cheese, margarine, alumunim foil, and an iron.
2. Heat the iron to medium-high.
3. Make a sandwich from the cheese, and butter both sides on the outside.
4. Wrap the sandwich in alumunim foil.
5. Place the iron on each side for about 20 seconds. (Check to see if you need more time.)

Using Numbers

Few people can visualize large quantities, such as millions or billions. Therefore it's useful if these figures are put into some kind of perspective. For example, your audience would probably be impressed to learn that a movie cost $35 million to make. However, if you relate this figure to the price of movie tickets, you will begin to speak in terms of the audience's pocketbook.

When you work with numbers, here are some simple rules to follow:

- If numbers are unusual or surprising, explain why. Usually the best way to do this is to quote an expert.
- Round off large numbers.
- If you have a lot of numbers, try to convert them to percentages.
- Look for opportunities to replace numbers with words. For example, it's easier to understand, "Over half the people said . . ." or "A majority believed . . . ."
- Try to relate numbers to something familiar or colorful. For example, "The number of people killed in the earthquake was equal to the entire student body of this college."
- If possible, try to compare numbers. For example, "Forty-five percent of the seniors but only three percent of the freshmen believed . . . ."
- Look for trends, especially from one year to another: "In 1981, the average TV viewer saw the majority of programming on the networks. By 1991, however, the average viewers were just as likely to watch cable or videos."
- Use graphs and other visual aids to make numbers more concrete.

Connecting the Known with the Unknown

When listeners are unfamiliar with a subject, a speaker can help them understand it by connecting the new idea to something they already know. For example, when a British student wanted to explain the game of cricket

> ## Try This Try This Try This
>
> Choose one of the following topics and list the main points you would make in preparing a speech on it:
>
> Using the library   Selecting a video for friends
>
> Writing a book review   Using time efficiently
>
> What makes a good sportswriter?   Playing a game

to her American classmates, she started by listing the ways that cricket was similar to baseball. Another student, explaining how a word processor works, started out comparing it to a typewriter. In both cases, after explaining how two things were similar, the speakers then went on to point out the differences.

Repeating and Reinforcing Ideas

Repetition in a speech is important because it helps the listeners remember keypoints. However, if it is overdone, the speaker runs the risk of boring the listeners. Let's look at a format that will enable you to spread out the repetition and reinforcement in a speech.

In your introduction, *tell your listeners what you plan to tell them.* In the introduction to her speech "Creating a More Effective Voice," Michelle listed her main points: "Today I want to talk about the three main steps for changing your voice. These steps are analysis, discipline, and production."

In the body of your speech, *tell your listeners your full message* (i.e., explain your points). In Michelle's speech, she explained each of her steps:

> *The first step in creating a more effective voice is analysis. You need to find your best pitch and a balanced tone, and you can do this only through an analysis of your own voice.*
>
> *The second step is discipline. By disciplining yourself to practice your natural, right voice in exercises and everyday conversation, you can use your voice to its best advantage.*
>
> *The third step in creating your best voice is production. You need to ease slowly and gradually toward producing the same pitch level whenever you speak.*

In your conclusion, *tell your listeners what you told them.* This is the place to summarize your main ideas. Michelle concluded her speech by saying:

> *Now you can see how you can go about creating a more effective voice. You need to analyze your voice, to discipline yourself to practice, and to work on producing a pitch that will show your voice at its best.*

Arousing Interest in Your Topic

So many things compete for each listener's attention that even though we might get attention at first, it is not always possible to keep it. You probably

This speaker is not speaking from behind a barrier. How does this choice affect audience response to the speech?

have had the experience of half-listening to a speaker while you wondered what was for lunch, mentally prepared a grocery list, and so on. What can you, as a speaker, do to compete with all these distractions?

AROUSE CURIOSITY

One way to make sure that you will be listened to is to create a desire to learn about your subject by stimulating your listeners' curiosity. For example, one speaker began her speech with "Have you ever wondered why you get so tired?" Another began his speech with "Do you know how to stop procrastinating?" Another started, "The real name of Captain Kangaroo is Bob Keeshan. The name of the river that flows over the Holland Tunnel is the Hudson. Five states border on the Pacific Ocean. Ever wonder why we are so fascinated by trivia?"

PRESENT ANECDOTES

An **anecdote** is a short, interesting story based on your own or someone else's experience. Although some speakers use them in their introductions, they are particularly useful in the body of your speech because they can get back audience attention if it is wandering.

Here is how a speaker used an effective anecdote from her own life to hold her audience members' interest:

During my freshman year [of college], I received a call that my mother had been seriously injured in a traffic accident. My father was unemployed at the time, and I was off at college. So who do you think was elected to take on the housework? Raise your hand if you think it was my father.

> *No???*
>
> *Does anybody think it was me?*
>
> *I am truly amazed at your guessing ability.*
>
> *Or is there something in our Hispanic cultures that says the women do the housework?*
>
> *Of course there is.*
>
> *So I drove home from Boulder every weekend; shopped, cleaned, cooked, froze meals for the next week, did the laundry, you know the list. And the truth is, it did not occur to me until some time later that my father could have done some of that. I had a problem, but I was part of the problem.*[16]

This next speaker built an anecdote from a newspaper article to startle his audience into paying attention.

> *A recent story from the pages of* The New York Times *shows just how little money and technology can buy these days.*
>
> *Last year a 26-year-old Pittsburgh woman named Cindy Martin became the first person to receive a new heart, liver, and kidney in the same operation. . . . At Pittsburgh's Presbyterian Hospital, medical personnel worked for 21 straight hours on Cindy: 11 surgeons, 6 anesthesiologists, 15 nurses, a physician's assistant, 2 blood technicians, and a liver technician.*
>
> *"They did everything they could," her husband, John Martin, said. "They tried to make her life better. But she suffered for four months in the hospital and nothing was accomplished." Cindy died after 113 days of intensive care. The bill was handed to John Martin's employer. It was for 1.25 million dollars.*[17]

BUILD ANTICIPATION

One way to build anticipation is to preview your points in the introduction. You could say, for example, that you are going to talk about the way to get the best buy on anything: haggle. Then say:

> *I want to give you some rules to sharpen your bargaining skills—rules like doing your homework, resisting the urge to make the first offer, avoiding a bid in round numbers, taking your time, and being creative.*

The audience is then more likely to listen for each of these points.

BUILD SUSPENSE

Building suspense is one of the best ways of keeping attention. One student decided to speak on the legal consequences in his state of driving while drunk. He built suspense this way:

*After a party one night, Joe got in his car to drive home. Because he had
had too much to drink, he lost control of his car on Route 150. He only
remembers waking up in the hospital. He wasn't badly hurt, and although
the car was destroyed, it was covered by insurance. Joe vowed never to
drink and drive again and breathed a sigh of relief for getting off so easily.
What he didn't know is that he had a whole lot of new problems coming
up.*

The student then went on to talk about the penalties in the state for
driving while drunk, such as fines, a police record, possible license suspension,
prison, and more.

Getting Listeners Involved

GET THE AUDIENCE TO PARTICIPATE

In a speech on aerobic exercises, the speaker had listeners try several of them.
In a speech on self-defense, a speaker had the class practice a few simple
moves. In a speech on note taking, the speaker had listeners take notes and,
as they did so, taught them some shortcuts and simplified procedures.

As every magician knows, choosing someone from the audience to
participate in an act is a good technique for keeping attention. Speakers can
do this too. In a speech on first aid, the speaker called for a volunteer from
the audience so she could point to pressure points. For a speech titled
"Appearance Sells," one student asked three classmates to come to class
dressed in a certain way: one was to dress casually, another in dressy clothes,
and the third in a businesslike way.

ASK RHETORICAL QUESTIONS

Some speakers use **rhetorical questions**—questions audience members answer mentally rather than out loud. Note how one speaker asked and answered
most of his own questions but left the critical one for audience members to
answer:

Question 1: *Which gets more status in our society?*
          a. learning
          b. sports
Answer: Sports

Question 2: *Which gets more hours of attention?*
          a. reading
          b. TV
Answer: TV

Question 3: *What causes more excitement?*
          a. a new idea
          b. a new car
Answer: A new car

Question 4: *What gets more promotion in our society?*
a. studying
b. shopping
Answer: *Shopping*

Question 5: *Essay question—Why do you think there's an education problem in our society?*[18]

SOLICIT QUESTIONS FROM THE AUDIENCE

Another device is to solicit questions from the audience following the speech. A question-and-answer session encourages listeners to get involved. You might even tell your listeners at the beginning that you will take questions when you finish, which may encourage them to pay attention in preparation for asking questions.

There are, however, some useful guidelines if you plan to solicit questions from your audience. First, make sure you listen to the full question before answering it. Sometimes speakers will cut off a questioner or will focus on irrelevant details instead of the main thrust of the question. Second, if a question is confusing, ask the questioner to rephrase it. If you are still confused, rephrase it yourself before answering it. For example, say "Let me make sure I have heard you right; what you are asking is . . . Am I right?" Finally, in responding to questions, try to keep your answers brief and to the point. This is no time for another speech. As a final check, it's also a good idea to ask "Does that answer your question?"

What are some of the ways that questions and answers can improve communication?

381

The Informative Speech

SAMPLE INFORMATIVE SPEECH

Here is an informative speech that uses a topical pattern of organization. A commentary of the speech is given at the right while a full transcription of the speech is at the left.

Title

New American Landmarks: Mountains of Trash

Specific Purpose

To inform my audience about the problems of disposing of trash and garbage.

Central Idea

Disposal of trash and garbage is a serious problem in the United States with few solutions in sight.

Here are some common household items that many of you might have bought. When you purchased them you probably bought them in this form because they are convenient. What you probably didn't know is that they all present problems when you throw them away.

The speaker works to get the attention of the audience by suggesting something is wrong with household items his audience is familiar with. He uses the actual objects (catsup bottle, peanut butter jar, disposable lighter) as visual aids.

Today I would like to talk about these items and others and how they create so much garbage that we have no place to put them when we're ready to throw them out.

Do you know that in your lifetime you will throw away 600 times your weight in garbage? That as an American you will generate twice as much garbage as any European? That in America, we throw away enough iron and steel to supply the U.S. auto makers continuously? That every three months we throw out enough aluminum to rebuild all the commercial airplanes in America?

Here he uses a series of rhetorical questions—all containing startling information.

The problem facing us is what to do with all of this garbage. I would like to begin by explaining what we are doing now with our garbage, along with some of the problems, and then I'll talk about what can be done to reduce waste.

In this transition he gives a brief idea of what he will be talking about.

The most common way of disposing garbage is to dump it in a landfill. A landfill is somewhat like a dump—the difference is that each day's waste is covered with six inches of earth. Also, many states require landfills to be lined.

The use of landfills for waste disposal first became popular in the 1960s. It was supposed to be an improvement over open dumping and backyard burn barrels. However, many early landfills leaked toxic pollutants into the local groundwater. Although the modern landfill is leak-proof, the landfill is still seen as dangerous to many people.

The amount of garbage and trash has increased by about 15 percent in the last ten years. However, the number of landfills has dropped by 75 percent. Very few new landfills are being opened because getting all the permits can take as much as two or three years. Often, the biggest obstacle to a new landfill project is what has been dubbed the NIMBY syndrome. NIMBY is an acronym for "Not In My Back Yard." Because of the negative image and pollution problems associated with landfills, there is usually a great deal of community opposition. As a result, new projects are often tied up in lengthy legal proceedings.

When landfills were built, however, it was discovered that they didn't quite work the way they were intended. Researchers have found that very little decomposes in a landfill. A recent article in *Audubon* magazine reported that a team of researchers from the University of Arizona in Tucson unearthed over 16,000 pounds of garbage from U.S. landfills. They found that the garbage and soil is so compacted in a landfill, that decomposition takes place very slowly, if at all. In fact, 40-year-old newspapers were described as being "so fresh you might read one over breakfast."

Here is the first main point: landfills. He defines a term that his audience might not know.

These statistics show trends.

The major alternative to the landfill is incineration. Incineration has proved to be a very efficient way of producing electricity. Instead of using coal or oil, garbage is burned to generate the electricity. For this reason, it is often looked at by small municipalities as a cure-all for their waste problems. However, incineration does not eliminate waste, it only reduces it. There is still a certain amount of ash to get rid of.

It is this waste that has caused a great deal of public concern. The incineration process reduces the ratio of toxic to nontoxic materials so much that the ash often must be disposed of as hazardous waste. In addition, even the most modern incineration facilities emit dioxin into the air. Dioxin was originally thought to cause cancer, and researchers are still debating whether it may also cause birth defects in both humans and animals. A state-of-the-art incinerator with a full array of pollution-control devices emits less dioxin than a wood-burning stove, for example. However, many experts feel that any dioxin released into the air is too much because they believe that it collects in our atmosphere.

The most common form of waste reduction is recycling. It was estimated that in March of 1990, only 2 percent of the counties in the United States were recycling 20 percent or more of their wastes. Unfortunately, the recent boom in recycling has caught the industry unprepared. Often, the paper and glass that's returned for recycling ends up stored in warehouses because there is either too little demand or no facilities to process it. Sometimes, the materials end up being burned or dumped anyway. Only aluminum is being recycled as quickly as it is turned in. The average aluminum can is back on the shelves within six weeks. However, 70 percent of our metals are still being used once and then thrown away.

Now he makes a transition to move to his second point: incineration.

Now he moves to his third point: recycling. Again he uses some statistics to show that recycling is not very widespread.

Although glass, newspaper, and aluminum are recycled in many areas, plastics present a problem. Plastics are more difficult to recycle because they are made in so many different ways. To recycle them, one has to know the kind of resin they were made from. The plastic industry has called for a voluntary labeling program to aid in the recycling process. As you can see, many plastic products have a recycling logo on them, with a number in the center. These numbers are used to identify the resin. Once the plastics are sorted by resin type, they are shredded and melted down to make other items. Some products, however, such as squeeze bottles, are made from several different plastics and cannot be recycled.

He holds up a plastic bottle and points to the number.

Another form of waste reduction is called precycling. Precycling is reducing household wastes by choosing products in containers that can be recycled. Groups such as the Environmental Action Foundation encourage everyone to avoid products that use excessive packaging. Nearly one third of your garbage is packaging that is thrown away immediately while nearly fifty percent of all the paper used in the United States is for packaging.

Here is his fourth point: precycling. Note that he defines it.

In most areas precycling means buying products packaged in cardboard, aluminum, and glass while avoiding plastic and styrofoam. If this peanut butter had been purchased in a glass container, the glass could have been recycled. According to the Earth Works Group, we could eliminate 144 million pounds of plastic from our landfills if only 10 percent of us bought products with less packaging 10 percent of the time.

Now he picks up the household items with which he began the speech.

Better still, you should buy products with little or no packaging. With this popcorn container you have a lot of waste. However, if you bought popcorn in a plastic bag and popped it in a pan, you'd have very little waste.

What about this little lighter? Did you know that Americans throw away over *500 million* disposable lighters every year? Waste can be reduced by not buying things like disposable cameras, flashlights, and razors and instead using products that are built to last.

Waste disposal is a complex problem. There are no easy solutions. Our landfills are reaching capacity and very few new ones are being built. Incinerators reduce garbage while generating electricity, but leave municipalities with the problem of disposing of hazardous wastes. Recycling works—sometimes. Precycling might work if enough people do it. Some states have proposed legislation to encourage the use of recycled materials. In the meantime, however, we still don't have enough recycling facilities to handle the quantity of waste being returned. If there isn't room to put all the garbage, perhaps it's time we learn not to make so much of it. Nine years from now, the highest point on the eastern seaboard will be New York City's Fresh Kills Landfill. We are in a sad state if our landmarks in the twenty-first century are going to be piles of garbage.

Note that he emphasizes this number because it is so big.

This transition, which is leading to his conclusion, is a brief summary of his main points.

His conclusion leaves his audience with a startling image. It may help them to remember the speech.

Source: This speech was given by Brian Smith during a science seminar at Lock Haven University in Lock Haven, Pennsylvania, 1991.

SUMMARY

Our society needs high-quality information, and one way of producing and delivering it is through the informative speech—a speech that defines, clarifies, instructs, or explains.

When giving a speech, one of the speaker's goals should be to attract and maintain attention by using information that is relevant and interesting to the audience. The speaker should work to increase understanding by making careful language choices, having the speech organized, and using illustrations and examples. Finally, the speaker should use emphasis and repetition to help the audience retain the information.

Definition is important to informative speaking—especially if the words or concepts might be new to the audience. Speakers will also find it useful to describe and explain information related to their topic. If the speech contains many numbers, or numbers that are large, the speaker should work to make them meaningful to the audience.

The speaker can get the audience involved in the speech by inviting volunteers to participate in the speech, by asking rhetorical questions, and by soliciting questions from the audience.

FURTHER READING

ANDERSON, JOHN R. *Cognitive Psychology and its Implications*, 2d ed. San Francisco: W. H. Freeman, 1985. This is an outstanding textbook that provides a comprehensive examination of the processes involved in knowing, learning, and thinking. For serious students interested in the theoretical underpinnings of effective informative communication.

BROWN, GEORGE. *Lecturing and Explaining*. London: Methuen. 1980. Although this book is designed for lecturers, it relates to the process of imparting information. It is an excellent, practical guide with numerous, specific suggestions for informative speakers.

DANIELS, TOM D., AND RICHARD F. WHITMAN. "The Effects of Message Introduction, Message Structure, and Verbal Organizing Ability Upon Learning of Message Information." *Human Communication Research.* (Winter 1981): 147–160. This research study focuses on organizational variables of verbal messages. It is useful because overall it supports the idea that organizational variables (especially initial material that serves to orient listeners to what follows in the speech) *do* benefit listeners.

MUDD, CHARLES S., AND MALCOLM O. SILLARS. *Speech: Content and Communication*, 5th ed. New York: Harper & Row, 1985. Using examples from real speeches and student-speech samples, these authors provide a comprehensive approach to public speaking. Their chapters on analyzing issues, analyzing the audience, and speaking to inform—just 3 of 22 chapters—are useful and well written. A very substantive textbook.

QUINE, W. V., AND J. S. ULLIAN. *The Web of Belief.* 2d ed. New York: Random House, 1978. Although it is complex, these authors offer a challenging discussion in Chapter 7 of three aspects of explanation: what, how, and why. For the serious student.

ROSS, RAYMOND S. *Speech Communication: Fundamentals and Practice.* 8th ed. Englewood Cliffs, NJ: Prentice-Hall, 1989. This is a popular public speaking textbook that has withstood the test of time. Ross's chapter, "Presenting Information," is especially strong because he first considers how people learn—from known to unknown, serial learning, and reinforcement. He examines primary objectives of the informative speaker and ends by considering audiovisual aids. A well-documented, readable, basic textbook.

SMITH, TERRY C. *Making Successful Presentations: A Self-Teaching Guide.* New York: Wiley, 1984. Smith offers a how-to book on planning, organizing, developing, and delivering presentations. His useful and practical book is a step-by-step guide supplemented by artwork showing charts, slides, and room setups. Also helpful are his checklists.

VERDERBER, RUDOLPH F. *The Challenge of Effective Speaking*, 8th ed. Belmont, CA: Wadsworth, 1990. Verderber includes one of the most extensive sections on informative speaking of any basic textbook. Besides covering the principles and the use of visual aids, he also has separate chapters on explaining processes, descriptive speeches, speeches of definition, and expository speeches. Complete approach supported with outlines and speeches to illustrate the basic types of informative speeches.

Chapter 16

The Persuasive Speech

CHAPTER OBJECTIVES	KEY TERMS
After reading this chapter, you should be able to:	analogy
	causal reasoning
1. Identify the four factors that make up credibility.	comparative advantage order
	deductive reasoning
2. Use logical appeals and emotional appeals in a speech.	dynamism
	emotional appeal
3. Tell how questions of fact, value, and policy can be used in a persuasive speech.	ethics
	expertise
4. Explain when to use one-sided versus two-sided arguments.	hierarchy of needs
	inductive reasoning
5. Organize a speech using each of the following: problem-solution, comparative advantages, and the motivated sequence.	logical appeal
	persuasion
	trustworthiness

*P*riya Mishra is in charge of the International Student Association (ISA) talent show. When the ISA meets, she gives a brief speech about the importance of the show and asks everyone to participate. Priya says that people may either perform in the show or work behind the scenes. She stresses that this show is a good opportunity to tell Americans about other cultures, and she hopes that all members will volunteer. After she finishes her speech and answers questions, she passes around a signup sheet asking for names and telephone numbers. Practically everyone volunteers.

Nancy Good gives a speech to her speech communication class about her own experiences with alcoholism. She points out that it is entirely possible to be an alcoholic at 19—she is one herself. She tells the class of the warning signs of alcoholism and urges them to get help if they or anyone they know is in difficulty. After her speech, she distributes handouts with the telephone numbers of all the Alcoholics Anonymous chapters in the city and the names of several drug and alcohol counseling centers. Although Nancy cannot assess the impact of her speech directly, she senses that her audience is paying careful attention. After the speech is over, several students tell her she made a strong impression.

Both of these speakers are engaged in the act of **persuasion**—the process of trying to get others to change their attitudes or behavior. Most of you engage in some sort of persuasion every day of your life. You try to persuade someone to join you for lunch or to join your study group. Others are involved in trying to persuade *you:* radio commercials exhort you to buy, telephone salespersons offer bargains on a variety of goods and services, professors try

Try This Try This Try This

*I*n what ways does persuasion touch your life? Which of the following have the power to persuade you directly? How about indirectly?

- Advertising
- Sales pitches
- Speeches
- Friends' communications
- Family communications
- Editorials in newspapers
- Members of groups you belong to
- Letters
- Teachers
- Religious leaders

Of these, which touch you the most directly? Which ones can change your attitudes or behavior? Why are some more powerful than others?

to persuade you to turn in your papers on time, and students running for student government try to persuade you to vote for them.

Since persuasion runs through every aspect of our society, it is important to study how it works. Understanding persuasion will help you evaluate the persuasive techniques of others. Studying persuasion will also help you develop your own persuasive messages in the most effective way possible.[1]

Persuasion Goals

When you are planning a persuasive speech, one of the first questions you should ask yourself is what you want your audience to do or think. As we have noted in previous chapters, this is called your specific purpose. For example, here are some specific purpose statements for persuasive speeches:

- To persuade audience members to eat less meat
- To persuade audience members to run for an office in student government
- To persuade the audience that deer hunting should be abolished

If you keep your specific purpose in mind, it will be easier to generate main points to support it. As you develop your purpose, remember that you will want your audience to respond in one or more of the following four ways:

1. *Take action.* For example, in the above specific purpose statements, the speakers want them to run for an office or to work to abolish deer hunting.

Persuasion takes many different forms. What are some of the persuasive messages the coach might be giving to the players?

2. *Continue what they are already doing.* In this case some audience members might already be doing what you are asking them to do. For example, if one of the students is planning to run for office, she will find the speech interesting because it *reinforces* what she is already doing.

3. *Avoid doing something.* Again, as in the above purpose statements, the speakers want them to avoid eating red meat or to stop deer hunting.

4. *Continue not doing something.* This goal is slightly different from the second goal. It works best if the audience is considering taking an action you're against. For example, if they're thinking about becoming deer hunters, you might be able to persuade them not to do so. The same is true of red meat—if your audience does not eat it, your speech might persuade them not to give in to peer pressure if they're out with a crowd at a hamburger joint.

In any audience, there probably will be listeners who represent every possible point of view on your subject. When you're planning your speech you should consider all of them. Figure 16-1 shows what each segment of the audience might be thinking.

Speaker Credibility

The likelihood of our being persuaded depends greatly on the person doing the persuading. You can probably think of people in your own life who are particularly persuasive. Why are some people more persuasive than others? Research on persuasion says we are more likely to be effective as persuaders if listeners consider us to be credible. **Credibility,** or believability, consists of

---

Consider This Consider This Consider This

*T*he ability to influence others shows up in childhood. "The studies showed that the personality traits that mark children as budding leaders included an ease at communicating, a sense of humor and the innate ability to arbitrate with other children. While some intelligent children shared these traits, intelligence itself was no guarantee of having them. Some studies found that intellectually gifted children were sometimes less popular than those of average intelligence because they offered advice to other children in an insensitive, domineering manner."

What makes people successful persuaders? "One of the most important skills, the research shows, is seen in people who have a nearly unerring ability to understand the motives and desires of others regardless of whatever is being said or done on the surface. These same people seem to understand themselves, to know what they are really driving at, regardless of what they find themselves saying."

Source: Daniel Goleman, "Influencing Others: Skills Are Identified." *The New York Times.*

"I'm going to get some seedlings and plant some trees."

"I'm glad we decided to use natural gas rather than a wood–burning stove."

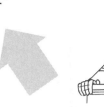

"My specific purpose is to persuade you that we should preserve our forests."

"We were going to cut down those trees to get a better view. I guess we shouldn't do it.

"I would like a paneled study. I wonder if I could find an alternative to wood?"

four qualities: expertise, dynamism, trustworthiness, and ethics. Let's look at each of them.[2]

Expertise

Someone who has **expertise** possesses special ability, skill, or knowledge. That is, he or she is an expert. A speaker who is perceived as an expert on his or her subject gains much credibility. For example, let's say that on the news one night you see a woman talking about the effects of long-term exercise on health. The anchorperson introduces her by saying that she is a medical doctor from Johns Hopkins Medical School who has been studying the effects of exercise. Since the results of her study are interesting, you listen closely. The next day you hear a student give a persuasive speech about the value of exercise. Some of his comments, however, contradict some of what you heard on the evening news. Which speaker do you believe? In this case there isn't much doubt. You believe the medical doctor because she is an expert.

EXPERTISE BASED ON PERSONAL EXPERIENCE

When you are a speaker trying to persuade an audience, it will help your credibility if you can show some expertise on your subject. Expertise does not depend only on book learning or specialized training; you can be an expert because of your personal experience. Nancy, for example, speaks of her own experience with alcoholism.

> *One night I went to a party. I remember the early part of the evening but that's about all. The next thing I remember was waking up in my own bed. I have no recollection of the end of the party or how I got home. When I woke up that morning and realized I didn't remember anything, I knew I was in serious trouble.*

You don't always have to relate such a dramatic experience as Nancy's. One student who had done volunteer work with the Red Cross persuaded classmates to serve as volunteers. Another student persuaded several class-mates to petition the dean of students for better food in the cafeteria. She knew that the food was poor, as did many members of her audience. Thus she used both her experience and the experience of audience members to make her point.

EXPERTISE BASED ON COMMITMENT

Another way to show expertise is by establishing your commitment to your topic. Listeners are more inclined to believe speakers who have taken actions that support their position. If you can show that you have donated blood, you are more likely to persuade others to donate. If you are trying to persuade people to become scout leaders and can point out that you have been a scout or have worked with scouts for many years, people are more likely to take you seriously.

EXPERTISE THROUGH RESEARCH

Expertise can also be built through research. By interviewing and reading articles and books, you can quote acknowledged experts, thereby making your speech more credible. When you are using information derived from experts, make that clear in your speech with such references as:

> *According to Dr. John Smith, a noted authority in this area . . .*
> *From an article in last week's* U.S. News & World Report . . .
> *As noted in Lee Iacocca's best-selling book . . .*

Dynamism

Speakers with **dynamism,** another aspect of credibility, show a great deal of enthusiasm and energy for their subject. For example, when a student tried to get his classmates to become more politically active, he spoke of his own work in a local politician's primary campaign as one of the most exciting times of his life. He described his experience so vividly that the audience was able to feel his excitement.

It's easy to be dynamic about a subject you're enthusiastic about. When Jane spoke about the Australian exchange program, she started this way:

> *When your classmates are fighting snow and ice, you will be on the sunny beaches of Australia. When it's winter here, it's summer there. You'll have a chance to talk with people who speak your language. You'll have a chance to see how a different political system works, and you'll have a chance to visit spaces that are more wide-open than you've ever dreamed of. A semester in Australia will change your life.*

Much of the dynamism in a speech will be created nonverbally. A speaker who stands up straight, projects his or her voice to the back of the room, and doesn't hesitate will be seen by the audience as more dynamic than one who doesn't do these things. Watch for the most dynamic speakers in your class and make some mental notes on how they convey their energy and enthusiasm nonverbally.

Trustworthiness

A speaker with **trustworthiness** is perceived as reliable and dependable. Sometimes we have no way of knowing whether a speaker is trustworthy unless he or she does something unreliable, like showing up an hour late for a speech. In a speech communication class, however, after a month or so, most students can identify classmates who are reliable and dependable. These are people who come on time for class, make their speeches on time, pull their weight in a group, and give evidence that they have spent time preparing for a speech. Because of their previous behavior in class, they are perceived as trustworthy and therefore worth listening to.

Ethics

Ethics is a matter of conforming to acceptable and fair standards of conduct. Ethics is particularly important to persuasion because you are trying to change people—often in a significant way. If your audience doesn't perceive you as ethical, your speech will fail. Here are some ethical principles that are particularly useful in persuasive speaking:

1. Treat your audience with respect. Assume that audience members are intelligent and mature and will respond to a well-reasoned and well-organized appeal.
2. Take care not to distort or exaggerate your facts. Find the best facts you can, and let them stand on their own.
3. Avoid lying or name calling. Even if you think that the opposing side is stupid or vicious, it's unacceptable to say so.

4. Avoid suppressing key information. If you discover important information that doesn't support your view, include it but find a way of refuting it.
5. If you have something to gain personally from your persuasive speech, tell your audience what it is.
6. Show respect for your opponent or the opposing side. Do not dismiss ideas from the opposition: show how your ideas are better.
7. Take the time to develop and organize the best possible speech you can. Make it worth the audience's time to listen to you.

Appealing to the Audience

Audiences can be persuaded in many different ways. Persuasion is very complex, and what persuades some listeners may have no effect on others. What may encourage one student to sign a petition asking the administration to buy more science equipment, may cause another student to think that the money should go for library books instead. While one person might be persuaded to join a group dedicated to banning nuclear weapons, another person might want to look at much more evidence before joining. This section discusses some of the different kinds of persuasion and when it might be appropriate to use a particular method.

Logical Appeals

A **logical appeal** is one that addresses listeners' reasoning ability. Evidence in the form of statistics or any other supporting material will help to persuade the audience. Chapter 12 explains in detail the kinds of supporting material you can use in a logical appeal.

A logical appeal may be argued in several ways: through deductive reasoning, inductive reasoning, causal reasoning, or reasoning by analogy.

Try This *Try This* Try This

Among all the persuaders you have heard recently, select one who has tried to persuade you of something. Is this person someone you know well or is he or she a stranger?

Using the concepts of expertise, dynamism, trustworthiness, and ethics, evaluate this person's credibility. Is this person credible? Do you accept what he or she says? Why or why not? Are you willing to question his or her credibility? Why or why not?

Do you think there is a way this person could increase his or her credibility? How?

How important is this person's credibility to his or her daily life? To his or her occupation? To his or her contact with others?

Speakers are often stereotyped by the way they look. Would that be likely to happen to this speaker?

DEDUCTIVE REASONING

Deductive reasoning moves from the general to the specific. Here is a deductive argument used by one student:

Acid rain is a problem throughout the entire northeastern United States.

Pennsylvania is a northeastern state.

Pennsylvania has a problem with acid rain.

Care is needed, however, with this pattern of reasoning. Have you ever heard someone say "It's dangerous to generalize"? A faulty generalization really is faulty deductive thinking—as in this example:

All college students procrastinate.

Mary is a college student.

Therefore, Mary procrastinates.

INDUCTIVE REASONING

Another logical technique is **inductive reasoning**—reasoning from the specific to the general. Usually when we use inductive reasoning we move from a number of facts to a conclusion. Here is how a student used inductive reasoning to persuade her audience that the college should require everyone to take a foreign language:

> *In some parts of the United States, you need to understand Spanish to get by.*
> *Americans are traveling more and more to countries where a language other than English is spoken.*
> *The mark of an educated person is that he or she can speak, write, and read at least one other language.*
> *Conclusion: Everyone should learn another language.*

When you use inductive thinking in a speech, you can organize it in the way that best suits your material. Sometimes it will work best to give the facts and then draw the conclusion; in other cases you might want to start with the conclusion and then support it with facts.

CAUSAL REASONING

Another way to reason is causally. **Causal reasoning** always uses "because"— either implied or explicitly stated: "I failed the class because I didn't complete the assignments" or "The basketball team is losing because it has an incompetent coach." This latter example points out some of the problems of causal reasoning. That the coach is incompetent may be a matter of opinion. The team might be losing because it doesn't have good players or because the other teams have taller players or because there is no way of recruiting good players. The causal pattern can be used for presenting evidence as well as for organizing an entire speech. The cause-and-effect pattern is one of the ways to organize a speech discussed in Chapter 12.

REASONING BY ANALOGY

Finally, you can reason by **analogy.** In this case you compare two similar cases and conclude that if something is true for one, it must also be true for the other. One student used analogy to argue that since the school supported child care leave for women, it should also support it for men.

Often speeches of policy use analogy. Advocates of a policy will look to see if the policy has succeeded elsewhere. For example, to argue that the United States should follow the British policy in treating heroin addicts, one student said:

> *The English do not treat heroin addicts as criminals. If someone is addicted to heroin in England, he or she can get the drug with a prescription from a doctor. Because heroin is available it is less desirable. The English addiction rate has changed very little over the past few years.*

Emotional Appeals

An **emotional appeal** focuses on listeners' needs, wants, desires, and wishes. Recent research shows that the people who are most successful at persuasion are those who can understand others' motives and desires—even when these motives and desires are not stated. To do this, researchers found, the persuader must be able to understand someone else's feelings without letting his or her own feelings get in the way.[3]

In a public speaking situation it is impossible to appeal to each person's motives and desires, and so it helps to know that there are some basic needs that we all have.

APPEALING TO NEEDS

Psychologist Abraham Maslow has proposed a model that arranges people's needs from relatively low-level physical needs to higher-level psychological ones.[4] This model, referred to as a **hierarchy of needs,** is shown in Figure 16-2. Let's take a look at the needs in the hierarchy and see how they can help you decide what emotional appeals to put in your persuasive speech.

As you can see at the bottom of Figure 16-2, the first needs all human beings have are *physiological needs*. Starving people do not care about freedom; their need for food is so great that it outweighs all other needs. Therefore, physiological needs must be taken care of before other needs can be met. Since we usually assume that basic needs are taken care of, they are generally not a basis for a persuasive speech.

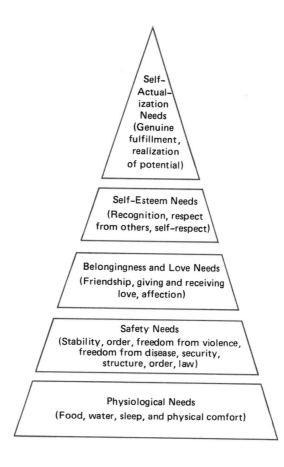

Figure 16-2
Maslow's Hierarchy of Needs

Safety needs are next in the hierarchy. The whole area of safety needs can be useful in persuasion, since all of us have these needs in varying degrees. Notice how this speaker appeals to the student audience's need for safety:

In the last three months there have been six assaults on this campus. Where have they occurred? All in parking lots with no lights. When? At night, after evening classes are over. Does this mean that you can't take any more evening classes without fearing for your life? Should you leave your car at home so you can avoid the campus parking lots?

Belongingness and love needs, the next level, also have a potent appeal. If you doubt this, turn on your television set and note how many commercials make a direct pitch to the need to be loved.

Here is how one student used the need to belong to urge freshmen to join "The Way"—a religious group on campus:

The freshman year is the hardest year of college. You are in a new environment and are faced with a bewildering array of choices. I felt this way when I was a freshman. Then I met someone from "The Way" who invited me to one of its meetings. The minute I walked in the door several people met me and made me feel welcome. Today some of these people are my best friends.

Self-esteem needs stem from our need to feel good about ourselves. We see a lot of persuasion based on these needs in self-help books. Typical themes are that you'll feel good about yourself if you change your fashion style, learn how to climb mountains, practice meditation, and so on. One student appealed to self-esteem needs when she gave a speech called "Try Something New":

I have a friend who, at the age of 35, decided to learn how to play the flute. She had never played an instrument before, but she loved music and thought it would be interesting to give it a try. Now that she has been studying for two years, she told me, "I will never be a great player but this has been a wonderful experience. I enjoy my records even more because I know what the musicians are doing because I understand so much more about music. It's wonderful to try something new." I am here today to urge you to try something new yourself. To see what you can discover about yourself.

At the top of his hierarchy, Maslow puts *self-actualization needs*—the need to recognize one's potential. This need involves our desire to do our best with what we have. An admissions director for a community college gave this speech when she talked to a group of older women in an attempt to persuade them to go to college.

I'm sure that many of you look back at your high-school days and think "I was a pretty good writer. I wonder if I still could write" or "I really liked my business courses. I would like to try my hand at bookkeeping again." I believe one of the saddest things that can happen to us is not to be able to try out things that we are good at, things that we have always wanted to do. Our new college program for returning adults will give you a chance to do just that—try out the things you are good at.

You have the best chance of choosing the right emotional appeal if you have done a thorough job of researching your audience. For instance, safety needs tend to be important to families—especially those with young children. On the other hand, younger audiences, such as college students, generally focus more on belonging, love, and self-esteem needs. If you were going to focus on safety needs to encourage the buying of savings bonds, a college audience probably wouldn't find it very interesting. Self-actualization needs probably appeal most to an older audience. Adults who are approaching midlife are the most likely to ask themselves whether they have made the right choices for their lives or whether they should make some changes. Age, of course, is only one factor to consider in assessing needs. The more information you have about your audience, the better the chance of selecting the right emotional appeals.

APPEALING TO OTHER EMOTIONS

Appeals can also be made to other emotions that all of us feel. In each of the examples that follows, the speaker is appealing to a common emotion.

In persuading her audience to be more aggressive in filing tax returns, this speaker used the emotion of fear:

When April rolls around, there is nothing the American taxpayer fears more than the Internal Revenue Service. I am here to tell you there is nothing to fear. I have been audited five times, and each time I have come out the winner.

In the next example, the speaker wanted audience members to consider taking a foster child. She used compassion as a way of getting them to feel sympathetic to the children:

What happens when a child has no home? When he is shunted around to five different foster homes in four years? This happens to thousands of American children every year. There is no place they can call home.

In this speech, the speaker used the emotion of anger to get her classmates to sign a petition to student government:

Every year each student pays $75 in student activity fees. What do we get for this money? Concerts by groups we have never heard of. Support for athletic teams that never win a game. A student newspaper that is written by illiterates. I am fed up and you should be too.

Sometimes you can appeal to a collective emotion. This student urged students to attend an honors convocation by appealing to their pride:

The most unsung heroes and heroines of this campus are those who have academic achievements. Do you know that 15 students from this school have scholarships to medical school next year? That for the past six semesters students from this campus have gone on highly competitive federal internships? That we are ranked as number four in the nation for our writing program?

When you are going to give a persuasive speech, think about the emotions you can appeal to that suit your subject. Emotions are powerful tools in persuasion. If you can find a good way of using them, they will add strength and power to your speech.

Structuring the Speech

Questions of Fact, Value, and Policy

Chapter 9 discussed using questions of fact, value, and policy in group discussion. Now let's see how these questions can be used for persuasive speeches.

QUESTIONS OF FACT

A question of fact deals with what is true or false. One student used a question of fact when he spoke on the question "Do Unidentified Flying Objects Really Exist?" The purpose of his speech was to persuade the audience that they did.

QUESTIONS OF VALUE

A question of value is concerned with some aspect of a moral issue: whether something is good or bad, right or wrong, beneficial or detrimental, and so on. Note how a student used a question of value to discuss the topic of plagiarism:

Specific Purpose: To persuade my audience that plagiarism of any kind is unacceptable.

Central Idea: Plagiarism may have short-term gains but it does long-term harm.

Main Points:
I. People's professional careers have been ruined when it was revealed that they had cheated in college.
II. People who plagiarize deny themselves the opportunity to learn new skills.
III. Plagiarism is theft; rather than take someone's possessions you steal his or her ideas and work.

QUESTIONS OF POLICY

Questions of policy deal with specific courses of action and usually contain such words as "should," "ought," or "must." Here are the main points for a speech based on a question of policy:

Specific Purpose: To persuade my audience that business should grant sabbaticals to administrators.

Central Idea: Sabbaticals are an effective solution to attracting and keeping workers, dealing with job stress and burnout, and broadening professional skills.

Main Points: I. Sabbaticals are an effective way to attract and keep workers.
 II. Sabbaticals are an effective way to deal with job stress and burnout.
 III. Sabbaticals are an effective way for workers to broaden their professional skills.
 IV. Sabbaticals should be granted to administrators.

One-Sided versus Two-Sided Arguments

Should persuaders present one side or both sides of an issue? When you know your listeners basically support your ideas, one side may be sufficient. For example, a student knew that she didn't have to persuade her audience of the pros and cons of being quiet in the library. Instead, she came up with some ideas for what her listeners could do to make the library quieter.

There are occasions, however, when speakers should present both sides of the picture. Often the presentation of both sides will boost credibility: a speaker who presents both sides is likely to be perceived as fairer and more rational. When an issue of public importance is controversial, it's a good idea to present both sides, since most people will probably have heard something about each side. When a student spoke on nuclear energy, he presented both sides because he knew there were strong feelings for and against. Another speaker chose to present both sides of the sex education issue. She thought sex education should be taught at home, but she wanted to let her audience know that others preferred it to be handled in the schools.

There has been extensive research comparing the one-sided versus two-sided speech. The results seem to indicate that: (1) a two-sided speech is more effective when the listeners have completed at least a high school education; (2) the two-sided speech is especially effective if the evidence clearly supports

---

Try This Try This Try This

Consider the following topics, and see if you can frame an argument for each side. Are there subjects where you are so firmly committed to one side that you can't even think of an opposing argument?

abortion	capital punishment	rock music
astrology	grades	seat belts
communism	exercise	prayer in schools
feminism	racism	organ transplants
freedom of speech	reincarnation	

the thesis; (3) the two-sided presentation is more effective when listeners oppose the speaker's position, but the one-sided approach is more effective when listeners already support the thesis.[5]

Order of Presentation

Certain ways of organizing speeches seem to be especially effective for a persuasive speech. As we discussed in detail in Chapter 13, the *problem-solution order* works well for persuasion. It lets the speaker build tension by describing the problem and getting listeners involved in it; then the speaker can relieve the tension by providing a solution.

Another organizational pattern that works well for persuasion is the **comparative advantage order.** When using this pattern, a speaker looks at some proposed solutions to a problem and then persuades the audience to choose a particular one by emphasizing its advantages. For example:

> *Several solutions have been proposed to alleviate the parking problem on campus. One is to build more parking lots. Another is to make everyone pay a hefty fee to get a decal to park on campus. The third is to provide some incentives for people to ride their bikes or walk to school. I favor this last solution because . . .*

The *motivated sequence*[6] was discussed in some detail in Chapter 13, but because of its popularity and usefulness for persuasion, we will review it here. The five steps of the motivated sequence, which is based on the problem-solution form, suggest five specific main points for developing a speech. Any problem-solving speech can be adapted to this form.

1. The *attention* step's purpose is to gain the attention of the audience. You do this by following the suggestions in the section "The Speech Introduction" in Chapter 13.
2. The *need* step points out a problem that affects audience members. In this step you create a sense of urgency about the problem.
3. The *satisfaction* step gives relief to the audience by providing a solution to the problem.
4. The *visualization* step lets the audience see how much better things would be if this solution were put into effect.
5. The *action* step urges the audience to go out and take some action that will help solve the problem.

Since the motivated sequence follows the human thought process, it is extremely easy to use. In fact, you might be using it without even knowing it. Here's how Maria tries to persuade her roommate Carlotta to move from the dorm to an off-campus apartment:

> *Attention:* Do you realize how small this room is? We don't have any place to store our clothes—let alone our books and tapes.

Need: We really need a space where we can spread out a little and invite our friends in without sitting nose to nose.

Satisfaction: See all the ads for off-campus housing? We can get an apartment in town for a little bit less than we are paying for the dorm.

Visualization: Just imagine—if we had our own apartment we could each have a separate room. We could have all our friends over at one time.

Action: Here's the list of apartments that are for rent. Let's start making some appointments to go and see them.

Now see how one student speaker developed a persuasive speech using the motivated sequence:

Specific Purpose: To persuade my audience that the campus newspaper should be funded directly by the activity fee rather than by student government.

Central Idea: When student government funds the newspaper, it often tries to control the news.

Main Points:
I. *Attention:* This week the student government says it will stop funding the newspaper unless the newspaper stops criticizing the government.

II. *Need:* This has been a problem for a long time. Whenever the government doesn't like what the paper says, it closes the paper down.

III. *Satisfaction:* The only way to solve this problem is to fund the paper directly with money from the student activity fee. If government doesn't control the funding, it can't control the newspaper.

IV. *Visualization:* The newspaper will be able to play its proper role as watchdog of government, and all of you will no longer find that the paper has not come out because the government has closed it down again.

V. *Action:* I have a petition addressed to the president of this university. I hope all of you will sign it.

SAMPLE PERSUASIVE SPEECH

Here is a persuasive speech that uses a problem-solution order. The full transcription of the speech is given at the left, and a commentary is on the right.

Title

Cigarettes: A Health Hazard to Non-smokers

Consider This Consider This Consider This

At this point in the semester you may have chosen so many topics for discussion and speeches that you've run out of ideas. This is a good time to use a data base in your school library to help you find a topic. The advantage of a data base is that you can feed it a broad, generalized heading, and it will give you some subheadings that will help you narrow your topic. Here are some headings and subheadings from InfoTrac, a common data base in college and university libraries. The information below for each item comes from one screen—there may be several more screens.

Animal Rights
  cases
  economic aspects
  evaluation
  law and legislation
  legal aspects
  moral and ethical aspects
  philosophy
  political aspects
  psychological aspects
  public opinion
  religious aspects
  social aspects
  study
Athletic Shoe Industry
  acquisitions and mergers
  advertising
  cases
  contributions, gifts, etc.
  directories
  earnings
  economic aspects
  finance

  history
  Hungary
  innovations
  management
Capital Punishment
  analysis
  anecdotes
  Arkansas
  death row
  electrocution
  executions and executioners
  for juvenile offenders
  for mentally handicapped
  hanging
  statistics
  stays of execution, proceedings, etc.
  United States
Cocaine
  cases
  control
  distribution

Specific Purpose

To persuade my audience to support legislation that will expand the Clean Indoor Air Act.

Central Idea

Secondary smoke from cigarettes is a serious health hazard, and nonsmokers must be protected from it.

If you smoke, you are a health hazard to those around you. Call it what you want—environmental tobacco smoke,

The speaker begins with a strong authoritative statement. The audience knows exactly where she passive smoking, involuntary smoking, secondhand smoke—the smoke from cigarettes, pipes, and cigars causes sickness and even death to innocent people around a smoker.

My mother and I both suffer from allergies and asthma, and I know that inhaling other people's smoke makes us suffer more.

The federal Environmental Protection Agency agrees. It says that exhaled tobacco smoke should be officially listed as a known cancer-causing agent. The

stands. She defines secondary smoke by using a series of synonyms.

She tells her own interest in the subject.

Now the speaker makes a transition by connecting her experience to expert testimony.

National Academy of Sciences reported in 1985 that at least 3 percent of the annual lung cancer deaths were caused by passive smoke.

I'll give you even more scary facts today, and I'll tell you what a lot of Americans are doing about this danger.

We should expand no-smoking laws to public places. The point is that we all need protection from secondhand smoke.

Here she states her central idea.

Do you know you can get lung cancer from inhaling someone else's smoke? American Cancer Society studies show that if you live with a smoker who smokes a pack a day at home, you have twice the risk of developing lung cancer. Involuntary smoke at home, on the job, and out in public can also aggravate chronic heart diseases and lung diseases such as asthma, bronchitis, and emphysema.

Now the expert testimony is applied to one's own home to illustrate the problem.

Secondhand smoke hurts infants and children. Pregnant women exposed to two hours of passive smoke a day will have lower-birth-weight babies. By-products of nicotine are found in the urine of infants because the smoke of those around them works its way into their systems. Children growing up in smoke-filled surroundings will grow and develop more slowly. In general, they are sicker and more likely to develop colds, bronchitis, pneumonia, ear infections, and reduced lung functions. They will have an increased risk of cancer as adults.

Here is evidence that has an emotional appeal too. No one wants harm to come to infants and children.

Do you doubt these facts? Do you think that it's unfair to accuse smokers of these offenses? It is true that the risks for nonsmokers depend on the amount of smoke they are exposed to. Nonsmokers do breathe less smoke than smokers. But the health risks to nonsmokers have been shown. All of us in public places face these risks. Is this fair?

This is a transitional paragraph that will lead to possible solutions. Here she acknowledges some arguments from the other side of the issue.

Public interest is growing for new legislation to protect the nonsmoker

This shows how some employers

from involuntary smoke. American businesses are working to cut their insurance costs by reducing the health risks from smoking. They are eliminating smoking on the job, and many are insisting that employees not smoke at all. In 1988, 6 percent of 283 companies in one study would not hire smokers. Turner Broadcasting, for example, has not hired a smoker since 1986. Companies want to get smoke out of the workplace and improve the health of their workers.

Some may argue that there are other ways to get rid of smoke in the workplace, such as through improved ventilation. But there is no filtration system that can get rid of all of the harmful effects of smoke, and any massive ventilation system would be very expensive. So companies choose to eliminate smoking for all their workers.

The move is on to reduce smoking in public places. Smoking is now banned on all domestic airplane flights under 6 hours. All U.S. government buildings have smoking restrictions. Thirty-three states have laws that address smoking in public workplaces, and fifteen have laws regarding private enterprises. More than 42 states and 400 local governments limit or restrict smoking in public places.

In 1989, the "Pennsylvania Clean Indoor Air Law" went into effect. It is designed to protect public health and comfort by regulating smoking in certain public places and events and some workplaces. Restaurants with 75 or more seats must provide a nonsmoking section. Employers are required to regulate smoking in their workplace. Public places such as museums, theaters, and health facilities are also required to regulate smoking and provide nonsmoking areas.

However these laws don't go far enough. Nonsmoking areas are not ade-

have solved the problem of smoke in the workplace.

This transition leads to a solution that the speaker feels might not work. This could be information the opposition might raise. Again, she raises an issue the opposition might consider. However, she is ready with superior evidence.

Again, she reminds us of the trend to ban smoking in public places.

Since the speaker is addressing an audience of Pennsylvanians she tells them what is being done in their state.

Now she tells why the present legislation isn't adequate.

quate, especially in some restaurants. I'm tired of going into restaurants where nonsmokers are two tables away from smokers. Nonsmokers are still exposed to involuntary smoke, and that means that we are still being subjected to very serious health risks. You can't even go to the grocery store and expect to be in a smoke-free environment.

Some smokers feel that they are already being inconvenienced by the non-smoking signs they encounter, but what about the innocent people affected by involuntary smoke? If smokers want to kill themselves, they are free to do so, but putting infants, children, and the rest of us at risk is taking away our rights to live in a smoke-free environment.

Let's stop this infliction and support new legislation which would extend the current Pennsylvania Clean Indoor Air Law to include a ban on smoking in all public-use buildings. Write to your state representatives urging them to take action against involuntary smoke in public-use buildings. Please join in this effort to protect our health and the health of future generations.

Here she tells the audience how they can help bring about changes and suggests a course of action.

Bibliography

American Cancer Society. *The Smoke around You: The Risks of Involuntary Smoking.* Atlanta: American Cancer Society, Inc., 1987.

Galloway, Arlene. *The Smoke-Free Guide.* Victoria, British Columbia: Qualy Publishing, 1988.

Pennsylvania Department of Health. *The Pennsylvania Clean Indoor Air Law.* Harrisburg, Pa.: Pennsylvania Department of Health, 1989.

Sipress, Alan. "Employers Exerting Control," *Centre Daily Times,* March 28, 1991, 1A, 11A.

Source: This speech was given by Carol E. Bubb in a speech class at Lock Haven University in Lock Haven, Pennsylvania, 1991.

Persuasion is the process of trying to change people's attitudes or behavior. Persuasion has four possible goals: to get people to take action; to get people to continue to do what they are already doing; to get people to avoid doing something; or to get people to continue not doing something. All these goals might be present in a single speech.

For a speaker to persuade an audience, he or she must have credibility. Credibility comes from four areas: expertise, dynamism, trustworthiness, and ethics. Expertise is gained by doing research and being informed on a subject. Dynamism is apparent when a speaker delivers a message with energy and enthusiasm. Trustworthiness depends on past experience; if you have been reliable in the past, people are more likely to trust you. An ethical speaker tells the audience if he or she has something to gain from the persuasion. The ethical speaker also looks for the best evidence, presents it fairly, and identifies its origin.

A persuasive message is usually made up of a combination of logical and emotional appeals. Logical appeals present evidence through deductive reasoning, inductive reasoning, causal reasoning, and reasoning by analogy. Emotional appeals play on the need for safety, the need to be loved and to belong, and the needs for self-esteem and self-expression. A speaker may also build emotional appeals into a speech by appealing to emotions we all feel, such as fear, pity, anger, and pride.

Structure is important to a persuasive speech. Some speakers like to organize their speeches around questions of fact, value, or policy. When a speaker is gathering supporting material for a speech, he or she must decide whether to present one side or both sides of the issue. Generally, two-sided arguments work best when the audience is educated and the subject is controversial.

Ordering a presentation depends on the subject. In persuasive speaking, speakers commonly use a problem-solution order, an order that gives comparative advantages, or the motivated sequence. The motivated sequence involves five steps: attention, need, satisfaction, visualization, and action.

FURTHER READING

ANDERSEN, KENNETH, AND THEODORE CLEVENGER. "A Summary of Experimental Research in Ethos." *Communication Monographs*, 30 (1963): 59–78. This article contains an excellent early summary of the research on credibility. It has become a classic reference piece.

BETTINGHAUS, ERWIN P., AND MICHAEL J. CODY. *Persuasive Communication*, 4th ed. New York: Holt, Rinehart and Winston, 1987. Bettinghaus and Cody examine the use of persuasion in contemporary situations. The book is useful for those concerned with public relations, labor management problems, advertising directed toward social issues, and social action programs. A solid, research-based textbook that is behavioral in orientation and theoretical in approach.

CAMPBELL, KARLYN KOHRS. *The Rhetorical Act*. Belmont, CA: Wadsworth, 1982. An excellent source that explains the nature of public speaking. For those interested in the classical roots of our discipline, Campbell uses Aristotelian terms to treat enthymemes, arguments produced cooperatively by speaker and audience. This, she feels, is "the substance of rhetorical persuasion."

FREELEY, AUSTIN J. *Argumentation and Debate: Critical Thinking for Reasoned Decision Making*, 7th ed. Belmont, CA: Wadsworth, 1990. The reason this book is included here is because of Freeley's excellent chapters on analyzing the problem, exploring the problem, evidence, tests of evidence, reasoning, and obstacles to clear thinking. With this material, your persuasion will have reasoned decision making as a fundamental base. A fine, comprehensive textbook.

LARSON, CHARLES U. *Persuasion: Reception and Responsibility*, 5th ed. Belmont, CA: Wadsworth, 1989. The major emphasis of this book is the need to become skillful consumers or receivers of persuasion. The second emphasis is on symbolic behavior—the language central to every persuasive act. The third emphasis is the impact of the media on persuasion, especially electronic media. In Chapter 11, Richard Johannesen explains the six major ethical perspectives—the most complete and well-researched discussion of the topic in any persuasion textbook.

LITTLEJOHN, STEPHEN W., AND DAVID M. JABUSCH. *Persuasive Transactions*. Glenview, IL: Scott, Foresman, 1987. These authors emphasize theory and analysis and treat practice in this conceptual context. Their underlying theoretical framework includes the following assumptions: persuasion is a transactional, rule-governed process; persuasion occurs in all communication contexts; persuasion is best understood through an eclectic approach; and persuasive competence involves a blend of theoretical understanding, sensitivity, and skill. A well-written, well-documented textbook.

SIMONS, HERBERT W. *Persuasion: Understanding, Practice, and Analysis*, 2d ed. New York: Random House, 1986. This is a classic textbook in persuasion. Simons provides a valuable blend of current perspectives, research, and applications.

SMITH, MARY JOHN. *Persuasion and Human Action: A Review and Critique of Social Influence Theories*. Belmont, CA: Wadsworth, 1982. This is an excellent source book for the theoretical underpinnings of research on persuasion. Smith provides a comprehensive overview of social influence theories.

TURNER, WILLIAM. *Secrets of Personal Persuasion*. Englewood Cliffs, NJ: Prentice-Hall, 1986. This is a self-help book on persuasion with numerous suggestions and success secrets—which are highlighted throughout the book. With no references, no documentation, and no suggestions for additional reading, Turner offers a practical, readable book full of skill builders. Included are "magic stories" and humorous examples to be used in speeches. A comfortable armchair approach to persuasion.

Notes

Chapter 1

1. Dan B. Curtis, Jerry L. Winsor, and Ronald D. Stephens, "National Preferences in Business and Communication Education," *Communication Education* 38 (1989): 6–14.

2. John R. Johnson and Nancy Szczupakiewicz, "The Public Speaking Course: Is It Preparing Students with Work-Related Public Speaking Skills?" *Communication Education* 36 (1987): 131–136.

3. David K. Berlo, *The Process of Communication: An Introduction to Theory and Practice* (New York: Holt, Rinehart, & Winston, 1960), p. 24.

4. Albert Mehrabian, *Silent Messages: Implicit Communication of Emotions and Attitudes*, 2nd ed. (Belmont, CA: Wadsworth, 1981), pp. 76–77.

5. See Carol Wilder, "The Palo Alto Group: Difficulties and Directions of the Transactional View for Human Communication Research," *Human Communication Research* 5 (Winter 1979): 171–186.

Chapter 2

1. Dean C. Barnlund, "Towards a Meaning-Centered Philosophy of Communication," *Journal of Communication* 12 (1962): 197–211.

2. Sandra Blakeslee, "How You See Yourself: Potential for Big Problems," *The New York Times*, February 7, 1991, p. B15.

3. Muriel James and Dorothy Jongeward, *Born to Win: Transactional Analysis with Gestalt Experiments* (Reading, MA: Addison-Wesley, 1971), pp. 68–100.

4. Robert K. Merton, *Social Theory and Social Structure* (New York: Free Press, 1957).

5. Philip E. Lampe, "The Problematic Nature of Interracial and Interethnic Communication," *The Social Studies* (May/June 1988): 116.

6. Ibid

7. Eva Hoffman, *Lost in Translation: A Life in a New Language* (New York: Penguin, 1990).

8. Janet E. Helms, "Towards a Theoretical Explanation of the Effects of Race on Counseling: A Black and White Model," *The Counseling Psychologist*, 12, 153–164.

Chapter 3

1. Michael J. Papa and Ethel C. Glenn, "Listening Ability and Performance with New Technology: A Case Study," *The Journal of Business Communication* 25 (Fall 1988): 13.

2. Andrew D. Wolvin and Carolyn Gwynn Coakley, *Listening*, 3rd ed. ((Dubuque, IA: William C. Brown, 1988), p. 208.

3. Sperry Corporation, *Your Personal Listening Profile* (Sperry Corporation, 1980), p. 4.

4. See Lyman K. Steil, Larry L. Barker, and Kittie W. Watson, *Effective Listening: Key to Your Success* (New York: Random House, 1983); and Florence I. Wolff, Nadine C. Marsnik, William S. Tacey, and Ralph G. Nichols, *Perceptive Listening* (New York: Holt, Rinehart & Winston, 1983).

5. Vincent DiSalvo, David C. Larsen, and William J. Seiler, "Communication Skills Needed by People in Business," *Communication Monographs* 25 (1976): 274.

6. American Federation of Teachers, "Listen, and Ye Shall Learn," *On Campus*, March 1988: p. 6.

7. William F. Eadie, "Hearing What We Ought to Hear," *Vital Speeches of the Day*, July 15, 1989, p. 588.

8. Neville Moray, *Listening and Attention* (Baltimore: Penguin Books, 1969), p. 23.

9. Paul G. Friedman, *Listening Processes: Attention, Understanding, Evaluation* (Washington, DC: National Education Association, 1978), p. 274.

10. Rebecca B. Rubin and Charles V. Roberts, "A Comparative Examination and Analysis of Three Listening Tests," *Communication Education* 36 (April 1987): 142–153.

11. Stanford E. Taylor, *Listening* (Washington, DC: National Education Association, 1964), p. 13.

12. Sperry Corporation, *Your Personal Listening Profile*.

13. Bert K. Pryor, K. Phillip Taylor, Raymond W. Buchanan, and David U. Strawn, "An Affective-Cognitive Consistency Explanation for Comprehension of Standard Jury Instructions," *Communication Monographs* 47 (1980): 69.

14. Ibid.

15. Deborah Tannen, *You Just Don't Understand* (New York: William Morrow & Company, 1990), pp. 49–53.

16. Gerald I. Nierenberg and Harry Calero, *Meta-Talk* (New York: Simon & Schuster, 1973), p. 12.

Chapter 4

1. Benjamin L. Whorf, "The Relation of Habitual Thought and Behavior to Language," *Language, Thought and Reality* (Cambridge, MA: MIT Press, 1956), pp. 134–159.

2. Barry Lopez, *Arctic Dreams* (New York: Charles Scribner's Sons, 1986), p. 274.

3. Neil Postman, *Crazy Talk, Stupid Talk* (New York: Delta, 1977), p. 9.

4. Erving Goffman, *Relations in Public* (New York: Basic Books, 1971), p. 62.

5. Esther Blank Greif and Jane Berko Gleason, "Hi, Thanks, and Goodbye: More Routine Information," *Language in Society* 9 (1980): 159–166.

6. Jim Barlow, "When Talk Turns to Mice Milking," *Houston Chronicle*, November 25, 1990, p. B1.

7. Chris Smith ed., "Fast Track," *New York*, May 28, 1990, p. 27.

8. Marsha Houston Stanback and W. Barnett Pearce, "Talking to 'The Man'; Some Communication Strategies Used by Members of 'Subordinate' Social Groups," *Quarterly Journal of Speech*, 67 (1981): 24–25.

9. Deborah Tannen, *You Just Don't Understand*, (New York: William Morrow & Company, 1990), pp. 42–43.

10. Ibid., p. 76.

11. Ibid., pp. 51–52.

12. Anthony Mulac, John M. Wiemenn, Sally J. Widenmann, and Toni W. Gibson, "Male/Female Language Differences and Effects in Same-Sex and Mixed-Sex Dyads: The Gender-Linked Language Effect," *Communication Monographs* 55 (1988): 316–332.

13. Tannen, *You Just Don't Understand*, p. 153.

14. Ibid., p. 245.

15. Ibid., pp. 255–256.

16. Faye Crosby and Linda Nyquist, "The Female Register: An Empirical Study of Lakoff's Hypothesis," *Language in Society* (1977): 314.

17. Eleanor Wilson Orr, *Twice as Less* (New York: W. W. Norton, 1987), pp. 1–14.

18. Wsveolod W. Isajiw, Review of *Ethnicity and Language*, Winston A. Van Horne and Thomas V. Tonnesan eds., Madison: University of Wisconsin System Institute on Race and Ethnicity, 1987) in *Contemporary Sociology* 18 (September 1989): 686.

19. Tannen, *You Just Don't Understand*, p. 62.

20. Craig E. Johnson, "An Introduction to Powerful Talk and Powerless Talk in the Classroom," *Communication Education* 36 (April 1987): 167–172.

21. Ibid.

22. As quoted in "Misusage Spells Trouble for Language: Professor Has Harsh Words for Bad Grammar," *The Salt Lake Tribune*, November 23, 1990, p. 30a.

23. C. Ray Penn, "A Choice of Words is a Choice of Worlds," *Vital Speeches of the Day*, December 1, 1990, p. 116.

24. Ibid., p. 117.

Chapter 5

1. Vincent Bozzi, "Tall, Dark First Date," *Psychology Today* (July/August 1989): 67.

2. Roberta Friedman, "Hand Jive," *Psychology Today* (June 1988): 10.

3. Daniel Goleman, "Studies Point to Power of Nonverbal Signals," *The New York Times*, April 8, 1986, pp. C1, C6.

4. Albert Mehrabian, *Silent Messages: Implicit Communication of Emotions and Attitudes*, 2nd ed. (Belmont, CA: Wadsworth, 1981), pp. 76–77.

5. Deborah Tannen, *You Just Don't Understand: Women and Men in Conversation* (New York: William Morrow, 1990), p. 246.

6. Ibid., pp. 235–236.

7. Mark L. Knapp, *Essentials of Nonverbal Communication* (New York: Holt, Rinehart & Winston, 1980), p. 237.

8. Loretta A. Malandro and Larry Barker, *Nonverbal Communication* (New York: Random House, 1983), p. 9.

9. Ibid., p. 280.

10. Mehrabian, *Silent Messages*, pp. 42–47. See also "Communicating Without Words," *Psychology Today* 2 (1968): 53.

11. James MacLachlan, "What People Really Think of Fast Talkers," *Psychology Today* 13 (November 1979): 113–117.

12. George B. Ray, "Vocally Cued Personality Prototypes: An Implicit Personality Theory Approach," *Communication Monographs*, 53 (1986): 272.

13. Ibid., p. 273.

14. Paul Ekman and W. V. Friesen, "The Repertoire of Nonverbal Behavior: Categories,

Origins, Usages, and Coding," *Semiotica* I (1969): 49–98.

15. Ernst Kretschmer, *Physique and Character: An Investigation of the Nature of Constitution and of the Theory of Temperament* (New York: Cooper Square, 1970), pp. 18–35.

16. William H. Sheldon, *The Varieties of Temperament* (New York: Hafner, 1942).

17. W. Wells and B. Siegel, "Stereotype Somatype," *Psychological Reports* 8 (1961): 77–78. Their work was confirmed by K. T. Strongman and C. J. Hart, "Stereotyped Reactions to Body Build," *Psychological Reports* 8 (1968): 77–78.

18. Mark L. Knapp, *Nonverbal Communication in Human Interaction*, 2nd ed. (New York: Holt, Rinehart & Winston, 1978).

19. Ellen Berscheid and Elaine Hatfield Walster, *Interpersonal Attraction*, 2nd ed. (New York: Random House, 1978).

20. Lawrence B. Rosenfeld, "Beauty and Business: Looking Good Pays Off," *New Mexico Business Journal* (April 1979): 22–26.

21. Nathan Joseph, *Uniforms and Nonuniforms*, (New York: Greenwood Press, 1986), p. 49.

22. Ibid., p. 50.

23. Ibid., pp. 2–3, 15.

24. Ibid., p. 143.

25. Ibid., pp. 168–169.

26. Ibid., pp. 124–125.

27. Edward T. Hall, *The Silent Language* (Greenwich, CT: Fawcett, 1959); and Edward T. Hall, *The Hidden Dimension* (Garden City, NY: Anchor Books, 1969).

28. Hall, *The Hidden Dimension*, pp. 116–125.

29. As cited in R. Winter, "How People React to Your Touch," *Science Digest* 84 (March 1976): 46–56.

30. Stanley E. Jones, "Sex Differences in Touch Communication," *The Western Journal of Speech Communication* 50 (Summer 1986): 227–241.

Chapter 6

1. Richard Morin, "Make Friends, Live Longer," *The Honolulu Advertiser*, December 27, 1988, p. A12.

2. Ibid.

3. John Powell, *Why Am I Afraid to Tell You Who I Am?* (Allen, TX: Argus Communications, 1969), p. 44.

4. William C. Schultz, *The Interpersonal Under-world* (Palo Alto, CA: Science and Behavior Books, 1966), pp. 18–20.

5. Penelope Eckert, *Jocks and Burnouts* (New York: Teachers College Press, 1989), pp. 2–3.

6. Daniel Goleman, "Feeling of Control Viewed as Central in Mental Health," *The New York Times*, October 7, 1986, pp. C1, C11.

7. Ibid.

8. Daniel Goleman, "High and Low Intensity: Two Emotional Cultures," *The International Herald Tribune*, March 19, 1987, p. 7.

9. Steven W. Duck, *Personal Relationships and Personal Constructs: A Study of Friendship Formation* (New York: Wiley, 1973), p. 20.

10. See Charles R. Berger and Richard J. Calabrese, "Some Explorations in Initial Interaction and Beyond: Toward a Developmental Theory of Interpersonal Communication," *Human Communication Research* 1 (1976): 99–112.

11. Sam Keen, "Why We Love Gossip," *Family Weekly*, June 5, 1983, pp. 4–8.

12. Jack Levin and Arnold Arluke, *Gossip: The Inside Scoop* (New York: Plenum Press, 1987), pp. 14–15.

13. Ibid., p. 16.

14. Ibid., pp. 20–21.

15. Tannen, *You Just Don't Understand*, p. 62.

16. Mark L. Knapp, Laura Stafford, and John A. Daly, "Regrettable Messages: Things People Wish They Hadn't Said," *Journal of Communication* 36 (1986): 40–57.

17. Lawrence R. Wheeless and Janis Grotz, "The Measurement of Trust and Its Relationship to Self-Disclosure," *Human Communication Research* 3 (Spring 1970): 250–257. Wheeless and Grotz explain the relationship between trust and self-disclosure.

18. Joseph Luft, *Group Process: An Introduction to Group Dynamics*, 2nd ed. (Palo Alto, CA: National Press, 1970), pp. 11–12.

19. Lawrence Rosenfeld, "Self-Disclosure Avoidance: Why Am I Afraid to Tell You Who I Am?" *Communication Monographs* 46 (March 1979): 63–74.

20. C. Arthur Vanlear, Jr., "The Formation of Social Relationships: A Longitudinal Study of Social Penetration," *Human Communication Research* 13 (Spring 1987): 299–322.

21. For a discussion of the relationship between liking and disclosure, see John H. Berg and Richard L. Archer, "The Disclosure-Liking Re-

lationship," *Human Communication Research* 10 (Winter 1983): 269–281.

Chapter 7

1. Leslie A. Baxter and Connie Bullis, "Turning Points in Developing Romantic Relationships," *Human Communications Research* 12 (Summer 1986): 469–493.

2. Mark L. Knapp, *Interpersonal Communication and Human Relationships* (Boston: Allyn & Bacon, 1984), pp. 35–44.

3. Mark L. Knapp, Roderick, P. Hart, Gustav W. Friedrich, and Gary M. Shulman, "The Rhetoric of Goodbye: Verbal and Nonverbal Correlates of Human Leave-Taking," *Speech Monographs* 40 (August 1973): 182–198.

4. For more information on how couples come apart see: Stephen P. Banks, Dayle M. Altendorf, John O. Greene, and Michael J. Cody, "An Examination of Relationship Disengagement: Perceptions, Breakup Strategies and Outcomes," *The Western Journal of Speech Communication*, 51 (Winter 1987): 19–41; and William W. Wilmot, Donal A. Carbaugh, and Leslie A. Baxter, "Communicative Strategies Used to Terminate Romantic Relationships," *The Western Journal of Speech Communication* 49 (Summer 1985): 204–216.

5. Margaret A. Farley, *Personal Commitments* (San Francisco: Harper & Row, 1986), p. 18.

6. Ibid., p. 21.

7. Deborah Tannen, "That's Not What I Meant!" (New York: William Morrow, 1986), p. 124.

8. Karen Tracy, Donna Van Dusen, and Susan Robinson, " 'Good' and 'Bad' Criticism: A Descriptive Analysis," *Journal of Communication* 37 (Spring 1987): 46–59.

9. Ibid., p. 48.

10. Ibid., p. 50.

11. Daniel Goleman, "Why Job Criticism Fails: Psychology's New Findings," *The New York Times*, July 26, 1988, p. C1.

12. Ibid., p. C15.

13. Rebecca J. Cline and Bonnie McD. Johnson, "The Verbal Stare: Focus on Attention in Conversation," *Communication Monographs* 43 (1976): 1–10.

14. Jack Gibb, "Defensive Communication," *Journal of Communication* 11 (1961): 141–148.

15. William Anthony Donohue, "An Empirical Format for Examining Negotiation Processes and Outcomes," *Communication Monographs* 45 (1978): 247.

16. Deborah Wieder-Hatfield, "A Unit in Conflict Management Communication Skills," *Communication Education* 30 (1981): 265–273.

Chapter 8

1. For an overview of the various types of interviews, see Michael Z. Sincoff and Robert S. Goyer, *Interviewing* (New York: Macmillan, 1984).

2. G. Barry Golson, The Playboy Interview, *Playboy Magazine*, September, 1962, p. 4.

3. E. G. Mishler, "Studies in Dialogue and Discourse: II. Types of Discourse Initiated By and Sustained Through Questioning," *Journal of Psycholinguistic Research* 4 (1975): 99–121. As cited in Laurie V. Babbitt and Fredrick M. Jablin, "Characteristics of Applicants' Questions and Employment Screening Interview Outcomes," *Human Communication Research* 11 (Summer 1985): 507–535.

4. William N. Yeomans, *1000 Things You Never Learned in Business School* (New York: McGraw-Hill, 1985), pp. 141–147.

5. Marc Silver, "Selling the Perfect You," *U.S. News and World Report*, February 5, 1990, pp. 70–72.

6. Ibid.

7. Much of the material about résumés and letters of applications is adapted from material written by Joan C. Welker, Director, Career Services, Lock Haven University.

8. Babbitt and Jablin, "Characteristics of Applicants' Questions," p. 529.

9. Charles J. Stewart and William B. Cash, Jr., *Interviewing: Principles and Practices* (Dubuque, IA: Brown, 1982), pp. 188–189.

10. Yeomans, *1000 Things You Never Learned in Business School*, p. 140.

Chapter 9

1. For a thorough overview of small-group communication, see B. Aubrey Fisher, *Small Group Decision Making: Communication and the Group Process*, 2nd ed. (New York: McGraw-Hill, 1980); Francis L. Ulschak, Leslie Nathanson, and Peter G. Gillan, *Small Group Problem Solving* (Reading, MA: Addison-Wesley, 1981); and Rodney W. Napier and Matti K. Gershenfeld, *Groups: Theory and Experience*, 2nd ed. (Boston: Houghton Mifflin, 1981).

2. John E. Baird, Jr., and Stanford B. Weinberg, *Communication: The Essence of Group Synergy* (Dubuque, IA: Brown, 1977), p. 126.

3. Elizabeth W. Flynn and John F. LaFaso, *Group Discussion as a Learning Process* (New York: Paulist Press, 1972), pp. 102–103.

4. Baird and Weinberg, *Communication*, p. 125.

5. R. Victor Harnack, Thorrel B. Fest, and Barbara Schindler Jones, *Group Discussion: Theory and Technique*, 2nd ed. (Englewood Cliffs, NJ: Prentice-Hall, 1977), p. 14.

6. Daniel Goleman, "The Group and the Self: New Focus on a Cultural Rift," *The New York Times*, December 25, 1990, pp. 37, 41k.

7. Ibid.

8. Ibid.

9. Bill Lawren, "Seating for Success," *Psychology Today* (September 1989): 16–20.

10. Steven A. Beebe and John T. Masterson, *Communicating in Small Groups: Principles and Practices*, (Glenview, IL: Scott, Foresman, 1982), p. 89.

11. I.L. Janis, *Victims of Groupthink* (Boston: Houghton Mifflin, 1972), p. 9.

12. Ronald B. Adler, *Communication at Work*, 2nd ed. (New York: Random House, 1986), pp. 227–228.

13. Goleman, "The Group and the Self: New Focus on a Cultural Rift," pp. 37, 41.

14. Ibid.

Chapter 10

1. William N. Yeomans, *1000 Things You Never Learned in Business School* (New York: McGraw-Hill, 1985), pp. 108–109.

2. Ibid., p. 108.

3. Hugh J. Arnold and Daniel C. Feldman, *Organizational Behavior* (New York: McGraw-Hill, 1986), pp. 120–121.

4. Robert A. Baron and Paul B. Paulus, *Understanding Human Relations*, 2nd ed. (Boston: Allyn & Bacon, 1991), pp. 241–245.

5. Ibid., p. 245.

6. P. Hersey and K. H. Blanchard, *Management of Organizational Behavior: Utilizing Human Resources*, 4th ed. (Englewood Cliffs, NJ: Prentice-Hall, 1982), pp. 152–155.

7. Kenneth D. Benne and Paul Sheats, "Functional Roles of Group Members," *Journal of Social Issues*, No. 4 (1948): 41–49.

8. Gloria Galanes and John K. Brilhart, *Communicating in Groups: Applications and Skills* (Dubuque, IA: William C. Brown, 1991), pp. 228–232.

Chapter 11

1. Steven Allen, *How To Make A Speech* (New York: McGraw-Hill), p. 40.

2. Alex Osborn, *Applied Imagination: Principles and Procedures of Creative Thinking* (New York: Scribner's, 1979).

3. Mortimer J. Adler, *How to Speak, How to Listen* (New York: Macmillan, 1983), pp. 71–72.

Chapter 12

1. Jesse Jackson, Excerpts from text of Jesse Jackson's remarks prepared for the Democratic Convention, *The New York Times*, July 18, 1984, p. 12A.

2. "This Year's College Freshmen: Attitudes and Characteristics," *The Chronicle of Higher Education*, January 30, 1991, pp. A30–A31. As cited in Alexander W. Astin, "The American Freshman: National Norms For Fall 1990" (American Council on Education and University of California at Los Angeles).

3. "Many See Mercy in Ending Empty Lives," *The New York Times*, September 23, 1984, p. 56.

4. Derived from *Toledo Blade*, October 30, 1978, p. 21.

5. See Jo Sprague and Douglas Stuart, *The Speaker's Handbook* (San Diego, CA: Harcourt Brace Jovanovich, 1984) for an excellent sourcebook for material on the principles of speech communication.

Chapter 13

1. Judy L. Haynes, *Organizing a Speech: A Programmed Guide*, 2nd ed. (Englewood Cliffs, NJ: Prentice-Hall, 1981).

2. Denise Foully, "Shape Up Your Pet!" *Prevention*, August 1984, pp. 58–63.

3. Douglas Ehninger, Alan H. Monroe, and Bruce E. Gronbeck, *Principles and Types of Speech Communication*, 10th ed. (Glenview, IL: Scott, Foresman, 1986), pp. 142–161.

4. Regina Schrambling, "Chop Phooey," *In Health*, March/April 1991, pp. 20–24.

5. Dan Moream, "Five Rules for Happy Haggling," *Changing Times*, April 1991, pp. 59–61.

6. Charles R. Gruner, "Advice to the Beginning Speaker on Using Humor—What the Research Tells Us," *Communication Education* 34 (April 1985): 142.

7. Rebecca C. Jann, "What They Should Have

Told Me When I Was a Senior," *Vital Speeches of the Day*, November 1, 1983, p. 51.

8. Roger B. Porter, "Conflict and Cooperation in the Global Marketplace: A Healthy Competition," *Vital Speeches of the Day*, January 1, 1991, p. 163.

9. Shirley Biagi, *Newstalk II* (Belmont, CA: Wadsworth, 1987), p. 165.

Chapter 14

1. See Alan Garner, *Conversationally Speaking* (New York: McGraw-Hill, 1981). Also see Les Donaldson, *Conversational Magic: Key to Poise, Popularity and Success* (West Nyack, NJ: Parker, 1981).

2. Timothy G. Hegstrom, "Message Impact: What Percentage Is Nonverbal?" *Western Journal of Speech Communication* 43 (Spring 1979): 134–142.

3. Evan Marshall, *Eye Language: Understanding the Eloquent Eye* (New York: New Trend, 1983).

4. See Jeffrey C. Hahner, Martin A. Sokoloff, Sandra Salisch, and Geoffrey D. Needler, *Speaking Clearly: Improving Voice and Diction*, 2nd ed. (New York: Random House, 1986).

5. "Teaching the 'Sir Winston' Method," *The New York Times*, March 11, 1990, p. F7.

6. Associated Press, "Weatherman Tells Phobics of His Panics," October 14, 1984.

7. Michael T. Motley, "Taking The Terror Out of Talk," *Psychology Today* (January 1988): 47.

8. Ibid.

9. William T. Page, "Helping the Nervous Presenter: Research and Prescriptions," *Journal of Business Communication* 22(2): 10.

Chapter 15

1. Peter Jaret, "The Cold Truth about Hard Workouts," *In Health*, March/April 1991, p. 38.

2. Douglas G. Bock and Margaret E. Munro, "The Effects of Organization, Need for Order, Sex of the Source, and Sex of the Rater on the Organization Trait Error," *Southern Speech Communication Journal* 44 (1979): 364–372.

3. Ray Ehrensberger, "An Experimental Study of the Relative Effects of Certain Forms of Emphasis in Public Speaking," *Speech Monographs* 12 (1945): 94–111.

4. Harold Burson, "Beyond 'PR'," *Vital Speeches of the Day*, December 15, 1990, p. 156.

5. Peter Granata, "Design in the 90's," *Vital Speeches of the Day*, September 15, 1990, p. 735.

6. Richard Kostyra, "Communications in the Future," *Vital Speeches of the Day*, October 15, 1990, pp. 21–22.

7. Mark L. Knapp, *Interpersonal Communication and Human Relationships* (Boston: Allyn and Bacon, 1984), p. 195.

8. Sarah Harder, "Equity by 2000," *Vital Speeches of the Day*, December 1, 1986, p. 111.

9. Ralph M. Baruch, "Lifestyle Revolutions in the Television Age," in *Contemporary American Speeches*, 5th ed., Wil A. Linkugel, R.R. Allen, and Richard L. Johannesen, eds. (Dubuque, IA: Kendall/Hunt, 1982), p. 48.

10. Douglas E. Olesen, "The Art of Waste Minimization," *Vital Speeches of the Day*, August 15, 1990, pp. 666–668.

11. Ibid.

12. Tom Logsdam, "Future Technology," *Vital Speeches of the Day*, September 15, 1987, p. 717.

13. Patrick Huyghe, "The Search for Bigfoot," *Science Digest* 92 (September 1984): 56.

14. Benjamin H. Alexander, "Why Be Ugly When You Can be Beautiful," *Vital Speeches of the Day*, January 15, 1987, p. 203.

15. James A. Joseph, "The Genesis of Community," *Vital Speeches of the Day*, October 1, 1990, p. 749.

16. Janice Payan, "Opportunities for Hispanic Women," *Vital Speeches of the Day*, September 1, 1990, p. 699.

17. Robert C. Winters, "Picking Sides in Health Care's Quality Revolution," *Vital Speeches of the Day*, January 15, 1991, p. 212.

18. James A. Kelly, "Establishing High Standards for the Teaching Profession," *Vital Speeches of the Day*, April 1, 1991, pp. 379–380.

Chapter 16

1. See Mary John Smith, *Persuasion and Human Action: A Review and Critique of Social Influence Theories* (Belmont, CA: Wadsworth, 1982) for a comprehensive overview of persuasion.

2. See Ruth Ann Clark, *Persuasive Messages* (New York: Harper & Row, 1984) for an up-to-date review of credibility in persuasion. See also James C. McCroskey, *An Introduction to Rhetorical Communication*, 4th ed. (Englewood Cliffs, NJ: Prentice-Hall, 1982).

3. Daniel Goleman, "Influencing Others: Skills Are Identified," *The New York Times*, February 18, 1986, pp. C1, C15.

4. Abraham H. Maslow, *Motivation and Personality*, 2nd ed. (New York: Harper & Row, 1970), pp. 80–92.

5. Wayne N. Thompson, *Responsible and Effective Communication* (Boston: Houghton Mifflin, 1978), p. 209. According to Thompson, research supporting these generalizations has been extensive. The original study was by Carl I. Hovland, Arthur Lumsdaine, and Fred Sheffield, *Experiments on Mass Communication*, vol. 3 of *Studies in Social Psychology in World War II* (Princeton, NJ: Princeton University Press, 1949), pp. 213–214.

6. Douglas Ehninger, Alan H. Monroe, and Bruce E. Gronbeck, *Principles and Types of Speech Communication*, 10th ed. (Glenview, IL: Scott, Foresman, 1986), pp. 145–161.

Glossary

Abstract(s) The summaries of written articles, texts, and documents that can be found in the library.

Abstract symbol A symbol that stands for an idea rather than a thing.

Active listener Someone who thinks about and evaluates what a person is saying.

Adaptors Nonverbal ways of adapting to a communication situation.

Affection The feeling of warm emotional attachment to other people.

Agenda A list of all the items that will be discussed during a group's meeting.

Aggression A physical or verbal show of force.

Analogy In reasoning, comparing two similar cases and concluding that if something is true for one it must also be true for the other.

Anecdote A short, interesting story based on an experience.

Articulation The ability to pronounce the letters in a word correctly.

Assessment Evaluating communication after it is over.

Attitudes The deeply felt beliefs that govern how one behaves.

Audience analysis Finding out what one's audience members know about a subject, what they might be interested in, and what their attitudes and beliefs are.

Authoritarian leader A leader who controls a group by deciding what should be discussed and who will do the talking.

Avoidance In relationships, refusal to deal with conflict or painful issues.

Beliefs One's own convictions; what one thinks is right and wrong, true and false.

Bibliography A list of sources (books, magazines, interviews, newspapers) used to prepare a speech or report.

Bilingualism The ability to communicate in two languages.

Body In a speech, all the material between the introduction and conclusion.

Body movement *See* Kinesics.

Brainstorming Coming up with as many ideas as possible without attempting to evaluate them until the ideas run out.

Catalog Contains information about all the material in a library and where it can be found. The catalog information is on small cards filed in a drawer or on a computer screen or printout.

Causal reasoning Reasoning that uses *because*—either implied or explicitly stated.

Cause-and-effect order Organization of a speech around why something is happening (*cause*) and what impact it is having (*effect*).

Central idea The main idea of the speech.

Channel In communication, the route a message travels as it goes between the sender-receivers.

Closed question A question worded in such a way that it restricts the answer.

Cohesiveness The feeling of attraction that group members have toward one another.

Commitment In a relationship, a desire by both parties for the relationship to continue.

Communication   A process in which people share information, ideas, and feelings.

Comparative advantage order   A method of arranging a speech that enables the speaker to compare the advantages of one solution over another.

Comparisons   Similarities between two or more things.

Composition   The makeup of a thing.

Conclusion   In a speech, the closing remarks.

Concrete symbol   A symbol that represents an object.

Conflict   Ideas among group members that may be different and incompatible.

Conflict resolution   Negotiation to find a solution to a conflict.

Connotative meaning   Feelings or associations one has about a word.

Consensus   The point at which all group members agree on an issue.

Contrasts   Differences between two or more things.

Control   In interpersonal communication, having some options and choices in life.

Costs and rewards   In a relationship, its disadvantages and advantages.

Credibility   The believability of a speaker based on the speaker's expertise, dynamism, trustworthiness, and ethics.

Critical listening   Evaluating and challenging what a speaker has said.

Criticism   A negative evaluation of a person for something he or she has said or done.

Database   A collection of information that can be read on a computer screen.

Deductive reasoning   Reasoning from the general to the specific.

Defensive communication   When one person engaged in communication attempts to defend himself or herself against the remarks or behavior of the other(s).

Definition   A brief explanation of what a word or phrase means.

Democratic leader   A leader who lets all points of view be heard and who lets group members participate in the decision-making process.

Demographic analysis   Data about characteristics of a group of people including such things as age; sex; education; occupation; race, nationality, ethnic origin; geographic location; and group affiliation.

Denotative meaning   The dictionary definition of a word.

Dialect   The habitual language of a community.

Displays of feeling   Facial expressions and body movements that show one's emotions.

Dynamism   In a speech, the amount of enthusiasm and energy speakers have for their topic.

Emblems   Body movements that have a direct translation into words.

Emotional appeal   An appeal that focuses on listeners' needs, wants, desires, and wishes.

Empathy   The ability to recognize and identify with another's feelings.

Employment interview   An interview used by an employer to determine if someone is suitable for a job.

Enunciation   How one pronounces and articulates words.

Ethics   Conforming to acceptable standards of conduct.

Ethnicity   A shared history, tradition, and culture among people.

Ethnocentrism   Feeling that one's own race or culture is superior to all other races and cultures.

Etymology   The study of the origin and development of words.

Evaluative statement   A statement that makes a judgment.

Example   An illustration that clarifies a point.

Expertise   Having the experience or knowledge of an expert.

Extemporaneous speaking   Speaking from notes.

External noise   Noise that comes from the environment and keeps the message from being heard or understood.

Factual information   The information obtained in an interview that deals with who, what, where, when, and the like.

Feedback   In communication, the response of the sender-receivers to each other.

Follow-up questions   Questions that arise out of the answers given by an interviewee.

Full-sentence outline   A complete map of what a speech will look like.

Function   How things perform or how they can be used.

General purpose   The intention of the speaker to inform or persuade.

Gossip   Talk of an intimate or personal nature.

Groupthink   A group in which the preservation of harmony becomes more important than the critical examination of ideas.

Hierarchy of needs   The relative order of the physical and psychological needs of all human beings.

Hypothetical example   An example that is made up to illustrate a point.

Illustrators   Body movements that accent, emphasize, or reinforce words.

Impromptu speaking   Speaking on the spur of the moment with little time to prepare.

Inclusion   In interpersonal communication, the need for involvement with others.

Indirect aggression   Refusing to do something or doing it in such an inept way that it is hardly worth the effort.

Inductive reasoning   Reasoning from the specific to the general.

Inflection   A change in pitch used to emphasize certain words and phrases.

Information interview   An interview with a goal of gathering facts and opinions from someone with expertise in a specific field.

Informative speech   A speech that concentrates on explaining, defining, clarifying, and instructing.

Internal noise   Noise that occurs in the minds of sender-receivers.

Interpersonal communication   Communication on a one-to-one basis—usually in an informal, nonstructured setting.

Interview   A series of questions and answers, usually involving two people.

Intrapersonal communication   Communication that occurs within us.

Introduction Of a speech, the opening remarks that aim to get attention and build interest in the subject.

Johari Window A model of self-disclosure that shows how much one does and does not disclose to others.

Key-word outline An outline containing only the important words or phrases of a speech that help to remind the speaker of the ideas he or she is presenting.

Kinesics The study of the relationship between nonverbal behavior and verbal communication.

Laissez-faire leader A leader who does not suggest any direction for or impose any order on a group.

Language environment A theory that states that language is made up of people, their purposes, the rules of communication, and the actual talk they use.

Leader A person who influences the behavior of one or more people in a group.

Leadership style The degree of control a leader exerts over a group of people.

Leading questions Questions that point an interviewee in a particular direction.

Listening Paying attention intellectually and emotionally to messages one hears.

Logical appeal The use of reasoning and evidence to advance an argument or point of view.

Main idea The central thought that runs through a message.

Main points Broad, general ideas and information that support the central idea in a speech.

Maintenance roles Roles that focus on the emotional tone of a meeting.

Messages Ideas and feelings that sender-receivers share.

Metamessages The meaning behind the words.

Minor points The specific ideas and information that support the main points.

Mixed messages Contradictory messages.

Monotone Little variety of pitch in a speech.

Motivated sequence Organization of a speech that involves five steps: attention, need, satisfaction, visualization, and action.

Neutral questions Questions that do not reveal how an interviewer feels about the subject.

Noise Interference that keeps a message from being understood or accurately interpreted.

Nonverbal communication Information or emotion one communicates without using words.

Nonverbal symbols Facial expressions, gestures, posture, vocal tones, appearance—all of which communicate nonverbally.

Norms Expectations group members have of how other members will behave, think, and participate.

Open-ended questions Questions that permit a person being interviewed to expand on his or her answer.

Outline   A way of organizing material in order to see all the parts and how they relate to the whole.

Pace   How fast or slowly one speaks.

Paralanguage   The way one says something.

Passive listener   Someone who listens without evaluation or mental questioning.

Perception   How one sees the world.

Periodicals   The inclusive name for magazines, journals, and newspapers.

Personal inventory   In order to find a topic for a speech, a look at one's own knowledge, experience, and interests.

Persuasion   The process of trying to get others to change their attitudes or behavior.

Persuasive speech   A speech in which the speaker takes a particular position and tries to get the audience to accept and support that position.

Pitch   The highness or lowness of the voice.

Policy information   The information obtained from an interview that focuses on how an organization should be run.

Polls   Surveys taken of people's attitudes, feelings, or knowledge.

Prediction   Anticipation of what is going to happen in a future communication.

Primary questions   Questions designed to cover a subject comprehensively.

Problem-solution order   Organization of a speech into two sections: one dealing with the problem and the other dealing with the solution.

Pronunciation   The ability to pronounce a word correctly.

Proxemics   The study of the space people maintain around themselves and how this relates to environmental and cultural factors.

Proximity   One's physical closeness and access to others.

Psychological risks   The risks that people who feel emotionally secure in a relationship are willing to take.

Psychological safety   The approval and support one gets from familiar people and surroundings.

Public communication   Communication, usually a speech, intended for an audience.

Quality   (in a voice) The overall sound.

Questions of fact   Questions of what is true and what is false.

Questions of policy   Questions about actions that might be taken in the future.

Questions of value   Questions of whether something is good or bad, desirable or undesirable.

Race   A group of persons related by common descent or heredity.

Rapport talk   Communication made up of intimate talk—generally more characteristic of women.

Rate   The speed at which one speaks.

Reflective listening   Trying to understand what a person is feeling from his or her point of view and reflecting those feelings back.

Regulators   Body movements that indicate when the speaker is finished speaking and when others should begin.

Report talk   Talk that trades information and attempts to gain status—generally used more by men.

Résumé   A written summary of one's professional life.

Rhetorical question   A question that audience members answer mentally rather than aloud. '

Ritual language   Conventional language expected on particular occasions.

Roles   The parts one plays and how one behaves with others.

Rules   Formal and structured directions for behavior.

Scripts   The lines or language one is taught to speak through social conditioning.

Selective attention   Focusing on what one wants or needs to hear.

Self-concept   How one sees oneself.

Self-disclosure   The process in which one person tells another something he or she would not tell just anyone.

Self-esteem   The value one puts on oneself.

Self-fulfilling prophecies   Predictions that come true because one (and others around one) expect them to.

Semantic noise   Noise caused by people's emotional reactions to words.

Sender-receivers   Persons who send and receive messages.

Setting   The place where the communication occurs.

Small group   Gatherings of three to thirteen members.

Small-group communication   Communication among a small group of people who meet together.

Small talk   Social talk with others about unimportant or impersonal information.

Spatial order   Organization of a speech by something's location in space (e.g., left to right, top to bottom).

Specific purpose   A statement for a speech that tells precisely what the speaker wants to accomplish.

Statistics   Facts in numerical form.

Stereotypes   Oversimplified or distorted views of people different from us, particularly those from another race or culture.

Study   An in-depth investigation of a subject.

Style   In communication, the way words and sentences are selected and arranged.

Substantive conflict   Conflict that arises when people have different reactions to an idea.

Supporting material   Information that backs up a main point and provides the main content of a speech.

Supporting points   Specific material that reinforces the main idea of any communication.

Symbols   Things that stand for something else.

Task roles   Assigned or assumed roles that help to get a job done.

Territory   The space one regards as one's own.

Testimony   Another person's statements or actions used to give authority to what the speaker is saying.

Time order   Organization (of a speech) by chronology or historical occurrence.

Topical order   Organization (of a speech) into subtopics.

Transactional communication   A theory of communication that states: people engaged in communication are sending messages continuously and simultaneously; communication events have a past, present, and future; participants in communication play certain roles.

Transitions   Comments that smoothly lead from one point to another.

Trustworthiness   In giving a speech, being perceived as reliable and dependable.

Verbal symbol   A word in the language that stands for a particular thing or idea.

Vertical file   Contains pamphlets and booklets written by various groups; generally filed by subject in the library.

Visual aids   Visual material that helps illustrate key points in a speech or presentation.

Vocal fillers   Sounds and words used to fill up sentences or to cover up when searching for words (i.e., "um," "you know").

Volume   (of vocal sound) How loud one speaks.

Credits and Acknowledgments

Text

27: From "The Stories We Live By?" by Sam Keen. *Psychology Today*, December 1988, p. 46. Reprinted with permission from *Psychology Today* magazine. Copyright © 1988 (Sussex Publishers, Inc.).

32: From Michael Rubin, *Men Without Masks*, Reading, MA: Addison-Wesley, 1980, pp. 187–188.

33: From *Lake Wobegon Days* by Garrison Keillor. Copyright © 1985 by Garrison Keillor. Used by permission of Viking Penguin, a division of Penguin Books USA Inc.

37: "The Investigation" by John Jonik. Copyright © 1984 by John Jonik. Reproduced by permission.

39–40: From Eva Hoffman, *Lost in Translation: A Life in a New Language*, New York: Penguin, 1990. Reprinted with permission.

39: (Table 2-1): Teun A. van Dijk, *Communicating Racism*, p. 59, copyright © 1987 by Sage Publications, Inc. Reprinted by permission of Sage Publications, Inc.

51: (Figure 3-1): Adapted from L. Barker et al., "An Investigation of Proportional Time Spent in Various Communication Activities by College Students," *Journal of Applied Communication Research*, 8 (1980), pp. 101–109. Used by permission of the University of South Florida.

54: Adapted from Harry Lorayne and Jerry Lucas, *The Memory Book*, New York: Dorset Press, 1989.

65: From *Brothers & Keepers* by John Edgar Wideman. Copyright © 1984 by John Edgar Wideman. Reprinted by permission of Henry Holt and Company, Inc.

79: From *Say It My Way* by Willard R. Espy. Copyright © 1980 by Willard R. Espy. Used by permission of Doubleday, a division of Bantam Doubleday Dell Publishing Group, Inc.

86: From Anne de Courcy, "Between Us: Male and Female English Spoken Here," *Chicago Tribune*, January 3, 1988, section 6, p. 4.

88: (Figure 4-2): *The New York Times*, November 17, 1985, p. 26. Copyright © 1985 by The New York Times Company. Reprinted by permission.

93: Reprinted with permission of Atheneum Publishers, an imprint of Macmillan Publishing Company, from *Miss Manners' Guide to Excruciatingly Correct Behavior* by Judith Martin. Copyright © 1979, 1980, 1981, 1982 by United Feature Syndicate, Inc.

105: Adapted from *The New York Times Magazine*, November 17, 1985 and *The [London] Times*, May 30, 1990.

107: From *The Gentle Art of Verbal Self-Defense* by Suzette Haden Elgin. Copyright © 1980 by Suzette Haden Elgin. Reprinted by permission of Suzette Haden Elgin.

110: Adapted from Bernice Kanner, "Color Schemes," *New York Magazine*, April 3, 1989, pp. 22–23.

112: Adapted from "Research Notes," *The Chronicle of Higher Education*.

118: (Figure 5-1): Adapted Figure 5-1 from *Realities of Teaching: Explorations with Video Tape* by Raymond S. Adams and Bruce J. Biddle, copyright © 1970 by Holt, Rinehart and Winston, Inc., reprinted by permission of the publisher.

123: Adapted from Daniel Goleman, "The Experience of Touch: Research Points to a Critical Role," *The New York Times*, February 2, 1988, pp. C1, C4.

124: From Letty Cottin Pogrebin, in Nancy R. Newhouse (ed.), *Hers, Through Women's Eyes*, New York: Villard Books, 1985, p. 6. Reprinted by permission of the author. Copyright © 1983 by Letty Cottin Pogrebin.

133: Adapted from Daniel Goleman, "Studies on Development of Empathy Challenge Some Old Assumptions," *The New York Times*, July 12, 1990, p. B8.

290, 294: From *How to Speak Like a Pro* by Leon Fletcher. Copyright © 1983 by Ballantine Books, a division of Random House. Reprinted by permission.

298: From Robert B. Rackleff, "The Art of Speech Writing," *Vital Speeches*, March 1, 1988. Reprinted with permission.

299–300: (Table 12-1): *The Gallup Poll Monthly*, November 1990, p. 21. Reprinted with permission.

301: (Table 12-2): *The New York Times*, June 26, 1987, p. 6, section 4. Copyright © 1987 by The New York Times Company. Reprinted by permission.

309: Taken from "The Writer's Art" column by James J. Kilpatrick. © 1984 Universal Press Syndicate. Reprinted with permission. All rights reserved.

343: *First Lady from Plains* by Rosalynn Carter. Copyright © 1984 by Rosalynn Carter. Reprinted by permission of Houghton Mifflin Company. All rights reserved.

346: From *Conversationally Speaking* by Alan Garner. Los Angeles, CA: Lowell House, 1991. Reprinted with permission.

347: Capp/Capp/Capp, *Basic Oral Communication*, © 1990, p. 247. Adapted by permission of Prentice-Hall, Inc. Englewood Cliffs, N.J.

348: Table from *Developing Your Speaking Voice*, 2nd ed. by John P. Moncur and Harrison M. Karr. Copyright © 1972 by John P. Moncur and Harrison M. Karr. Reprinted by permission of HarperCollins Publishers.

351: From Terry C. Smith, *Making Successful Presentations: A Self-Teaching Guide*. Copyright © 1984 by John Wiley & Sons, Inc. Reprinted by permission of John Wiley & Sons, Inc.

353: (Figure 14-1): *The New York Times*, May 6, 1991, p. A1. Copyright © 1991 by The New York Times Company. Reprinted by permission.

354: (Table 14-1): Lou Fabian, Lock Haven University, Lock Haven, Pennsylvania, 1991.

356: (Figure 14-5): Lou Fabian, Lock Haven University, Lock Haven, Pennsylvania, 1991.

361: From "Personal Best" by Dr. George Sheehan. In (Toledo) *Blade*, November 13, 1987. Reprinted by permission of Dr. George Sheehan.

382–386: Brian Smith, "New American Landmarks: Mountains of Trash." Reprinted by permission of Brian Smith.

392: From Daniel Goleman, "Influencing Others: Skills Are Identified," *The New York Times*, February 18, 1986. Copyright © 1986 by The New York Times Company. Reprinted by permission.

399: (Figure 16-2): "Hierarchy of Needs" from *Motivation and Personality* by Abraham H. Maslow. Copyright 1954 by Harper & Row, Publishers, Inc. Copyright © 1970 by Abraham H. Maslow. Reprinted by permission of HarperCollins Publishers.

405–410: Carol E. Bubb, "Cigarettes: A Health Hazard to Nonsmokers." Reprinted by permission of Carol E. Bubb.

406–407: InfoTrac is a registered trademark of Information Access Company. Reprinted with permission.

Photos

v and vi: Werner Bokelberg/The Image Bank; **ix:** Comstock; **xi:** Garfield/The Stock Market; **xiii:** Gabe Palmer/The Stock Market; **xiv:** Superstock; **xvi:** Ed Bock/The Stock Market; **2:** Fernando Bueno/The Image Bank; **9:** Gabe Palmer/The Stock Market; **12:** Anthony Edgeworth/The Stock Market; **17:** Comstock: **24:** John Kelly/The Image Bank; **30:** David Pollack/The Stock Market; **35:** Sandy Roessler/The Stock Market; **38:** Tim Davis/Photo Researchers; **48:** Sven Martson/Comstock; **57:** Erika Stone/Photo Researchers; **63:** Hugh Rogers/Monkmeyer; **74:** Steve Takatsuno/The Picture Cube; **77:** Jan Lukas/Photo Researchers; **90:** Martin Miller/Positive Images; **102:** Tim Davis/Photo Researchers; **109:** Joel Gordon; **117:** *top left,* Donna Jernigan/Monkmeyer; *top right,* Roswell Angier/Stock, Boston; *bottom left,* Bettye Lane/Photo Researchers; *bottom right,* Merrim/Monkmeyer; **120:** *top,* UPI/Bettmann Newsphotos; *bottom,* Reuters/Bettmann Newsphotos; **130:** Comstock; **134:** Lew Long/The Stock Market; **141:** Richard Hutchings/Photo Researchers; **146:** Comstock; **152:** Erik Leigh Simons/The Image Bank; **160:** John Feingersh/The Stock Market; **167:** Lawrence Migdale/Photo Researchers; **173:** Comstock; **178:** David Powers/Stock, Boston; **190:** Owen Franken/Stock, Boston; **199:** Kathy Sloane; **210:** Bill Bachman/Photo Researchers; **218:** McGraw-Hill photo by Stacey Pleasant; **221:** Martin Miller/Positive Images; **228:** Nita

Index